The Joan Palevsky  Imprint in Classical Literature

In honor of beloved Virgil—

"O degli altri poeti onore e lume . . ."

—Dante, *Inferno*

The publisher gratefully acknowledges the generous support of the
Classical Literature Endowment Fund of the University of
California Press Foundation, which was established
by a major gift from Joan Palevsky.

Controlling Contested Places

Controlling Contested Places

Late Antique Antioch and the Spatial Politics of Religious Controversy

Christine Shepardson

BR
1085
A58 S54
2014

WEB

UNIVERSITY OF CALIFORNIA PRESS

Berkeley   Los Angeles   London

University of California Press, one of the most distinguished university
presses in the United States, enriches lives around the world by advancing
scholarship in the humanities, social sciences, and natural sciences. Its
activities are supported by the UC Press Foundation and by philanthropic
contributions from individuals and institutions. For more information,
visit www.ucpress.edu.

University of California Press
Berkeley and Los Angeles, California

University of California Press, Ltd.
London, England

© 2014 by The Regents of the University of California

Library of Congress Cataloging-in-Publication Data

Shepardson, Christine C.
    Controlling contested places : late antique Antioch and the spatial
politics of religious controversy / Christine Shepardson.
        p.   cm.
    Includes bibliographical references and index.
    ISBN 978-0-520-28035-9 (cloth, alk. paper)
    1. Antioch (Turkey)—Church history.   2. Antioch (Turkey)—Religious
life and customs.   3. Church history—Primitive and early church, ca.
30–600.   I. Title.
BR1085.A58S54   2014
275.64'8—dc23   2013032091

Manufactured in the United States of America

23   22   21   20   19   18   17   16   15   14
10   9   8   7   6   5   4   3   2   1

In keeping with a commitment to support environmentally responsible and
sustainable printing practices, UC Press has printed this book on Natures
Natural, a fiber that contains 30% post-consumer waste and meets the
minimum requirements of ANSI/NISO Z39.48-1992 (R 1997) (*Permanence
of Paper*).

For my parents, Carl and Margie Shepardson,
for sharing their love of maps and wilderness places

CONTENTS

ACKNOWLEDGMENTS

I have had the enormous good fortune to have the support and aid of innumerable colleagues, friends, and family members as I researched and wrote this book. While I cannot list them all by name, I am extremely grateful to them.

Elizabeth Clark continues to be a wonderful mentor and role model, and I thank her for all she has given to the field and the kindness and generosity she has shown to me over many years. I owe a special thanks to Wendy Mayer, who welcomed me so warmly to the study of Antioch and John Chrysostom, a figure whom she knows so well. She has offered me more support than I could have imagined, and I am grateful for her friendship and reading suggestions. Philip Rousseau has also been a generous and longtime supporter of this project. His invitation to a conference on Antioch in 2009 provided the opportunity for me to meet many scholars whose work is cited below. Similarly, Catherine Saliou included me in the first seminar on Antioch that she organized in Paris in 2010, and I benefited greatly from the scholars I met there, including Klaus-Peter Todt. I am grateful for the conversations I have had with these and other scholars of fourth-century Antioch, including Silke-Petra Bergjan, Gunnar Brands, Raffaella Cribiore, Chris De Wet, Susanna Elm, Blake Leyerle, Jaclyn Maxwell, Hatice Pamir, and Isabella Sandwell.

During the years that it took to produce this book, I received several grants and fellowships, without which the research would not have been possible. Some of this research was assisted by the ACLS/SSRC/NEH International and Area Studies Fellowship Program of the American Council of Learned Societies, made possible by funding from the National Endowment for the Humanities. I am grateful for the ACLS/SSRC/NEH Fellowship in 2009–10; the Individual Research Grant in 2009–10 from the American Academy of Religion; the Franklin Research Grant in

2008 from the American Philosophical Society; the NEH Summer Stipend in 2008 from the National Endowment for the Humanities; and the Professional Development Award in 2006 from the University of Tennessee, Knoxville. Alan Rutenberg read many drafts of my grant proposals, and I appreciate his tireless feedback.

It is also my great pleasure to be able to thank here the people who made my research trips to Turkey and Syria so wonderful and productive. On my first trip to Turkey in 2006, Claudine Nagel facilitated a welcome at the Istanbul airport by her friends Ingrid and Can Karatay, whose gracious hospitality first introduced me to the country. I then flew to Antakya (the Roman city of Antioch) where I happened to meet Hulya and Ercan, two wonderful university students who adopted me on my first days in the city and even helped me locate the remains of the Roman hippodrome with nothing but Glanville Downey's map of the Roman city and my wild gesticulations. They have continued to be delightful hosts on my subsequent trips to the city, and I am grateful for their kindness.

My visits to Antakya have also been enriched beyond measure by the generosity of p. Domenico Bertogli, the priest in charge of Antakya's Katolik Kilisesi. He welcomed me to the city in 2006, 2008, and again in 2010, and has been a rich source of wisdom about the Roman and Christian sites in the area. He has been an exquisite host, and I thank him for sharing his knowledge, for making available his church's beautiful guesthouse, and especially for the tour of Symeon the Younger's monastery and Seleucia Pieria. I look forward to delivering a copy of this book to his new library as a small token of my great appreciation.

The friends and family who joined me on different parts of my research trips also made the experience much easier and more pleasurable. I thank my colleagues Melanie Johnson-DeBaufre and Laura Nasrallah, who joined me partway through my trip in Turkey in 2006; my mother, who joined me in Istanbul and Şanliurfa (the Roman city of Edessa) in 2008; and Dayna Kalleres, Wendy Mayer, and Wendy's husband, Dan, who joined me in Antakya in 2008. I am also very pleased to have made the acquaintance of Nicola Dinç from Antakya.

In 2010 I had the wonderful opportunity to do research in Syria. It was an incredible trip that would not have been possible, nor nearly so enjoyable, without the company, good humor, and adventurous spirit of Dayna Kalleres. Even so, we would not have been able to visit half of the (considerable number) of Roman sites we saw without the knowledge, kindness, patience, and excellent navigation and language skills of Muhammad Moubarak from Aleppo. Dayna, Hammad, and I shared not only many adventures at the Roman ruins in the Syrian countryside, and the chance to wade in the Euphrates River, but also an evening of ice cream, shisha, and conversation that I will cherish always. He and his family have been much on my mind during the crisis in Syria that began soon after we left, and I hope that they are safe.

I thank all those who have offered feedback on conference papers and articles, and in informal conversations, during the years of this project: Michael Kulikowski for years of friendship and conversations about all things Roman, many of which took place on the hiking trails of the Great Smoky Mountains; the participants of the faculty research seminar on late antiquity at the University of Tennessee; Maura Lafferty for her friendship, insight, and Latin expertise; Tom Burman for his encouragement; Amy Elias and Derek Alderman for some useful readings; and J. P. Dessel for his knowledge of the ʿAmuq Valley. I thank my colleagues in the University of Tennessee's Department of Religious Studies and the Marco Institute for Medieval and Renaissance Studies as well as my students for their inspiration and feedback.

In addition to those named above, I am extremely grateful for the many other scholars of late antiquity who have helped as both colleagues and friends, including Catherine Chin, Maria Doerfler, Andrew Jacobs, Aaron Johnson, Nicole Kelly, Todd Krulak, Ellen Muehlberger, Michael Penn, Jeremy Schott, Caroline Schroeder, Adam Schor, and Kristi Upson-Saia. David Brakke, Patout Burns, Bart Ehrman, Charlotte Fonrobert, Paula Fredriksen, Susan Ashbrook Harvey, David Hunter, Robin Jensen, Derek Krueger, Patricia Cox Miller, Dennis Trout, and Lucas Van Rompay have also mentored me during this project, and I am indebted to them.

A special thanks goes to my colleague Gregor Kalas, who undertook the herculean task of offering detailed, constructive feedback on the entire manuscript of this book. His own work on topography in fourth-century Rome proved very valuable in helping me think through the final stages of this project, and I am grateful for his advice and friendship. I also thank my uncle Fred, my father, and the professional reviewers and editors of University of California Press—all of whose feedback was helpful. The project is better for their assistance. Eric Schmidt has been a patient and encouraging editor, Marian Rogers has been a wonderful copy editor, and Cindy Fulton has been an efficient and gracious project editor. Of course the responsibility for any errors that remain is mine alone.

The two maps appear thanks to the skills of Will Fontanez, and the financial support of the Department of Religious Studies and the Marco Institute for Medieval and Renaissance Studies at the University of Tennessee, Knoxville. The photograph of the fifth-century mosaic from Antioch's suburb of Daphne that is on the cover of this book was taken by Dick Osseman from Amsterdam, and I appreciate his permission to use it. I am grateful for permission to include in this book some material previously published elsewhere. Chapter 2 includes material from three articles: "Rewriting Julian's Legacy: John Chrysostom's *On Babylas* and Libanius' *Oration 24*," *Journal of Late Antiquity* 2.1 (2009): 99–115; "Burying Babylas: Meletius and the Christianization of Antioch," *Studia Patristica* 37 (2010): 347–52; and "Apollo's Charred Remains: Making Meaning in Fourth-Century Syria," *Studia Patristica* 38 (2013): 297–302. Chapter 3 includes material from "Controlling Contested Places: John Chrysostom's *Adversus Iudaeos* Homilies and the Spatial Politics of Religious Controversy," *Journal of Early Christian Studies* 15.4 (December 2007): 483–516.

This book is dedicated to my parents, Carl and Margie Shepardson, so I will end with a few words to my family. Lyn Hartman has filled my life with joy and adventure, and introduced me to the rich cultural heritage of Appalachia. I am grateful for her caring support while I worked long hours and her healthy insistence on making time for friendships and fresh air; I thank her for her love, her heart, and the compassion and goodness that she brings to this world. I thank Randy for reminding me that there is always a more interesting way, and Bridey for defying the ordinary in all things. Finally, there is no doubt that my love of maps and adventures stems from my family's many canoe trips throughout the Canadian wilderness. This book in many ways owes its topographical theme to my parents for these exceptional childhood travels, and I dedicate it to them with my love.

ABBREVIATIONS

ACW   *Ancient Christian Writers.* 66 vols. Mahwah, NJ: Paulist Press, 1978–.

CSEL   *Corpus scriptorum ecclesiasticorum latinorum.* 99 vols. Vienna: Akademie Verlag, etc., 1866–.

FC   *The Fathers of the Church: A New Translation.* 118 vols. Washington, DC: Catholic University of America Press, 1947–.

GNO   *Gregorii Nysseni Opera.* Leiden: Brill, 1921–.

PG   *Patrologia graeca.* Edited by J.-P. Migne. 161 vols. Paris: Migne, 1857–66.

PL   *Patrologia latina.* Edited by J.-P. Migne. 217 vols. Paris: Migne, 1844–65.

SC   *Sources chrétiennes.* 564 vols. Paris: Éditions du Cerf, 1943–.

ROMAN EMPERORS AND BISHOPS OF ANTIOCH

ROMAN EMPERORS, 325–455 C.E.

Constantine (306–37)

Constantine II (337–40)

Constans (337–50)

Constantius II (337–61)

Julian (361–63)

Jovian (363–64)

Valentinian (364–75)

Valens (364–78)

Gratian (367–83)

Valentinian II (375–92)

Theodosius (379–95)

Arcadius (383–408)

Honorius (393–423)

Theodosius II (408–50)

Valentinian III (425–55)

Marcian (450–57)

BISHOPS OF ANTIOCH, 325–415 C.E.

Alexander — Meletian-Nicene bishop who succeeded Porphyrius ca. 412/3

Dorotheos — Homoian bishop who succeeded Euzoius by 378; died in 381

Eudoxius — Homoian bishop who succeeded Leontius

Eulalius — Homoian bishop who succeeded Paulinus of Tyre

Euphronius — Homoian bishop who succeeded Eulalius

Eustathius — Attended the Council of Nicaea (325) and supported its outcome; deposed in 330/1

Euzoius — Homoian bishop elected in 361 by those who deposed Meletius

Evagrius — Nicene bishop who succeeded Paulinus in 388/9

Flacillus — Homoian bishop who succeeded Euphronius

Flavian — Meletian-Nicene bishop who succeeded Meletius in 381; died in 404

Leontius — Homoian bishop who succeeded Stephen

Meletius — Elected in 359/60 as Eudoxius's successor, but soon deposed; endured three exiles; died in 381 as a supporter of the Council of Nicaea

Paulinus — Nicene bishop elected in 361/2 to continue Eustathius's community; supported by Jerome, Athanasius, and Ambrose; died in 388/9

Paulinus of Tyre — Homoian bishop who succeeded Eustathius in 330/1

Porphyrius — Meletian-Nicene bishop who succeeded Flavian in 404; died ca. 412/3

Stephen — Homoian bishop who succeeded Flacillus

Vitalis — Apollinarian bishop ordained in 375 by Apollinaris of Laodicea

TIMELINE OF KEY EVENTS

351/2	Council of Antioch
351–54	Caesar Gallus in Antioch, translates Babylas's relics to Daphne
353	Libanius gives guest lecture in Antioch's *bouleutērion*
354	Libanius returns to live in Antioch
356	Libanius, *Oratio* 11
357/8	Bishop Leontius dies, succeeded by Eudoxius
358	Council of Antioch under Bishop Eudoxius accepts Second Creed of Sirmium
359	Bishop Eudoxius deposed at Council of Seleucia
359/60	Meletius becomes bishop of Antioch
360	Eudoxius becomes bishop of Constantinople
361	Bishop Meletius exiled under Constantius II, succeeded by Euzoius
	Council of Antioch under Bishop Euzoius and Constantius II
	Constantius II dies, succeeded by Julian who recalls exiled bishops
361/2	Paulinus ordained bishop of Antioch
	Bishop Meletius returns to Antioch
362	Julian visits Antioch, has Babylas's relics returned to cemetery
	Fire destroys temple of Apollo in Daphne
	Julian temporarily closes the Great Church
363	Julian, *Misopōgōn*
	Julian dies, succeeded by Jovian
	Council of Antioch under Bishop Meletius and Jovian
363–80	Ammianus Marcellinus lives in Antioch
364	Jovian dies, succeeded by Valens and Valentinian
	Bishop Meletius loses control of church buildings, holds services outdoors
365	Bishop Meletius exiled by Valens
	Athanasius of Alexandria visits Bishop Paulinus in Antioch
365–69	Bishop Meletius returns to Antioch
367	Gratian becomes co-emperor
369	Bishop Meletius exiled again by Valens
373	Athanasius of Alexandria dies
374	Libanius circulates much of *Oratio* 1
	Ambrose becomes bishop of Milan
375	Vitalis ordained bishop of Antioch
	Valentinian dies, succeeded by Valentinian II
376–78	Bishop Dorotheos succeeds Euzoius
378	Valens dies
378/9	Bishop Meletius returns
379	Council of Antioch under Bishop Meletius
	Theodosius becomes emperor

379/80	Bishop Meletius builds new church for Babylas's relics
380	Bishop Meletius ordains John Chrysostom deacon
	Theodosius issues *cunctos populos* edict
381	Council of Constantinople under Theodosius
	Bishop Meletius dies, succeeded by Flavian
	Gregory of Nyssa, *Oratio funebris in Meletium episcopum*
	Codex Theodosianus 16.5.6: "heretics" deprived of churches
	Bishop Dorotheos dies, not replaced
383	Gratian dies
	Arcadius becomes emperor
384	Famine in Antioch
ca. 384	Egeria visits Antioch
385–90	Libanius, *Oratio* 30
385–86	Ambrose of Milan argues with Valentinian II over church buildings
386	Bishop Flavian ordains John Chrysostom presbyter
	John Chrysostom, *De sancto Meletio*
386–87	John Chrysostom, *Adversus Iudaeos* and *De incomprehensibili natura dei*
387	Statues Riot in Antioch
	John Chrysostom, *De statuis*
388	Bishop Paulinus dies, succeeded by Evagrius
	New Latin chair in Antioch
392	Valentinian II dies
	Serapeum destroyed in Alexandria
393	Honorius becomes emperor
ca. 393	Theodoret born in Antioch
ca. 394	Libanius dies
395	Theodosius dies
398	John Chrysostom becomes bishop of Constantinople
404	John Chrysostom exiled
	Bishop Flavian dies, succeeded by Porphyrius
407	John Chrysostom dies
408	Arcadius dies
	Theodosius II becomes emperor
412/3	Bishop Porphyrius dies, succeeded by Alexander
415	Bishop Alexander reconciled with Paulinus's community

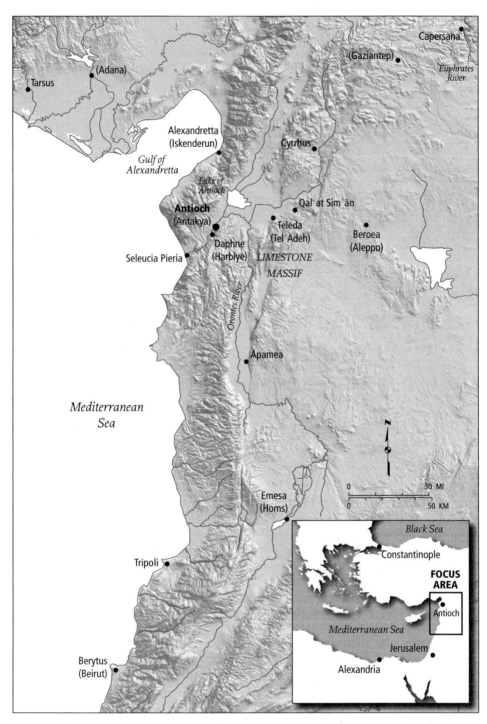

Tarsus

(Adana)

Alexandretta
(Iskenderun)

Gulf of
Alexandretta

Lake of
Antioch

Antioch
(Antakya)

Daphne
(Harbiye)

Seleucia Pieria

*Mediterranean
Sea*

Orontes River

Capersana

(Gaziantep)

*Euphrates
River*

Cyrrhus

Qal' at Sim' ān

Teleda
(Tel 'Adeh)

Beroea
(Aleppo)

*LIMESTONE
MASSIF*

Apamea

N

0   30 MI
0   50 KM

Emesa
(Homs)

Tripoli

Berytus
(Beirut)

Black Sea

Constantinople

**FOCUS
AREA**

Antioch

Mediterranean Sea

Jerusalem

Alexandria

MAP 1. Region of Antioch. Present-day place names are in parentheses.

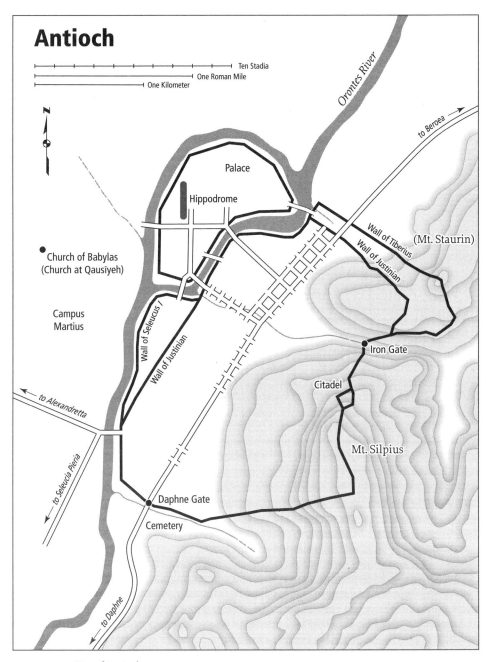

Antioch

Ten Stadia

One Roman Mile

One Kilometer

N

Orontes River

to Beroea

Palace

Hippodrome

Wall of Tiberius

(Mt. Staurin)

Wall of Justinian

● Church of Babylas
(Church at Qausīyeh)

Campus
Martius

Wall of Seleucus /

Wall of Justinian

Iron Gate

to Alexandretta

Citadel

to Seleucia Pieria

Mt. Silpius

Daphne Gate

Cemetery

to Daphne

MAP 2. City of Antioch.

Introduction

The Lay of the Land

From constructing new buildings to describing places controlled by their rivals as morally and physically dangerous, early Christian leaders fundamentally shaped their physical environment and thus the events that unfolded within it. Historical narratives that overlook the manipulation of physical places have obscured some of the powerful forces that structured the development of early Christianity. Mapping the city of Antioch (present-day Antakya, Turkey) through some of the topographically sensitive vocabulary of cultural geographers will demonstrate the critical role of physical and rhetorical spatial contests in this city during the tumultuous fourth and fifth centuries C.E. The strength of theological claims and political support were not the only significant factors in determining which of the Roman Empire's competing Christian communities gained authority around the Mediterranean. Rather, Antioch's urban and rural places, far from being an inert backdrop against which events transpired, were also ever-shifting sites of, and tools for, the negotiation of power, authority, and religious identity.

Antioch offers a particularly fruitful site for studying the processes through which Christian orthodoxy developed. Indeed, it is difficult to exaggerate the religious and political complexity of Roman Antioch, or the historical impact of the fourth century, as all later Christians are defined by the creeds and doctrines that resulted from fourth-century negotiations. Antioch was one of the largest cities in the later Roman Empire, a winter residence for emperors, and home to one of the most influential Christian bishoprics in the world. The voluminous Antiochene writings of the Greek teacher Libanius (ca. 314–94) and his student the Christian preacher John Chrysostom (ca. 347–407), among others, provide an unusual wealth of literary material for the fourth-century city, in addition to

1

archaeological, legal, and other resources. This study investigates the contested ownership and valuation of religiously charged places in fourth-century Antioch against a background of turbulent events: changes in imperial rule, divisions in Christians' political and religious loyalties, and the temporarily revived imperial patronage of traditional temple rituals under the emperor Julian. In particular, this study traces physical and rhetorical efforts to control the city's landscape, and thus shape the experiences of its inhabitants, although the limitations of the extant material evidence, due in part to the city's continuous habitation, have necessitated a strong focus on Roman authors' narrative constructions. In Antioch, religious and local politics collided in the concrete details of claiming church buildings, the city's bishopric, and the definition of religious orthodoxy. More than five decades of episcopal schism within Antiochene Christianity ended by 415 C.E. Aided by imperial legislation, Bishop Meletius and his followers, including the "golden-mouthed" preacher, John Chrysostom, eventually succeeded in establishing their Christian community as "orthodox" and their leader as the rightful bishop. This study demonstrates that Meletius and his colleagues, like leaders elsewhere in the empire, prevailed in part because of their skilled and aggressive efforts to reshape and control Antioch's physical topography.

Although historians cannot know what most ancient individuals thought, said, or did, we can more often know what their leaders encouraged them to think, say, or do. The types of evidence that survive for late antique Antioch tell us more about the efforts of the elite and powerful than about their followers, and more about the rhetorical narratives of the city's leading figures than about the physical layout of the city's buildings. It would not be reasonable to assume that leaders were always or entirely successful in shaping the identities and behaviors of those who lived in Antioch and the surrounding region. "Desire lines" in the landscape, such as a well-worn footpath through the grass created by people taking a shortcut rather than following the planned walkways, and Michel de Certeau's observations in his essay "Walking in the City" provide clear examples of individuals' choices to reject planned efforts to control their movements.[1] Likewise, postcolonial scholarship has clearly demonstrated the variety of forms of resistance that are possible apart from positions of political dominance, and Jaclyn Maxwell has documented well the opportunities that John Chrysostom's fourth-century congregants took to resist their preacher's rhetorical ideals, in addition to the ways in which Chrysostom's rhetoric could shape a listener's habits.[2] Éric Rebillard emphasizes that, like us, every Roman participated in a variety of communities and identities, so that it

---

1. Michel de Certeau, *The Practice of Everyday Life,* trans. Steven Rendall (Berkeley: University of California Press, 1984), 91–110.

2. Jaclyn Maxwell, *Christianization and Communication in Late Antiquity: John Chrysostom and His Congregation in Antioch* (New York: Cambridge University Press, 2006), esp. 144–75.

is predictable that many people whom John Chrysostom, for example, considered "Christian" did not behave in the ways that he expected ideal Christians to behave, in part because their "Christianness" was not always the primary identity being triggered in any given context.[3] Although ideally my investigation would map rhetorical descriptions of the city onto its physical topography, the limited archaeological remains allow only a provisional comparison between the two. Always keeping in mind that the texts of Libanius, John Chrysostom, and another Antiochene native, Theodoret (ca. 393–457), bishop of Cyrrhus, provide us with rhetorical descriptions rather than "reality," this study focuses on the efforts that educated Antiochenes made to shape the behavior and identities of their fellow citizens.

The late antique sources from Antioch reveal that the city's leaders encouraged their audiences to consider seriously the religious implications of where in the city and the surrounding region they did and did not go. More specifically, physically controlling the appearance and use of places and rhetorically shaping perceptions of them were significant, though as yet largely unrecognized, means through which ancient leaders negotiated the complex power struggles of their times. Focusing on the fourth century, and primarily the second half of that century, allows a thorough examination of the powerful place-oriented rhetoric that participated in defining religious orthodoxy around the empire at a time when Nicene Christian leaders' success was not yet clear. This study does not focus on large-scale imperial building projects, such as those undertaken by the emperor Constantine; nor does it focus on the capital cities of Rome and Constantinople, or the places associated directly with the life and death of Jesus in and around the city of Jerusalem. Rather, this study traces the ways in which local leaders encouraged their followers to modify their daily behaviors and transform their interpretation of the world (and landscape) around them in ways that were imitable around the empire. Although most of my investigation is centered on Antioch and its surrounding territory, it will also demonstrate that the examples from that city were echoed around the Mediterranean world in late antiquity, and that similar types of physical and rhetorical manipulations of powerful places continue to shape the politics of identity and perceptions of religious orthodoxy to this day.

CONSTRUCTING AND REMEMBERING PLACES

Although scholars have long worked to reconstruct the theological debates that surrounded questions of early Christian orthodoxy, little work has been done to include the significant influence of either spatial politics or the rural areas surrounding Antioch in these controversies. Several recent monographs demonstrate Antioch's

3. Éric Rebillard, *Christians and Their Many Identities in Late Antiquity: North Africa, 200–450 C.E.* (Ithaca, NY: Cornell University Press, 2012), esp. 3, 92.

position as a religious and political center during the fourth century and contribute substantially to our knowledge of the city. Jaclyn Maxwell's study of John Chrysostom's preaching highlights the interaction between preacher and audience in the construction of fourth-century expectations for Christian behavior and belief;[4] Isabella Sandwell's analysis compares and contrasts Libanius and John Chrysostom in relation to their construction of religious identity;[5] Raffaella Cribiore's investigation of Libanius reveals his pedagogical networks and the practices related to education in fourth-century Antioch;[6] and Emmanuel Soler's study synthesizes the widespread data for festival practices in fourth-century Antioch, and the processes by which they became increasingly associated with Christianity.[7] Edward Schoolman's comparison of Ravenna and Antioch, and the physical transformations each underwent from late antiquity to the early Middle Ages, also contributes to our knowledge of both cities.[8] In addition, Wendy Mayer and Pauline Allen have published a comprehensive analysis of the extant evidence for the churches and other Christian sites in Roman Antioch;[9] and Catherine Saliou has collected a useful series of essays presenting the sources for the physical topography of Antioch.[10] Gunnar Brands and Hatice Pamir have led a new Turkish-German archaeological survey of Roman Antioch, although their full report has not yet been published.[11] Even this scholar-

4. Maxwell, *Christianization*.

5. Isabella Sandwell, *Religious Identity in Late Antiquity: Greeks, Jews, and Christians in Antioch* (New York: Cambridge University Press, 2007).

6. Raffaella Cribiore, *The School of Libanius in Late Antique Antioch* (Princeton, NJ: Princeton University Press, 2007). Although regrettably Raffaella Cribiore's newest book came out after my manuscript was completed, it provides another excellent and relevant study of Libanius: *Libanius the Sophist: Rhetoric, Reality, and Religion in the Fourth Century* (Ithaca: Cornell University Press, 2013).

7. Emmanuel Soler, *Le sacré et le salut à Antioche au IVe siècle apr. J.-C.: Pratiques festives et comportements religieux dans le processus de christianisation de la cité* (Beirut: Institut français du Proche-Orient, 2006); Soler, "Sacralité et partage du temps et de l'espace festifs à Antioche au IVe siècle," in *Les frontières du profane dans l'antiquité tardive*, Collection de l'École Française de Rome 428, ed. Éric Rebillard and Claire Sotinel (Rome: École française de Rome, 2010), 273–86.

8. Edward Schoolman, "Civic Transformation of the Mediterranean City: Antioch and Ravenna, 300–800 C.E." (PhD diss., University of California, Los Angeles, 2010). See also Maria Francesio's examination of Libanius's literary presentation of his city: Francesio, *L'idea di città in Libanio* (Stuttgart: Franz Steiner Press, 2004).

9. Wendy Mayer and Pauline Allen, *The Churches of Syrian Antioch (300–638 C.E.)* (Walpole, MA: Peeters, 2012).

10. *Les sources de l'histoire du paysage urbain d'Antioche sur l'Oronte: Actes des journées d'études des 20 et 21 septembre 2010* (Paris: Université Paris 8, Vincennes-Saint-Denis, 2012), published online at www.bibliotheque-numerique-paris8.fr/fre/ref/146505/COLNH1. Note particularly Wendy Mayer, "The Topography of Antioch Described in the Writings of John Chrysostom," in *Les sources de l'histoire*, 81–100.

11. Hatice Pamir has released some initial observations: Pamir, "Preliminary Results of the Recent Archaeological Researches in Antioch on the Orontes and Its Vicinity," in *Les sources de l'histoire*, 259–70. The results of this project are planned in a three-volume series currently in preparation. Also soon to be published are Gunnar Brands, "Antiochia in der Spätantike" (forthcoming); Brands, "Antioch on

ship, however, rarely addresses leaders' constructive manipulation of the city's topography, or analyzes the interactions between the city and the surrounding Syrian countryside.[12] Most recently, Dayna Kalleres has perceptively identified some of the processes through which Antioch, Jerusalem, and Milan became more visibly marked by Christianity, although her focus on what she terms "diabolizing" rituals distinguishes her work from my own.[13]

These publications, of course, draw on the foundational work on Roman Antioch by scholars such as Paul Petit, Glanville Downey, and J. H. W. G. Liebeschuetz. Many aspects of their work from the middle of the twentieth century remain valuable, including the careful collection of the relevant literary and archaeological data available at that time and observations about the changes in some civic structures, such as the role of the *curiales*. Nevertheless, this earlier work is marked by not having had access to all of the relevant materials that are currently available, and by a tendency to read the texts without the "hermeneutics of suspicion" and other methodological preferences prevalent in contemporary scholarship. Given the training of these earlier authors, it is no surprise that they focus on topics such as the governance of the city, economic shifts, the role of the military, and prosopography.[14] Liebeschuetz's emphasis on "decline" is well known, even though most scholars now prefer to speak of the "transformation" of the late Roman cities

the Orontes," in *Archaeology of Late Antiquity*, ed. Leonard Rutgers, Olof Brandt, and Jodi Magness (Cambridge: Cambridge University Press, forthcoming); and Gunnar Brands and Ulrich Weferling, "Ein neuer Stadtplan für Antiochia," *Jahrbuch des Deutschen Archäologischen Instituts* (forthcoming). On the process of Christianization in other Roman regions, see Gunnar Brands, "Die spätantike Stadt und ihre Christianisierung," in *Die spätantike Stadt und ihre Christianisierung: Symposion vom 14. bis 16. Februar 2000 in Halle/Saale*, ed. Gunnar Brands and Hans-Georg Severin (Wiesbaden: Reichert Press, 2003), 9; and Jens-Uwe Krause and Christian Witschel, eds., *Die Stadt in der Spätantike—Niedergang oder Wandel?* (Stuttgart: Franz Steiner Press, 2006).

12. Wendy Mayer's work is an exception, as she occasionally discusses the changing landscape, such as in Mayer, "Antioch and the Intersection between Religious Factionalism, Place, and Power in Late Antiquity," in *The Power of Religion in Late Antiquity*, ed. Andrew Cain and Noel Lenski (Burlington, VT: Ashgate, 2009), 357–68; Mayer and Allen, *Churches*, 200–208. In addition, Emmanuel Soler's work investigates the changing behaviors in the city's landscape (Soler, *Le sacré et le salut*), and Schoolman's archaeological project addresses some of the physical urban changes, with a particular focus on bathing and burial practices (Schoolman, "Civic Transformation"). Chris de Wet has begun to apply the concept of psychogeography to John Chrysostom's writings; see de Wet, "A Walk through the City with John Chrysostom: Toward a Psychogeography of the Urban Ascetic," *Religion and Theology* (forthcoming).

13. Dayna Kalleres, *City of Demons: Violence, Ritual, and Christian Power in Late Antiquity* (Berkeley: University of California Press, forthcoming).

14. See, for example, Paul Petit, *Libanius et la vie municipale à Antioche au IVe siècle après J.-C.* (Paris: Libraire Orientaliste Paul Geuthner, 1955); Glanville Downey, *A History of Antioch in Syria: From Seleucus to the Arab Conquest* (Princeton, NJ: Princeton University Press, 1961); Downey, *Ancient Antioch* (Princeton, NJ: Princeton University Press, 1963); and J. H. W. G. Liebeschuetz, *Antioch: City and Imperial Administration in the Later Roman Empire* (Oxford: Clarendon Press, 1972).

and empire.[15] A.-J. Festugière's work stands out for its focus on religious interactions, but it, too, has been largely superseded by the more methodologically sophisticated discussions of scholars such as Isabella Sandwell.[16] These earlier works therefore differ significantly in method and focus from more recent scholarship, including the current study.

Similarly, earlier studies of the "Christianization" of the Roman Empire often spoke of Christianity monolithically and focused on topics other than topography. Ramsay MacMullen's *Christianizing the Roman Empire, A.D. 100–400*, for instance, highlights the appeal of Christian theology, law, and financial incentives in the religion's growth.[17] Although Frank Trombley's two-volume study, *Hellenic Religion and Christianization c. 370–529*, recognizes that the "conversion" of places was one important aspect in the process of "Christianizing" the empire, it focuses more on theological and political efforts to change practices and allegiances than on ideological efforts to reshape the landscape. Furthermore, Trombley's use of archaeological and epigraphic sources leads him to focus primarily on the fifth century rather than earlier.[18] The sensitivity to the spatial aspects of Roman culture in Laura Nasrallah's insightful recent study of the second century, on the other hand, has allowed her to present the development of Christianity in a new light.[19] Some scholars of late antiquity have conducted spatially sensitive studies, often of particular locations, but most continue to perpetuate the assumption that local places provided a static context in which fourth-century events transpired, despite cultural geographers' critical discussions of the means by which space is constructed and controlled.[20]

---

15. See, for example, J. H. W. G. Liebeschuetz: *The Decline and Fall of the Roman City* (New York: Oxford University Press, 2001), esp. 414–16; "Transformation and Decline: Are the Two Really Incompatible?," in *Die Stadt in der Spätantike—Niedergang oder Wandel?*, ed. Jens-Uwe Krause and Christian Witschel (Stuttgart: Franz Steiner Press, 2006), 476–78; "The Uses and Abuses of the Concept of 'Decline' in Later Roman History, or, Was Gibbon Politically Incorrect?," in *Recent Research in Late-Antique Urbanism*, ed. Luke Lavan, Journal of Roman Archaeology Supplementary Series 42 (Portsmouth, RI: Journal of Roman Archaeology, 2001), 233–38.

16. A.-J. Festugière, *Antioche païenne et chrétienne: Libanius, Chrysostome et les moines de Syrie* (Paris: Éditions E. de Boccard, 1959); Sandwell, *Religious Identity*.

17. Ramsay MacMullen, *Christianizing the Roman Empire, A.D. 100–400* (New Haven, CT: Yale University Press, 1984).

18. Frank Trombley, *Hellenic Religion and Christianization, c. 370–529*, 2 vols. (Leiden: E. J. Brill, 1993).

19. Laura Nasrallah, *Christian Responses to Roman Art and Architecture: The Second-Century Church amid the Spaces of Empire* (New York: Cambridge University Press, 2010).

20. I am indebted to earlier scholarship on the significance of topographical changes in the late Roman Empire, including Harry Maier, "Private Spaces as the Social Context of Arianism in Ambrose's Milan," *JTS* 45 (1994): 72–93; Maier, "The Topography of Heresy and Dissent in Late-Fourth-Century Rome," *Historia: Zeitschrift für alte Geschichte* 44.2 (1995): 232–49; and Christopher Haas, *Alexandria in Late Antiquity: Topography and Social Conflict* (Baltimore: Johns Hopkins University Press, 1997). See also James Goehring, "The Dark Side of Landscape: Ideology and Power in the Christian Myth of the

While Kim Knott, Thomas Tweed, and Jonathan Z. Smith—and of course, earlier, Mircea Eliade—are among the scholars of religion who have examined particularly religious uses and constructions of places, I have avoided the more ethereal concept of "sacred space" and have largely relied directly on geographers for the spatial vocabulary of this project on Roman antiquity.[21] Geographers such as Henri Lefebvre, Yi-Fu Tuan, Gill Valentine, Benedict Anderson, and David Sibley demonstrate that the rhetorical and physical manipulation of places plays a significant role in the development of the events that take place in and around them. Edward Soja has long been an advocate of this "spatial turn" in the social sciences and the humanities, and he has provided a brief history of its development.[22] Elsewhere he eloquently describes its broad significance:

> [Places are] products of collective human action and intention, and therefore susceptible to being modified or changed. This infuses all (socially constructed) scales of human spatiality, from the local to the global, not just with activity and intentionality, but also with built-in tensions and potential conflicts, with openness and freedom as well as enclosure and oppression, with the perpetual presence of geohistorically uneven development, and hence with politics, ideology, and what, borrowing from Michel Foucault, can be called the intersections of space, knowledge, and power.[23]

Unveiling the ways in which Antioch's urban and rural places played a critical role in the monumental fourth-century struggles to define religious orthodoxy will require scholars to recognize the local and locative politics involved in the development and eventual prominence of Nicene Christianity in the Roman Empire.

Contemporary critical geographers challenge the existence of undifferentiated absolute space, much like the more general challenge that modern critical theorists have leveled against the possibility of empirical objectivity, and this has significant implications for the study of late antiquity. Human geographers such as Doreen Massey argue that we cannot fully understand events outside of their particular locations; the events do not exist independently of some neutral space, but rather the space and the event work hand in hand in shaping each other, the space

Desert," in *The Cultural Turn in Late Ancient Studies: Gender, Asceticism, and Historiography,* ed. Dale Martin and Patricia Cox Miller (Durham, NC: Duke University Press, 2005), 136–49. Additional works are cited in the discussion below.

21. Thomas Tweed, *Crossing and Dwelling: A Theory of Religion* (Cambridge, MA: Harvard University Press, 2006); Kim Knott, *The Location of Religion: A Spatial Analysis* (Oakville, CT: Equinox Press, 2005); Jonathan Z. Smith, *To Take Place: Toward a Theory of Ritual* (Chicago: University of Chicago Press, 1987); and Mircea Eliade, *The Sacred and the Profane: The Nature of Religion* (San Diego: Harcourt Brace Jovanovich, 1959).

22. Edward Soja, "Taking Space Personally," in *The Spatial Turn: Interdisciplinary Perspectives,* ed. Barney Warf and Santa Arias (New York: Routledge, 2009), 11–35.

23. Edward Soja, *Postmetropolis: Critical Studies of Cities and Regions* (Oxford: Blackwell, 2000), 7.

affecting the course of the event, and the event in turn shaping the understanding of the space.[24] This scholarship encourages historians no longer to presume that the location of an event is simply an inert staging ground that could easily have been different in design or location and still have produced the same event. Rather, the location is itself another participant that shapes and influences what takes place there; and as a participant, the location is in turn affected by the events. Scholars following the work of Henri Lefebvre differentiate between *space* and *place* by understanding place to be "a particular form of space, one that is created through acts of naming as well as the distinctive activities and imaginings associated with particular social spaces."[25] In this vocabulary, fourth-century Antioch was rich with the construction of places, as leaders struggled to define and control the city's spaces and thus solidify the competing religious identities of Antioch's citizens.

Geographers' observations that physical places are not culturally neutral have prompted scholars across numerous disciplines to explore the power dynamics of place-construction, and scholars of late antiquity have begun to benefit from these conversations.[26] If places are constructed, then there are agents who actively shape them, and some people who benefit more than others from their representation. To construct a place in Roman Antioch, whether physically or rhetorically, is thus inherently to wield power, and to engage in the politics associated with those power dynamics.[27] Chris Philo and Gerry Kearns's nuanced discus-

---

24. See Felicity Callard, "Doreen Massey," in *Key Thinkers on Space and Place*, ed. Phil Hubbard, Rob Kitchin, and Gill Valentine (Thousand Oaks, CA: Sage Publications, 2004), 219–25; and Doreen Massey, *Space, Place, and Gender* (Cambridge: Polity Press, 1994).

25. Hubbard, Kitchin, and Valentine, "Editors' Introduction," in Hubbard, *Key Thinkers*, 5.

26. See, for example, Kay Anderson and Fay Gale, *Inventing Places: Studies in Cultural Geography* (Melbourne: Longman Chesire/Wiley Halsted Press, 1992). Feminist scholars have demonstrated the gendered constructions of places that have facilitated the perpetuation of male dominance; e.g., Massey, *Space, Place, and Gender*. There has also been a growing academic interest in "the household" in late antiquity, and its implications regarding gendered uses of space, and their narrative portrayal. See, for example, Kristina Sessa, ed., "Holy Households: Space, Property, and Power," special issue, *Journal of Early Christian Studies* 15.2 (2007); Shelley Hales, *The Roman House and Social Identity* (New York: Cambridge University Press, 2003); Lisa Nevett, *Domestic Space in Classical Antiquity* (New York: Cambridge University Press, 2010); Beryl Rawson and Paul Weaver, eds., *The Roman Family in Italy: Status, Sentiment, Space* (Oxford: Clarendon Press, 1997); Kate Cooper, *The Fall of the Roman Household* (New York: Cambridge University Press, 2007); Kim Bowes, *Private Worship, Public Values, and Religious Change in Late Antiquity* (New York: Cambridge University Press, 2008); Kim Bowes, *Houses and Society in the Later Roman Empire* (London: Duckworth, 2010). Jaś Elsner's work on Roman art complements this discussion of the changing Roman landscape: Elsner, *Art and the Roman Viewer: The Transformation of Art from the Pagan World to Christianity* (New York: Cambridge University Press, 1995).

27. For examples of political uses of local landscapes in the ancient world, see Adam Smith, *The Political Landscape: Constellations of Authority in Early Complex Politics* (Berkeley: University of California Press, 2003).

sion of places as commodities that are shaped for a particular audience is useful, for example, in understanding some of the power dynamics of John Chrysostom's rhetoric regarding the burned temple of Apollo in Antioch's suburb of Daphne.[28]

Such spatial manipulations and their effects are visible not only in the events of history,[29] but also in the ways in which history is remembered.[30] Since places call to mind events associated with them, or are "culturally constructed to connote and consolidate the possession of past events associated with their own use or ownership,"[31] they are mutable. "Memory practices and experiences shift over time," according to Lynn Meskell, "as perceptions of the past are reworked in the context of the present and also in anticipation of the future."[32] Not surprisingly, these changes intervene in local and global power dynamics, as, in the words of

28. Gerry Kearns and Chris Philo, eds., *Selling Places: The City as Cultural Capital, Past and Present* (New York: Pergamon Press, 1993), 1–32.

29. See, for example, Marc Boone, "Urban Space and Political Conflict in Late Medieval Flanders," *Journal of Interdisciplinary History* 32.4 (2002): 621–40; John Curran, "The Christianization of the Topography of Rome, AD 337–384," in *Pagan City and Christian Capital: Rome in the Fourth Century* (Oxford: Clarendon Press, 2000), 116–57; Ton Derks, "The Transformation of Landscape and Religious Representations in Roman Gaul," *Archaeological Dialogues* 4.2 (1997): 126–47; W. J. Thomas Mitchell, *Landscape and Power* (Chicago: University of Chicago Press, 2002); Jon May, "Globalization and the Politics of Place: Place and Identity in an Inner London Neighbourhood," *Transactions of the Institute of British Geographers* 21 (1996): 194–215; and Doreen Massey and John Allen, *Geography Matters! A Reader* (New York: Cambridge University Press, 1984).

30. See Paul Ricoeur, *Memory, History, Forgetting*, trans. Kathleen Blamey and David Pellauer (Chicago: University of Chicago Press, 2004); Dydia DeLyser, "When Less Is More: Absence and Landscape in a California Ghost Town," in *Textures of Place: Exploring Humanist Geographies*, ed. Paul Adams, Steven Hoelscher, and Karen Till (Minneapolis: University of Minnesota Press, 2001), 24–40; Aleida Assmann, *Cultural Memory and Western Civilization: Functions, Media, Archives* (New York: Cambridge University Press, 2011); Gregor Kalas, *Transforming Public Space in Rome: The Late Antique Revision of the Roman Forum* (Austin: University of Texas Press, forthcoming); and Kalas, "Writing Restoration in Rome: Inscriptions, Statues, and the Late Antique Preservation of Buildings," in *Cities, Texts, and Social Networks, 400–1500: Experiences and Perceptions of Medieval Urban Space*, ed. Caroline Goodson et al. (Surrey: Ashgate, 2010), 21–43. Other scholars have focused on archaeology and memory, such as Norman Yoffee, *Negotiating the Past in the Past: Identity, Memory, and Landscape in Archaeological Research* (Tucson: University of Arizona Press, 2007); and Ruth Van Dyke and Susan Alcock, eds., *Archaeologies of Memory* (Malden, MA: Blackwell Publishing, 2003). See also Pamela Stewart and Andrew Strathern, eds., *Landscape, Memory, and History: Anthropological Perspectives* (Sterling, VA: Pluto, 2003); and Alexandra Walsham, *The Reformation of the Landscape: Religion, Identity, and Memory in Early Modern Britain and Ireland* (New York: Oxford University Press, 2011).

31. Michael Rowlands, "The Role of Memory in the Transmission of Culture," *World Archaeology* 25 (1993): 44.

32. Lynn Meskell, "Back to the Future: From the Past in the Present to the Past in the Past," in Yoffee, *Negotiating the Past*, 221; see also Meskell, "The Intersections of Identity and Politics in Archaeology," *Annual Review of Anthropology* 31 (2002): 279–301.

Catherine Lyon Crawford, "memory (both collective and individual) is integral to [the] process of legitimization and assimilation."³³ Memory is thus inherently related to the physical landscape with which events are associated and to the identity of the people whose memories they are. Norman Yoffee writes: "Landscapes, thus, form the material of 'memory communities' (as Alcock, using Maurice Halbwach's term, puts it), and such communities provide important aspects of people's identities. These identities then 'overarch' other, local identities; the landscapes of everyday life are the sites where the various and diverse levels of identity are negotiated."³⁴ Landscapes, memories, and individual and collective identities work symbiotically with one another; to change physically or rhetorically how a place is perceived is to affect the politics and identities associated with it, as the discussion below shows regarding the Apollo temple in Daphne and the relics of the Christian saint Babylas.

Scholars' work on the politics of mapping has also shaped my study of fourth-century presentations of the Antiochene region's landscape. According to Angèle Smith, for example, "Maps, as representations of landscape, are political tools."³⁵ J. B. Harley and Geoff King emphasize that every map represents a particular perspective, and thus shapes the reader's view of the places it portrays.³⁶ The differing representations of Antioch and its environs in the writings of Libanius, John Chrysostom, and Theodoret confirm the political and individual nature of these Antiochene authors' narrative maps. Examining Antioch through the lens of spatial politics will reveal that fourth-century leaders' manipulation of the city's landscape was one means by which they actively engaged in the tumultuous local and imperial contests over religious and political power. Their activities not only changed the topography of the city and its surrounding region, but also in the process furthered the "Christianization" of the Roman Empire and redefined the shape of religious orthodoxy.

33. Catherine Lyon Crawford, "Collecting, Defacing, Reinscribing (and Otherwise Performing) Memory in the Ancient World," in Yoffee, *Negotiating the Past,* 2.

34. Norman Yoffee, "Peering into the Palimpsest: An Introduction to the Volume," in Yoffee, *Negotiating the Past,* 3; see also Susan Alcock, *Archaeologies of the Greek Past: Landscape, Monuments, and Memories* (New York: Cambridge University Press, 2002); and Maurice Halbwachs, *On Collective Memory,* ed. and trans. Lewis A. Coser (Chicago: University of Chicago Press, 1992).

35. Angèle Smith, "Landscape Representation: Place and Identity in Nineteenth-Century Ordnance Survey Maps of Ireland," in Stewart and Strathern, *Landscape, Memory, and History,* 71.

36. J. B. Harley, "Deconstructing the Map," *Cartographica* 26 (1989): 1–20; Harley, "Maps, Knowledge, and Power," in *The Iconography of Landscape: Essays on the Symbolic Representation, Design and Use of Past Environments,* ed. Denis Cosgrove and Stephen Daniels (New York: Cambridge University Press, 1988), 277–311; Geoff King, *Mapping Reality: An Exploration of Cultural Cartographies* (New York: St. Martin's Press, 1996).

ANTIOCHENE CHRISTIANITY IN SCHISM:
THEOLOGY AND POLITICS IN LATE ANTIQUITY

While those living in fourth-century Antioch continued to attend religious festivals, buy and sell in the markets, and visit the theater and baths largely as they had in the past, new emperors and a surplus of local bishops, each with his own doctrines and politics, meant that Antiochenes' city and world were constantly changing around them. By the fourth century, Christians in Antioch could look to their sacred scripture for evidence that they were among the oldest Christian communities in the empire, visited by the apostles Paul and Peter, and living where the followers of Jesus were first called Christians (Acts 11.26). This scriptural fame was supplemented by the admiration and renown given to the city's late first-century bishop and martyr Ignatius. The city's size, wealth, and political significance further contributed to its fame and importance in the empire quite apart from its early Christian community, and by the fourth century the city was one of the largest in the empire, with its winter palace used by many of the fourth-century emperors. Militarily well positioned with respect to the hostile border with the Persian Empire, the city had a military drill field (*campus martius*) across the river and a variable number of troops in residence.

Antioch's significance may provide some insight into why so many people cared so deeply to claim the right to be bishop of this city in the important decades of the fourth century while leaders publicly debated the first imperial definitions of Christian orthodoxy. It also suggests that the shifting religious topography of Antioch, and its implications for the definition of religious orthodoxy, relate not only to Christianity in this one city but have much wider influence. Many of the most influential leaders in the empire, from Athanasius and Jerome to the emperors themselves, passed through Antioch and sought to influence the politics there.[37] A brief overview of the complexities of Antioch's fourth-century ecclesiastical controversies will provide the necessary background for the following chapters, as well as for the ways in which the struggle to represent religious orthodoxy in Antioch was intricately intertwined with local and imperial concerns.

When the emperor Constantine convened the first ecumenical Council of Nicaea in 325 C.E., he seems to have hoped that the empire's bishops would settle the most pressing intra-Christian disputes and create a measure of Christian orthodoxy for the empire. While the council addressed many topics, the most

---

37. Athanasius not only visited Antioch, but in 362 addressed a letter to its citizens regarding the episcopal schism in the city (Athanasius, *Tomus ad Antiochenos*). Regarding the council in Alexandria that preceded the letter, see Thomas Karmann, *Meletius von Antiochien: Studien zur Geschichte des trinitätstheologischen Streits in den Jahren 360–364 n. Chr.*, Regensburger Studien zur Theologie 68 (Frankfurt: Peter Lang, 2009), 168–92; for more on the letter itself, see 193–305; on Meletius and Athanasius in Antioch, see 412–25.

divisive—at the council and in the decades that followed—centered on the question of the proper description for the relation between the first and second Persons of the Christian Trinity. In the years preceding the council, the priest Arius had entered into a local dispute with his bishop in Alexandria, Alexander, who was strongly and vocally supported by his deacon Athanasius, who succeeded Alexander as bishop in 328. In his efforts to preserve Christian monotheism, Arius argued that it could not be possible for the second Person of the Trinity to be of the same substance as the Father, as that would result in two gods. His opponents, intent on preserving the narrative of Christian salvation as they understood it, argued that unless the second Person of the Trinity were consubstantial with the Father, then his incarnation, death, and resurrection could not effect human salvation. By the end of the lengthy deliberations of 325, a majority of the bishops at the Council of Nicaea voted to include in the Christian creed that the second Person, the Son, was consubstantial (*homoousios*) with God the Father, and Arius's teachings were anathematized, setting the stage for decades of controversy in Antioch and around the empire between those who supported the council's creed and those who still thought that the second Person was in some way subordinate to, and thus at least slightly different from, the first Person of the Trinity.[38]

Even after the council, therefore, there remained strong support for a more subordinationist Christian doctrine, especially in much of the eastern empire, and Christian leaders continued to argue over the details.[39] Eustathius was Antioch's bishop when the Council of Nicaea was called, and he attended the famous gathering, lending his support to the winning side. Nevertheless, although Eustathius supported the council's outcome, and thus Alexander and Athanasius of Alexandria, the eastern empire predominantly supported a homoian theology that subordinated the Son to some degree. Thus, even though Eustathius's Nicene followers in Antioch continued to consider him the rightful bishop, he was deposed from

38. For an overview of these complicated controversies, see, for example, Lewis Ayres, *Nicaea and Its Legacy: An Approach to Fourth-Century Trinitarian Theology* (New York: Oxford University Press, 2004); R. P. C. Hanson, *The Search for the Christian Doctrine of God: The Arian Controversy, 318–381* (Grand Rapids, MI: Baker Academic Press, 1988); Timothy D. Barnes, *Athanasius and Constantius: Theology and Politics in the Constantinian Empire* (Cambridge, MA: Harvard University Press, 1993); David Gwynn, *The Eusebians: The Polemic of Athanasius of Alexandria and the Construction of the "Arian Controversy"* (New York: Oxford University Press, 2007). For an effort to reconstruct the homoian side of the conversation, see especially Hanns Christof Brennecke, *Studien zur Geschichte der Homöer: Der Osten bis zum Ende der homöischen Reichskirche* (Tübingen: J. C. B. Mohr/Paul Siebeck, 1988). Although I have been unable to access Robin Ward's graduate thesis, Wendy Mayer has noted its relevance: Robin Ward, "The Schism at Antioch in the Fourth Century" (PhD diss., King's College, London, 2003).

39. The term "subordinationist" refers to a wide number of different theological positions, all of which rejected the term *homoousios* from the Council of Nicaea, and none of whom voluntarily chose to be associated with Arius or his teachings, which had been anathematized.

his see ca. 330/1.[40] Those who supported his removal appear to have most vocally hoped that the homoian leader Eusebius, then bishop of Caesarea, would take his place, but Eusebius seems to have been unwilling to move to Antioch. The sources are not unanimous, but it seems that there was a brief struggle to agree on a suitable replacement, during which time Eusebius's friend and fellow homoian Paulinus of Tyre became bishop of Antioch for six months, followed briefly by Eulalius, and then the homoian Euphronius, who was soon succeeded upon his death by another homoian bishop, Flacillus, who was in place by 335.[41] The forced removal of the Nicene bishop Eustathius, and his replacement by a series of homoian appointees, led to a schism in Antioch's episcopacy that lasted for decades and is at the center of the fourth-century struggles to claim the title of Christian orthodoxy, and all the political advantages it conferred.

Upon Constantine's death in 337, his son Constantius II became emperor in the East and patronized homoian Christianity.[42] Constantius II's early years as emperor were a time of a great deal of conflict in Antioch, both between the homoian Christians, who had the political support of the emperor, and their opponents, who had the doctrinal support of the Council of Nicaea, as well as internally within each group. By the time of Constantius II, Athanasius, then bishop of Alexandria,[43] had become the most vocal opponent of subordinationist theology—and its numerous and varied proponents—in the empire, and was actively blurring their distinctions by creating terms such as "Arianism" and "Ariomaniacs" to cover all of their theological permutations.[44] Athanasius met with Constantius II in Antioch in 346, and the bishop's strident political and theological claims would later directly influence Antiochene politics when two different Nicene factions emerged, Paulinus's clearly associated with Athanasius and Antioch's earlier bishop Eustathius, and Meletius's further distanced from the controversial Alexandrian bishop, in opposition to their mutual homoian rivals.

It was also during the early years of Constantius II's reign that the Dedication Council met in Antioch in 341 to memorialize the completion of the extravagant

40. See Downey, *History,* 352; Mayer and Allen, *Churches,* 262–66; Hanson, *Search,* 208–38. The traditional date of Eustathius's deposition is 330/1, though others have argued for an earlier date, such as Henry Chadwick's suggestion of 326, which Hanson rejects. See Henry Chadwick, "The Fall of Eustathius of Antioch," *JThS* 49 (OS) (1948): 27–35; and R. P. C. Hanson, "The Fate of Eustathius of Antioch," *Zeitschrift für Kirchengeschichte* 95 (1984): 171–79.

41. See, for example, Downey, *History,* 352; Hanson, *Search,* 259, 277, 388.

42. Barnes's book-length study of the relationship between Constantius II and Athanasius is insightful and useful to the reconstruction of this history (Barnes, *Athanasius and Constantius*).

43. Athanasius became bishop of Alexandria in 328, although he was exiled by Constantine from 335 to 337, by Constantius II from 339 to 346 and again from 356 to 362, by Julian from 362 to 363, and by Valens from 365 to 366.

44. See Ayres, *Nicaea,* 105–30.

Great Church and concurrently develop a creed that avoided the most controversial language from the Council of Nicaea, a new creed that they intended should at least clarify, if not outright supplant, that from the council of 325.[45] There was also occasional trouble among Antioch's homoian Christians in these years, which added to the complexity. Illicit plotting by the homoian bishop Stephen seems to have led to his removal in 344, and Leontius took over the see. While Nicene Christians in Antioch continued to consider Eustathius their rightful bishop until his death, the episcopacy and the city's main church buildings belonged to their homoian opponents under the emperor Constantius II, and leaders who supported the Council of Nicaea sought new ways to regain control of the city's (and the eastern empire's) churches.[46]

The second decade of Constantius II's reign continued to be tumultuous for religious leaders in Antioch and around the empire. The emperor issued legislation that forbade ritual sacrifice and impeded access to temples (*CTh* 16.10.2–6), and sometime between 351 and 354 Caesar Gallus had the relics of Antioch's third-century Christian martyr, Babylas, moved from the cemetery that was outside the city's gate to the grounds of the famous Apollo temple in Daphne. Gallus was friendly with another Antiochene Christian leader, Aetius, an extreme subordinationist who was ordained as a deacon in Antioch in 350 and taught in the city until Bishop Leontius dismissed him.[47] By 357 Athanasius had been exiled from Alexandria for the third time, and homoian Christians had gained the upper hand around the empire. Bishop Leontius's death in Antioch soon afterward led to the election of Eudoxius, a Christian whose theology was even more distant from the creed of Nicaea than Leontius's had been, as Eudoxius supported the teachings of Aetius and denied any resemblance between the first and second Persons of the Trinity. As bishop, Eudoxius hosted a council in Antioch in 358 that confirmed the validity of the Second Creed of Sirmium, a creed that was actively hostile to the decisions of the Council of Nicaea. Eudoxius's subsequent election as the bishop of Constantinople in 360 confirmed that the decisions and politics of Antioch engaged in empire-wide conversations, and raised the challenge for Antiochenes to find yet another new bishop for their tension-fraught community, which consisted not only of those Christians in favor of the creed from 325 at Nicaea, but also a variety of Christians who found it unsatisfactory.[48] In the decades after 360, Christian leaders most explicitly appear to have used the city's topography to negotiate an outcome to this schism that would have been advantageous for their version of Christianity.

---

45. Ayres, *Nicaea*, 119.
46. See Mayer and Allen, *Churches*, 269.
47. Downey, *History*, 363.
48. Regarding Eudoxius, see Brennecke, *Studien*, esp. 48–55, 63–67.

Given the turmoil within Antiochene Christianity, it was not easy to choose a new bishop for the city, and the man they elected, Meletius, found himself quickly exiled.[49] Although Meletius's theological affiliations changed over time, Thomas Karmann concludes that the bishop was exiled so soon after his election not, as most scholars have concluded, over questions about his doctrine, which arose only later, but primarily because of controversial administrative choices he was making.[50] Meletius moved to Antioch from Beroea (present-day Aleppo, Syria), a small city east of Antioch.[51] Past gestures, such as his support for the homoian leader Acacius in 357, had caused Meletius to have a reputation that made some leaders hope that he would be sympathetic to the reigning homoian orthodoxy and yet able to provide a bridge to Christians who approved of the Council of Nicaea, healing the schism that still rent the city's Christian communities. Meletius was exiled soon after his election, however, perhaps even a month or less after his appointment (John Chrysostom, *De sancto Meletio* 1, 2/4, 6), and was replaced by the homoian leader Euzoius.[52]

In 361 the emperor Constantius II died and was succeeded by his cousin Julian, whose primary religious interests as emperor were in reestablishing "Hellenism" and bringing back state-sanctioned sacrifices to the gods.[53] During Julian's brief reign (361–63), Christian churches had to compete for resources and followers with temples, whose patronage was being rejuvenated by Julian quite actively and personally in Antioch and its suburb Daphne, and with Jewish communities, whom Julian admired in light of the religion's antiquity and its history of ritual sacrifice. Julian visited Antioch as emperor and had the Christian martyr Babylas's relics returned from the site of Apollo's temple back to the cemetery at Antioch. Bishop Meletius returned to Antioch when Julian recalled all exiled bishops around the empire, and the years of Julian's reign were ones of continued upheaval for Antioch's competing clergy.[54]

49. See Brennecke, *Studien*, 66–77; Barnes, *Athanasius and Constantius*, 149.

50. Karmann, *Meletius von Antiochien*, 135–49. See also Franz Dünzl's investigation of the theological nuances, politics, and social networks behind this exile in Dünzl, "Die Absetzung des Bischofs Meletius von Antiochien 361 N.C.," *Jahrbuch für Antike und Christentum* 43 (2000): 71–93. Johannes Zachhuber also investigates the complicated theology of Meletius in Zachhuber, "The Antiochene Synod of AD 363 and the Beginnings of Neo-Nicenism," *Zeitschrift für antikes Christentum* 4.1 (2000): 83–101.

51. For more detail, see Karmann, *Meletius von Antiochien*, 51–74.

52. The Greek text of *De sancto Meletio* is in PG 50.515–20. I note first the PG paragraph numbering, followed by the paragraphs of Wendy Mayer's recent English translation: Wendy Mayer with Bronwen Neil, *St. John Chrysostom: The Cult of the Saints: Select Homilies and Letters* (New York: St. Vladimir's Seminary Press, 2006), 39–48.

53. See the discussion in Scott Bradbury, "Julian's Pagan Revival and the Decline of Blood Sacrifice," *Phoenix* 49.4 (1995): 331–56; Susanna Elm, *Sons of Hellenism, Fathers of the Church: Emperor Julian, Gregory of Nazianzus, and the Vision of Rome* (Berkeley: University of California Press, 2012).

54. For more detail, see Karmann, *Meletius von Antiochien*, 150–67.

Bishop Meletius's exile under Constantius II, and Euzoius's subsequent election, initiated a period of severe schism in the city. When Julian recalled all exiled bishops, the Christian leaders in Antioch were forced to compete for control of the city even more sharply, as both bishops were in residence at the same time, and neither had clear imperial support. During this time, Bishop Euzoius and his followers appear to have maintained control of Antioch's newest and largest Great Church, thanks to the support they had received from Constantius II until his death, while Bishop Meletius and his followers appear to have held services most regularly in the old Apostolic Church.[55] To add to the confusion, however, a Christian named Paulinus was also ordained as another bishop for Antioch at this time.

While Meletius was in the process of returning to Antioch, Lucifer of Cagliari hastily consecrated Paulinus, a Nicene Christian who followed in the footsteps of Antioch's earlier bishop Eustathius and was a strong supporter of Athanasius of Alexandria, as yet a third bishop of Antioch after Bishop Euzoius's appointment and immediately before Bishop Meletius's return.[56] Thus under the emperor Julian, three distinct Christian communities survived in Antioch, each with its own clergy. The homoian Christians of Antioch, following the bishop Euzoius, were a community with political control in the city and around the empire after decades of favorable imperial status. After some early uncertainty about Meletius's theology, some Christians in Antioch who supported the Council of Nicaea, though not so strongly the controversial and highly politicized bishop Athanasius of Alexandria, came to follow this bishop, the first officially appointed successor to Bishop Eudoxius. Meletius's community seems to have been quite large, with the support of some powerful regional leaders like Basil of Caesarea, and it was able to survive decades of imperial hostility. Other Nicene Christians, however, had continued to support Bishop Eustathius after he was deposed in 330/1 and were aligned politically and theologically with Athanasius of Alexandria and his supporters, and these Antiochene Christians followed the new bishop Paulinus.[57] Although Paulinus seems to have had a small community with perhaps more support outside of

55. Mayer summarizes this history of church possession: Mayer and Allen, *Churches*, 269.

56. See, for example, Barnes, *Athanasius and Constantius*, 155–56; Hanson, *Search*, 509, 643–44; Ayres, *Nicaea*, 176, 226; Karmann, *Meletius von Antiochien*, 306–21.

57. According to Zachhuber, "It is clear from all the texts that have been investigated that there is no indication of Athanasius' not accepting Meletius as bishop of Antioch. On the contrary, it was the latter who, apparently, rejected the Alexandrian pope" (Zachhuber, "Antiochene Synod," 99). Tom Elliott counters Zachhuber's interpretation of the evidence, however, arguing that Athanasius's *Tomus ad Antiochenos* supports Paulinus's episcopacy over Meletius's, an argument that I find persuasive: Tom Elliott, "Was the *Tomus ad Antiochenos* a Pacific Document?," *Journal of Ecclesiastical History* 58 (2007): 1–8. Karmann adds more nuance to this discussion, speculating about some of the reasons that might have influenced Athanasius's preference of Paulinus over Meletius: Karmann, *Meletius von Antiochien*, esp. 204–19, 234–44.

Antioch than inside (including support from Athanasius of Alexandria, Jerome, and Ambrose of Milan), this Antiochene faction seems to have been tolerated by both of Antioch's larger Christian factions. The followers of Paulinus continued to hold separate worship services in the city even during the alternating exiles of the competing bishops of the other two Christian communities.

With three bishops competing to control one city, it is little surprise that conflicts soon arose over who could lead services in which places. When the Christian Jovian became emperor after Julian's unexpected death at war in Persia in 363, Bishop Meletius hosted a council to rally support for his branch of Antiochene Christianity, during which brief time he appears to have had imperial support and thus control of Antioch's Great Church.[58] Jovian died soon thereafter, however, and, with the homoian Christian Valens's ascension to the throne in 364, Meletius lost control of Antioch's Great Church and even the old Apostolic Church and apparently had to hold services outdoors (e.g., Theodoret, *HR* 2; *HE* 4.22). Soon after, in 365, Valens exiled Meletius, although his congregants continued to 'worship apart from the other two Antiochene Christian communities even in his absence, meeting at the foot of Mount Silpius and then in the military training grounds across the Orontes River outside the city walls.[59] Bishop Euzoius and his homoian supporters, meanwhile, regained control of the city's Great Church, while the bishop Paulinus and his supporters were allowed to continue worshipping in a small church in the city.[60]

This tripartite episcopal schism continued in Antioch through the reign of Valens (r. 364–78) and the death of Athanasius (d. 373), and gained one more complication with Apollinaris of Laodicea's consecration around 375 of a fourth bishop of Antioch, Vitalis. Under Valens, Bishop Meletius was exiled twice, but his priests Flavian and Diodore seem to have led his followers in his absence. Meletius returned from his second exile around 369, but was exiled again soon after,[61] and finally returned to Antioch upon Valens's death in 378, when John Chrysostom also appears to have returned to public life in his native city.[62] The homoian community in Antioch also underwent some changes in these years, as by 378 they elected a new

58. Brennecke, *Studien,* 173–78; Mayer and Allen, *Churches,* 269; Karmann, *Meletius von Antiochien,* 341–54.

59. The date of Meletius's return from his second exile is uncertain (Hanson, *Search,* 792), but Mayer suggests he returned only in 369, to be exiled again later in the same year (Mayer and Allen, *Churches,* 45).

60. Mayer and Allen, *Churches,* 269. Socrates (*HE* 4.2) notes that Paulinus was allowed to continue meeting his community as always during this time.

61. Mayer and Allen, *Churches,* 45.

62. Although Palladius claims that John Chrysostom withdrew from Antioch to practice a more rigorous asceticism (*Dial.* 5), Martin Illert has challenged the veracity of that claim in light of evidence in Chrysostom's own texts favoring a "Syrian" form of asceticism that did not necessitate withdrawal from the city: Illert, *Johannes Chrysostomus und das antiochenisch-syrische Mönchtum: Studien zu Theologie, Rhetorik und Kirchenpolitik im antiochenischen Schrifttum des Johannes Chrysostomus* (Zurich:

bishop, Dorotheos, to replace Euzoius, although both Dorotheos and his rival Meletius died only three years later in 381. While Dorotheos does not appear to have
been replaced, bringing the Antiochene schism one step closer to an end, John
Chrysostom attests to continued conflict in the following years with Anomeans and
other Christians, all of whom he considered to be heretical, although there is no
mention of Antioch's Anomean Christians having a separate bishop.[63]

With the privilege of hindsight, it is clear that with the accession of Theodosius
to the throne as the Eastern emperor in January 379, the days of the homoian
Christians' success around the empire were numbered. Given the upheaval of the
recent decades, however, this could not have been clear at the time. Theodosius
became a very active patron of Nicene Christianity, and his administration supported Meletius rather than Paulinus as the rightful bishop of Antioch.[64] Under
the emperor Theodosius, therefore, Bishop Meletius and his followers regained
control of the Great Church in Antioch, as well as at least most of the city's other
Christian places. Soon after Meletius's return from his third and final exile, he
began building a new church to house the relics of saint Babylas. Theodosius
quickly provided legislative and conciliar support for the Nicene Christians, first
through the so-called *cunctos populos* edict that required Nicene orthodoxy of the
empire's citizens (*CTh* 16.1.2); then by calling the Council of Constantinople, which
took place May–July 381, and reaffirmed the orthodoxy of the Council of Nicaea
with new decisions in light of the past decades of controversy; and finally with the
further legislation that immediately followed the council, which required all
church buildings to be in the hands of Christians who were orthodox by the
empire's new definition (*CTh* 16.1.3). Meletius had the honor of presiding over the

Pano Press, 2000), 95–110. Wendy Mayer takes up Illert's challenge to Palladius's portrayal in her study
of John Chrysostom's ascetic practices: Mayer, "What Does It Mean to Say That John Chrysostom Was
a Monk?," *Studia Patristica* 41 (2006): 451–55. More recently J. H. W. G. Liebeschuetz accepted Illert's
claim that John Chrysostom's asceticism was influenced by distinctively Syrian ascetic practices (in
contrast to developing Egyptian traditions), but also Palladius's claim, rejected by Illert, that Chrysostom withdrew to one of the mountain retreats outside Antioch: Liebeschuetz, *Ambrose and John
Chrysostom: Clerics between Desert and Empire* (New York: Oxford University Press, 2011), 3–4.

63. John Chrysostom, *De incomprehensibili natura dei; De s. Pelagia*. It is noteworthy that this
development differed significantly in the western Mediterranean, where an imperial edict of 386
allowed those who adhered to the Council of Ariminum (359), many of whom would have been
disenfranchised homoians in the East, to continue to claim rights to orthodoxy and property in the
West (*CTh* 16.1.4).

64. It is interesting to note, though, that the bishop of Antioch was left out of an imperial list from
381, soon after the death of Meletius. David Hunt has suggested that this could have been due to the
controversy over who would succeed Meletius as Antioch's imperially sanctioned bishop, indicating
further the uncertainty at this time among Flavian, John Chrysostom, and their contemporaries about
the future of Antioch's episcopal leadership: Hunt, "Christianising the Roman Empire: The Evidence
of the Code," in *The Theodosian Code*, ed. Jill Harries and Ian Wood (Ithaca, NY: Cornell University
Press, 1993), 150.

ecumenical council in 381, although he died there during the proceedings, and his body was carried back with great pomp to Antioch, where it was buried in the church that he had recently built for Saint Babylas.

Flavian succeeded Meletius as bishop of Antioch in 381, and it was under Bishop Flavian's leadership that John Chrysostom became a presbyter in 386. When Bishop Paulinus died in 388, he was succeeded by Evagrius. Flavian himself died in 404 after being recognized by the bishops of Alexandria and Rome as the rightful bishop of Antioch, and Flavian was replaced by Porphyrius and then his successor Alexander, who finally ended the schism with the smaller Nicene community in Antioch by 415. Another equally fraught schism soon split the Antiochene Christian community again, however, between those who supported the outcome of the Council of Chalcedon in 451 and those who did not, a schism that remains until today. The following chapters will reveal the persistent rhetorical and physical manipulations of Antioch's topography that facilitated Meletius's, Flavian's, and John Chrysostom's ultimately successful efforts to shape local perceptions of religious orthodoxy in their favor in this chaotic formative period.

ANTIOCH'S CHURCHES

The limited availability of Antioch's physical remains, largely buried beneath the present-day city of Antakya, Turkey, have led me to focus this project on rhetorical more than material manipulations of Antioch's landscape. Nevertheless, a general overview of the city's church buildings and martyria will aid in understanding the negotiations described in the following chapters. In recent years renewed scholarly attention has focused on Roman and early Byzantine Antioch after the archaeological excavations by a Princeton team in the 1930s, and the substantial early work on Antioch by Glanville Downey.[65] The extant information about Antioch's church buildings, cemeteries, and martyria has recently been analyzed by Emmanuel Soler, and collected and published with thorough study by Wendy Mayer and Pauline Allen;[66] more archaeological data has been collected by the Turkish-German project led by Hatice Pamir and Gunnar Brands. This information supplements the

---

65. These excavations were published in a series of volumes: *Antioch-on-the-Orontes, Publications of the Committee for the Excavation of Antioch and Its Vicinity,* vol. 1, *The Excavations of 1932,* ed. George W. Elderkin (Princeton, NJ: Princeton University Press, 1934); *Antioch-on-the-Orontes,* vol. 2, *The Excavations, 1933–1936,* ed. Richard Stillwell (Princeton, NJ: Princeton University Press, 1938); *Antioch-on-the-Orontes,* vol. 3, *The Excavations, 1937–1939,* ed. Richard Stillwell (Princeton, NJ: Princeton University Press, 1941); *Antioch-on-the-Orontes,* vol. 4.1, *Ceramics and Islamic Coins,* ed. Frederick O. Waagé (Princeton, NJ: Princeton University Press, 1948); *Antioch-on-the-Orontes,* vol. 4.2, *Greek, Roman, Byzantine, and Crusaders' Coins,* ed. Dorothy B. Waagé (Princeton, NJ: Princeton University Press, 1952); Downey, *History;* and Downey, *Ancient Antioch.* See also Festugière, *Antioche;* Liebeschuetz, *Antioch.*

66. Soler, *Le sacré et le salut;* and Mayer and Allen, *Churches,* esp. 32–125.

numerous Roman and early Byzantine authors who provided textual evidence, as did early medieval travelers, pilgrims, Crusaders, and early modern travelers.[67] Since this information is readily available, a summary will suffice to sketch what we know of the physical Antiochene Christian landscape of the fourth and early fifth centuries.

A visitor to Antakya today will quickly be pointed to the pilgrimage site of St. Peter's Grotto as the earliest Christian meeting place in Antioch, donated—as tradition has it—by Luke the Evangelist, who was a native of Antioch; visited by Barnabas, Cephas, and Paul (Acts 11, 15; Gal 2); and the apparent worship place for first-century Christians in Antioch.[68] The New Testament stories in Acts and Galatians provide good textual support for the survival of these traditions, and the impressive and towering Crusader-era façade that marks the cave's entrance stands witness to the fact that medieval Western Christians were persuaded that this was a site worth memorializing and marking for Christian pilgrims in the centuries to come. Theodoret also records a tradition that there was a cave at the foot of the mountain in Antioch associated with the apostle Paul (HR 2.18). Despite remnants of a mosaic floor from the Roman period, however, the critical historian recognizes the lack of verified evidence that first-century Christians used this cave. Thus while Acts provides textual references to Christians in Antioch from the earliest apostolic times, and while there is a modern pilgrimage site claiming to be a first-century place of Christian worship, we do not have clear historical testimony about the location of any particular first-century Christian places in the city.

Our more specific knowledge of Antioch's church buildings begins with textual evidence for a church alternately called the Old Church (sometimes left in Greek by translators as the Palaia) or the Apostolic Church.[69] Mayer notes that John Chrysostom also refers to this church as "the mother of the Antiochene (Nicene) Christians and the mother of all its churches," and elsewhere seems to refer to it simply as "mother."[70] This church is attested in several late fourth-century texts by John Chrysostom, in Theodoret's fifth-century Historia ecclesiastica, and in the anonymous seventh-century Chronicon paschale; Mayer describes it as "the only

67. See, for example, the sources collected in Krijnie Ciggaar, "Antioche: Les sources croisées et le plan de la ville," in Les sources de l'histoire, 223–34; and Guy Meyer, "L'apport des voyageurs occidentaux (1268–1918)," in Les sources de l'histoire, 235–58.

68. See, for example, M. Grazia Zambon, Domenico Bertogli, and Oriano Granella, Antioch on the Orontes: "Where the Disciples Were First Called Christians" (Parma, It.: Edizioni Eteria, 2005), esp. 55.

69. As Mayer and Allen note (Churches, 100–102), scholars have posited different interpretations of the name's origin, whether because of its position in the old part of the city (see W. Eltester, "Die Kirchen Antiochias im IV. Jahrhundert," ZNTW 36 [1937]: 251–86) or because of its age (see Downey, History, 336).

70. Mayer and Allen, Churches, 101–2, referring to the beginning of John Chrysostom's second homily on Acts, and a homily Chrysostom delivered on Pentecost.

church at Antioch for which we have evidence that dates from the period before Constantine."[71] Theodoret, who like John Chrysostom was a native of Antioch, records that the church building had been destroyed sometime in the late third or early fourth century, and was rebuilt by the early 320s (*HE* 1.2). Certainly it was used during the fourth century, as there are references to its use in the 360s, and by Chrysostom himself in the 380s, after which time other churches appear to have overshadowed it, since it is not mentioned again after the end of the fourth century.[72] The fact that it seems to have been rebuilt soon after its destruction suggests that it was significant to many Antiochene Christians. Nevertheless, with the rise of the Great Church not long after the Apostolic Church's renovation, the older church seems to have fallen in relative prestige in the city. By the time John Chrysostom was writing, the Great Church was the site of the imperially sanctioned bishop. This raises the question of whether Chrysostom's references to the Old Church as the mother of all of Antioch's Christians and churches was a conscious effort to deploy its antiquity and apostolic claims as a means of raising its status, and that of the Christians like himself who preached there, in competition with his homoian opponents who controlled the prestigious new Great Church.

The Great Church, so called by Ammianus Marcellinus, who lived in the city in the late fourth century, and later by Theodoret and Malalas, was also called "the golden church" by Jerome, "the new church" by John Chrysostom, "the domed church" in a seventh-century Syriac chronicle, and "the octagonal church" by Theophanes in the ninth century; according to Eusebius it was started by Constantine as one of his numerous Christian building projects.[73] When Constantine died in 337 before the project was finished, his son Constantius II continued its funding, and the church's completion was celebrated with a personal visit by the emperor in 341 with the so-called Dedication Council. The church was temporarily closed by the emperor Julian, but it soon reopened and continued to be controlled by whichever Antiochene Christians currently had the emperor's support. While little is known for certain about the church or its location, numerous references attest to its importance, wealth, and beauty for over a century after its completion, although it had aged noticeably by the early sixth century. Traditionally scholars have located the church on the large island in the Orontes, with the newer part of the city and the imperial palace, but Mayer cautions against jumping to conclusions with evidence that is not clear.[74] Catherine Saliou similarly concludes that despite

---

71. Mayer and Allen, *Churches*, 100.

72. See Mayer and Allen, *Churches*, 102.

73. For a thorough collection and discussion of this evidence, see Mayer and Allen, *Churches*, 76–77. See also Ana Maria Goliav's recent reconsideration of this church, its architecture, and its context: Goliav, "Proposal for the Reconstruction of the Golden Octagon," in *Les sources de l'histoire*, 159–77.

74. Mayer and Allen, *Churches*, 68–76.

presumptions about the church's location, a recent survey of the evidence reveals that the church's location is still unknown.[75] We do know, though, that it does not seem to have been a basilica-style church, which is unusual, and that it was impressive in both size and wealth when it was built.

The Great Church played a significant role in the politics of fourth-century struggles to claim episcopal authority in the city, as it was the church where the city's bishop presided, and thus changed hands several times during the second half of the fourth century. Mayer and Allen write, "It is at the dedication of the Great Church that we first find evidence for the role of churches in the power-plays at Antioch that became associated with religious factionalism."[76] Saints' relics played a significant role in the politics of claiming many religious places in fourth-century Antioch, from the translation of the martyr Babylas to the precincts of Daphne's famous Apollo temple and then to a new church outside the city, to the rearrangement of saints' relics in the floor of a building at the Romanesian Gate, but no relics are known to have been housed in the Great Church until the arrival of the ascetic Symeon the Stylite's body (d. 459). I agree with Wendy Mayer's observation that the absence of relics from the Great Church until the middle of the fifth century "is of considerable interest" in light of relics' roles elsewhere around Antioch,[77] but I would note that this may well be evidence that unlike the fourth-century places that housed relics, the Great Church had been built within the city walls. Although fourth-century Christians began to reshape Roman attitudes toward bodily remains through the veneration of saints' relics, it took longer to overcome the ancient tradition that relegated the dead to places outside the walls of the city.

The clearest example of relics being used effectively to grant authority to a group that did not at that moment have imperial patronage and control of the Great Church involves the Church of St. Babylas, also called in scholarship "the cruciform church" and "the church at Kaoussie [Qausīyeh]," named for the suburb of Antakya in which the remains were discovered. Wendy Mayer persuasively demonstrates that we should be wary of downgrading this building to a "martyrion" if we understand the latter term to be distinct from a church in that it would be used primarily only for festival days of the martyr(s) buried there, since the building that housed Babylas's relics was clearly used more frequently.[78] Mayer and Allen comment that it is with the movement of Babylas's relics "that we observe the

75. Catherine Saliou, "À propos de la ταυριανὴ πύλη: Remarques sur la localisation présumée de la grande église d'Antioche de Syrie," Syria 77 (2000): 217–26. See also Goliav, "Proposal," 159–77.

76. Mayer and Allen, Churches, 133.

77. Mayer and Allen, Churches, 74.

78. Wendy Mayer, "The Late Antique Church at Qausīyeh Reconsidered: Memory and Martyr-Burial in Syrian Antioch," in Martyrdom and Persecution in Late Antique Christianity: Festschrift Boudewijn Dehandschutter, Bibliotheca Ephemeridum Theologicarum Lovaniensium 241, ed. J. Leemans (Leuven: Peeters, 2010), 161–77; and Mayer and Allen, Churches, 167–74.

beginning of a series of events in which religious buildings are more explicitly drawn into imperial and ecclesiastical discourse and become a significant part of the polemic between competing religions and religious factions."[79]

The textual references to this church will be discussed in detail in chapter 2. It should be noted here that it was a church started by Bishop Meletius early in 380 as a martyrion for the relics of Babylas,[80] and its floor was tiled under Meletius's successor, Flavian, in 387. Meletius's own body was also buried in the church, which was finished at least before John Chrysostom's homily on Meletius, *De sancto Meletio*, which he presented in the church in 386.[81] This church appears to be the same building that was uncovered by archaeologists in 1934. Given that the textual sources match this excavated structure on three significant matters—that it was constructed before 387 (known archaeologically from the mosaic inscriptions with this date), that it was located across the Orontes River from the main city, and that there were tombs in the church floor—Wendy Mayer agrees with earlier scholars that "it is with reasonable certainty, then, that we can say that the excavated church complex is the Church of St. Babylas," a church that we know from the textual sources played a significant role in the efforts of Bishop Meletius and his followers to bolster their authority in the midst of the fourth-century schisms and political turmoil.[82] The book by Mayer and Allen contains a detailed summary of the archaeological evidence for this church, which was reburied at the end of the excavations after the removal of the mosaic inscriptions, and which currently resides under modern housing buildings in Antakya's growing urban sprawl. Mayer adds significantly to our understanding of this archaeological data in her careful discussion, reading the evidence in ways that open new possibilities for reconstructing the church, its uses, and its development over time.

Numerous other Christian places of worship also dotted the landscape of Antioch and its surrounding region in the fourth and fifth centuries, although we now know the specific locations of only a few. Several of Antioch's early church buildings have only scattered extant references, and there is no way to know for certain when they were first built, or where in the city they were located. Mayer and Allen summarize what is known about the Church of Cassian, which is unlikely to have existed as early as the fourth century but had become important by the early sixth century;[83] a church dedicated to the Maccabees that Augustine mentioned, which

79. Mayer and Allen, *Churches*, 135.

80. On the dating, see Christine Shepardson, "Rewriting Julian's Legacy: John Chrysostom's *On Babylas* and Libanius' *Oration 24*," *Journal of Late Antiquity* 2.1 (2009): 99–115.

81. For the setting of this homily, see Mayer with Neil, *Cult of the Saints*, 39–41.

82. Mayer and Allen, *Churches*, 45.

83. The location of this church has been unknown in modern scholarship. When Wendy Mayer, Dayna Kalleres, and I were in Antakya together in 2008, however, a story by the Capuchin leader of the local Roman Catholic church, Domenico Bertogli, prompted Wendy Mayer to wonder if the current

may have existed already in the time of John Chrysostom; the Church of the Holy Prophets, which was rebuilt under Justinian; a church dedicated to John the Baptist, which appears in a story about Symeon the Younger's childhood during the earthquake of 526; a Church of St. John attested in 507; the Church of the Theotokos, which Mayer convincingly suggests was most likely built after the Council of Ephesus in 431; and a Church of Michael the Archangel, which appears to have been built in the later fifth century.[84] A reference from John Chrysostom mentions a large martyrion, perhaps the one that Palladius described as being at the Romanesian Gate. The slim evidence raises the question, based on the tombs known to have been in its floor, of whether this is the same church as the Babylas church, or if not, then whether we know for certain which of these two was uncovered by archaeologists and identified as the Babylas church.[85] In addition, a surviving inscription may provide evidence for a church completed in Antioch under Caesar Gallus (r. 351–54); and material remains still exist of churches to the west in Antioch's port city of Seleucia Pieria, and on the Limestone Massif to the city's east.[86]

Fifth-century church historians also recorded that Meletius's followers held some church services on the *campus martius* across the Orontes River from the city when they did not have access to any of Antioch's church buildings.[87] While Meletius was expelled from Antioch ca. 365–69 during the reign of Valens, Meletius's followers, according to Theodoret, sometimes "taking over the foot of the mountain, would hold the holy assemblies there," whereas other times "they made the bank of the river the site of prayer, and at other times the military exercise ground that is in front of the city's north gate, for the enemies did not permit the pious to settle in one site" (*HR* 2.15).[88] Theodoret claims that during this time a rumor spread

---

Habibi Neccar Cami might stand on the site of the earlier Church of Cassian, which would place it in a central location at the crossroads of two main Roman roads through the city (see Mayer and Allen, *Churches*, 54).

84. Mayer and Allen, *Churches*, 80–83, 90–91, 98–99, 107–9. Mayer notes that it is unclear from the evidence whether or not the Church of St. John is a different church from the one associated with John the Baptist.

85. Mayer and Allen, *Churches*, 94–95. See also Catherine Saliou, "Le palais imperial d'Antioche et son contexts à l'époque de Julien: Réflexions sur l'apport des sources littéraires à l'histoire d'un espace urbain," *Antiquité Tardive* 17 (2009): 235–50.

86. Mayer and Allen, *Churches*, 58–67, 116–17; Ross Burns, *The Monuments of Syria: A Guide* (New York: I. B. Taurus, 2009).

87. Mayer and Allen, *Churches*, 51–52.

88. All translations from Theodoret's *Historia religiosa* are my own from the Greek text edited by Pierre Canivet and Alice Leroy-Molinghen in *Théodoret de Cyr, Histoire des moines de Syrie (I-XIII)*, vol. 1, SC 234 (1977; repr., Paris: Les Éditions du Cerf, 2006). In this chapter I consistently and exclusively translate the Greek word χωρίον as "site." An English translation of this work by Theodoret can also be found in Richard Price, *A History of the Monks of Syria, by Theodoret of Cyrrhus* (Kalamazoo, MI: Cistercian Publications, 1985).

that the ascetic Julian Saba supported a homoian theology, and Meletius's priests Flavian and Diodore sent messengers to persuade the ascetic to come to Antioch to denounce this charge and show his support for Meletius. Upon his arrival in the city, Julian Saba made his way "to the assembly of the pious," for which he had to pass through the palace gates and cross the river (Theodoret, *HR* 2.19). "The whole crowd of the town," Theodoret writes, "flowed together, and the military exercise ground became filled with those running together" (*HR* 2.19; cf. *HR* 8.8). Given the chronological limits of Valens's succession and Julian Saba's death, this story is set between 364 and 367 and shows that church buildings were not the only local places of Antiochene Christian assembly and worship.

The evidence for Christian martyria in the region is also helpful in identifying places of Christian ritual, although again their specific locations are rarely known. The primary site for Christian burials, of saints and otherwise, was of course the cemetery, and Antioch's main cemetery just outside the Daphne Gate became home to numerous early martyria, including the relics of Babylas and the unnamed children associated with him (until they were later moved into Daphne and then back to Antioch).[89] John Chrysostom provides evidence for other specific saints who were buried in this cemetery and were honored by Antioch's Christians on their individual feast days, including the Christian martyr Julian (until he was moved into a church built for him by the sixth century) and the female saint Drosis.[90] In addition, there is sixth-century evidence for a martyrion of Saint Dometius; a shrine dedicated to Bishop Ignatius, whose relics Theodosius II (r. 408–50) translated into a former Tychaeum in the city; a martyrion of Stephen, which might also have included a shrine to Thecla; a martyrion of Romanus; and another martyrion in Daphne that for a time housed the relics of Babylas.[91] The martyrs Juventinus and Maximinus were also remembered locally.[92]

89. It appears that the bodies of three children were also moved with Babylas's relics, and so were among the earliest relics to be translated, although the narrations prioritize Babylas as the saint whose bones are so powerfully effective. For a recent discussion of the evidence regarding the bodies of the children, and whether they were buried in one sarcophagus with Babylas, or in a second sarcophagus near Babylas, see Mayer and Allen, *Churches*, 48, 86–87, 137, 191–93, 196. See also the fourth-century reference by John Chrysostom (*In Iuventinum et Maximum*), the fifth-century reference by Theodoret (*HE* 3.10), and the sixth-century reference by the Piacenza pilgrim (*Ant. plac. itin. recensio* 1). For a more in-depth and annotated discussion of Roman burials and Christian martyria, see chapter 5 below.

90. See John Chrysostom, *In s. Iulianum martyrem* and *De s. Droside*; Mayer and Allen, *Churches*, 85–88.

91. Mayer and Allen, *Churches*, 68, 81, 96–97, 102–4.

92. John Chrysostom, *In Iuventinum et Maximum*; Mayer and Allen, *Churches*, 88. The origins of this tradition are unknown, but Hanns Christof Brennecke speculates that the tradition began within the homoian Christian community of Antioch, which he argues was particularly active in martyr traditions, especially during the reign of the emperor Julian (Brennecke, *Studien*, 144–45).

While the relatively small amount of available archaeological evidence prevents us from being able to map Antioch's fourth- and fifth-century churches and martyria precisely, it does allow us to see that Antioch was a large urban center with multiple churches, and more being built, and that Christian space did anything but stop at the city gates. John Chrysostom's homilies reveal that there were numerous martyria outside the city walls, some farther away than others, starting in the cemeteries just outside the city gates and spreading across the landscape (and eventually inside the walls into the churches themselves). While fourth-century church leaders saw in Antioch's landscape a host of places that threatened their congregants and were ripe for transformation, the churches and martyria that existed provided the basis for intra-Christian conflicts, as competing bishops struggled to maintain control of Antioch's Christian places.

• • •

The variety of places associated with Christianity in and around Antioch, in addition to powerful places associated with Judaism or the gods, combine with the unique complexities of Antioch's Christian leadership in the fourth century to produce a rich case study for demonstrating not only the power that places can wield, but also the ways in which leaders shaped those places and thus manipulated the authority associated with them. The following chapters demonstrate the role that the physical and, especially, rhetorical manipulation of places played in making the late Roman Empire more visibly marked by Nicene Christianity. While the examples focus most closely on late fourth-century Christian leaders' struggles in the city of Antioch, they fit a pattern both locally among Christian and non-Christian leaders, and around the empire more generally, revealing the far-reaching benefits of looking at this material through this new lens.

Beginning with a brief introduction to Roman education, chapter 1 examines the processes by which Antioch's famous fourth-century teacher Libanius worked his way from humbly teaching a few students in his home to proudly teaching crowds of students in the city's most prestigious public classroom. Libanius's explicit discussions reveal that he was aware of, consciously manipulated, and benefited from the power that came from controlling prominent teaching places vis-à-vis other Antiochene teachers, local rulers, and even the emperor Julian during his visit to Antioch. In particular, sociolinguistic sensitivities to Libanius's narratives highlight the spatial power dynamics in a person's attendance (or refused attendance) at particular places. Libanius's discussions of the relative prestige that related to teaching in different places in Antioch thus provides an informative comparison with the competition of Christian bishops over controlling the best preaching places in the city.

Chapter 2 focuses on the spatial politics related to the body of Babylas, an early Antiochene Christian bishop, martyr, and saint whose relics came to be at the center of power struggles between Christians and the emperor Julian as well as among various Antiochene Christian factions. Babylas's relics were moved to the site of an oracular Apollo temple in Daphne by Caesar Gallus in the early 350s, a juxtaposition that raised Julian's ire on his imperial visit to Antioch in the early 360s. Julian required Babylas's relics to be returned to their original resting place, but the fire that soon destroyed Apollo's temple caused heated speculation about the relative power of the deities involved and affected the perception of the contested temple precinct and martyrion. When Babylas's relics finally came to rest in a new church that Bishop Meletius built to house them, they not only shaped the perceptions of this Antiochene place, but also participated in the intra-Christian power struggle between the local Nicene and homoian communities. Cultural geographers' discussions of the benefits that can be gained by promoting a particular view of a place are useful regarding the competition to claim and define Apollo's temple complex, particularly after the fire that left it in ruins. Scholars' discussions of the role that politics play in the construction of community memories also help to illuminate the rhetorical narratives surrounding Babylas's relics. The sites associated with Babylas demonstrate some of the concrete ways in which imperial officials and local leaders alike physically manipulated Antioch's landscape to their own advantage, and to the disadvantage of their opponents.

Chapter 3 complements the discussion of physical manipulations of the city by demonstrating that leaders such as John Chrysostom also rhetorically shaped the cityscape toward similar ends. The chapter focuses on two series of homilies delivered by John Chrysostom in the years 386–87, the homilies *Adversus Iudaeos* and *De incomprehensibili natura dei*. The homilies *Adversus Iudaeos* demonstrate Chrysostom's clear association of religious orthodoxy (and orthopraxy) with attendance at, and absence from, certain places in Antioch and Daphne that carried with them specific religious connotations. Chrysostom describes, for example, synagogues and other places that he defined by association with Judaism, as filled with demons and as spiritually and physically dangerous for Christians to approach, explicitly hoping to curb what he understood to be the inappropriate attendance of those in his church congregation at Jewish services and festivals. Yi-Fu Tuan's concept of *topophilia* gives nuance to the love of the synagogue that John Chrysostom hoped to disrupt, and Gill Valentine's discussion of "imagined geographies" and the "imagined communities" that they produce brings texture to Chrysostom's descriptions of how he wished people would see the city.[93] A comparison of Chrysostom's

---

93. Yi-Fu Tuan, *Topophilia: A Study of Environmental Perception, Attitudes, and Values* (Englewood Cliffs, NJ: Prentice-Hall, 1974). Note that the fourth-century author Libanius prefers the term φιλοχωρία rather than *topophilia* (Libanius, *Or.* 11.117). Gill Valentine, "Imagined Geographies: Geographical Knowledges of Self and Other in Everyday Life," in *Human Geography Today*, ed. Doreen Massey, John Allen, and Philip Sarre (Malden, MA: Polity Press, 1999), 47–48. See also Benedict Anderson, *Imagined Communities: Reflections on the Origin and Spread of Nationalism* (London: Verso, 1983).

anti-Anomean homilies with those against the Judaizers reveals that his spatial rhetoric contained further nuance, differentiating not only "Christians" from "Jews," but also spiritually stronger from weaker Christians. The former he encouraged to endure dangerous places for the sake of bringing others to Nicene Christianity, while he reminded the weaker Christians to avoid such places for fear that they might be led astray. The value, and especially the revaluation, of particular local places thus played a significant role in John Chrysostom's rhetorical efforts to define and influence perceptions of Christian orthodoxy and orthopraxy.

Chapter 4 uses the vocabulary of transgression to explore the narrative distinctions that John Chrysostom and Libanius constructed between urban and rural places in the *territorium* of Antioch. Tim Cresswell's nuanced discussion of topographical transgressions, and the transformations that boundary crossing can produce, encourages reading John Chrysostom's homilies following the "Statues Riot" of 387 in a new light.[94] By rhetorically manipulating Roman stereotypes of urban and rural places, largely inverting them, Chrysostom contributed to shifting local power dynamics and perceptions of the topography, elevating the prestige and authority of his church in the process. Despite a common assumption that urban life and urban dwellers were far superior to their ostensibly uneducated and less-advantaged rural counterparts, Chrysostom's rhetoric depicts the city, identified with such places as the marketplace (*agora*) and theater, as a corrupt place whose citizens do not live lives of Christian orthodoxy, while the space outside the city, represented by such places as ascetics' caves and martyrs' shrines, was inhabited by those who embodied true Christianity. In Chrysostom's rhetoric, the civic chaos of the urban riot of 387, in which numerous Antiochenes fled to the mountains and mountain ascetics flocked to the city, allowed a significant momentary transformation—in this case, Christianization—of Antioch's people and places. The transgression of the urban/rural divide thus allowed in Chrysostom's rhetoric the topographical transformation of the city, as he again relied on spatial rhetoric to narrate and shape religious orthodoxy and orthopraxy.

Chapter 5 examines the ways in which temples, ascetics, and martyrs' shrines contributed to Christian leaders' proactive reshaping of the topography of Antioch and its surrounding countryside. Geographers' studies of mapping highlight the politics and perspectives in creating any map, and offer a fruitful means of analyzing the unique narrative maps that Libanius, John Chrysostom, and Theodoret present. Edward Soja's conception of Thirdspace, a terrain that is at once both real and imagined, provides another useful tool for analyzing the relationship between

94. Tim Cresswell, *In Place/Out of Place: Geography, Ideology, and Transgression* (Minneapolis: University of Minnesota Press, 1996).

the physical and rhetorical landscapes of late Roman Antioch.[95] The writings of both Libanius and Theodoret depict Christian ascetics co-opting or destroying places outside of Antioch that were associated with the gods and the rituals that honored them. In addition to this depiction of the role of living saints, John Chrysostom's homilies on earlier Christian martyrs who were buried in the vicinity of Antioch reveal numerous ways in which he encouraged the transformation of the city's cemeteries and festival celebrations to be more closely in line with his view of Nicene Christian orthopraxy. His hope that those in his audience would avoid the region's traditional holiday celebrations, visit regularly the shrines of the holy martyrs, and curb their behavior in ways that reflected Christian abstinence from excessive drinking, laughter, and other raucous activities demonstrates his effort to map Nicene Christianity onto the people and places in and around Antioch. Evidence from Chrysostom about the behavior of his bishop Flavian also provides an interesting example of how Nicene Christian leaders manipulated saints' relics in Antioch at the expense of their homoian Christian opponents.

Chapter 6 surveys a series of examples from around the empire to show that while Antioch offers some of the best-preserved and complex examples of spatial manipulation in the course of fourth-century theological conflicts, it was by no means the only locus of such activities. Examining imperial legislation and data from Milan, Jerusalem, Minorca, North Africa, and Alexandria demonstrates that while Antioch is unique in its wealth of relevant extant sources from this period and in the particular details of its examples, these phenomena were widespread in the late fourth-century empire.

The conclusion presents a synthetic analysis and a return to the broader implications of the study beyond scholarship on late antiquity. There is power involved in rhetorically shaping places' connotations as well as in physically controlling places of religious and civic authority. Being attentive to these topographical dynamics makes visible mechanisms that shape history by controlling the very ways in which people view and define their relationship to the physical places that surround them.

95. Edward Soja, *Thirdspace: Journeys to Los Angeles and Other Real-and-Imagined Places* (Malden, MA: Blackwell Publishing, 1996).

1
___

The Power of Prestigious Places
Teaching and Preaching in Fourth-Century Antioch

The Greek sophist Libanius recounts in his autobiography the struggle that he faced when he returned to his hometown of Antioch in the middle of the fourth century, intending to teach there after years abroad. At first confined to teaching in his home to a small group of students, he eventually acquired a classroom at the edge of the marketplace (*agora*), and then finally the coveted right to lecture at the *bouleutērion*, the city hall, where he gained numerous students, and his authority increased exponentially. Libanius's manipulation of Antioch's places also reveals itself through the numerous interactions that he narrates with local and imperial officials, from the praetorian prefect Strategius to the emperor Julian. In particular, the power dynamics of attendance (or avoidance) at strategic locations throughout Antioch demonstrate the authority that Libanius was able to wield through his control of the city's topography. In these same decades, as many as four Christian leaders concurrently claimed the title of bishop of Antioch, each elected by a different Christian faction. This led to sharp and long-lived competition about who could preach in which of Antioch's church buildings (and who was exiled altogether). This chapter will examine Libanius's competition for Antioch's most prestigious teaching places, and the power attendant on teaching in the prime *bouleutērion* classroom, setting the stage for comparisons with Christian leaders' competition to control the city's most prestigious preaching places. Together the Christian disputes and Libanius's narratives reveal the complexity of the spatial power dynamics in fourth-century Antioch. Roman leaders of all types took advantage of the benefits that came from controlling identifiably powerful places, in terms of the numbers of people they could influence and the local authority they would gain.

ROMAN CLASSROOMS

While Christian leaders were busy competing over Antioch's churches, Libanius suggests that the city's teachers likewise competed not only for students, but also for the best classrooms in the city, where they could gain visibility in areas with large audiences. Unlike the churches, however, which at least have some extant textual and occasionally even archaeological evidence for when and where they existed, Antioch's classrooms are less recoverable, not least because many of them would have been rooms that were also (and sometimes primarily) used for purposes other than teaching.

Roman education consisted of several different levels, from the basic reading and writing skills that the elementary *didaskalos* taught to the more advanced study offered by the grammarians to the elite higher education provided by teachers of rhetoric. The locations of education at any of these levels were quite varied and are difficult to reconstruct with much clarity. When Stanley Bonner gathered much of the textual evidence for Roman teaching places, he lamented the dearth of evidence: "There is scarcely any part of the study of Roman education in which precise information is so difficult to obtain as that which concerns the localities and premises in which teaching took place."[1] As discussed below, more recent excavations, such as in Egypt; further analysis of textual references, including newly available papyri from Oxyrhynchos; and material culture, such as scenes portrayed in vase paintings, have led to some more detailed academic discussions, although much still remains unknown. Raffaella Cribiore has outlined the numerous possibilities for teaching places in the Roman world: "Besides occupying a private or public building, a school could have been located within the perimeter of an ancient temple, in the cell of a monastery, in a private house, or even in the open air, at a street corner or under a tree."[2] New evidence for what appear to have been classrooms has come to light from large auditoria in excavations in Alexandria and from a room with poems painted on the wall in excavations in the Dakhleh Oasis of western Egypt.[3] Likewise, parts of some Roman baths, the forum of Trajan in Rome, and various *stoai* appear to have had educational uses.

---

1. Stanley Bonner, *Education in Ancient Rome: From the Elder Cato to the Younger Pliny* (Berkeley: University of California Press, 1977), 115 (see 115–25 for his summary of places that were used for education). On late Roman education more generally, see also Robert Kaster, *Guardians of Language: The Grammarian and Society in Late Antiquity* (Berkeley: University of California Press, 1988); Henri Marrou, *Histoire de l'éducation dans l'antiquité* (Paris: Éditions du Seuil, 1948).

2. Raffaella Cribiore, *Gymnastics of the Mind: Greek Education in Hellenistic and Roman Egypt* (Princeton, NJ: Princeton University Press, 2001), 21.

3. See, for example, Tomasz Derda, Tomasz Markiewicz, and Ewa Wipszycka, eds., *Alexandria: Auditoria of Kom el-Dikka and Late Antique Education,* Journal of Juristic Papyrology Supplement 8 (Warsaw: Journal of Juristic Papyrology, 2007); Raffaella Cribiore, Paolo Davoli, and David M. Ratzan, "A Teacher's Dipinto from Trimithis (Dakhleh Oasis)," *Journal of Roman Archaeology* 21 (2008): 170–91.

While some urban centers, like Antioch, had public teaching places and publicly funded teachers, most education in the Roman Empire seems to have taken place in more individually owned settings, including especially the homes of wealthier Romans. Other teachers seem to have taught their students in their own homes, as Libanius mentions doing when he first returned to his home city of Antioch (*Or.* 1.101).[4] Still other teaching places seem to have been public multipurpose rooms. Suetonius, for example, mentions the possibilities of teaching in a patron's *domus,* in the open air, in open roofed areas in front of shops or homes, and in one's own house, which Robert Kaster understands to be among the best of Suetonius's options.[5] Augustine refers to curtains on the doors of grammarians' schools, suggesting makeshift classrooms that would only be classrooms while the day's lessons were actively in session.[6] Because of classrooms' often private and transitory nature, it is difficult to learn much about the actual locations of the majority of teaching places in the Roman Empire—with some important exceptions.

Some recent archaeological discoveries from Alexandria and Libanius's textual evidence from Antioch suggest that in these two cities there seem to have been large auditoria available for publicly supported Roman education,[7] and there is textual evidence that there were large lecture halls for teaching law in fourth-century Berytus (present-day Beirut, Lebanon).[8] Athens seems to have had private lecture rooms away from the center of the city in late antiquity, and there has been speculation that recently unearthed buildings on the slope of the Areopagus in Athens were used by teachers, and that their large halls were *theatra* for teaching and lecturing.[9] Athens further provides evidence that the house belonging to Julianus, and then Prohaeresius, the city's official sophists, had a marble lecture room for classes and declamations;[10] and Himerius mentions a small lecture room

---

4. I rely on the Greek text edited by A. F. Norman in *Libanius: Autobiography and Selected Letters,* vol. 1 (Cambridge, MA: Harvard University Press, 1992); all translations of Libanius's *Or.* 1 are my own from Norman's Greek text.

5. See C. Suetonius Tranquillus, *De grammaticis et rhetoribus,* ed. and trans. Robert Kaster (New York: Clarendon Press, 1995) 1.2, 2.2, 7.2, 17.2, 18.2. In his notes on Suetonius's text, Kaster comments that those who were not tutors in someone else's *domus* had to find space elsewhere, noting that those who had their own home were likely to use it as their classroom, while others taught outdoors (120).

6. See Augustine, *Sermo* 400.9; see also Augustine, *Conf.* 1.13, 22; *Sermo* 178.8.

7. See Derda, Markiewicz, and Wipszycka, *Alexandria;* Libanius, *Or.* 22.31; and the scholarship of Raffaella Cribiore on this topic, especially her useful summary of much of this evidence: Cribiore, *The School of Libanius in Late Antique Antioch* (Princeton, NJ: Princeton University Press, 2007), 43–47.

8. See Libanius, *Expositio totius mundi et gentium;* Cribiore, *School,* 44.

9. Cribiore, *School,* 44–45.

10. Cribiore, *School,* 44, using evidence from Eunapius, *Vitae sophistarum.* Edward Watts has usefully demonstrated some of the personal investment in Eunapius's collection of biographies, not least of which was the documentation of Eunapius's own "intellectual family tree" (Watts, *Riot in Alexandria: Tradition and Group Dynamics in Late Antique Pagan and Christian Communities* [Berkeley: University

in a temple to Hermes and the Muses in Athens where he learned to declaim.[11] Thus, there are enough references to places of learning in the Roman Empire to demonstrate the variety of types of classrooms, even though there are relatively few examples of specifically identifiable locations in any particular city.

Not surprisingly, our information about teaching places in fourth-century Antioch comes primarily from Libanius's numerous writings.[12] Libanius visited his native city in 353, and he returned to stay permanently in 354. Following some struggles, he was offered the city's chair of rhetoric and recognized as the leading sophist in the city. *Oratio* 31 reveals that Libanius had four other teachers working under him as his assistants by 361, when he addressed Antioch's city council on their behalf (*Or.* 31, esp. 31.8). By that time Libanius was well established in the city and was teaching in the classroom that he most coveted there, a lecture hall that was part of the prominent city hall. Libanius depicts this classroom as "a roofed theater and four colonnades (*stoai*) surrounding a courtyard in the middle that had been made into a garden" (22.31),[13] which he used for "his students' declamations and for regular classes."[14] According to Cribiore, "It was a monumental room with an imposing entrance and, on the opposite side, there were two seats, one of which was [the sophist's] chair (*thronos*)."[15] The size of the teaching space, the formal *thronos* that it contained, and the prominence of its attachment to the *bouleutērion* all contributed to the authority of the teacher who controlled this classroom.

Libanius also provides some information about other teachers and teaching places in Antioch, although more about the former than the latter. In the year 388, for example, the city of Antioch sponsored a new Latin chair, which brought Liba-

---

of California Press, 2010], 37). While Watts reveals that Eunapius's collection is not as comprehensive as it presents itself to be, there is little reason to doubt the general reliability of the evidence that his text provides for teaching places in Athens (see Watts, *Riot*, 37–45).

11. Himerius, *Or.* 64; Cribiore, *School*, 45.

12. Although outdated, Paul Petit's studies of Libanius still deserve mention: Petit, *Libanius et la vie municipale à Antioche au IVe siècle après J.-C.* (Paris: Libraire Orientaliste Paul Geuthner, 1955); Petit, *Les étudiants de Libanius* (Paris: Nouvelles Éditions Latines, 1955). Cribiore lucidly summarizes the weaknesses of Petit's work in light of recent methodological trends, noting that Petit's work provides a useful foundation for later scholarship, but his belief "in isolating facts as irreducible entities" and that Libanius's works "could be interpreted objectively," and his presumption of "a rather rigid pattern of schooling" mean that his conclusions are no longer the most plausible (Cribiore, *School*, 9–10).

13. All translations of Libanius's *Oratio* 22 are my own from the Greek text edited by A. F. Norman in *Libanius: Selected Orations*, vol. 2 (Cambridge, MA: Harvard University Press, 1977).

14. Cribiore, *School*, 44.

15. Cribiore, *School*, 44. In conversation, Wendy Mayer made two intriguing associations, discussed more below, between the sophist's chair (*thronos*) in the *bouleutērion* in Antioch and contemporaneous Christian material: Sozomen's description of Meletius being placed by his followers on the bishop's chair (*thronos*) in one of the churches outside Antioch's city walls when he returned from exile and found himself competing with Paulinus (Sozomen, *HE* 7.3), and the "northwest-Syrian U-shaped bema found in the Babylas church with its bema-throne."

nius competition, as previously he held the only chaired teaching position in the city.[16] Libanius also mentions many teachers who were beneath him in status, pay, and prestige in the city.[17] Although he complains that Constantinople was draining all the good teachers from Antioch, his narration of his days before he became the city's chaired sophist reveals that a sufficient number of teachers remained in the city to create competition for students and teaching places.[18] The evidence for places of Roman education is rather sparse in comparison with some other aspects of daily Roman life, but Libanius remains a fruitful source of information about the Antiochene competition over classrooms.

TEACHING PLACES: CONTROLLING ANTIOCH'S CLASSROOMS

Libanius was one of Antioch's most famous fourth-century citizens. Born in Antioch in 314, he left to be a student in Athens in 336. Four years later he moved to Constantinople to begin teaching, but he left after only two years, arriving in Nicomedia by 344 to become the city's sophist, a position that he held for five years. In the year 349, Libanius accepted an official chaired position in Constantinople and returned to the eastern capital for five more years. Apparently homesick for Antioch and not fond of Constantinople, Libanius returned to his hometown for a visit in 353, and in 354 he left Constantinople permanently for Antioch, where he lived the remaining forty years of his life.[19] Much of our knowledge of Libanius's life comes not only from his letters and orations, but also from his autobiography, which details many of the prominent events in his life, including his travels, the ill health that plagued him, and his encounters in Antioch with the emperor Julian.[20] In this text, most of which (*Or.* 1.1–155) first circulated in 374, Libanius places a strong emphasis on his struggles to gain and maintain control over a prominent place in Antioch from which he could teach a large audience. Combined with his

16. See Libanius, *Or.* 1.255; *Or.* 3.24. Libanius's disapproval of the rise of Latin's prominence in Eastern education is well known. See, for example, J. H. W. G. Liebeschuetz, *Antioch: City and Imperial Administration in the Later Roman Empire* (Oxford: Clarendon Press, 1972), 242–55.

17. See especially Libanius, *Or.* 43, from 385, in which he addresses other teachers in the city, hoping to get them to form a union and refuse to allow their students (or their students' parents) to take advantage of them by playing one against the other.

18. For his complaints, see, for example, Libanius, *Ep.* 368.1.

19. For Libanius's life, see the introduction in A. F. Norman, *Antioch as a Centre of Hellenic Culture as Observed by Libanius* (Liverpool: Liverpool University Press, 2000), xi–xviii; Cribiore, *School;* Liebeschuetz, *Antioch,* esp. 1–39; and Jorit Wintjes's more thorough biography: Wintjes, *Das Leben des Libanius* (Rahden/Westf.: Marie Leidorf Press, 2005).

20. For an important discussion of the methodological challenges of recreating historical events through the use of a retrospective autobiography, see Paula Fredriksen, "Paul and Augustine: Conversion Narratives, Orthodox Traditions, and the Retrospective Self," *JThSt* 37.1 (1986): 3–34.

discussions of other cities and their (poor) educational facilities, Libanius relates his efforts to construct and claim significant places in Antioch.

From the beginning of his autobiography, Libanius establishes the importance that he placed on education and study, and he consistently locates this conversation geographically, in terms of less worthy places that competed for his attention. He laments his early indifference to studying, remembering that his mother indulged him more than he later wished she had, and did not press him to study diligently despite the money that she paid to educate Libanius and his two brothers (*Or.* 1.4). He explains that as a result he and his brothers "spent most of the year in the country (*agros*) rather than in study (*logous*)" (1.4). The leisurely countryside emerges immediately from Libanius's narrative in opposition to the urban place of study. As he matured, Antioch rose further and further in his estimation until it surpassed not only the countryside but also the major centers of Athens and Constantinople in the high quality of its educational opportunities, and thus its civility and other qualities that Libanius considered to be the fruits of *paideia*.[21]

Libanius's carefree childhood did not last, however. At the age of fifteen, as he recounts, "a sharp love of study" took hold of him and reshaped his life, and thereafter "the charms of the country were neglected: the pigeons were sold . . . ; the horse competitions and everything of the stage were renounced"; he claims that he "astonished both young and old" with his preference for his studies over the country and the spectacle of the theater (*Or.* 1.5). Despite newly clinging to his books (instead of to other places of entertainment in the city) and having a good teacher, however, Libanius claims that he still did not attend lectures as much as he should have (1.5; 1.8). Just as he outgrew his childhood apathy toward studying, though, so too he eventually developed a renewed desire to attend lectures, which required him to frequent certain places and avoid others. After the death of his promising lecturer, Libanius attended several other teachers' lectures, but found them all wanting. Rather than frequent inferior lectures, he chose to study more elementary material under a teacher who better engaged his interest; Libanius claims that he attended this teacher's classes regularly: "Indeed I devoted myself entirely to this [teacher], such that I would not even depart from him after the students had departed," following him "even through the *agora*" (1.8). Luke Lavan notes the significance of the *agora* in fourth-century Antioch, and that the company one visibly kept there reflected one's social status.[22] Libanius's identity was strongly tied

21. For a discussion of Christian perceptions of the potential benefits and dangers of a traditional Greek education, see A.-J. Festugière, *Antioche païenne et chrétienne: Libanius, Chrysostome et les moines de Syrie* (Paris: Éditions E. de Boccard, 1959), 211–40.

22. Luke Lavan, "The *agorai* of Antioch and Constantinople as Seen by John Chrysostom," in *Wolf Liebeschuetz Reflected: Essays Presented by Colleagues, Friends, and Pupils*, ed. John Drinkwater and Benet Salway (London: Institute of Classical Studies, University of London, 2007), 157–67, esp. 162.

to his education and then to his own role as a teacher, and for him both of these were intimately connected with where he went.

In 354 Libanius returned to Antioch from Constantinople, a city that he describes as corrupt with a population that "abounded in the pleasures of the theaters" rather than in education, and from Nicomedia, a city that he much preferred to Constantinople and whose citizens he characterizes as reveling "in the fruit of *paideia*" (*Or.* 1.52). Libanius remembers that in Nicomedia he had given lectures everywhere in the city, even in the public baths: "Thus the whole city had become a *mouseion* for us" (1.55).[23] Despite this idyllic image of his time in Nicomedia, Libanius left for Constantinople and Antioch, where he found that, in contrast, the whole city was very clearly not his lecture room, and he had to struggle to attract students and gain control of classrooms whose location granted a level of authority and visibility that he found acceptable.

In his autobiography, Libanius recalls the sharp contrast that he experienced between 353 and 354 with respect to the lecture halls of Antioch. When he visited in 353 from his post in Constantinople, he carried enough prestige to speak as a guest in the *bouleutērion*. Not only was he warmly welcomed on this occasion, but he portrays an overwhelmingly enthusiastic crowd that attended and cheered his public declamation: "First of all, it was not necessary for anyone to gather each one with flattery, but rather it was sufficient that they knew I would speak. Then, without waiting for the sun, they crowded the *bouleutērion*, and for the first time it appeared to be insufficient" to hold the throngs of people (*Or.* 1.87). Although we should expect rhetorical exaggeration in this self-aggrandizement, Libanius wrote this autobiography in the same city where the events took place, and it seems plausible that he was genuinely honored on his visit by a warm reception. The crowd's enthusiasm only grew during the speech itself, according to Libanius: "How could I adequately speak about the weeping over the prologue, which not a few left having learned thoroughly, and about the frenzy concerning what followed" (1.88). He claims that the crowd kept interrupting him, demanding that the emperor release him from his position in Constantinople to return to his own people, and that even after his speech they followed him around the city, each one wanting to touch his body (1.88–89). While this is Libanius's idealized reminiscence of decades gone by, the story nevertheless highlights the significance of Antioch's *bouleutērion* as the city's most prestigious place for public speaking, a site associated with powerful aristocrats and large audiences.

When Libanius returned to live in Antioch, he relates that he did not receive the same welcome that he had during his earlier visit. Libanius narrates that his visit in 353 already created competition with "a certain Phoenician" teacher who was

---

23. A *mouseion* most literally refers to a place, or temple, devoted to the Muses, but it also came to refer to a place where the works inspired by the Muses were taught, or a classroom.

"admired for his skill" (*Or.* 1.90). Despite the fact that at that time Libanius was only visiting from his position in Constantinople, the Phoenician teacher not only returned to Antioch to claim his students before they left to follow Libanius, but, Libanius claims, immediately "began a fight" with him (1.91). When Libanius arrived in 354, he came as a teacher who would be competing for students with those who already lived and taught in Antioch, and he leads his reader to believe that he constituted a severe threat to those who were established in the city before him. Dayna Kalleres notes that Libanius's discovery of a dead chameleon in his lecture hall led him to conclude that one of his competitors had put a curse on him, highlighting the competition that he imagined surrounded him (1.243–50; 36).[24] Libanius claims that in the face of his own successful teaching, his rival's "followers were again withdrawing even more readily," suggesting that they became Libanius's students instead (1.110).[25]

Although Libanius was born into a curial family, most of the family's property had been confiscated in 303/4 after the revolt of Eugenius, and his mother sold what remained while Libanius was abroad in Athens. When he returned to Antioch, he narrates that in the beginning he did not teach publicly, let alone in the *bouleutērion* itself: "I was at home with my fifteen students," most of whom he claims had come with him when he moved from Constantinople (*Or.* 1.101).[26] In what was a far cry from his jubilant performance in the *bouleutērion* in 353, Libanius blames those teachers with whom he competed for space and students for this lackluster start to his Antiochene teaching career. While Suetonius portrayed teaching in one's home as a common and comfortable context, preferable to most of the alternatives, Libanius saw his relegation to his house as a significant loss in prestige, and determined to reenter the more public sphere. All teaching places were not equal to Libanius, and he understood the location of his classroom to speak strongly to the quality of his teaching and his rhetorical ability, which in turn reflected his own relative position of authority within the city.

Libanius again emphasizes the importance of place when he relates that he fell into a despondent depression about his humble classroom until an elderly man

24. Dayna Kalleres, *City of Demons: Violence, Ritual, and Christian Power in Late Antiquity* (Berkeley: University of California Press, forthcoming), chap. 1.

25. This is ironic in light of his oration from the winter of 386/7 that condemns students who switch teachers (Libanius, *Or.* 43). A letter from Libanius to Anatolius confirms, however, that Libanius did entice students away from other teachers (Libanius, *Ep.* 4.11; cf. *Ep.* 6). On the frequent exchange of students in both Antioch and Athens, see Raffaella Cribiore, "The Value of a Good Education: Libanius and Public Authority," in *A Companion to Late Antiquity,* ed. Philip Rousseau (Malden, MA: Wiley-Blackwell, 2009), 235; cf. Harald Völker, "Spätantike Professoren und ihre Schüler: Am Beispiel von Himerios und Libanios," in *Gelehrte in der Antike: Alexander Demandt zum 65. Geburtstag,* ed. Andreas Goltz, Andreas Luther, Heinrich Schlange-Schöningen (Cologne: Böhlau Press, 2002), 171–73.

26. Compare Libanius's reference to his seventeen early students in Antioch in *Ep.* 6.4, for which I rely on the Greek text edited by Norman in *Libanius,* vol. 1 ; all translations of Libanius's *Ep.* 6 are my own from Norman's Greek text.

reminded him that if he wanted his fortune to change, he needed to teach in the public eye, preferably at "any of the temples," where many were "thirsting to learn" (*Or.* 1.102). "In this," Libanius says, "I did not listen to the elderly man, but having changed a certain one of those from the *agora* to another part of the complex, I went down and settled myself there, touching the *agora*" (1.102). In other words, Libanius seems to have persuaded someone to relinquish a place in the busy *agora* so that Libanius himself could teach there. Not only does this pericope demonstrate the significance of civic space in the context of gaining public recognition and authority, but it further elaborates on Libanius's understanding of the city and the role of education. By highlighting that his new classroom was "touching the *agora*," Libanius implies that this city square represented an urban center that granted him the respect and wider audience that he was seeking. He comments that "this site (*chōrion*) did a lot" to double the number of his students, although he still laments that others had the advantage of teaching in the *mouseion* (1.102).

While Libanius attributes the course of his life to Fortune (and sometimes to the Muses and the gods), he nonetheless recognizes that he was actively engaged in a struggle with people he considered to be his rivals. In his autobiography, he regularly speaks not only of the places that he taught, but also of his rivalries with other teachers, with whom he competed for students, fame, and classrooms. Jorit Wintjes notes the lineage of Antioch's rhetors, and that Libanius had earlier experienced more severe rivalries in Athens.[27] When Libanius returned to Antioch, he expected the sophist Zenobius to acknowledge the returning sophist as his successor, but Zenobius retained his position, so that Libanius found himself at odds with some of the other teachers in the city, and was soon in the midst of heated competition over students.[28] In his autobiography (e.g., *Or.* 1.90) Libanius portrays a mutually hostile relationship with another teacher, identified by such scholars as A. F. Norman, P. Wolf, Cribiore, and Wintjes as Acacius from Caesarea (e.g., *Or.* 1.156–59).[29] Libanius pleaded with Calliope for assistance from his position in the *stoa,* and soon thereafter, he found his rivals vanquished, and he brags with pleasure: "I had been established in the *bouleutērion* and . . . there was such a flock [of students] that it was not possible to get through them all before the sun set" (1.104). Cribiore concludes that Libanius "ruled over a student population that reached eighty in the best years," and reminds readers that when he taught in the

27. Wintjes, *Das Leben*, 38, 100.

28. Samuel Lieu briefly discusses this interaction in "Libanius and Higher Education at Antioch," in *Culture and Society in Later Roman Antioch*, ed. Isabella Sandwell and Janet Huskinson (Oxford: Oxbow Books, 2004), 13–23.

29. See P. Wolf, *Vom Schulwesen der Spätantike: Libanius-Interpretationen* (Baden: A. Reiff & Cie. Press, 1951), 93–94; Norman's note on *Or.* 1 in Norman, *Libanius*, 1:155; Cribiore, *School*, 39; Wintjes, *Das Leben*, 101. Although the *PLRE* associates these references with Eubulus instead of Acacius (6), I follow Cribiore and Wintjes in concluding that Wolf's identification of Acacius is persuasive.

city hall he had at least four assistants, though he rarely mentions them.[30] Thus, having begun with a small classroom in his home, Libanius surpassed his rival Zenobius and regained the power and prestige of place that he had been granted upon his earlier visit. Libanius understood his classroom to reflect his ability and status, with better classrooms bringing more students in a cycle that continuously benefited those who were already on top.[31]

Libanius demonstrated clearly the influence that went hand in hand with teaching in the *bouleutērion,* as his acquisition of the official teaching chair and its associated classroom helped make him the spokesperson for many of the city's citizens (*Or.* 1.107). Libanius thus became a key figure in the patronage networks of Antioch,[32] although Wintjes cautions that Libanius's influence in Antioch was due not only to his position as rhetor, but also to the status of his family in recent generations in the city.[33] Libanius does not hesitate to mention that such behavior by the citizens of Antioch upset his main teaching rival, presumably because of the authority that it demonstrated Libanius held in the city by virtue of his new post (1.109).

The end of Libanius's autobiography provides a fitting conclusion to his earlier efforts to gain control of the lecture hall in the *bouleutērion,* as illness eventually confined him at home. Libanius describes his distress at his adult son's injury, the death of his son's mother, and his own growing illnesses, claiming that the events were so debilitating to him that he could not even be moved on his bed; yet, despite the personal tragedies and physical failings, he rejoices at his ability to speak and teach as well as he had before: "As a gift from the gods, words remained in my mouth as earlier" (*Or.* 1.280). He notes that it was no longer necessary to go to large halls such as the *bouleutērion* in order to fulfill his duty to his students, because "students came from many places" to hear his orations in his house (1.281).[34]

---

30. Cribiore, "Value," 234; cf. Libanius, *Or.* 31.

31. Interestingly, Libanius elsewhere recalls his rise to fame in Antioch in happier terms, without the struggles recounted in his autobiography (Libanius, *Ep.* 6.5–6; *Ep.* 4.10). He portrays himself as so quickly popular that even when he did nothing but work all day, he was still unable to satisfy the pressing demand for his public lectures (Libanius, *Ep.* 4.11).

32. See also Liebeschuetz, *Antioch,* 192–208. Compare Adam Schor's recent discussion of Theodoret's role as a mediator in Antioch's social networks in the middle of the fifth century, and the power dynamics involved in such negotiations: Schor, *Theodoret's People: Social Networks and Religious Conflict in Late Roman Syria* (Berkeley: University of California Press, 2011).

33. Wintjes, *Das Leben,* 62. See also the discussion of Libanius's use of patronage in Edward Schoolman, "Civic Transformation of the Mediterranean City: Antioch and Ravenna, 300–800 C.E." (PhD diss., University of California, Los Angeles, 2010), 87–88.

34. Libanius uses the word θεάτροις to refer to the large halls where the audience used to hear him speak. While Libanius does not explicitly use the word "house" or "home" for the place he entertains his students during his illness, the fact that he was resting from illness on a bed from which (and even on which) he could not be moved (*Or.* 1.280) justifies Norman's translation: "Pupils came from many quarters, my declamations being composed and delivered at home" (Norman, *Libanius,* 1:333).

In this narrative, the politics of place have come full circle. Whereas upon his return to Antioch in 354 Libanius craved access to the *bouleutērion* as a way of affirming his prestige and granting himself greater authority and visibility within the city, by the end of his career, he portrayed himself as a sufficient attraction to bring students to the more modest place of his own home. By the end of his life Libanius was content to teach from home, because his home no longer held the same connotations as it had when he first returned to the city. As the location and classroom of the city's well-known sophist, his home at the end of his career commanded the respect associated with him and his teaching; no longer did he rely primarily on a prestigious place to bring students to his lectures, but his own renown brought prestige and students to whatever place he taught.

LOCATION, LOCATION, LOCATION: LIBANIUS, OFFICIALS, AND THE SPATIAL EXERCISE OF POWER

Because Libanius's negotiations of the power dynamics of Antioch's places come to us through his written texts, the critical analysis of sociolinguists such as Miriam Locher offers insight into the processes by which Libanius negotiates power through his manipulation of his and others' attendance at Antioch's places. According to Locher, "Power cannot be possessed like a commodity: it is constantly negotiated in and around relationships," and efforts to exercise power are always open to resistance.[35] Sociolinguists recognize that most relationships interweave space, status, and education as components of power dynamics. Libanius and the emperor Julian negotiated in Antioch, for example, and although Julian's status as emperor was superior to Libanius's status as a citizen, Libanius's seniority over the younger Julian and his status as a sophist compared to Julian's role as a student complicated the power dynamics between the two. Reading Libanius's autobiography through the lens of sociolinguistic descriptions of the exercise of power and resistance further highlights the place-related negotiations of power that Libanius undertook, particularly with respect to representatives of imperial authority.

An incident with the praetorian prefect Strategius demonstrates the political clout that Libanius claims to have wielded.[36] First, Libanius explains that Strategius

---

35. Miriam Locher, *Power and Politeness in Action: Disagreements in Oral Communication* (New York: Mouton de Gruyter, 2004), 37; cf. also Stewart Clegg, *Frameworks of Power* (London: Sage, 1989), 207.

36. Danielle Slootjes notes that Libanius is not hesitant to criticize local governors (Libanius, *Or.* 33, 45), and that certain administrative changes under Diocletian and a changing Roman elite had made such actions less dangerous than they had been earlier: see Slootjes, "Between Criticism and Praise: Provincials' Image of the Governor in the Later Roman Empire," in *The Representation and Perception of Roman Imperial Power: Proceedings of the Third Workshop of the International Network 'Impact of Empire' (Roman Empire, c. 200 B.C.–A.D. 476), Netherlands Institute in Rome, March 20–23, 2002,*

requested of him a panegyric, which alone reflects Libanius's high standing. More notably, Libanius announces that he would only deliver the requested panegyric to the prefect "if Strategius left his house and received the work in the *bouleutērion*," a behavior that Libanius explicitly comments "was something new for the prefect to do" (*Or.* 1.112). Strategius (Strategius Musonius) was already well acquainted with Libanius, and had years earlier succeeded in persuading the Athenians to offer Libanius a chair of rhetoric, which Libanius refused after noting what a great honor it was to be invited (1.81–86, 106).[37] Furthermore, Libanius suggests that he had spent a great deal of time with Strategius in Antioch, taking advantage of the prefect's respect by obtaining his leniency in legal matters for those Antiochenes whom Libanius wished to be indebted to him (1.106–8). The incident of Libanius's panegyric for Strategius, and the sophist's insistence on its performance in his lecture hall, thus participated in a long history of patronage and exchange between the two men.

For Libanius, there was great power in his successful persuasion of the prefect to attend the lecture hall. Not only did this likely mean that a larger and more diverse crowd might attend, thus leading to the greater circulation and wider acclaim of his work, but it also demonstrated his ability to encourage particular behaviors of this government official, indicating even more clearly Libanius's authority generally, and his status with respect to the prefect specifically. In addition to the personal influence that this event reveals, it also confirms the significant power inherent in the location where Libanius regularly taught. More than a classroom for students, the lecture hall in the *bouleutērion* was a grand and public place associated with civic authorities and host to the emperor's spokesperson in the region. Finally, not only did Strategius's requested attendance reinforce the authority that Libanius and his classroom held in the public eye, but the event of the lecture itself became a new piece of the classroom's history, adding to the collective memory of that place and the connotations that passersby would associate with it ever after.

Not one to miss an opportunity, Libanius recounts about Strategius: "He said he would do the honor, though most did not believe, but indeed he was present," and when the length of the work made it necessary for him to return a second, and even a third, time, he did (*Or.* 1.112). Taking full advantage of the situation, Libanius persuades the prefect to attend Libanius's lecture room not only one time, but three, as if to flaunt the sway that he held over this official both in persuading him

---

ed. Lukas De Blois, Paul Erdkamp, Olivier Hekster, Gerda De Kleijn, and Stephan Mols (Amsterdam: J. C. Gieben, 2003), 138–26. Richard Saller observes that local officials participated in the ubiquitous patronage system, offering their influence, particularly in legal matters, in exchange for *gratia* such as monumental dedications, orations in their honor, or monetary gain: Saller, *Personal Patronage under the Early Empire* (New York: Cambridge University Press, 1982), esp. 145–68. Saller uses Libanius's interactions with Strategius on behalf of other Antiochenes as one example of this patronage system.

37. T. M. Banchich demonstrates that Libanius also declined an honorary title from another emperor (Banchich, "Eunapius on Libanius' Refusal of a Prefecture," *Phoenix* 39.4 [1985]: 384–86).

to appear in his classroom and in controlling the powerful place that commanded such respect. Libanius explains with pleasure in his autobiography that soon everyone in the city respected him, having heard not only about the incident and who it involved, but also specifically "where in the city" it took place (1.112).

Libanius's manipulation of the praetorian prefect Strategius provides an example of what Richard Watts defines as the "exercise of power."[38] When Libanius claims that he persuaded Strategius to break with custom (and Strategius's initial intention) and to hear the panegyric in the city hall instead of the prefect's house, Libanius portrays himself as exercising power over the praetorian prefect. By declining to resist Libanius's request, Strategius positioned himself under Libanius's power, despite his status as praetorian prefect. Stewart Clegg observes that people "'possess' power only insofar as they are relationally constituted as doing so,"[39] and Libanius here narrates his resistance to Strategius's exalted position, renegotiating through language and physical attendance the relative power between these two men.

Throughout his autobiography Libanius relates other similar examples in which he affects the behavior of a government figure, choosing where to stage his appearances so as to lend himself prestige. Libanius mentions, for example, a certain well-respected Archelaus who honored him. Libanius claims that Archelaus intended to visit him, instead of vice versa, which would have been customary, and that the visit never took place only because Libanius asked him to remain where he was, thus exercising power in changing Archelaus's stated intentions (Or. 1.166). Physical location becomes a key factor in this complex power exchange. To begin, the story suggests that both Libanius and Archelaus understood it to be a mark of authority for Libanius to receive Archelaus as a guest, rather than having Libanius be the visitor.[40] The architect Vitruvius from the first century B.C.E. noted that

---

38. "A exercises power over B," Richard Watts writes, "when A affects B in a manner contrary to B's initially perceived interests, regardless of whether B later comes to accept the desirability of A's actions" (Watts, Power in Family Discourse [New York: Mouton de Gruyter, 1991], 62; cf. Locher, Power, 18–19).

39. Clegg, Frameworks, 207.

40. Scholars in a variety of fields, from sociology and anthropology to tourism, have studied the complex issues surrounding the practice of hospitality, and particularly the host/guest relationship. While much of the work focuses on tracing the historical expectations of hospitality in various contexts, and of the obligations incumbent upon both host and guest, scholars such as Martha Robinson and Paul Lynch have also explicitly discussed the power dynamics involved: Robinson and Lynch, "The Power of Hospitality: A Sociolinguistic Analysis," in Hospitality: A Social Lens, ed. Conrad Lashley, Paul Lynch, and Alison Morrison (New York: Elsevier, 2007), 141–54. Paul Lynch, Jennie Germann Molz, Alison McIntosh, Peter Lugosi, and Conrad Lashley likewise acknowledge the "politically laden questions about power, identity, violence and equity" that surround practices of hospitality (Lynch et al., "Theorizing Hospitality," Hospitality & Society 1.1 [2011]: 5). Peter Brown specifically comments on the power dynamics in Libanius's context, writing, "Not to agree to receive such a visit was a sign, on Libanius' part, of disapproval of the governor" (Brown, Power and Persuasion in Late Antiquity: Towards a Christian Empire [Madison: University of Wisconsin Press, 1992], 31–32).

people of higher status always received at their homes visitors of lower status, but the opposite was not true (*De architectura* 6.5). Through the retelling of this story, Libanius demonstrates not only that he was worthy of Archelaus's intention to visit him, despite Archelaus's high status, but in the vocabulary of Thomas Wartenberg, Libanius had "power over" Archelaus in constraining his actions by persuading him to change the visit, showing Libanius's ostensible influence over where this notable figure did and did not go.[41]

Libanius follows this account with a series of examples of the power dynamics involved in his ability to visit, decline to visit, and host local rulers.[42] He comments that Protasius, the *consularis Syriae*, was told by some of his followers "that he would be a really bad governor if he did not bar his doors to me" (*Or.* 1.167). In his autobiography, Libanius rhetorically dismisses Protasius's apparent refusal to see him, suggesting that he would not have visited Protasius in any case (1.168). The advice to Protasius as well as Libanius's response acknowledge that it was not without significant meaning that Libanius or a local ruler might visit or refuse one another. If Protasius exercised his authority to refuse to host Libanius, as his advisers suggested, Libanius nevertheless narrates the story to suggest that it was he who withheld his attendance from Protasius because they were not on friendly terms.

A series of similar narrations follows. Protasius's unnamed successor also engaged in power contests over visitations, according to Libanius, who records that the official "hoped for an invitation to [my] orations," but Libanius invited others and demonstrated that he "had no great need" of the official (*Or.* 1.169). Libanius describes the consul's anger at this slight, and his effort to punish some of Libanius's students unjustly, presumably in an effort to demonstrate the force that he wielded in the face of Libanius's suggestion that Libanius's authority was not subordinate to that of the consul. Libanius elsewhere in his autobiography refers to an Antiochene governor's unhappiness over a custom (*nomos*) that prevented him from visiting Libanius at his home (1.211), as well as to Libanius withholding attendance from Proclus, the *comes Orientis,* and the virtue that Libanius felt that his refusal had demonstrated (1.223–24). In each case, Libanius presents himself as engaged in negotiations of power with a government official through attendance at, or resistance to invitations to, particular places.

41. Thomas Wartenberg writes, "A social agent *A* has *power over* another social agent *B* if and only if *A* strategically constrains *B*'s action-environment" (Wartenberg, *The Forms of Power: From Domination to Transformation* [Philadelphia: Temple University Press, 1990], 85; cf. Locher, *Power,* 22).

42. Schouler has examined some of the political roles that Libanius's classroom afforded him, including his training of future government officials, and his own adoption of the Greek philosopher's ideal of *parrēsia* (B. Schouler, "Le rôle politique de l'école au temps de Libanios," in *Antioche de Syrie: Histoire, images et traces de la ville antique; Colloque de Lyon [octobre 2001]*, Topoi Suppl. 5, ed. B. Cabouret, P.-L. Gatier, and C. Saliou [Lyon: Maison de l'Orient et de la Méditerranée, 2004], 97–115).

In a similar encounter that recalls the struggle with Strategius, Libanius writes that following the emperor Valens's death at Adrianople in 378, Libanius and others in Antioch celebrated the nomination of Hypatius, who was in Antioch at the time, as the prefect of the city of Rome. After all the other speakers had presented their addresses, it was time for Libanius to present his oration, and he claims that Hypatius wanted his speech to be presented where the new prefect was, in front of a small audience; Libanius, however, wanted it to take place "in the *bouleutērion*" so that many people could attend (*Or.* 1.180). Although in this case Hypatius does not seem to have granted Libanius's request, the story represents another example of Libanius's efforts—at least in the rhetorical self-presentation in his autobiography—to manipulate his power and prestige vis-à-vis local rulers through his command over the locations of his speeches, his attendance, and the attendance of others.

A story that Libanius recounts about Eubulus, and Eubulus's influence on Festus, the *proconsul Asiae,* suggests that Libanius was not alone in recognizing the dynamics involved in such acts of attendance. Libanius claims that once a crowd had gathered to hear him in his lecture hall when the proconsul Festus tried to disperse them by calling them to hear a letter from the emperor, demonstrating his exercise of power over those who were subject to the authority of his position by threatening them if they did not attend (*Or.* 1.157). Norman observes that the council members' need to hear the reading of a letter from the emperor resulted in an act that "removes the cream of Libanius' audience from his declamation."[43] Libanius claims that Festus even posted people at Libanius's lecture to record the names of any who did not attend the summons. Libanius reconciles himself to Festus's success in using his role as a representative of the emperor to take these members of Libanius's audience by describing the audience as unwilling to leave, even though they felt that they had no choice but to do so (1.157). Although Festus took the initiative in this story, according to Libanius, the proconsul was directly influenced in these actions by Libanius's rival Eubulus. Each of these stories of Libanius's interaction with a government official in Antioch leaves no doubt that Libanius narrates these events with a keen awareness of the power inherent in places, and in attendance at those places.

As with local rulers, Libanius also demonstrates his authority in urban space when the emperor Julian visited Antioch in 362–63.[44] Libanius praises Julian's adherence to ancient traditions, in sharp contrast to the orator's clear disdain for

---

43. See Norman, *Libanius,* 1:224.

44. Hans-Ulrich Wiemer has published a thorough study of the long and complex relations between Libanius and Julian: Wiemer, *Libanios und Julian: Studien zum Verhältnis von Rhetorik und Politik im vierten Jahrhundert n. Chr.* (Munich: C.H. Beck'she, 1995). Wintjes has more recently updated this discussion in his chapter on the relation between these two figures (Wintjes, *Das Leben,* 119–33). See also Reinhold Scholl's study of Libanius's Julianic orations: Scholl, *Historische Beiträge zu den julianischen Reden des Libanios* (Stuttgart: Franz Steiner Press, 1994).

Christians and Christianity's rejection of traditional practices, values, and education.[45] Libanius's pleasure in Julian's accession to the throne is clear in his praise of Julian's love of wisdom and his restoration of traditional practices (Or. 1.118).[46] Libanius conveys his personal joy at the rise of someone who valued education and the classical heritage as Libanius himself did: "I laughed and leapt, and put together and gave my speeches with pleasure, as the altars received blood, smoke carried the savor of burnt sacrifice to heaven, the gods were honored through festivals" (1.119). Julian's reign had such restorative possibility for the empire in the rhetoric of Libanius's memories that Libanius claims that Romans took courage from Julian's accession to the throne, and the barbarians suffered (1.119). Despite such praise, however, Libanius claims that his own authority in the city of Antioch had grown to such a level that he could successfully persuade the new emperor concerning where and which events the sophist would attend.[47]

45. Wiemer traces the relationship between Libanius and Julian even before the latter became emperor (Wiemer, Libanios und Julian, esp. 13–48). Certainly their shared love for education and the gods gave them much in common. Although Wiemer posits a temporary estrangement between the two at Julian's elevation to caesar, Wintjes questions whether the evidence supports this interpretation of the gap in extant correspondence between the two from 353 to 358 (Wiemer, Libanios und Julian, 18–28; Wintjes, Das Leben, 121–23). Regardless of the reason for this epistolary silence, there is no doubt that their interactions in Antioch were complex in light of their long history.

46. Jean Bouffartigue has noted that Libanius presents a highly favorable, "partisan" image of Julian as a leader given by the gods for the mission of restoring traditional religious practices (Bouffartigue, "L'image politique de Julien chez Libanios," Pallas 60 [2002]: 183). Bouffartigue further argues that Libanius presents Julian as a liberator to contradict others' accusations that he was a tyrant, and that Libanius's writings suggest that nothing could be as advantageous for the empire as to have a leader who is in direct communication with the gods (Bouffartigue, "L'image," 182–85).

47. Libanius's reported behavior with respect to local and imperial rulers is far from unique. Jonas Palm has studied Greek orators' self-presentation regarding emperors and notes that the orators tended to present themselves as superior (Palm, Rom, Römertum und Imperium in der griechischen Literatur der Kaiserzeit [Lund: Gleerup, 1959]). Compare Jaap-Jan Flinterman, "Sophists and Emperors: A Reconnaissance of Sophistic Attitudes," in Paideia: The World of the Second Sophistic, ed. Barbara Borg (New York: Walter de Gruyter, 2004), 359–76. Flinterman follows Elizabeth Rawson in distinguishing between rhetors and sophists, who typically praised imperial authority, and philosophers, who more frequently challenged emperors (Flinterman, "Sophists," 376; Elizabeth Rawson, "Roman Rulers and the Philosophic Advisor," in Philosophia Togata: Essays on Philosophy and Roman Society, ed. M. Griffin and J. Barnes [New York: Oxford, 1989], 253). Nevertheless, Flinterman cites examples of sophists who were occasionally described as having refused imperial invitations in much the same way that Libanius claims to do in his autobiography ("Sophists," 364). Compare also Odile Lagacherie, "Libanios, rhétorique et politique à propos des discours 50 et 45: Le principe de réalité," in Approches de la Troisième Sophistique: Hommages à Jacques Schamp, ed. Eugenio Amato (Brussels: Editions Latomus, 2006), 460–68; Carsten Drecoll, "Sophisten und Archonten: Paideia als gesellschaftliches Argument bei Libanios," in Griffin and Barnes, Philosophia Togata, 403–17; and Bernadette Cabouret, "Le gouverneur au temps de Libanios, image et réalité," Pallas 60 (2002): 191–204.

Libanius narrates a struggle with Julian that Libanius ostensibly won in defining the terms of his attendance at particular places in Antioch. Libanius's autobiography establishes Julian's allegedly great admiration for Libanius upon the emperor's first approach to the city, which, along with their long history of respect for one another, set the stage for Libanius's boldness in the interactions that soon followed (*Or.* 1.120).[48] Libanius relates that every day the emperor would sacrifice "under the trees in the garden of the palace, and many came regularly" to participate in the service to the gods (1.121). Libanius explains his reticence to attend Julian's sacrificial rituals, offering the excuse that he had never been invited and would not attend simply in order to flatter the emperor (1.121).[49] Thus, Libanius was drawing further lines about where in the city and in what circumstances his status would allow him to go. In particular, Libanius's reticence to attend the emperor without an invitation led to his absence from the sacrificial altars that Julian used. In light of his celebration that under Julian "the altars received blood, smoke carried the savor of burnt sacrifice to heaven, the gods were honored through festivals" (1.119), it is questionable whether Libanius would have avoided the altars primarily because of an objection to the sacrifices themselves.[50] His language suggests that much like his authoritative insistence that the prefect Strategius attend an oration at the place of Libanius's dominance, so too in this case Libanius's choice not to frequent Julian's altars was an assertion of Libanius's decision to avoid compromising his standing. Hans-Ulrich Wiemer also interprets Libanius's actions with respect to Julian in the weeks following his arrival in Antioch, as narrated in his autobiography, as a bold effort to demonstrate his independence and status, although Wiemer plausibly suggests that Libanius was not always withholding his presence from the emperor from a position of authority, as Libanius claims.[51] Glen Bowersock notes of Libanius's choice not to attend: "Libanius acted from a proper sense of his own dignity and station (and possibly a

---

48. The details of Julian's imperial entrance into Antioch are the subject of some debate. Whereas Bidez describes this encounter between Julian and Libanius as an immediate reconciliation of their previous estrangement, Wiemer argues that some tension remained and Libanius was disappointed that Julian's greeting was not warmer than it was (J. Bidez, ed., *L'Empereur Julien, Oeuvres complètes*, vol. 2 [Paris: Les Belles Lettres, 1932], 109; Wiemer, *Libanios und Julian*, 41–43). Wintjes, however, understands Libanius to be satisfied with Julian's greeting (*Das Leben*, 127).

49. Ugo Criscuolo reminds readers that Libanius could be quite willing to accept direct invitations from Julian, such as the emperor's public request for a speech from Libanius (Criscuolo, "Libanio e Giuliano," *Vichiana* 11 [1982]: 77).

50. Festugière makes a strong argument that it is possible that Libanius was not comfortable with Julian's excessive public ritual sacrifices: Festugière, *Antioche païenne et chrétienne*, 234. For the discomfort of fourth-century Antiochenes more generally regarding cult sacrifice, see Emmanuel Soler, *Le sacré et le salut à Antioche au IVe siècle apr. J.-C.: Pratiques festives et comportements religieux dans le processus de christianisation de la cité* (Beirut: Institut français du Proche-Orient, 2006), 40–42.

51. Wiemer, *Libanios und Julian*, 43–45.

recollection of the similar way in which the great second-century sophist Aristides had behaved toward Marcus Aurelius)."[52] At least in Libanius's retelling, altars became sites for the negotiation of status, even in relation to the emperor himself.

Libanius's struggle with Julian continued to escalate during Julian's stay in the city. "Once [Julian] came to sacrifice at the altar of Zeus Philius," Libanius says, "and he saw the others, for they wished and would do anything to be seen. I alone of all of them was not watching" (*Or.* 1.122). When Julian wrote to Libanius to ask why he had not attended, Libanius sent his reply, explaining his absence from Zeus's altar in the same way that he explained to his reader his absence from the daily sacrifices in the palace garden, that he had not received an invitation. The emperor's reproof was apparently not sufficient to effect Libanius's attendance, as he claims that by choice even after this exchange he still "kept away from the garden" (1.123). According to Richard Watts's model, Libanius would "possess power" if he "has the freedom of action to achieve the goals [he] has set [himself], regardless of whether or not this involves the potential to impose [his] will on others."[53] By exercising his freedom of action in withholding his presence, Libanius reveals the ability to negotiate the status that he possesses in relation to the emperor. Resistance is, according to Wartenberg, "the attempt by the subordinate agent to change her circumstances in regard to the dominant agent so as to diminish the dominant agent's power over her."[54] By resisting Julian's expectations of his attendance, Libanius rejected the emperor's presumption of control, and in the process renegotiated the power dynamics between them.

The honor eventually granted by the emperor's official invitation to Libanius, with the emperor ostensibly forced to request the favor of Libanius's presence, finally resolved the issue.[55] Locher describes the power of "action-restriction" in relation to Wartenberg's comment that a powerful figure "changes the social space of the agents over whom she has power."[56] In the Antiochene example, Libanius "strategically constrains" Julian's "action-environment" by persuading Julian to change his behavior by issuing a formal invitation if he would like Libanius's attendance.[57] By orchestrating an event at the *agora,* one of the most important public places in the city, Libanius allegedly overturned the expected influence of the

---

52. G. W. Bowersock, *Julian the Apostate* (Cambridge, MA: Harvard University Press, 1978), 97.

53. Watts, *Power,* 60.

54. Wartenberg, *Forms of Power,* 102; cf. Locher, *Power,* 23.

55. Bidez understands the resolution of this conversation between Libanius and Julian, which he takes at face value as presented in Libanius's autobiography, to signify the reestablishment of a closer friendship between them: J. Bidez, *La vie de l'Empereur Julien* (Paris: Société d'Édition "Les Belles Lettres," 1965), 279.

56. Wartenberg, *Forms of Power,* 74; Locher, *Power,* 21. Compare Teun van Dijk, "Structures of Discourse and Structures of Power," *Communications Yearbook* 12 (1989): 20.

57. Wartenberg, *Forms of Power,* 85; Locher, *Power,* 22.

emperor over a citizen: "I was invited as the *agora* became full, and [the emperor] who had invited me was at a loss and hung his head to the ground," indicating to Libanius that the emperor regretted his earlier poor behavior and ceded control of the situation to Libanius (*Or.* 1.123). According to Wartenberg's model for power dynamics, Libanius would "influence" Julian "if and only if" Libanius "*communicatively* interacts" with Julian in such a way that, as a result, Julian "alters his assessment of his action-environment in a fundamental manner."[58] When Julian reconsidered and issued an invitation to Libanius at the sophist's insistence, Libanius demonstrated influence over the emperor in the context of those particular negotiations. Libanius's narration of the emperor bowing his head in respect to the sophist in the midst of the crowded *agora* paints a very public display of Libanius's high standing and the prominent places in which he received imperial recognition.

Libanius claims that he put off his attendance not only at the emperor's ritual sacrifices but also at the emperor's table until he received an invitation. Even once the emperor invited Libanius to join him for a meal, Libanius continued to negotiate, as he declined the emperor's first and second invitations, only to have the emperor request that he visit often (*Or.* 1.124). Part of the power inherent in an invitation lies in its potential to be refused, and thus the one who is invited is able to assert control over the one who offers the invitation. By carefully delimiting where he would and would not go, and under what circumstances, Libanius highlights the political force that attendance in particular locations could have, and he describes himself as successfully constructing spatial boundaries in order to demonstrate his status with respect to the emperor Julian. These actions in turn increased Antiochenes' perception of Libanius's power, as he claims that when Julian left the city in anger in 363 they chose Libanius to plead their case to Julian, in part because they considered Julian to be Libanius's student (15.6).[59]

Julian himself also recognized the significance of withholding his presence, and wielded this same power against Antioch after he felt that the city had unforgivably insulted him and the gods. The citizens of Antioch so offended Julian that he claimed he would not return to their city. In his infamous satirical work, the *Misopōgōn*, Julian insists, "I determined to depart and withdraw from this city [Antioch]," disgusted by the corruption and frivolous life of luxury preferred there, and insulted by the citizens' treatment of the emperor and of the gods (*Misopōgōn*

---

58. Wartenberg, *Forms of Power*, 105; Locher, *Power*, 24.

59. For Libanius's *Oratio* 15 I rely on the Greek text edited by Norman in *Libanius*, vol. 1; all translations of *Or.* 15 are my own from Norman's Greek text. Many scholars have written extensively about Libanius's role as Julian's companion and as a mediator between the emperor and the city's curia and citizens. See, for example, Wintjes, *Das Leben*; Wiemer, *Libanios und Julian*, esp. 48–68, 189–246; and Wiemer, "Die Rangstellung des Sophisten Libanios unter den Kaisern Julian, Valens und Theodosius, mit einem Anhang über Abfassung und Verbreitung von Libanios' Rede für die Tempel (*Or* 30)," *Chiron* 25 (1995): 89–130.

364–65; cf. Libanius, *Or.* 15.55).[60] As Emmanuel Soler and others have recognized, Julian shared an educated disdain for Antiochenes' alleged love of spectacle and pleasure, criticized also by others who knew the city well, including Libanius, Ammianus Marcellinus, and John Chrysostom.[61] Offended by the behavior of Antioch's citizens, Julian recognized that withholding his presence from the city was an effective form of censure and a demonstration of his strength, much as he closed the Great Church to censure the Christian communities in 362 after the fire at Apollo's temple.[62] Libanius's pleas on behalf of Antioch's citizens demonstrate that the full force of Julian's behavior was apparent to his audience (*Or.* 15.55–56). Imagining the impending disaster that would follow, Libanius laments that Antiochenes would be rejected around the world and have to conceal the place of their origin (15.57). As a result, Libanius found himself in the weakened position of extending an invitation to the emperor, one he knew well might be refused: "What I ask . . . is that you do as you did, Emperor, making the second [trip] resemble the first stay. Marching from the west you were with us; stay now also, returning from having been victorious" (15.14–15). These texts confirm that both Libanius and Julian recognized the power of controlling their public appearances, and the authority that the places in which they appeared could confer. This competition adheres to the same pattern as Libanius's struggles with his rival teachers to gain students, demonstrating Libanius's attention to and control over where and with whom he went.

PREACHING PLACES: CONTROLLING
ANTIOCH'S CHURCHES

Teachers such as Libanius were, however, far from the only fourth-century Antiochenes competing to gain control of the city's best teaching places. Antioch's Christian leaders struggled to gain control over church buildings much as Libanius competed for students and classrooms with his rival teachers. By the fourth century,

60. All translations from the *Misopōgōn* are my own from the Greek text edited by Wilmer Cave Wright in *The Works of the Emperor Julian*, vol. 2 (New York: Putnam, 1923). See also the discussion of this text in Soler (*Le sacré et le salut*, 43–64). Nicholas Baker-Brian highlights the different perceptions of virtue between Antiochenes and the emperor Julian that were on prominent display in the *Misopōgōn*: Baker-Brian, "The Politics of Virtue in Julian's *Misopogon*," in *Emperor and Author: The Writings of Julian the Apostate,* ed. Nicholas Baker-Brian and Shaun Tougher (Swansea: The Classical Press of Wales, 2012), 263–80.

61. Soler, *Le sacré et le salut,* esp. 29–32; Soler, "Sacralité et partage du temps et de l'espace festifs à Antioche au IVe siècle," in *Les frontières du profane dans l'antiquité tardive,* Collection de l'École Française de Rome 428, ed. Éric Rebillard and Claire Sotinel (Rome: École française de Rome, 2010), 273–86; cf. Marinela Casella, "Les spectacles à Antioche d'après Libanios," *Antiquité Tardive* 15 (2007): 99–112.

62. See Bowersock, *Julian,* 104–5.

Constantine's patronage helped Christianity to flourish around the empire, although the new political climate also led to ecumenical councils, beginning with the Council of Nicaea in 325, that limited the possibilities of who could legitimately claim to represent "orthodox" Christianity. Shifting political patronage and corresponding imperial definitions of Christian orthodoxy in the decades that followed also brought competing claims to episcopal sees around the empire, but few places more so than Antioch. Concurrently, Antioch was a center for church councils,[63] Olympic games,[64] and emperors themselves, as the imperial palace in the city was intermittently occupied by Constantius II, Julian, Jovian, and Valens.[65] In this complex landscape, Antioch's Christian leaders competed not only with those of other religious communities but also with each other to gain control of the city's powerful preaching places and its citizens' attendance at them. A brief overview of the shifting control of Antioch's churches will reveal the possibilities for fruitful Christian comparisons to Libanius's skirmishes, and will thus lay a foundation for the in-depth analysis in the following chapters.[66]

As seen in the introduction, fourth-century Antioch was rife with intra-Christian divisions, fueled by the political and theological controversies around the empire, especially from the Council of Nicaea (325) to Theodosius's issuing of the *cunctos populos* edict (380). During these decades, Antioch's population had choices between multiple concurrent Christian leaders, for a time as many as four different bishops, and even more numerous places where they could gather to hear

63. For the numerous church councils in Antioch in this period, see Glanville Downey, *A History of Antioch in Syria: From Seleucus to the Arab Conquest* (Princeton, NJ: Princeton University Press, 1961), 357–60, 370, 388, 415–17. For a more recent discussion and contextualization of the councils and canon law associated with Antioch, see Hermann Hess, *The Early Development of Canon Law and the Council of Serdica* (Oxford: Oxford University Press, 2002), esp. 14, 48–54, 80–85.

64. Downey lists evidence for Olympic games in Antioch, including in the years 332, 336, 380, 384, 388, and 404 C.E. (Downey, *History*, 435–40). See also Glanville Downey, "The Olympic Games of Antioch in the Fourth Century A.D.," *Transactions and Proceedings of the American Philological Association* 70 (1939): 428–38; Liebeschuetz, *Antioch*, 136–44; Petit, *Libanius et la vie municipale*, 123–44; Catherine Saliou, "Antioche décrite par Libanios: La rhétorique de l'espace urbain et ses enjeux au milieu du quatrième siècle," in Amato, *Approches de la Troisième Sophistique*, 273–85.

65. Downey refers to Ammianus Marcellinus to locate Constantius II in Antioch intermittently from 338 to 349, and again briefly in the winter of 360–61, Julian from May 362 through March 363, Jovian from October to November 363, and Valens for some months in 370 and then from November 371 to spring 378 (Downey, *History*, 356–72, 398–402); see Wendy Mayer and Pauline Allen, *The Churches of Syrian Antioch (300–638 C.E.)* (Walpole, MA: Peeters, 2012), 132, 263.

66. Wendy Mayer made the useful observation in conversation that we have some information about Christian catechesis in late fourth-century Antioch that might allow for a constructive comparison with Libanius's descriptions of classrooms. While there is no question that such a comparison would be productive, this current project focuses on places that were sites of competition, and not places of education for their own sake.

these leaders preach.[67] Possession of the most desirable place, whether the *bouleutērion* or the Great Church, was a matter of imperial appointment. Nevertheless, just as Libanius competed with other teachers to claim the most prestigious lecture hall as his classroom, and just as doing so facilitated his acquisition of a much larger audience and greater number of students, so too Christian leaders vied to control the most powerful preaching places, and could expect that control over those places to aid the spread of their version of Christianity to more people, and the growth of their congregations.

Theodoret, who grew up in Antioch, records an intra-Christian conflict over places that recalls Libanius's negotiations with the praetorian prefect Strategius. Theodoret's story involves a conflict between Leontius, the homoian bishop of Antioch from 344 to the late 350s, and two ascetics who were later ordained into the priesthood by Bishop Meletius—namely, Flavian and Diodore. Theodoret claims that Flavian and Diodore "gathered together the lovers of God's works in the dwellings of the martyrs, praising God with them in song the whole night" (*HE* 2.24.9).[68] According to Theodoret, Bishop Leontius interpreted these actions as a challenge to his authority. Recognizing that "the multitude was extremely well disposed toward these excellent men," Leontius "did not consider it safe to try to hinder them, but . . . he required from them that this ministry (*leitourgian*) take place in the churches" (Theodoret, *HE* 2.24.10; cf. Sozomen, *HE* 3.20.9).[69] Just as Libanius understood there to be a powerful significance in his ability to request that the praetorian prefect attend him in his own classroom, so this story suggests that Bishop Leontius thought that he could retain his authority over Antioch's Christian community if the charismatic ascetics led their followers in a place that was clearly under the bishop's control. For Libanius and Bishop Leontius, the loca-

---

67. The places were more numerous than the bishops, because the bishops were not the only Christian leaders who led church services. John Chrysostom mentions, for example, times when he preached in one of Antioch's churches while Bishop Flavian concurrently held another service at a martyr's shrine outside of the city (*De sanctis martyribus* 1). Chrysostom also mentions preaching in different churches in Antioch (e.g., *In illud: In faciem ei restiti;* see also Wendy Mayer, "John Chrysostom and His Audiences: Distinguishing Different Congregations at Antioch and Constantinople," *Studia Patristica* 31 [1997]: 70–75; Mayer, "Who Came to Hear John Chrysostom Preach? Recovering a Late Fourth-Century Preacher's Audience," *Ephemerides Theologicae Lovanienses* 76.1 [2000]: 73–87).

68. All translations of Theodoret's church history are my own from the Greek text edited by Léon Parmentier and Günther C. Hansen in *Théodoret de Cyr, Histoire ecclésiastique,* vol. 1 (I–II), SC 501 (Paris: Les Éditions du Cerf, 2006). References are to the chapters and verses in this edition, although they differ from the numbering used in the more widely accessible English translation in the Nicene and Post-Nicene Fathers series.

69. All references to Sozomen's church history are to the Greek text in Günther C. Hansen, ed. and trans., *Sozomenos, Historia ecclesistica: Kirchengeschichte,* vol. 2, Fontes Christiani, no. 73/2 (Turnhout, Belgium: Brepols Publishers, 2004); all translations of Sozomen's history are my own from the Greek text in this volume.

tion of the public performance was critical to the negotiation of the power dynamics among the participants. Theodoret's fifth-century description suggests that Christians like himself, and possibly Leontius, Flavian, and Diodore, recognized the spatial politics of authority.[70]

Another fifth-century church historian, Sozomen, also wrote Antioch's history in ways that echo some of Libanius's stories. He notes, for instance, that when Athanasius of Alexandria visited Antioch during the episcopacy of Leontius, he found the Nicene Christians who opposed the homoian Antiochene bishop gathering "in private houses," and asked the emperor Constantius II to provide one of the church buildings under Bishop Leontius's control to the Nicene community (*HE* 3.20.4). Regardless of the historical accuracy of Sozomen's text, the parallel between Libanius's narrative of his struggle to move from teaching in his home to a place in the *agora* to the prestigious *bouleutērion*, and Sozomen's account of Nicene Christians' struggle to move from worshipping in a home to a small church building to the Great Church, reveal the familiarity of such spatial narratives and the assumption that there was a direct relation between location and power. This comparison can be carried even further by considering Sozomen's claim that years later Bishop Meletius's followers "caused him to mount the episcopal throne (*thronos*) in one of the churches before the city" upon his return from exile (*HE* 7.3.3). Much like Libanius's *thronos* in the *bouleutērion*, the *thronos* of Sozomen's story explicitly signifies the authority—in this case the episcopal authority—of the person who sits in it.

The five tumultuous years of 359–64 provide the most concentrated example of the shifting imperial patronage of Christian leaders in the schisms following the Council of Nicaea, and of the local changes of episcopal fortune and control that accompanied them. Meletius's almost immediate exile after his appointment as bishop in 359/60, and the election of the homoian Christian Euzoius to replace him, created two stark Antiochene Christian communities, each of which had been granted an imperially supported bishop within the year.[71] With Julian's accession to the throne in 361 and his recall of all exiled bishops, both Euzoius and Meletius were in residence in Antioch, along with Paulinus, who had been appointed bishop just before Meletius returned. Meletius hosted a council in Antioch under the emperor Jovian (r. 363–64), but Jovian's successor Valens returned imperial patronage to Bishop Euzoius later in 364.[72]

---

70. I thank Wendy Mayer for suggesting the comparisons between Libanius and the church histories.

71. On the homoian Christian community during these years, see Hanns Christof Brennecke, *Studien zur Geschichte der Homöer: Der Osten bis zum Ende der homöischen Reichskirche* (Tübingen: J. C. B. Mohr/Paul Siebeck, 1988), 87–157.

72. On the difficulty of defining Jovian's church politics, see Brennecke, *Studien*, 158–81. See also Thomas Karmann, *Meletius von Antiochien: Studien zur Geschichte des trinitätstheologischen Streits in den Jahren 360–364 n. Chr.*, Regensburger Studien zur Theologie 68 (Frankfurt: Peter Lang, 2009), 341–54.

Much as the *bouleutērion* was rightfully the lecture hall of the city's appointed sophist, the beautiful Great Church of Antioch became the domain of the imperially recognized bishop and his congregation—both were prominent and respected public places that were closely associated with imperial power. In the midst of the complex politics of the years 359–64, the Great Church changed from homoian Christian control since the time of its dedication in 341 under the emperor Constantius II (r. 337–61) to Meletius's brief control upon his appointment around 360 to the homoian bishop Euzoius's control after Meletius was quickly exiled. When Meletius returned to Antioch under the emperor Julian by 362, Euzoius appears to have maintained control of the Great Church for the homoian community for a time, but lost control of it again to Meletius late in 363 when Jovian became emperor. With Valens's accession to the imperial throne months later in 364, the Great Church returned to Euzoius, and Meletius was exiled again, although he and his successor Flavian would regain control of the Great Church with the accession of the emperor Theodosius fifteen years later. It is easy to understand how this political chaos, church schism, and shifting control of the Great Church could have led Meletius and his followers John Chrysostom and Flavian to take a particularly active interest in shaping the physical topography of Antioch in the decades that followed, and in creating (and controlling) powerful new Christian places that would not shift as easily from the control of one Christian community to another, regardless of changing imperial support.

The Great Church, though, was not the only significant Christian meeting place in the fourth-century city, and just as Libanius reports his advancement from teaching in his own home to teaching in a room on the edge of the *agora* to teaching in the *bouleutērion* itself, so, too, Christian leaders in Antioch moved from one location to another for a variety of reasons. While some moves were ritually necessary, such as Bishop Flavian preaching at a martyr's shrine on the day of the celebration of that martyr, other moves were not voluntary, such as those forced by the exile of Bishop Meletius. As noted in the introduction, when the emperor Valens exiled Meletius in 365, Meletius's congregants lost control of the Great Church, and it appears that in this period they did not have access to any of the city's church buildings, as Theodoret records that for a time the community gathered to worship at the foot of Mount Silpius and then in the military training grounds across the Orontes River (*HR* 2.15, 2.19). While Antioch's rhetors and sophists do not usually seem to have competed directly with the city's Christian leaders for the same places, teachers and preachers alike competed among themselves to gain control over the places that held the greatest prestige, and thus influence, within their community.

Just as the end of Libanius's autobiography exemplifies, however, that the values of places were not static, there are comparable Christian examples. Although the *bouleutērion* was a prestigious place, and Libanius's home did not initially hold much value as a classroom in the city, by the end of his life Libanius narrates that this had changed: his own prestige as a renowned teacher turned his home class-room into a place that attracted numerous students because of his presence there. Likewise, although Antioch's Great Church held prestige within the city as the ornate and impressive new church built with imperial patronage, other buildings could become significant places if something or someone powerful inhabited them. John Chrysostom records, for example, that many Antiochenes, even some who attended Chrysostom's church services, considered the Jewish synagogue to be a fearsome place, in part because it housed the sacred scriptures (*Adv. Iud.* 1.5; 6.6).[73] During the fourth century, martyrs' relics became extraordinarily powerful objects that brought religious authority to the places where they were located.[74] Thus occasionally teachers and preachers alike could increase the prestige of a place, rather than being forced to change their location to a place that already had greater potency in order to raise their status. This increased respect for a place could thus convey greater authority to the leader who controlled it, a dynamic that Bishop Meletius found particularly useful in the face of his forced exile from the city's church buildings. The most dramatic example of this, which will be discussed more fully in the following chapter, is the decades-long manipulation of the relics of the early Christian saint Babylas, and Bishop Meletius's appropriation of Baby-las's relics to grant greater authority to a new structure that he built to house them.

The intentional relocation of Babylas's relics in order to reshape the connota-tions and relative power of places in and around Antioch connects the Christian story to Libanius's also through the involvement of the emperor Julian. Whereas Libanius depicts himself engaging with the emperor in a complex dance around the offering and acceptance of invitations, and thus controlling his and the emper-or's attendance at particular places, John Chrysostom also describes Christian leaders engaging with Julian over the manipulation of places and the influence associated with them. Thus, during the same months that Libanius was allegedly involved in delicate spatial negotiations with Julian, raising Libanius's own status by refusing his attendance at Julian's invitations, Julian was involved in much more explicit manipulations of the region's topography, exhuming Babylas's bones from the grounds of Apollo's temple to regain control of that place for the Greek god, wresting it away from Christian control. While Julian successfully forced the removal of the remains from the temple grounds, he was unable to lessen the power associated with the relics. Whether teaching Greek rhetoric or Christian orthodoxy, whether struggling against their most immediate colleagues or with

---

73. For further discussion, see chapter 3 below; and Christine Shepardson, "Controlling Contested Places: John Chrysostom's *Adversus Iudaeos* Homilies and the Spatial Politics of Religious Contro-versy," *JECS* 15.4 (2007): 483–516.

74. A fuller discussion of the evidence for the power of relics and their role in Christianity in late antiquity, and recent academic investigations of these topics, follows in chapters 2 and 5 below.

the emperor Julian, whether seeking to gain control of already potent places or seeking to make more potent the places that they already controlled, these Antiochene leaders reveal the power that was at stake in fourth-century Antioch through the reshaping of physical places.

CONCLUSION: TEACHING AND PREACHING

Antioch's role in imperial politics during the fourth century, as well as the complexity of its religious history and the wider influence of the city's church leaders, made it particularly significant to the development of the definition of Christian orthodoxy in the eastern empire, as well as to the erratic spread of Christians' influence and visibility around the Mediterranean in late antiquity. Amid this complexity, Antioch's teachers and preachers recognized the importance of controlling local places that were associated with status and authority, and actively manipulated them in their favor.

Libanius returned to Antioch in 354, hoping that his years of education and teaching would garner him recognition and prestige in his hometown, such as he had received on his recent visit to the city. He expresses disappointment and frustration that upon his return he was at first able to attract only small numbers of students, and that he was forced to teach them in his own home, since he did not have access to more public teaching places in the city. In particular, he writes at length about his yearning to teach in the most prestigious place in the city, where he had spoken so successfully on his visit. When he finally earned the appointment to the official chair of rhetoric, and the right to teach in the *bouleutērion,* he provides further information about the location itself, its impressive size, and the official *thronos* that was set so visibly opposite the room's main entrance and that marked the authority and honor associated with his new post. Libanius's rhetoric reflects a distinct awareness that initially the amount of respect he received as a teacher was directly tied to the location of his classroom, and he narrates in detail his painful though eventually triumphant efforts to move from teaching in his home to teaching in the city's largest classroom. Libanius extends this sense of the importance of physical location into his dealings with imperial officials, and even with the emperor Julian when he was resident in the city. From persuading the prefect Strategius to come to Libanius instead of vice versa, to declining to attend the emperor's rituals, Libanius portrays his careful control over his attendance at the city's places, and in the process manipulates the status of those places, his classroom, and himself.

Christian preachers concurrently vied for control in the city, and like Libanius they did so amid a great deal of competition. It seems as if the old Apostolic Church was likely the most prestigious church through the reign of Constantine, but it seems to have been quickly overshadowed by the completion of the Great Church, dedicated in 341 under Constantine's son Constantius II. The schism in

Antioch's episcopacy meant that for decades there were multiple distinct Christian communities in Antioch, each with its own bishop, and each bishop anxious to preach in the most prestigious places and thus demonstrate his authority and hopefully win over the rest of the city to his community. Throughout the fourth century each new Eastern emperor gave his support to a different Christian community than the emperor before him, from Constantius II to Julian to Jovian to Valens to Theodosius. Shifting imperial patronage aggravated the internal struggles, as bishops from different Antiochene factions alternately found themselves promoted to control of the Great Church, demoted to control of a smaller church, or exiled altogether.

In this chaotic climate, Bishop Meletius and his followers seem to have been active in their efforts to control and define Antioch's urban and rural places, as will be demonstrated in the following chapters. Emmanuel Soler has observed that the project of Meletius and his followers was to make Antioch an exclusively Nicene Christian city.[75] Given the preponderance of evidence for leading figures' recognition of the power of controlling such places, it is likely, as Hanns Christof Brennecke suggests, that Meletius's Christian rivals were likewise engaged in related efforts that unfortunately do not survive as clearly in the extant sources.[76] In some cases, these Christian leaders fought primarily against other Antiochene Christian factions for control of powerful Christian places in the city, in order to be the ones to define Christian orthodoxy in Antioch (and they hoped in the empire). In other cases, these Christian leaders struggled against those who respected the gods to redefine the city's significant places. This overview of the cityscape of fourth-century Antioch, and of the competition to control the city's teaching and preaching places, provides the framework for a closer examination of some of the specific manipulations and transformations that the city's leading figures effected, and the results of those changes for perceptions of religious orthodoxy.

75. Soler, *Le sacré et le salut*, 140.
76. Brennecke, *Studien*, 87–157.

2

Burying Babylas

Place-Marketing and the Politics of Memory

In the midst of the intra-Christian controversies in fourth-century Antioch, Christians undertook to acquire and redefine not only other Christians' places, but also places associated with Greek and Roman gods and with Judaism. The emperor Julian's interest in rebuilding the Jerusalem Temple inflamed Christian anti-Jewish rhetoric around the empire,[1] and his support of places and practices associated with the gods further complicated Christians' relations with their neighbors in Antioch.[2] These latter tensions increased during the conflict involving Daphne's famous oracular temple of Apollo. Although other scholars have used the complex history of Babylas's relics as an example of fourth-century contests to control memory, places, and religious orthodoxy, none have synthesized all of the relevant writings of Libanius, Julian, and John Chrysostom, nor located the actions of Gallus, Julian, Libanius, Meletius, and John Chrysostom within a broader narrative of the spatial manipulations of Antioch's fourth-century landscape, which are the goals of the current chapter.[3]

---

1. For the ancient sources for Julian's efforts, see David Levenson, "The Ancient and Medieval Sources for the Emperor Julian's Attempt to Rebuild the Jerusalem Temple," *Journal for the Study of Judaism* 34.4 (2004): 409–60.

2. See Socrates, *HE* 3.18; Sozomen, *HE* 5.19; Rufinus, *HE* 10.36.1; Libanius, *Or.* 60.5–6; Theodoret, *HE* 3.6; Ammianus Marcellinus, *Res gest.* 22.12.8.

3. See, for example, the earlier studies of Glanville Downey, *A History of Antioch in Syria from Seleucus to the Arab Conquest* (Princeton, NJ: Princeton University Press, 1961), 387–88; Susanna Elm, *Sons of Hellenism, Fathers of the Church: Emperor Julian, Gregory of Nazianzus, and the Vision of Rome* (Berkeley: University of California Press, 2012), e.g., 280–81; Elizabeth Digeser, "An Oracle of Apollo at Daphne and the Great Persecution," *Classical Philology* 99.1 (2004): 57–77; Hanns Christof Brennecke,

During his brief time as caesar in the early 350s the future emperor Julian's half brother Gallus built a martyrion in Antioch's suburb of Daphne in the precinct of the temple of Apollo and had the relics of the third-century Christian martyr Babylas, and the unidentified children buried with him, translated there from a cemetery outside Antioch's city wall. Susanna Elm has observed that Antioch's homoian bishop Leontius may have instigated the translation, even though Gallus received the credit.[4] She notes that John Chrysostom's later narrative transfer of responsibility from a local homoian bishop to an imperial caesar may have downplayed, to Chrysostom's advantage, the early association of Babylas's relics with the homoian Christian community in Antioch.[5] Gallus's ties with the strongly subordinationist Antiochene native Aetius, however, may not have made the relics' association with him much better for Chrysostom. Regardless, when Julian visited Antioch as the emperor in the summer of 362, he was apparently informed that the oracle at Apollo's temple could no longer function because of the nearby (Christian) corpses.[6] Julian quickly required that Babylas's remains be moved out of the temple precinct, presumably in the hope of restoring the famous oracle.

A fire destroyed much of the Apollo temple soon after Julian had forced the removal of Babylas's relics, leading to heated conversations over the symbolic meaning of the series of events and their implications for the relative power of Apollo and the Christian God. Around the time of the emperor Theodosius's accession to the throne, Bishop Meletius worked to have a new church for Babylas built across the Orontes River from the main part of Antioch, and moved Babylas's relics there by the time of his own death in 381, when he was interred in the church near the relics that he had worked to house and honor. In a modern context, cultural geographers Gerry Kearns and Chris Philo have described intentional efforts

---

Studien zur Geschichte der Homöer: Der Osten bis zum Ende der homöischen Reichskirche (Tübingen: J. C. B. Mohr/Paul Siebeck, 1988), 137–38; Wendy Mayer, "Antioch and the Intersection between Religious Factionalism, Place, and Power in Late Antiquity," in *The Power of Religion in Late Antiquity,* ed. Andrew Cain and Noel Lenski (Burlington, VT: Ashgate, 2009), 357–68; Edward Schoolman, "Civic Transformation of the Mediterranean City: Antioch and Ravenna, 300–800 C.E." (PhD diss., University of California, Los Angeles, 2010), esp. 337–40; Juana Torres, "Emperor Julian and the Veneration of Relics," *Antiquité Tardive* 17 (2009): 205–14; Justin Stephens, "Ecclesiastical and Imperial Authority in the Writings of John Chrysostom: A Reinterpretation of His Political Philosophy" (PhD diss., University of California, Santa Barbara, 2001), esp. 24–44. See also Mary Carruthers, *The Craft of Thought: Meditation, Rhetoric, and the Making of Images, 400–1200* (New York: Cambridge University Press, 1998), 46–57; Emmanuel Soler, *Le sacré et le salut à Antioche au IVe siècle apr. J.-C.: Pratiques festives et comportements religieux dans le processus de christianisation de la cité* (Beirut: Institut français du Proche-Orient, 2006), e.g., 37–38, 58–62, 205.

4. Elm, *Sons of Hellenism,* 280.

5. See also Brennecke, *Studien,* 137–38.

6. Cf. Glen Bowersock, *Julian the Apostate* (Cambridge, MA: Harvard University Press, 1978), 99.

to change the connotations of specific physical places as "place-marketing."[7] Although capitalist connotations of contemporary Western economic markets do not cohere with the Roman world, the work of these geographers demonstrates that distinctive politics surround manipulations of a local landscape, how such places are physically and rhetorically shaped to appeal to a particular audience, and how they are remembered—all of which helps illuminate the events surrounding Babylas's relics.[8] Babylas's relics proved to be a particularly potent tool by which leaders in Antioch shaped the religious topography of the region and, with it, increased their own authority.[9]

(RE)MOVING BABYLAS'S RELICS

The power of successful marketing is visible in the sale of commodities in the world around us, but it is also a productive concept for understanding the nuances of historical development; the ubiquitous images of well-marketed places, from the Statue of Liberty to Walt Disney World, reveal that places become commodified. One important aspect of place-marketing often involves the location's physical restructuring, such that the place becomes best molded for its new intended purpose and audience. Geographer Mark Goodwin observes that human changes to a local landscape are not politically neutral: "Urban change, then, is never pregiven, or guaranteed, but instead is actively shaped by competing social forces."[10] An exploration of the social, political, and religious forces that were competing in

7. See, for example, Chris Philo and Gerry Kearns, "Culture, History, Capital: A Critical Introduction to the Selling of Places," in *Selling Places: The City as Cultural Capital, Past and Present,* ed. Gerry Kearns and Chris Philo (New York: Pergamon Press, 1993), 1–32.

8. The example of the Nicene and homoian burials at the Christian memorial place at the Romanesian Gate offers an additional example that will be discussed in chapter 5 in the context of other extramural transformations. Wendy Mayer has also noted the comparison with Chrysostom's homily *De coemeterio et cruce.*

9. Wendy Mayer discusses the ways in which Babylas's relics Christianized Antioch's topography ("Antioch and the Intersection," 357–68). Although she focuses primarily on the actions of Gallus and Meletius, and does not include the related rhetorical projects undertaken by Julian, Libanius, and John Chrysostom, she nevertheless highlights the power that Babylas's relics had in Antioch's landscape. Edward Schoolman reiterates these events in his study ("Civic Transformation," esp. 337–40). For an introduction to the role that saints' relics began to play in the fourth century more generally, see Peter Brown, *The Cult of the Saints: Its Rise and Function in Latin Christianity* (Chicago: University of Chicago Press, 1981); Yvette Duval, *Auprès des saints, corps et âme: L'inhumantion "ad sanctos" dans la chrétienité d'Orient et d'Occident du IIIe au VIIe siècle* (Paris: Études Augustiniennes, 1988); James Howard-Johnston and Paul Antony Hayward, eds., *The Cult of Saints in Late Antiquity and the Middle Ages: Essays on the Contribution of Peter Brown* (New York: Oxford University Press, 1999).

10. Mark Goodwin, "The City as Commodity: The Contested Spaces of Urban Development," in Kearns and Philo, *Selling Places,* 149.

fourth-century Antioch reveals the significance of the topographical changes that surrounded Babylas's relics.

Andrew Fretter narrates some of the steps that go into his decisions regarding place-marketing as the head of economic development in Gwent County (Wales); he instructs marketers, after outlining a vision for the place's future, to "define your customers," "adapt and improve your product to customer requirements," "know your competitors," "find a real point of difference," and speak "with one voice."[11] Applying these instructions loosely to the places associated with Babylas's relics highlights the ways in which different stages of those contested places' development would have been particularly meaningful to different Antiochene communities, and reveals some of the processes by which Christian leaders changed a temple of Apollo and a homoian martyrion into places that were associated with Nicene Christianity. In the words of geographer Briavel Holcomb, "The primary goal of the place marketer is to construct a new image of the place to replace either vague or negative images previously held by current or potential residents."[12] Fourth-century representations of the locations of Babylas's relics reveal the contests over how those places should be perceived, and the effects of changing topographical perceptions on those who lived there.

Babylas's relics are among the first Christian relics known to have been translated from their original place of burial for purposes of veneration when they were moved by caesar Gallus. Elizabeth Digeser has made a persuasive suggestion that when Christians had the authority to do so under the emperor Constantius II, they targeted the Apollo temple at Daphne as the location most in need of what she calls "cleansing" by martyrs' relics, in part because this temple had been the site of an oracle that had prompted the so-called Great Persecution under the emperor Diocletian. The evidence as she reconstructs it suggests that in 299 Caesar Galerius attempted to consult some entrails near the palace in Antioch, but the haruspices were unable to produce any messages; Galerius then consulted the oracle at the Daphne temple of Apollo where the anti-Christian attendant Theotecnus reported an oracle blaming Christians for the failed auspices, which was in turn the catalyst for Diocletian's first anti-Christian edicts. Digeser's hypothesis is strengthened by her observation that Diocletian turned in February 303 to the Apollo oracle at Didyma, with the result that he issued even more wide-reaching anti-Christian edicts, and that the Apollo temple at Didyma seems to have been very close behind Daphne as one of the earliest sites to which Christians translated relics.[13]

11. Andrew Fretter, "Place Marketing: A Local Authority Perspective," in Kearns and Philo, *Selling Places*, 168–72.

12. Briavel Holcomb, "Revisioning Place: De- and Re-constructing the Image of the Industrial City," in Kearns and Philo, *Selling Places*, 133.

13. See Digeser, "Oracle of Apollo," 57–77, esp. 74–76.

Allegedly killed for forbidding an unrepentant (and unnamed) murderous emperor entry into his third-century church building, Babylas became a local symbol of Christian strength and orthodoxy. Chrysostom was a child in the city when Gallus transferred the relics to Daphne, and he later wrote about these events in his text *De sancto Babyla*: when "a long time had passed after [Babylas's] burial, so that only bones and dust were left in the coffin, one of the subsequent emperors decided to return the coffin to this suburb of Daphne" (*De s. Babyla* 67).[14] Their move under Gallus turned out to be the first of several fourth-century moves for these relics, each of which significantly reshaped the way in which passersby interpreted the religious landscape of the region. Hanns Christof Brennecke notes that the circumstances of Babylas's translation to Daphne reveal that Nicene Christians were not the only ones interested in efforts to change the local landscape.[15] Wendy Mayer and Pauline Allen similarly note that the "Nicene bias" of most of our extant sources means that we do not receive a comprehensive description of the activities of homoian Christians.[16] While much of the homoian Christian side of the struggle to reshape Antioch's topography is not extant, the initial translation of Babylas's relics may well be one such effort that remains opaquely visible.[17]

In *De sancto Babyla*, Chrysostom portrays God as having inspired Gallus's action as a means of impeding traditional practices at the temple, and of fostering Christianity in the region: "For when [God] saw the site being tyrannized by the licentiousness of the young, and in danger of becoming impassable to those who were more reverent and who wanted to live moderately, [God] pitied this [site] of spiteful abuse and sent the one who would ward off the wantonness" (*De s. Babyla* 67).[18] Chrysostom's narrative highlights the significance of the particular physical places involved in this relocation. The oracular temple had long been considered to be the site where Apollo had chased the beautiful young Daphne, who had been saved from Apollo's desire by being transformed into a laurel tree (Ovid, *Metamorphoses* 1.525–52). According to Chrysostom, when Apollo, "the intemperate lover, lost his beloved, he intertwined himself with the tree, occupied both the plant and

14. All translations from *De s. Babyla* are my own from the Greek text in SC 362 (1990), 90–274. In this chapter I consistently and exclusively translate the Greek word προάστειον as "suburb." An English translation of *De s. Babyla* is also available in Margaret Schatkin and Paul Harkins, *Saint John Chrysostom: Apologist*, FC 73 (Washington, DC: Catholic University of America Press, 1983). Sozomen also retells the story (*HE* 5.19).

15. Brennecke, *Studien*, 137. See also Soler, *Le sacré et le salut*, 37–38, 205; Elm, *Sons of Hellenism*, 280–81.

16. Wendy Mayer and Pauline Allen, *The Churches of Syrian Antioch (300–638 c.e.)* (Walpole, MA: Peeters, 2012), 140–41.

17. Another example that Brennecke does not mention relates to the burials near the Romanesian Gate, discussed in chapter 5 below.

18. In this chapter I consistently and exclusively translate the Greek word χωρίον as "site." See also the discussion of these texts and events in Mayer and Allen, *Churches*, 135–40.

the place, and henceforth was always near the site, and he embraced and loved this [site] most of all the earth" (*De s. Babyla* 68).[19] Chrysostom claims that straightaway the famous temple was founded on the spot, "so that the *daimōn* might be able to assuage his madness through the place," and Apollo "occupied the site with a crowd of corrupt youths and the abodes of *daimones*" (68).[20] It is understood to be this same powerful place, which Apollo continued to occupy in memory of his attraction for Daphne and where, according to Chrysostom, "those licentious among the youths . . . ran riot," that received Babylas's relics in the early 360s (69).

The site in Daphne was a notable place dedicated to Daphne and Apollo, and associated for fourth-century Christians with the oracular roots of imperial persecution. It is thus difficult to interpret Gallus's movement of Babylas's relics to that very spot as anything other than an overt effort to redefine the place and co-opt for Christianity generally, and possibly for a specific Christian community that rejected the Council of Nicaea, the power associated with it—an interpretation that reflects Chrysostom's own later understanding of the events. In the vocabulary of Andrew Fretter, Christians constituted a new public audience, or customer base, and Gallus began to "adapt" the region's landscape to appeal to Christian "customers" like himself.

For Chrysostom, Babylas's relics showed Gallus's intention to change perceptions of, and behavior in, the suburb, to deliver it "from such an evil" by bringing "the doctor to the sick"; Gallus was not to be disappointed, as "the martyr was able to destroy the power of the *daimōn* and to restrain the merriment of the youths," changing the activities and associations Antiochenes would have with the area (*De s. Babyla* 69). Chrysostom describes the shrine of Babylas as eminently visible upon entering Daphne from Antioch such that it chastised visitors as a parent or teacher would do, dissuading them from inappropriate behavior: "As soon as one stops in Daphne and sees the martyrion from the entrance of the suburb, [the visitor] is humbled . . . and becoming more reverent by the sight, and imagining the blessed one, immediately hastens to the coffin; and when s/he comes there, greater fear takes hold and casting out all negligence and becoming winged, s/he thus goes forth" (70).[21] Likewise, on the visitors' way out of Daphne, Chrysostom claims, the

---

19. In this chapter I consistently and exclusively translate the Greek word τόπος as "place."

20. I have chosen to leave the Greek δαίμων transliterated, to convey its complex connotations, concurrently invoking a potentially positive traditional image of a god and a hostile Christian image inherent in the English translation "demon." See also the discussion of the process by which Christians transformed gods into the Christian sense of *daimones*: Frank Trombley, *Hellenic Religion and Christianization c. 370–529* (Leiden: E. J. Brill, 1993), 1:98–108.

21. Dayna Kalleres adeptly contextualizes this comment within fourth-century Antiochene understandings of demons, magic, and moral transformation. See chapter 2 of Dayna Kalleres, *City of Demons: Violence, Ritual, and Christian Power in Late Antiquity* (Berkeley: University of California Press, forthcoming).

shrine again received them, suggesting that it was a highly visible and prominently Christian landmark for those coming and going between the suburb and the city (70; cf. *De s. hierom. Babyla* 9). Chrysostom records Gallus's translation of the relics with a distinct emphasis on the prominence of the location, first as a temple for Apollo and then as a resting place for Babylas. This explicit restructuring and redefinition of the landscape carried with it clear consequences for religious practice and identification in the region, bringing Christian associations to a significant location in Daphne that had been associated with Apollo, sacrifice, and oracles.

The result of this manipulation of Daphne's topography for Chrysostom was that the region became more visibly Christian. Referring to the earlier time, when Babylas's relics had remained in the cemetery outside Antioch's gate, Chrysostom writes, "For since some people because of laziness and some because of worldly concerns do not care to present themselves at the graves of the martyrs, God managed by this means [of Babylas's new and more centralized shrine] for these to be caught in a net and to enjoy spiritual healing" (*De s. Babyla* 71). Chrysostom suggests that Babylas's new resting place was so much more centrally located than his cemetery martyrion that even those who had no interest in visiting the martyr would now have little choice but to do so. According to Chrysostom, this forced interaction with the martyr's relics had a significant effect on the religious makeup of those who lived in the region; "in time they were healed," and Chrysostom rejoices that "desire for the saint" began to replace desire for luxury as the reason "most" people went to Daphne (72). Samuel Lieu speculates, "The devotees of paganism might have found the sight of throngs of hymn-singing worshippers venerating the bones of a dead man repulsive and become reluctant, therefore, to consult the oracle."[22]

Thanks to Babylas, the place of the Daphne temple precinct, and the visitors as well, became, at least in Chrysostom's idealized rhetoric, closer to his Christian ideals; it was no longer a place of Apollo's power, affirming Goodwin's observation that "competing social forces" regularly lead to the redefinition of key places in a landscape.[23] Even the famous oracle of Apollo, which in Daphne was thought to speak through signs from the god's statue rather than through a priestess as at Delphi or Didyma, was made silent by Babylas's presence:[24] "As if being censured by a master, the martyr, [Apollo] ceased howling," Chrysostom writes, "and did not utter a sound" (*De s. Babyla* 73). Chrysostom relates that at first the silence of

---

22. Samuel Lieu, *The Emperor Julian: Panegyric and Polemic, Claudius Mamertinus, John Chrysostom, Ephrem the Syrian,* Translated Texts for Historians, Greek Series 1 (Liverpool: Liverpool University Press, 1986), 53.

23. Goodwin, "City as Commodity," 149.

24. Digeser provides an excellent overview of the Roman history of Apollo's oracles, and their distinctive lack of a human mediator in Syria, including at Daphne ("Oracle of Apollo," 63–69).

Apollo's oracle was interpreted as the result of the fact that the Christian presence in the temple precinct put an end to offerings and the other services associated with religious cult, but that later Apollo "was proved to be bound by strong necessity" (74–75). Chrysostom finds evidence for this latter claim in the fact that even the emperor Julian, who removed Babylas's relics and reinstituted sacrifice at the temple's altar in 362, could not reawaken the oracle. The physical move by Gallus and the rhetorical efforts by John Chrysostom clearly hoped to foster as much as possible Antiochenes' increased contact with places associated with Christian saints, and to limit their contact with places associated with the gods, changing the perceived religious identity of those who frequented the site.

Although Gallus's actions ostensibly deactivated the temple as a site of Apollo's power, the temple remained standing, giving the emperor Julian an opportunity to undo Gallus's work a decade later. When Julian objected to Babylas's proximity to (and apparent interference with) the oracle at the temple, he required the Christians to move Babylas's relics back to their former resting place in Antioch's cemetery.[25] In contrast to Gallus, Julian actively patronized the empire's temples and sacrificed at their altars.[26] The Apollo temple's destruction by fire, which followed the forced removal of Babylas's relics, set the stage for a highly charged controversy, during which the emperor appears to have further manipulated Antioch's places by closing the Great Church, under homoian Christian control at the time, in a stark reminder of the power involved in controlling the city's places (Theodoret, *HE* 3.12.1; Ammianus Marcellinus, *Res gest.* 22.13.2). That the emperor Julian retaliated for the fire against the homoian-controlled Great Church may reinforce the argument that Babylas's relics were associated with that particular community ever since their move by Gallus,[27] even as John Chrysostom's homily later emphasized that Babylas's relics should symbolize the victory of (Nicene) Christian "orthodoxy" over the Greek gods.

---

25. Juana Torres nicely contextualizes Julian's response to Babylas's relics within the larger context of Julian's policies toward corpses and burials ("Emperor Julian," 58–62).

26. See Scott Bradbury, "Julian's Pagan Revival and the Decline of Blood Sacrifice," *Phoenix* 49.4 (1995): 331–56. Polymnia Athanassiadi-Fowden's intellectual biography of Julian further details his developing engagement with Hellenism and traditional Greek ritual and philosophy: Athanassiadi-Fowden, *Julian and Hellenism: An Intellectual Biography* (New York: Oxford University Press, 1981). Other scholars have also provided biographies of this compelling historical figure. See, for example, J. Bidez, *La vie de l'Empereur Julien* (Paris: Société d'Édition "Les Belles Lettres," 1965); Robert Browning, *The Emperor Julian* (Berkeley: University of California Press, 1976); Bowersock, *Julian*; L'Association pour l'Antiquité Tardive, ed., *L'Empereur Julien et son temps:* Antiquité Tardive 17 (Turnhout, Belgium: Brepols, 2009); and Elm, *Sons of Hellenism*. Note, though, Jean Bouffartigue's caution about the seductive coherence of constructed biographies: Bouffartigue, "Julien entre biographie et analyse historique," *Antiquité Tardive* 17 (2009): 79–89.

27. Brennecke, *Studien*, 137–38. Compare the discussion of Julian's engagement with Antioch's cityscape in chapter 1.

From a Christian perspective, the events of 362 were filled with religious significance strongly in Christians' favor. Chrysostom later described, in the presence of people who were eyewitnesses to the events, that when Julian came to Antioch, he frequently went up to Daphne with numerous animals for sacrifice and "caused torrents of blood to flow from the slaughter of animals" (*De s. Babyla* 79, 80; cf. Ammianus Marcellinus, *Res gest.* 22.12.6–8). Believing that Babylas's strength prevented Apollo from speaking, Chrysostom recounts that the oracle "gave a pretext for the silence," claiming, "the site of Daphne is full of corpses, and this hinders the oracle" (*De s. Babyla* 80–81). Interpreting the oracle, Julian "immediately came after the blessed Babylas" (81).[28] Chrysostom ridicules Julian: "Why did you mention corpses namelessly and indiscriminately while you heard with discrimination a certain named one and, leaving behind the others, moved only the saint?" (81). Nevertheless, Chrysostom argues that when Julian "ordered [Babylas's] coffin to be brought down" to Antioch, he made Babylas's power over Apollo clear to all (87).

Far from the punishing banishment that Julian may have intended, Christians later described the return of Babylas's remains to Antioch as a festive moment, as in their view it demonstrated the force that Babylas wielded over the gods: "The coffin was dragged along the whole road, and the martyr returned like an athlete carrying a second crown into his own city where he had received the first" (*De s. Babyla* 90; cf. Theodoret, *HE* 3.10.3).[29] Chrysostom boasts that those all over the region thereafter saw the empty martyrion that had held Babylas's coffin in Daphne and interpreted it as evidence of Apollo's weakness in the face of the Christian martyr: "Not only those living in the city, the suburb, and the country, but also people far removed from these sites, when they did not see the coffin lying there, and then investigated the cause, immediately learned that the *daimōn*, being expected by the emperor to give an oracle, said that he could not do this until someone moved blessed Babylas away from him" (*De s. Babyla* 87).[30] Christians were certain that the fire that soon followed was a further sign of the triumph of the Christian martyr and God. Both Gallus and Julian physically manipulated the

28. Ammianus Marcellinus describes this event, and suggests that Julian understood himself to be imitating the Athenians' earlier cleansing of bodies from the grounds of a temple to Apollo (*Res gest.* 22.12.8; cf. Herodotus, *Hist.* 1.65; Thucydides, *Hist.* 3.104.1). Elizabeth Digeser examines the evidence regarding the prophetic springs at Daphne, concluding that they remained closed from Hadrian's order until the time of Julian, who tried to reopen them; nevertheless, Julian does not seem to know of their successful reopening, since he continues to use another oracular tradition during his time in Daphne— namely, hearing directly from the statue of Apollo: see Digeser, "Oracle of Apollo," 64–66.

29. Theodoret describes a joyful parade with the crowd singing the Psalms (the reference is to the Greek text in Parmentier and Hansen). Note, however, Susanna Elm's caution that these texts are later Christian interpretations of the forced removal of Babylas's relics, and it is difficult to know whether the translation was celebrated so triumphantly at the time (Elm, *Sons of Hellenism*, 279).

30. In this chapter I consistently and exclusively translate the Greek word ἀγρός as "country."

landscape by reshaping Apollo's temple precinct through the transfer of Babylas's relics. As Holcomb has observed more generally about such place-marketing, in this instance Gallus and Julian seem to have been striving to construct a new image for the place of Apollo's temple. In both cases, however, it appeared to John Chrysostom that Christians were most persuasive in their manipulations, in arguing that first the presence and then the absence of Babylas's remains in Daphne equally signified to viewers (Nicene) Christianity's power over Apollo.

READING THE RUINS: THE BURNED TEMPLE OF APOLLO AND THE POLITICS OF MEMORY

Beyond the physical restructuring of a place for a new audience, its narrative redefinition affects its position in the collective memory, and thus the identity, of the region's inhabitants.[31] Emmanuel Soler notes that Meletius and his followers built their legitimacy largely through the construction and rearrangement of the city's martyria, which reinforced their efforts to change "the collective memory" of Antioch's religious history to their benefit.[32] The history of the burned remains of Apollo's temple in Daphne reveals competition over not only the physical display of the site, but also the memory of its story, what Harriet Flower refers to as "memory wars."[33] Every community, according to Flower, "needs a memory story to explain its identity and past."[34] Such collective memories, Paul Ricoeur argues, reflect "a concerted manipulation of memory and forgetting by those who hold power," who mobilize memory "in the service of the quest, the appeal, the demand for identity."[35] Following the fire, the charred remains of Apollo's temple became the site of intensive negotiations over meaning, memory, and identity. Because, as Paul Connerton writes, "our experience of the present very largely depends upon our knowledge of the past," it is "surely the case that control of a society's memory largely conditions the hierarchy of power."[36] Recognizing these dynamics, fourth-century leaders worked to shape perceptions of the *temenos* of Apollo's Daphne temple in ways that legitimated their own community's claim to power. As is clear

31. Some of the material in this section appeared in Christine Shepardson, "Apollo's Charred Remains: Making Meaning in Fourth-Century Syria," *Studia Patristica* 38 (2013): 297–302.

32. Soler, *Le sacré et le salut*, 241.

33. Harriet Flower, *The Art of Forgetting: Disgrace and Oblivion in Roman Political Culture* (Chapel Hill, NC: University of North Carolina Press, 2006), 67. Mary Carruthers uses the events surrounding Babylas's relics in her discussion of collective memory, the contested ways in which events are remembered, and the politics of those memories (*Craft of Thought*, 46–57).

34. Flower, *Art of Forgetting*, 7.

35. Paul Ricoeur, *Memory, History, Forgetting,* trans. Kathleen Blamey and David Pellauer (Chicago: University of Chicago Press, 2004), 80–81.

36. Paul Connerton, *How Societies Remember* (New York: Cambridge University Press, 1989), 1–2.

from the example of the burned temple of Apollo, memories are not static, and they are often shaped in such a way so as to "legitimate certain developments in the present."[37]

The earliest extant descriptions of the fire come from Julian and Libanius, two influential leaders who witnessed the events and who mourned the temple's destruction, in contrast to Christian interpretations that used the destruction to denigrate the gods and their ritual practices.[38] Julian's *Misopōgōn* dates from February 363, a mere few months after the October fire. Julian's description of the events is brief, as the story serves the larger purpose of the *Misopōgōn*—namely, to satirize the antagonistic relationship between Julian and the Antiochenes,[39] whom Julian characterizes as lavish and concerned primarily with theater and banquets rather than with the gods of their ancestors or intellectual pursuits.[40] Julian argues that Antiochenes should interpret the temple's remains as a shameful reminder of their mistreatment of Julian and the gods.

Julian narrates the destruction as the result of human mischief and impiety, a sign of Apollo's authority rather than a challenge to it. He condemns the Antiochenes because, despite his warnings, they "overturned the altars that had just been raised" (*Misopōgōn* 361B).[41] Julian thus contextualizes the fire in a series of events that featured Antiochenes acting aggressively against Julian and the gods. He refers specifically to his removal of Babylas's body, and suggests that, out of spite, the Antiochenes allowed disgruntled Christians to retaliate: "And when I sent the corpse away from Daphne, some of you . . . handed over the precinct (*temenos*) of the god of Daphne to those who were irritated about the remains of the corpse" (361B-C).[42] Ammianus Marcellinus also mentions the fire and Julian's suspicion that Christians had set it (*Res gest.* 22.13.1–2). But even still Julian does not blame Christians per se for the temple's destruction, as he accuses a wider Antiochene audience: "and others of you, whether knowingly or not," caused the fire that, he insists, "made strangers who were visiting shudder, but brought pleasure to your people" (361C). In this text, Julian does not claim to know the exact

37. Chris Philo and Gerry Kearns, "Culture, History, Capital: A Critical Introduction to the Selling of Places," in Kearns and Philo, *Selling Places*, 25.

38. Soler discusses the fire and the literary responses to it in *Le sacré et le salut*, 16–18.

39. See the discussion in Elm, *Sons of Hellenism*, 327–31; Bowersock, *Julian*, 101–5.

40. Soler has noted that this criticism of Antioch's citizens is shared among Julian, Libanius, Ammianus Marcellinus, and John Chrysostom: Soler, *Le sacré et le salut*, 29–32; Soler, "Sacralité et partage du temps et de l'espace festifs à Antioche au IVe siècle," in *Les frontières du profane dans l'antiquité tardive*, Collection de l'École Française de Rome 428, ed. Éric Rebillard and Claire Sotinel (Rome: École française de Rome, 2010), 273–86.

41. All translations from the *Misopōgōn* are my own from the Greek text edited by William Cave Wright in *The Works of the Emperor Julian*, vol. 2 (New York: Putnam, 1923).

42. See Elm's discussion of these events and this text in *Sons of Hellenism*, 277.

origin of the fire, but he places the blame for the devastation quite clearly on the entire population of Antioch, and finds the destruction to be consonant with the disrespectful and self-indulgent character of the city.[43] Julian's rhetoric thus attempts to instill remorse in those who saw the charred remains as a sign of the city's rash behavior against the emperor and the gods.

Nevertheless, in a time when events such as a temple's destruction by fire were regularly understood to represent divine intention and power (or impotence), the fire at Apollo's temple put Julian in the position of needing to explain how a god could have allowed his temple to be destroyed.[44] To address this, Julian claims that Apollo had already abandoned the temple, so that the fire was of no consequence to the god and certainly should not malign his reputation. Julian writes, "Now, to me the god seems to have left the temple behind even before the fire, for when I first entered, the statue [so] indicated to me" (*Misopōgōn* 361C). Julian further recalls a warning that he addressed to the Antiochenes about the disgraceful state of the temples, predicting that the gods themselves would find it displeasing. He follows his recollection with a regret: "These are the things I remember saying at the time, and the god [Apollo] bore witness to my words—would that he had not!—forsaking the suburb that he had protected for so long" (363C). Because the people had abandoned the temples, Julian believes, the gods abandoned the people; the fire is for the emperor simply proof that the gods had left. Julian places himself and the gods on the same side, and Antiochenes on the other as antagonistic to both, driving Apollo and other gods to abandon Antioch and its citizens, as Julian did soon thereafter. In Julian's text, the ruined temple site should be seen as a sharp reminder of Apollo's punishment of Antioch's badly behaved citizens.

Julian was not, though, the only one to offer an interpretation of the fire or to suggest how the burned remains should be understood by passersby. Libanius's *Oratio* 60 is a mournful monody on the temple's destruction, although unfortunately the only extant fragments of the text survive in the quotations that John Chrysostom inserted into *De sancto Babyla*, composed over fifteen years later. The surviving fragments of Libanius's text highlight the ironic timing of the temple's destruction, and blame the fire on human mischief. Whereas John Chrysostom's commentary on Libanius emphasizes the impotence of Apollo, Libanius's surviving fragments lament the loss of the temple, particularly at the very time when Julian had started to lavish attention on the site and the god after many years of neglect. While similar to Julian's *Misopōgōn* in interpreting Apollo's temple as abandoned, and casting this as a regrettable state of affairs, Libanius's excerpts capture more

43. Compare Elm, *Sons of Hellenism*, 277–78. See also Bowersock, *Julian*, 99.

44. Compare the relation of divine power (and messages) to the first-century destruction of the Jewish Temple in Jerusalem: Christine Shepardson, "Paschal Politics: Deploying the Temple's Destruction against Fourth-Century Judaizers," *Vigiliae Christianae* 62.3 (2008): 233–60.

concern than Julian's text about how to explain Apollo's leaving. Like Julian, Libanius appeals to an audience who still had positive memories of Apollo's once-thriving temple. Seeking an explanation that would allow for Apollo's continued viability, Libanius engages more directly with the explanations that later Christian leaders recorded as their own, specifically that the destruction at the time of Julian's support reflected poorly on Apollo and the gods more broadly.

Libanius provides the earliest full description of the events. Unable to deny the fire, he is left to lament the temple's destruction, which he defines as unjust and as an evil (*Or.* 60.9).[45] He describes it in some detail, as he was living in Antioch at the time and writes not long after its destruction, recounting the panic of Apollo's priestess, who roused the town while the magistrate frantically tried to learn how the fire had started. In the temple itself, "beams were swept down, carrying the fire that destroyed whatever it approached: Apollo immediately, since he [i.e., his statue] was only a small distance from the roof, and then the other things" (Libanius, *Or.* 60.12). Libanius strongly condemns the human mischief that he says caused the fire. He cannot deny the fire and the destruction, but he chooses not to read a deeper religious meaning into the events than the simple tragedy of a human miscreant's destructive act.

Libanius's sadness is clear as he laments the transformation of this place, though understandably he dwells on its past glory. He mourns its current state in contrast to what it was before: "O Zeus, what a resting place for a weary mind we have had taken away. The site of Daphne was so free from clamor and the temple more so, what a harbor upon a harbor, made by nature itself. Both [Daphne and the temple] were sheltered from the waves, but the second offered greater rest" (*Or.* 60.6). In the same passage Libanius remembers the peaceful rest that the temple once gave, as if to suggest that the place of its remains should be remembered for what it had been, a site of Apollo's strength, rather than a place of desolation and loss. Whereas Chrysostom later presents a Christian interpretation that the destroyed temple became a new site with new religious meanings, Libanius wishes to have passersby remember in the remains what it had been at the height of its strength and beauty. In this "memory war," Libanius hopes that the temple's recent destruction would be overshadowed by its earlier history in Antiochenes' memories of the place and the community identity that it fostered.

Libanius wonders aloud what the destruction suggested about Apollo's power, but whereas Julian claims to have been informed that Apollo would abandon the temple because of the lack of worship there, Libanius seems not to have a clear answer to this pressing concern, and can only contrast its previous strength with

---

45. Libanius's *Oratio* 60 has been reconstructed from the fragments quoted in John Chrysostom's *De s. Babyla*. All translations of *Or.* 60 are my own from the Greek text in Richard Foerster, *Libanii Opera* (Leipzig: Teubner, 1908), 4:298–321.

its current desolation. Libanius recalls the triumph of Apollo at that very temple when the Persian leader Shapur I captured Antioch and set the city on fire, sparing the temple of Apollo out of respect for the god; Shapur, "throwing away the torch, fell down and worshipped Apollo" (*Or.* 60.2).[46] Libanius savors this image, describing Shapur a second time: "He, leading an army against us, thought it better for himself that the temple be saved; and the beauty of the statue prevailed against the barbaric anger" (*Or.* 60.3). This earlier felicitous outcome stands in sharp contrast to the disaster of 362. Libanius asks, "But now, Sun and Earth, who or whence is this enemy, who without hoplites, or cavalry, or light infantry, undid everything with a small spark?" (*Or.* 60.3). Chrysostom's citation of Libanius attributes to him regret not only that Apollo's temple fell, but that it disappeared without so much as a whimper: "And what is more, a great deluge did not sweep away our temple, but it was brought down in fair weather and when the cloud had passed by" (Libanius, *Or.* 60.4). Libanius appears to have been aware that the destroyed temple site could provoke challenges to Apollo's effectiveness, and strives to preserve a memory of the place at the pinnacle of its power.[47]

Even as Libanius presents his narrative of the temple's greatness, however, he also wrestles with the irony of the destruction's timing. After all, under Julian's patronage, the temple had once again started to receive animal sacrifices and imperial attention after years of neglect. Libanius reminds Apollo about the time before Julian became emperor: "When your altars were thirsting for blood, Apollo, you remained a careful guard of Daphne, and having been left, being abused and plundered of your outward ornaments, you remained constant" (*Or.* 60.5). The reference to the temple's loss of its outward ornaments is vague, but suggests more about the transformation of the site in the years under the emperor Constantius II. It was, though, under Julian, when the temple was being restored to its earlier glory that disaster struck. "But now," Libanius writes, "after many sheep and many bulls," after Julian, the emperor himself, had honored the god and offered sacrifices and even moved the troublesome corpse of Babylas, then and only then Apollo "leapt away from the midst of your attendants"; and Libanius wonders, "How will we still strive for honor among men who are mindful of temples and images?" (*Or.* 60.5). Libanius appears to have been acutely cognizant of the potential for interpretations of the temple's destruction that reflected poorly on Apollo and those

---

46. See also Arthur Darby Nock, "Sapor I and the Apollo of Bryaxis," *American Journal of Archaeology* 66.3 (1962): 307–10.

47. Catherine Saliou has noted Libanius's manipulation of Antioch's history and city layout in order to construct a particular memory of the city in *Oratio* 11: Saliou, "Les fondations d'Antioche dans l'*Antiochikos (Oratio* XI) de Libanios," *ARAM* 11–12 (1999–2000): 357–88; cf. Saliou, "L'*Éloge d'Antioche* (Libanios, discours 11 = *Antiochikos*) et son apport à la connaissance du paysage urbain d'Antioche," in *Les sources de l'histoire du paysage urbain d'Antioche sur l'Oronte* (Paris: Université Paris 8, Vincennes-Saint-Denis, 2012), 43–56.

who honored him, and he pleads that Apollo follow the fire with a powerful act that would restore him to a place of prominence and respect in the eyes of the region's inhabitants (*Or.* 60.14).

While Julian becomes angry and blames the Antiochenes for what he represents as Apollo's choice to abandon the temple, Libanius appears to have been upset by the fire and embarrassed by its possible implications. Libanius writes with concern: "The Olympics are not very far-off, and the festival will convene the cities, and they will come bringing bulls as an offering for Apollo. What should we do? Where should we hide?" (*Or.* 60.7). Despite his efforts to see in the temple's remains their former glory, these fragments suggest that Libanius is well aware that the most compelling interpretations of the site after the fire are those that echo Christian narratives of Apollo's impotence. If, as Connerton claims, perceptions of the past shape identity in the present, a great deal was at stake in shaping the collective memory of this fraught site, and it is little surprise that Libanius lashes out sharply at the human culprit he thinks caused the fire that challenged local perceptions of the gods' power (*Or.* 60.8).[48]

The Christian version of these efforts to shape what viewers understood the temple ruins to signify is represented by John Chrysostom, whose lengthy treatise *De sancto Babyla* addresses this issue in depth more than fifteen years after the fire.[49] After the emperor Valens's sudden death in 378, Julian's legacy—and the valuation of traditional religious practices—were again foremost in some debates as Valens joined Julian in suffering a death in battle and again called into question the strength of the Greek gods and the homoian Christian God who should have protected Julian and Valens, respectively. With the emperor Theodosius's accession to the throne, John Chrysostom rekindles the earlier efforts to define the memory of the burned temple site, arguing that it witnessed indisputably to the positive benefits of the Christian martyr and his God. Chrysostom argues that Babylas's relics reshaped the landscape physically in ways that signified Christianity's superiority over "Greek superstition," such that passersby could read this message when they saw the ruined site.[50] It is this text that comments explic-

---

48. Connerton, *How Societies Remember,* 1–2. Note that Libanius's *Ep.* 1376, "To Heliodorus," may also address the events following the fire.

49. Another study narrows the most likely date to between spring 379 and spring 380, with the possibility that the text was written for Babylas's feast day, January 24, 380: Christine Shepardson, "Rewriting Julian's Legacy: John Chrysostom's *On Babylas* and Libanius' *Oration 24*," *Journal of Late Antiquity* 2.1 (2009): 99–115. Note that Chrysostom revived similar rhetoric years later in *De s. hierom. Babyla.*

50. See the analysis of Chrysostom's use of Babylas to condemn "Hellenism" in Jean-Noël Guinot, "L'*Homélie sur Babylas* de Jean Chrysostome: La victoire du martyr sur l'hellenisme," in *La narrative cristiana antica: XXIII Incontro de studiosi dell'antichità cristiana,* Studia Ephemeridis Augustinianum 50 (Rome: Istituto Patristico Augustinianum, 1995), 323–41.

itly on the temple's central location for those coming and going from Daphne, and claims that the visible destruction was striking and made visitors ask what had happened, with the result that they would be told of Christianity's superiority (*De s. Babyla* 70). As Theodosius took over the eastern empire, John Chrysostom's interpretation carried both local and imperial significance.[51] Chrysostom's reiteration of these sentiments later in *De s. hierom. Babyla* 9 ensured that the narrative would continue to be familiar to Antiochenes and associated with Babylas's relics, which by then rested in the new martyrion built by Meletius.

In *De sancto Babyla* John Chrysostom uses the story of Babylas and the destruction of Apollo's temple as local evidence to portray (Nicene) Christianity's triumph (esp. *De s. Babyla* 1–21, 40–50). So powerful were Christian saints, Chrysostom claims, that even after Babylas's death he continued to demonstrate his strength, particularly over Apollo, as witnessed by the charred temple remains that were still visible when Chrysostom wrote this text more than fifteen years after the fire. Chrysostom revels in the power of the martyr's relics as demonstrated by Apollo's (and Julian's) objections to their burial in Daphne (64–72). Retelling the tale of the fire, Chrysostom notes that Babylas silenced Apollo and caused a fire whose damage was too fortuitous to be natural (73–75, 94). Chrysostom mocks Julian for so fearing Babylas's potency that Julian declined to retaliate or destroy the martyr's relics, only asking that the Christians move them to another location (96).[52] Finally, Chrysostom claims that Babylas forced Apollo to flee Daphne altogether, despite Apollo's preference to reside there (100–103). Chrysostom comments, "Such is the power of the saints, so invincible and formidable, both to emperors and to *daimones* and to the leader of the *daimones* himself" (127). Thus in Chrysostom's view, not only the Christian God, Christianity itself, and Christians, but even the relics of Christian saints have the ability to overwhelm the gods and their clients. For Chrysostom, "when [Babylas] died and went away, he brought an end to the power of the *daimōn,* refuted the deceit of the Greeks, revealed the nonsense of divination, crushed its mask, and displayed all its naked hypocrisy, having curbed and thrown down by the greatest vehemence the one who seemed to have power over him" (127). Referring to the burned ruins of the temple and the martyrion currently empty of its relics, Chrysostom writes, "Both the temple and the martyrion stand as reminders of [Julian's] madness and of the power of the blessed Babylas" (126; cf. *De s. hierom. Babyla* 9). Chrysostom wants the Daphne site to call this narrative to viewers' minds in ways productive for shaping a new collective Christian identity.

Chrysostom not only uses Babylas and the destruction of Apollo's temple as evidence of the potency of Christianity and the Christian God, but he concurrently

51. See the full discussion of this in Shepardson, "Rewriting," 99–115.

52. Soler notes that Julian might have been motivated in this apparent leniency by his law requiring respect of funerary monuments (Soler, *Le sacré et le salut,* 62).

highlights the powerlessness of traditional cult and its gods, and the fact that they would soon be gone altogether. He claims in this text that "Greek superstition (*deisidaimonia*)," as he labels traditional religion, was radically weakened in his lifetime and in the process of dying (*De s. Babyla* 13).[53] Chrysostom supports his remarks about the dilapidated state of traditional practices by observing the neglect that allegedly took place immediately with the rise of Christian emperors: "everywhere in the temples of the idols" one would see spider webs all over the walls, and "on the statues dust such that neither the nose nor the eye nor any other part of the face will be visible" (41). The altars were in disrepair, with only the ruins of some remaining and others overgrown so much that they were unrecognizable; no longer expecting feasts of meat or other recompense, the incentive to honor the statues was gone. Thus, according to Chrysostom the fact that Christianity superseded earlier practices reflected the falseness of the superstition that had motivated the old practices. He compares the dying traditions to an elderly body that died without injury from anyone: "Similarly the error of Greek superstition . . . crumbled and collapsed into itself," even though no one ever did it harm (13). Chrysostom appeals to his audience to recognize this story in the landscape around them.

Chrysostom focuses these generalizations on Babylas and Apollo, specifically detailing the powerlessness of the Greek god in the face of the martyr's relics, embedding his argument within Daphne's physical landscape. Chrysostom's description of the encounter between Babylas and Apollo is lengthy and detailed, as he works through every aspect that in his view so clearly demonstrated this greatest example of Apollo's impotence and Christianity's superiority. Chrysostom ridicules Apollo whose oracle allegedly was unable to function in the presence of Babylas's relics, despite the unprecedented number of sacrifices offered to the god by Julian (e.g., *De s. Babyla* 80–87). Chrysostom mocks Apollo's weakness (80), and derides his pathetic excuse for not performing: "A good person will not be hindered by a dead body either from deliberating over that which is useful or from accomplishing that which is necessary," and each artisan also will work unhampered not only when near corpses, but even when building "the memorials of the departed" (84). Even everyday people, Chrysostom argues, were able to perform their work in the proximity of corpses. "One alone out of everyone, Apollo, claims to be hindered by corpses from foreseeing the future" (84). Others who prophesied did not complain of such difficulties, even when they were surrounded by impurities (85). Only Apollo, Chrysostom asserts, used this excuse, because "the *daimōn* . . . could not prophesy but, in order not to seem at a loss, was forced to allege . . . ridiculous things" (85). Retold in this way, the events of Apollo's oracular silence

---

53. Related to the word δαίμων, this Greek word, δεισιδαιμονία, suggests an inappropriate or superstitious fear of the gods to the Christian Chrysostom, although others used the word in a positive sense. See Dale Martin, *Inventing Superstition: From the Hippocratics to the Christians* (Cambridge, MA: Harvard University Press, 2004).

in 362 suggest clear evidence of Apollo's overwhelming weakness in the face of the Christian saint.

John Chrysostom insists that Apollo's limitations in prophesying stemmed from the same source as his physical defenselessness in allowing his statue and temple to be burned. Not only was Apollo bothered by the relics, but he was even unable to protect himself from insult and injury. Chrysostom challenges claims made by Libanius regarding Apollo's ability to see the future, and ruthlessly mocks both Apollo and those like Libanius who honored the god, noting that even a person (let alone a god) should have noticed the fire that destroyed Apollo's statue and temple (*De s. Babyla* 108). Far from an omnipotent deity, Apollo emerged from Chrysostom's description as inferior even to humans in strength and foreknowledge. With that established, Chrysostom observes that it would be ridiculous to honor such a being: "If you claim to have greater skill and experience than the *daimōn,* there is no need to honor the one who is more ignorant and weaker in the things in which you say he conquers all" (109). Chrysostom concludes that in the face of his evidence it is irrefutable that Apollo abandoned Daphne under the compulsion of a greater power (100).[54]

Chrysostom's revival of the "memory wars" over Apollo's temple, and the religious identity that memory could nurture in Antioch's citizens, is further revealed in Chrysostom's direct refutation of the claim that Julian presents in his *Misopōgōn*—namely, that Apollo left the temple before the fire destroyed it. Chrysostom notes that the fire happened at exactly the time when the god was receiving an unprecedented amount of cultic attention, even from the emperor himself, and that this took place "so that it would not be possible for you to deceive yourselves further and to say that being angry and accusing you about the offerings and blaming you regarding the other [temple] services, [Apollo] withdrew of his own free will" (*De s. Babyla* 100). Chrysostom's countering of explanations used in the writings of Libanius and Julian demonstrates the struggle to define which social memories would be visible at the temple's remains.

In Chrysostom's retelling, Julian's death soon after the fire reinforced a narrative of Christian superiority, and when people saw the site in Daphne they should remember the fire and Julian's death as two equal warnings regarding the Christian God's power. Chrysostom explicitly and implicitly makes the connection between Julian and the third-century emperor who persecuted Babylas. Explicitly he connects Babylas's deeds of the third and fourth centuries: "for each leads toward the other, and it is not possible to separate them" (*De s. Babyla* 22). In particular, Chrysostom highlights that in each event Babylas angered the reigning emperor, and that memory of one should also recall the other. Furthermore, in the third century, Bishop Babylas drove the emperor from the church building, while in 362

54. He also argues that the other gods were equally helpless (John Chrysostom, *De s. Babyla* 113).

Babylas's relics forced the god from his temple; Babylas's speech angered the emperor during his lifetime, and his bones angered Julian after his death (John Chrysostom, *De s. Babyla* 90). Chrysostom claims that by confronting these emperors, Babylas demonstrated the force of Christianity, and therefore the places associated with his relics—their current resting place and their previous site in Daphne—should recall this story.[55]

In addition to explicit comparisons between Babylas's third-century imperial opponent and the emperor Julian, Chrysostom also uses several other rhetorical strategies to connect the two leaders. One such association is Chrysostom's emphasis in both stories on bloody sacrifice, the relation of which to the violent murder of the saint himself would not have been lost on Chrysostom's audience. Through the bloody images of animal sacrifice and human murder, Chrysostom suggests a connection between the idolatrous sacrifices that he describes Jesus as coming to earth in order to overturn, the murder of Babylas, and Julian's well-documented bloody temple sacrifices, implying that Julian's actions tied him not only to Babylas's murderer, but to ungodly pre-Christian human sacrifices. Chrysostom argues that Jesus came in part to overcome the *daimones,* who were the center of pre-Christian Roman cult, and whom Chrysostom portrays as commanding that "their altars be reddened with the human blood" of children slain by their parents (*De s. Babyla* 3; cf. 4–5). This emphasis on human sacrifice as part of the cult of the gods would heighten the grotesqueness of ritual practices that Chrysostom associates with Julian, and color audiences' associations with local temple sites.[56]

Beyond the associations of sacrifice, Chrysostom also draws a parallel between the roles that Babylas's murderer and Julian played in relation to the Christian God, and argues that both emperors provided God with an opportunity to demonstrate a love of humanity (*philanthrōpia*) in the hope that the emperor would repent (*De s. Babyla* 125), but were ultimately both visibly punished for persevering in their wrongdoing, providing a long-lasting message for Chrysostom's audience. Chrysostom suggests that some in his audience might be curious as to why God allowed the third-century emperor to murder: "And certain ones are probably wondering how it was he was not struck by a divine blow for such recklessness, or how it was God did not discharge a thunderbolt at him from above" (28). Likewise, Chrysostom addresses those who questioned why Apollo's temple was destroyed, but Julian initially remained unharmed, "the reason why God vented his anger not on the

55. Justin Stephens investigates the relative power of the Christian God and the Roman emperor in order to demonstrate John Chrysostom's early interest in imperial and ecclesial power relations: Stephens, "Religion and Power in the Early Thought of John Chrysostom," in *The Power of Religion in Late Antiquity,* ed. Andrew Cain and Noel Lenski (Burlington, VT: Ashgate, 2009), 181–88.

56. The accusation of human sacrifice, of course, reflects the force of Chrysostom's Christian polemic more than the historicity of such sacrifice. Schatkin notes this in a footnote to her translation (*Saint John Chrysostom,* 77 n.10).

emperor but on the *daimōn,* and why the fire did not destroy the whole temple but abated after having destroyed the roof and the idol simultaneously" (114). Chrysostom suggests that the temple's ominous and enduring remains offered an explanation for why God did not punish Julian immediately, namely, because it would have been too quickly forgotten: "For the one who sees everything before it happens also knew this, among other things, that if the thunderbolt had been brought against the emperor, those who were present and beheld the blow would be afraid at the time, but after two or three years the memory of the event would perish," while the temple's long-lived remains would announce "the anger of God more clearly than any herald not only to those then but also to all thereafter" (114). God's initial patience did not persuade either emperor to repent, however, and eventually they received a just punishment for their crimes (124). Julian's "greater punishment" came, according to Chrysostom, when he was humiliatingly defeated in battle and killed in Persia; the lingering rubble in the Apollo precinct in Daphne remained for Chrysostom a visible warning and reminder of the Christian God's power in these events.

The charred remains of the Apollo temple thus acted as a potent site for the negotiation of religious orthodoxy and cultural memory both at the time of the fire in the writings of Julian and Libanius, and also many years later in the writings of John Chrysostom. In *Selling Places: The City as Cultural Capital, Past and Present,* Gerry Kearns discusses the "politics of memory," or the effects that particular constructions of places have on the ways in which they are remembered,[57] and Susan Alcock and others have similarly highlighted the power dynamics involved in specifically landscape-related memories.[58] Through the fire and the multiple narratives that interpreted its meaning, the place of Apollo's Daphne temple was redefined, and the new perceptions brought with them new power structures and cultural significance, what Angèle Smith calls "the politics of perception."[59] Mary Carruthers writes: "The deserted ruin of charred beams and destroyed columns mourned by Libanius is 'turned,' like the trope it is, in a different 'direction' by Chrysostom. The key to 'forgetting' Apollo in this incident is not to destroy his temple but to re-position it and remember it, in a different, though closely related,

57. Gerry Kearns, "The City as Spectacle: Paris and the Bicentenary of the French Revolution," in Kearns and Philo, *Selling Places,* 63.

58. Ruth Van Dyke and Susan Alcock, eds., *Archaeologies of Memory* (Malden, MA: Blackwell Publishing, 2003); Norman Yoffee, "Peering into the Palimpsest: An Introduction to the Volume," in *Negotiating the Past in the Past: Identity, Memory, and Landscape in Archaeological Research,* ed. Norman Yoffee (Tucson: University of Arizona Press, 2007), 3; Susan Alcock, *Archaeologies of the Greek Past: Landscape, Monuments, and Memories* (New York: Cambridge University Press, 2002). See the fuller discussion in the introduction above.

59. Angèle Smith, "Landscape Representation: Place and Identity in Nineteenth-Century Ordnance Survey Maps of Ireland," in *Landscape, Memory, and History: Anthropological Perspectives,* ed. Pamela Stewart and Andrew Strathern (Sterling, VA: Pluto, 2003), 71.

'story.'[60] John Chrysostom's retelling upended the political power structures preferred by Julian and Libanius, positioning Christianity, and for him specifically Nicene "orthodoxy," at the top of a new hierarchy. In the words of Harriet Flower, Chrysostom's *De sancto Babyla* offers a "memory story" that grounds a public Christian identity in Antioch's landscape.

Representations of places, physical and/or rhetorical, are imbued with significance. "There are," Angèle Smith writes, "multiple ways of perceiving and understanding the landscape as well as the social memories and meanings that are encoded in the landscape," and representations of any place are, therefore, "sites of cultural negotiations in which competing perceptions and experiences of the landscape and its social history are manipulated."[61] Libanius's and John Chrysostom's narrative depictions of the burned temple and its history present new interpretations of a familiar landmark to their respective audiences. Amid the rich religious patchwork of the city,[62] John Chrysostom identifies the year after Theodosius's accession to the imperial throne as a strategic time in which to renew negotiations over the meaning and memories associated with the burned Apollo temple in Daphne. Memory in the earlier Julio-Claudian period, Flower writes, "was consistently and variously recreated to suit the political needs of the moment. . . . Each new ruler effectively faced the challenge of how to shape the memory of his predecessor(s)."[63] Like these emperors, John Chrysostom reads the history of the ruined temple in ways that promoted the growing new authority of Bishop Meletius's Christianity over a landscape that had once belonged to the gods and over a martyrion that appears to have had associations with Antioch's homoian Christian community.

Writing in response to Libanius's efforts to recover the emperor Julian's legacy (Libanius, *Or.* 24), and with the new emperor Theodosius's religious policies not yet solidified, Chrysostom turns to the powerful local landmark of the Apollo temple precinct in Daphne to reinscribe his narrative of Christian superiority. Carruthers concludes that Apollo's temple after the fire "is dis-placed into a different associational map. Burnt and broken, it serves as a memory cue 'for the chastisement' of future generations, who can remember both the pagan 'thing' associated with the [temple's] column and that this 'thing' is now broken and has been re-placed."[64] For

60. Carruthers, *Craft of Thought,* 52. Charles Hedrick has written persuasively about partial Roman erasures and silences that cause Romans to remember to forget, thus preserving with dishonor rather than obliterating the memory of the subject: Hedrick, *History and Silence: The Purge and Rehabilitation of Memory in Late Antiquity* (Austin: University of Texas Press, 2000), esp. xii-xiv, 89–130.

61. Smith, "Landscape Representation," 72.

62. Soler notes that in relying on the large literary corpora of Libanius and John Chrysostom, scholars should beware not to overlook the variety of significant religious communities in fourth-century Antioch besides these authors' own, particularly the Jews but also Manichaeans and the wide variety of other Christian groups (Soler, *Le sacré et le salut,* 2–3, 5).

63. Flower, *Art of Forgetting,* 197–98.

64. Carruthers, *Craft of Thought,* 53.

Chrysostom the ruined temple site functions as Hedrick describes a *damnatio memoriae*, a "grand and eloquent gesture" that intends "to dishonor memory, not to destroy it."[65] Explicitly using the landscape to reify Christian triumph over the Greek gods, Chrysostom writes:

> The temple and the martyrion memorialize both [Julian's] madness and the power of blessed Babylas, the one [temple] is desolate and the other [martyrion] has the same energy that it had before. The coffin has not yet been brought up again, and God arranged this too in order that knowledge of the accomplishments of the saint might become clearer to those who come along. (*De s. Babyla* 126)

Chrysostom concludes that the physical relocation of Babylas's relics was doubly forceful, first in Babylas's presence and again in his absence: "Babylas, having been in Daphne and again having left it behind, thus gives the greatest benefit" (126). "Such is the power of the martyrs," Chrysostom insists, "while living and dead, both when they are present in places and again when they leave them behind" (127). Chrysostom is explicit in his recognition that reshaping physical places and the memories associated with them could redefine local religious and political power dynamics. With Apollo's temple precinct having been physically transformed by Gallus and then by Julian through the movement of Babylas's relics, Chrysostom attempts rhetorically to insure that the skeletal temple remains and the absence of Babylas's relics from the Daphne martyrion continued to signify his message of Christian superiority to those who saw them. Years later Chrysostom would return again to the significance of Babylas's relics in light of their further movement by his bishop, Meletius.

"THE MINISTRY OF THE BODY": BISHOP MELETIUS IN ACT AND MEMORY

The case of Meletius's manipulation of Babylas's relics presents an appropriate conclusion to the previous discussion, as knowledge about Meletius's physical restructuring of the landscape survives primarily in John Chrysostom's memory-shaping narratives, demonstrating the symbiosis between the physical and rhetorical strategies of redefinition.[66] Anthropologists Pamela Stewart and Andrew Strathern comment, "We see history as involved continuously in the making and remaking of ideas about place, realigning or differentiating place in relation to notions of

---

65. Hedrick, *History and Silence*, xii. The modern phrase "damnatio memoriae" conflates a variety of Roman practices, none of which were as totalizing or systematic as the modern concept suggests. See Friedrich Vittinghoff, *Der Staatsfeind in der römischen Kaiserzeit: Untersuchungen zur* damnatio memoriae (Berlin: Junker and Dunnhaupt, 1936); and Flower, *Art of Forgetting*, xix.

66. Some of the material in this section has been published earlier: Christine Shepardson, "Burying Babylas: Meletius and the Christianization of Antioch," *Studia Patristica* 37 (2010): 347–52.

community."[67] Meletius and John Chrysostom's joint efforts indisputably realigned and differentiated Antiochene space for the benefit of their Nicene Christian community at the expense of their opponents.

Bishop Meletius had a new church built to house Babylas's relics across the river in the military fields just outside Antioch's city wall soon before his own death in 381. This moment in Meletius's episcopal career was not, however, an isolated instance of his efforts to shape religious orthodoxy in Antioch. Examination of texts by Basil of Caesarea, Gregory of Nyssa, and John Chrysostom suggest that Meletius's actions are best interpreted as self-conscious efforts to shape the religious landscape through the recognition of the authority associated with the location(s) of Babylas's relics. Meletius's entire episcopal career entailed struggles in local and imperial politics: imperially he worked to locate himself safely within the complicated and ever-shifting theological conflicts that surrounded claims to Christian orthodoxy, and locally he engaged in lengthy contests with other bishops who claimed his see to assert his version of orthodoxy within the city of Antioch.[68] For the latter, Babylas proved to be particularly helpful.[69] While we can never know for certain the motivations behind Meletius's actions, our knowledge of several particular events, combined with Basil of Caesarea's, Gregory of Nyssa's, and John Chrysostom's comments about Meletius's life, suggest that he was aware of their politicized consequences. We can, therefore, speak of Meletius's manipulation of the authority that comes with the control of powerful local places through his construction of a new church, and of his interest in spreading his particular Christian doctrine in the city. One important mechanism through which Meletius helped his Christianity become Antiochene orthodoxy amid competing bishops and theologies was through the manipulation of Babylas's relics.

As mentioned in the introduction, Meletius's episcopal career was tumultuous.[70] Born in Melitene in Armenia, Meletius replaced the denounced Eustathius as bishop of Sebaste in 358. Meletius did not last very long in Sebaste, however, and lived in Beroea before becoming bishop of Antioch in 360 and briefly controlling the city's Great Church after Bishop Eudoxius. It seems to have been only a matter of weeks, however, before he was exiled and Euzoius was elected bishop of Antioch

67. Stewart and Strathern, *Landscape, Memory, and History*, 3.

68. For the details of these controversies, see Thomas Karmann, *Meletius von Antiochien: Studien zur Geschichte des trinitätstheologischen Streits in den Jahren 360–364 n. Chr.*, Regensburger Studien zur Theologie 68 (Frankfurt: Peter Lang, 2009), esp. 1–13, 121–34, 463–69.

69. Soler has persuasively demonstrated the similar Antiochene struggle to define the memory of Bishop Eustathius, although that contest was less clearly spatially located (Soler, *Le sacré et le salut*, 141–46).

70. For a recent study of Meletius, see Karmann, *Meletius von Antiochien*. Karmann focuses on the first years of Meletius's episcopacy at Antioch.

in his place (John Chrysostom, *De sancto Meletio* 1, 2/4, 6).[71] Meletius returned to control the Apostolic Church in Antioch in 362 under the emperor Julian, competing with both Euzoius and Paulinus to claim the city's see.[72] Jovian became emperor after Julian's unexpected death in Persia in June 363, and Meletius held a council in Antioch that autumn, showing his active interest in rallying support for his branch of Christianity.[73] Jovian died just months later in February 364, and with the homoian emperor Valens's ascension to the throne Meletius lost control of even the Apostolic Church and had to hold services in a field outside the city. In 365, the same year that Athanasius came to Antioch to celebrate the Eucharist with Bishop Paulinus, Valens exiled Meletius altogether, although his congregants continued to worship apart from Paulinus's and Euzoius's communities in his absence. Theodoret provides evidence that the military training ground across the river, beyond the palace and the city wall, became recognizably associated with Meletius's congregation in these years (*HE* 4.25–26; cf. *HR* 2.15, 8.5–8).[74] Meletius returned to Antioch between 365 and 369 and was again exiled by Valens for the final time ca. 369, returning after Valens's death in 378.[75] Only two years later Meletius had built a new church for Babylas, gained control of Antioch's Great Church, and was chosen to oversee the ecumenical Council of Constantinople of 381, where he died. The emperor Theodosius had Meletius's remains returned to Antioch, where they were buried next to Babylas's as Meletius appears to have planned.

In this complex situation, struggling for his own authority as well as the success of Christian "orthodoxy," Meletius took concrete actions to ensure that his congregation prospered. In exile, Meletius participated in a complex network of communications as one means of maintaining powerful ties and attesting to his orthodox status. During his final exile, Meletius returned to Getasa in Armenia where he visited with his friend Theodotus in Nicopolis and communicated with Basil of Caesarea through one visit and several letters that provide useful witnesses

71. All translations from *De sancto Meletio* are my own based on the Greek text in Migne, PG 50.515–20. I note first the PG paragraph numbering, followed by the paragraphs of Wendy Mayer's recent English translation: Wendy Mayer with Bronwen Neil, *St. John Chrysostom: The Cult of the Saints: Select Homilies and Letters* (New York: St. Vladimir's Seminary Press, 2006), 39–48. See also Brennecke, *Studien,* esp. 66–81.

72. See Downey, *History,* 370, 396; W. Eltester, "Die Kirchen Antiochias im IV. Jahrhundert," *ZNTW* 36 (1937): 251–86; Timothy D. Barnes, *Athanasius and Constantius: Theology and Politics in the Constantinian Empire* (Cambridge, MA: Harvard University Press, 1993), 149; R. P. C. Hanson, *The Search for the Christian Doctrine of God: The Arian Controversy, 318–381* (Grand Rapids, MI: Baker Academic Press, 1988), 384; J. N. D. Kelly, *Golden Mouth: The Story of John Chrysostom—Ascetic, Preacher, Bishop* (London: Duckworth, 1995), 12, 16.

73. Brennecke, *Studien,* 173–78; Karmann, *Meletius von Antiochien,* 341–54.

74. This reference is to the Greek text in Parmentier and Hansen.

75. Mayer places Meletius's exiles in 361, 365, and 369 (Mayer and Allen, *Churches,* 45).

regarding perceptions of Meletius's episcopacy. During 373–75 Basil had a falling-out with Eustathius of Sebaste, and subsequently courted Meletius's and Theodotus's friendship. Through such social networks, by hosting a council in Antioch upon his return in 379, by building a new church for Babylas's relics, and by ordaining the golden-mouthed orator, John, as his deacon in the winter of 380–81, Meletius proactively shaped the successful future of his congregation.[76]

Whereas most early Christian leaders have come down to us primarily through their writings, it is Meletius's actions that most clearly survive, narrated through the writings of others, such as his protégé John Chrysostom. There is no question that the effects of Meletius's acts were to make his version of Christianity more visible in Antioch and its environs, and to further the success of Meletian orthodoxy in the Antiochene schism. Basil of Caesarea, Gregory of Nyssa, and John Chrysostom all describe Meletius as actively engaged in producing and promoting a particular orthodoxy in the midst of the complex struggles for authority in Antioch. The ultimate shape of Antiochene Christianity's history, with Babylas, Meletius, Flavian, and John Chrysostom adopted as saints by the Nicene Christianity that triumphed, shows the success that Meletius's actions helped to bring about. This image of Meletius suggests that the bishop's manipulation of such a powerful object as Babylas's relics was not by chance, and that the boost that this adoption of Babylas gave Meletius's congregation in the midst of the Hydra-like split in Antiochene Christianity would have come as no surprise to their seasoned orchestrator.

Basil of Caesarea's letters provide one important contemporary witness to Meletius's authority and his efforts to define and represent Christian orthodoxy, as well as to the fact that many Christian leaders outside of the city recognized Meletius as Antioch's rightful bishop. Basil's relationship with Meletius began in a web of shifting allegiances, but during Meletius's third exile in the 370s, Basil actively courted his support.[77] In the process of writing letters to him, Basil references Meletius's significance in Antioch and Basil's own strong support for the exiled bishop. Basil honors Meletius, praising his "wisdom" and referring to "the profitable lessons" of his voice (*Ep.* 57; cf. *Ep.* 89.1).[78] Basil tried to intervene on Mele-

76. While the precise date of John Chrysostom's ordination to the diaconate is unknown, Kelly argues that it had to be at the end of 380 or the very beginning of 381, before Meletius traveled to Constantinople for the ecumenical council (Kelly, *Golden Mouth,* 38). This brings a little more precision to Baur's earlier observation that it happened in 381 before the May council: Chrysostomus Baur, *John Chrysostom and His Time* (Westminster, MD: The Newman Press, 1959), 1:143. Both scholars begin their calculations from Palladius's observations (*Dial.* 5).

77. See the discussion in Philip Rousseau, *Basil of Caesarea* (Berkeley: University of California Press, 1994), 239–45; Lewis Ayres, *Nicaea and Its Legacy: An Approach to Fourth-Century Trinitarian Theology* (New York: Oxford University Press, 2004), 225–29.

78. All translations from Basil's letters are my own from the Greek text in Yves Courtonne, ed. and trans., *Saint Basile: Correspondance,* vol. 1 *(Lettres 1–100)* (Paris: Les Belles Lettres, 2003). Basil's

tius's behalf in 375 when Basil learned that Bishop Paulinus had received new support from the West (*Ep.* 216). Basil's description suggests that Meletius spent his episcopacy actively and self-consciously working to win the claim to his see and the right to define religious orthodoxy in Antioch and the wider region.

Although Gregory of Nyssa, like Basil of Caesarea, did not live in Antioch, he was at the Council of Constantinople where Meletius died suddenly in 381, and he was one of many leaders who presented a funeral oration on the occasion, a text that like Basil's letters presents Meletius as an active and respected proponent of religious orthodoxy in the eyes of many present in Constantinople for the council.[79] Given that Gregory was less familiar with Meletius than some of those who were speaking at his funeral, he primarily praises Meletius in general terms as a great leader and mourns the Christian community's loss (*Oratio funebris in Meletium episcopum*, pp. 442, 445, 446). Gregory refers to Meletius's death as "a misfortune" that caused "sufferings" for orthodox Christians, particularly for the "city of Antioch," whose "ornament has been stripped away" (pp. 442, 446, 447). Gregory's descriptions not only of the life that Meletius had lived, but also of his death and funeral preparations, highlight Meletius's popularity and authority, referring to how much Antioch loved him and looked to him as a leader, even when he was in exile. Gregory predicts that when the report of Meletius's death spread, "then the roads will be full of mourners" (p. 452). Gregory exhorts those who would bear the body to Antioch to tell Meletius's followers of the crowds in Constantinople who recognized Meletius's greatness and mourned his death, how crowds of thousands "formed a sea around the procession of the body" (p. 456). Those present at Meletius's death bore witness to his sanctified status by grasping at his body for relics, and even the emperor honored him. "The napkins on his skin," Gregory writes, "were plucked away to become amulets for the faithful. Let it be added to the narrative that the emperor bore a sad face because of the misfortune, and rose from his throne, and how the whole city joined the procession of the saint" (pp. 456–57).

In the context of the Council of Constantinople over which Meletius had presided, as well as the context of the ongoing Antiochene schisms, it is little surprise that Gregory also specifically mentions Meletius's active role in fighting heresy and promoting orthodoxy. Gregory describes Meletius as "that magnificent sail that was always being guided by the Holy Spirit," as "the steadfast rudder of our souls by means of which we sailed without suffering over the huge waves of heresy," as

---

choice to seek assistance from Meletius is colored not only by his need to defend his own orthodoxy after Eustathius of Sebaste apparently started rumors about him, but also by his desire to settle conflicts in parts of Armenia. Meletius's ties with the region would have made him a particularly useful ally. See Rousseau, *Basil*, 239–45.

79. Gregory mentions that many others have spoken before him. All translations of *Oratio funebris in Meletium episcopum* are my own from the Greek text in *Gregorii Nysseni Opera* 9.441–57. I have cited *Or. fun. in Mel. episc.* here by the page numbers in *GNO*.

an "immovable anchor of intelligence," and as an "excellent pilot who directed our ship straight toward its goal above" (*Or. fun. in Mel. episc.*, p. 444). These images are active, granting Meletius agency in stemming the tide of heresy that threatened to overwhelm Antioch, and suggesting that Meletius fought to help his orthodoxy prevail. Meletius spoke "with pure devotion to truth," and exhibited "zeal for the faith" (pp. 446, 449). During his exiles, Meletius is depicted by Gregory as an active athlete, engaging in contests for the church, repelling attacks in his three exiles, and "contending in strenuous contests on behalf of truth" (p. 450). Gregory's funeral oration from 381 suggests that Meletius was the respected leader of a vibrant group of Antiochene Christians who fought "the confusion of heresy" (p. 453).[80] With Meletius's death, Gregory mourns that there would no longer be anyone left "to lead us" through the current trials (p. 453). Gregory's oration portrays Meletius as having proactively struggled to assert his understanding of Christian orthodoxy in Antioch, and to gain support for his cause within the wider empire.

It is, though, from John Chrysostom's local testimony that we learn the more specific means by which Meletius progressed in his struggle. Chrysostom recounts Meletius's efforts at some length in two different texts: *De sancto Meletio*, which demonstrates that Meletius's own relics had created a powerful place of authority and religious orthodoxy in Antioch, and *De sancto hieromartyre Babyla*, which provides some of the details of Meletius's physical manipulation of the Antiochene landscape during his lifetime through the construction of a church for Babylas. Chrysostom presented *De sancto Meletio* in 386, five years after Meletius's death, when Chrysostom was ordained presbyter by Meletius's successor, Bishop Flavian. When Chrysostom delivered this homily at Meletius's coffin in the church of Babylas (*De sancto Meletio* 1/1),[81] there seems already to have been an annual remembrance of his death. Chrysostom refers to the numerous people in attendance: "You, who after so long are flying around the body of the blessed Meletius like bees around honeycomb, are eyewitnesses" (3/9). He notes Antioch's enthusiasm for Meletius since the beginning of his episcopacy (1/1), and comments on how many families named children after him to show their devotion (1/2–3). Even when Meletius was in exile in Armenia, Chrysostom claims, he was always in the mind of his congregants, as if they still heard and saw him (2/5). These descriptions further demonstrate that Meletius's congregation continued to thrive during the Antiochene conflict, and that Meletius became a respected saint upon his death.

<hr />

80. See also the discussion of Gregory's confrontation with "Arians" in Johan Leemans, "Preaching and the Arian Controversy: Orthodoxy and Heresy in Gregory of Nyssa's Sermons," *Journal of Eastern Christian Studies* 60 (2008): 127–42.

81. See also Julia Alissandratos, "The Structure of the Funeral Oration in John Chrysostom's *Eulogy of Meletius*," *Byzantine Studies* 7.2 (1980): 182–98.

Like Gregory, Chrysostom notes Meletius's active engagement in the struggles for control of Antiochene Christianity, and how much he did to promote and define Christian orthodoxy. Noting Meletius's "zeal for the faith," Chrysostom describes Meletius's exiles within the context of his fight for control of Antiochene Christianity: "Immediately as [Meletius] entered, he was expelled from the city, since those who hate truth drove him out" (*De sancto Meletio* 3, 1/7, 4). Chrysostom claimed that Meletius arrived in Antioch "just as Moses into Egypt" and "freed the city from the deception of heresy, and by cutting off from the rest of the body the limbs that had been rotting and were incurable, brought back uncontaminated health to a large part of the church" (1/4). According to Chrysostom, it was on account of this active advocacy of Christian orthodoxy that "those who hate truth, not enduring reform, and urging on the emperor of the time, expelled him from the city, expecting by this to subvert the truth and overturn the reform of events" (1/4). Meletius's congregation clung stalwartly to his leadership after less than a month of his episcopacy, demonstrating for Chrysostom Meletius's great "skill at teaching" (1, 2/4, 6). With the added authority of firsthand knowledge of Meletius and Antiochene politics, John Chrysostom portrays Meletius as a leader proactively engaged in resolving Antioch's religious schisms in his favor. Chrysostom even explains Meletius's death in Constantinople as having the advantage that others could follow his exemplary model, stating that he died in Thrace so that "bishops all over the world" could have a clear example and role model for how they ought to administer and govern the churches" (3/7). Preaching in the church of Babylas that also housed Meletius's relics, Chrysostom simultaneously remembers Meletius's active engagement in making Antioch correctly Christian during his lifetime and demonstrates that his relics continued to be a regional force for strengthening religious orthodoxy after his death.

In the second text, *De sancto hieromartyre Babyla*, Chrysostom describes in detail sometime between 386 and 397 the significant relation between Babylas and Meletius, and how toward the end of his life Meletius had joined the ranks of Gallus and Julian by using Babylas's relics to reshape Antioch's topography.[82] This homily provides the most direct evidence about Meletius's manipulation of Babylas's relics in light of Antioch's doctrinal and episcopal schisms. Chrysostom links Meletius with Babylas through Meletius's actions regarding Babylas's relics as well as by comparing the lives and religiosity of both bishops. Chrysostom claims that

---

82. The date of the second homily is less certain, since Wendy Mayer has challenged the traditional date of 388 and posited instead 386–87, 391–92, or 396–97, but the consensus remains that John first delivered the sermon on Babylas's festival day, January 24. See Mayer's introduction to her English translation: Johan Leemans, Wendy Mayer, Pauline Allen, and Boudewijn Dehandschutter, *"Let Us Die That We May Live": Greek Homilies on Christian Martyrs from Asia Minor, Palestine, and Syria (c. AD 350- AD 450)* (New York: Routledge, 2003), 141.

Meletius shared the same dignity as Babylas, and "for the sake of religion showed forth equal frankness (*parrēsia*)" (*De s. hierom. Babyla* 10).[83] Likewise, he praises Meletius's asceticism as the equivalent of Babylas's martyrdom, and comments that Babylas was destined to have "a neighbor and a cohabitant having the same way of life" (10). Equally important for Chrysostom, however, was not just that Meletius and Babylas were both saints, but that Meletius had self-consciously forged a relationship with Babylas while he was still alive, and thus rightfully enjoyed his place next to him in death.

Chrysostom is explicit in this text about Meletius's building of a new church to house Babylas's relics, and about the outcome that these actions had. Chrysostom claims, "For [Meletius] toiled such a long time there [at Babylas's church], sending letters continually to the emperor, troubling the authorities, and contributing the ministry of the body for the martyr" (*De s. hierom. Babyla* 10). The "ministry of the body" in this case consisted of the self-conscious physical labor undertaken by Meletius, ostensibly on behalf of Babylas, although Chrysostom does not wait long before demonstrating that Meletius's own congregation benefited greatly from the deeds. Chrysostom details Meletius's manual labor to an audience that included those who were eyewitnesses to the events of 379/80:

> For you know, of course, and remember that in the middle of the summer when the midday rays occupied the heaven, [Meletius], together with his companions, walked there every single day, not as a spectator only but also as one who would be a sharer in what was happening. For he even often brought along stone and dragged a rope and even before those who were working he attended to the need of any one of the builders. (10)

Chrysostom claims that Meletius "knew what rewards lay in store for him for these things" (10), likely referring to his status as a saint in his own right, but also suggesting that Meletius performed these acts of devotion well aware that they would have future positive repercussions for his Antiochene Christianity.

The location of Meletius's new church building also contributes to our knowledge of the appropriation of local places. There is evidence that this region across the river in the field where the military performed its practice drills had been associated with Meletius's congregation for years by the time Meletius built the church. When Meletius was exiled by Valens in the mid-360s, Theodoret records that his followers gathered in this field for their meetings (*HE* 4.25–26).[84] Theodoret claims that during this exile, sometime between 364 when Valens came to power and 367 when the ascetic Julian Saba died, Meletius's priest Flavian, who was car-

83. John Chrysostom, *De s. hierom. Babyla* 10. All translations of *De s. hierom. Babyla* are my own from the Greek text in SC 362 (1990), 294–313. See also the English translation available in Leemans et al., "*Let Us Die*," 140–48.

84. This reference is to the Greek text in Parmentier and Hansen.

ing for the congregation in his bishop's absence, brought Julian Saba to the field to address his congregants. Theodoret describes him as proceeding from "the caves at the foot of the mountain" where he first rested when he entered Antioch, to "the gathering of the devout," which for Theodoret refers to the congregation under the exiled Meletius (*HR* 2.18, 2.19).[85] Narrating the location of this place, Theodoret writes that Julian "went through the gates of the palace," which was located on a large island in the river on the other side of the city from the mountains, suggesting Julian was headed toward the *campus martius* where Meletius later built the Babylas church; Theodoret confirms that this was his destination by noting that in anticipation of listening to him, "all the people of the town streamed together, and the military drill-ground (*to polemikon gymnasion*) became full of those running together" (2.19). Meletius's construction of a church in this area confirms that this place was associated with his community, at the same time that it concretized that association by the establishment of a physical church building that with the interment of Meletius next to Babylas soon after his death in 381 could have been expected to remain clearly in the hands of his particular Christian faction.[86]

Since Meletius seems to have prepared the site for his burial before his death, his interment in the new church that he had built for Babylas can be interpreted as his final act of manipulating Antioch's topography in the service of promoting his Christian community as the local representatives of religious orthodoxy. Wendy Mayer has recently published a careful analysis of the available data about the presumed tombs of Bablyas and Meletius,[87] and concludes that whether scholars interpret John Chrysostom's reference to Meletius as Babylas's "neighbor and co-inhabitant" to mean that the two saints shared a single tomb (*De s. hierom. Babyla* 10), or interpret Sozomen's reference to Meletius's burial near Babylas's tomb to mean that the two saints were buried close by one another (*HE* 7.10.5), "the excavated church suits either interpretation."[88] Thus, whether they were buried together in what appears to be a double tomb in the floor of the church at Qausīyeh on the edge of the *campus martius,* or whether they occupied two of the separate tombs

85. All translations from Theodoret's *Historia religiosa* are my own from the Greek text edited by Pierre Canivet and Alice Leroy-Molinghen in *Théodoret de Cyr, Histoire des moines de Syrie (I-XIII)*, vol. 1, SC 234 (1977; repr., Paris: Les Éditions du Cerf, 2006). There is an English translation in Richard Price, *A History of the Monks of Syria, by Theodoret of Cyrrhus* (Kalamazoo, MI: Cistercian Publications, 1985).

86. As Mayer has noted, "The location of this church was strategic" (Mayer, "Antioch and the Intersection," 361).

87. See Mayer and Allen, *Churches*, 32–48; and Wendy Mayer, "The Late Antique Church at Qausīyeh Reconsidered: Memory and Martyr-Burial in Syrian Antioch," in *Martyrdom and Persecution in Late Antique Christianity: Festschrift Boudewijn Dehandschutter*, Bibliotheca Ephemeridum Theologicarum Lovaniensium 241, ed. J. Leemans (Leuven: Peeters, 2010), 161–77. See also the discussion of this church in the introduction above.

88. Mayer and Allen, *Churches*, 45.

that archaeologists uncovered during their excavations, the church that Meletius had built in order to contain Babylas's relics seems quite early to have become a location for the practice of *depositio ad sanctos,* or the burial near a recognized saint for the purpose of benefiting from the sanctity of the holy person.[89] Meletius was buried there shortly after Babylas himself, and the archaeological evidence shows that in later years additional tombs were added in the floor.[90] Meletius's burial near Babylas's relics highlights the power of the third-century saint's remains as well as of the place where they lay, but it also strengthens the potency of the church because of Meletius's own status as a saint, leaving the church and his community after his death with the memory and relics of not just one, but two saints.

For someone who was as deeply engaged in Antioch's theological conflicts as the extant texts describe Meletius to have been, it is hard to imagine that Meletius would not have foreseen the advantages to his own community if he could successfully claim ownership of the relics of the local martyr-saint Babylas, bringing this Antiochene hero under the control of a church that he had built and that his congregation and successors controlled in the years after his death. Having been forced to move from the Great Church to the old Apostolic Church and then to the fields outside the city, knowing that Babylas's relics had connections with Antioch's homoian Christian community in the 350s and 360s, and having watched homoian bishops control the Great Church during his exile, Meletius lived his episcopacy enmeshed in the politics of controlling significant landmarks in Antioch's topography. When Meletius built "magnificent buildings" for Antioch's martyrs and held "continuous feasts" in their honor, he co-opted for his congregation and his successors the power of these respected saints, particularly Babylas, whose martyrion church he built (John Chrysostom, *De s. hierom. Babyla* 10). In so doing, Meletius reaped an additional reward in that his own body, too, came to be a Christian relic, further drawing Antioch's Christians to the church that he had built. By so definitively linking Babylas with himself and the church that he built, Meletius gained a persuasive tool that would outlast his own life for shaping the religious affiliations of Antioch and its environs.

In the end, *De sancto Meletio* and *De sancto hieromartyre Babyla,* delivered by one of Meletius's clergy to a crowd of Antioch's Christians gathered in the church that Meletius had built and marking the annual saints' festivals for Meletius and Babylas, respectively, demonstrate the success of Meletius's maneuverings to

89. For more on this custom as it developed in Christian late antiquity, see especially Duval, *Auprès des saints.*

90. See Mayer and Allen, *Churches,* 32–40; Jean Lassus, "L'église cruciforme Antioche-Kaoussié 12-F," in *Antioch-on-the-Orontes (Publications of the Committee for the Excavation of Antioch and Its Vicinity),* vol. 2, *The Excavations, 1933–1936,* ed. Richard Stillwell (Princeton, NJ: Princeton University Press, 1938), 114–56.

reshape Antioch's topography in a way that brought authority, and many congregants, to his church, despite his long exile from the local episcopal Great Church. Recognizing the significance of places in the politicized episcopal schisms, and refusing to allow imperial and episcopal policies to overshadow his role as Antioch's bishop, Meletius co-opted Babylas's relics to construct a new church whose local significance could rival that of the imperial church and whose possession resided in the hands of Meletius's congregation. While there are numerous factors involved in the definition of Antiochene orthodoxy, Meletius's topographical "ministry of the body" demonstrates one significant means by which Meletian Christianity succeeded over that of its rival claimants to Antioch's see.

The influence of Meletius's actions, however, was intensified by their memorialization in John Chrysostom's homilies on Meletius and Babylas, which are significant as sources for information about Meletius's activities as well as for Chrysostom's later engagement in this struggle. These two homilies not only provide a picture of how Meletius used saints' relics, Babylas's and his own, to reshape the Antiochene landscape both in life and in death, but they show that John Chrysostom continued Meletius's work by renarrating the events on the anniversaries of their respective deaths. By keeping Meletius's efforts alive and their significance clearly defined in the memory of each member of his audience years after Meletius's death, Chrysostom ensured that Meletius's and Babylas's relics continued to mark a place of power and Meletian orthodoxy.

Sociologist Paul Connerton describes generally the ways in which "commemorative ceremonies"—like those referenced in John Chrysostom's memorial homilies—construct and maintain social memory, claiming that in a commemorative ceremony "a community is reminded of its identity as represented by and told in a master narrative."[91] Through an annual commemoration of Meletius at the memorial site that the deceased bishop shared with Babylas, Chrysostom not only recounted Meletius's productive reshaping of Antioch's physical landscape, but reenacted the reshaping narratively by reinforcing the (Nicene) Christian affiliation of his audience and of the place in which they met. As Pamela Stewart and Andrew Strathern remark, "Perceptions of and values attached to landscape encode values and fix memories in places that become sites of historical identity."[92] John Chrysostom not only recalls these saints' status and Meletius's efforts to spread Christian orthodoxy in Antioch, but by retelling their stories annually he reifies that power, creating it anew through his homilies, reminding those who know the story and teaching it to those who do not yet know it. Chrysostom's rhetorical constructions, much like the narratives by the emperor Julian and Libanius and like Chrysostom's earlier *De sancto Babyla*, worked to shape the way in which

91. Connerton, *How Societies Remember*, 70.
92. Stewart and Strathern, *Landscape, Memory, and History*, 1.

Antiochenes viewed their religious landscape, just as Meletius shaped their views through his movement of the relics and building of the church.

CONCLUSION: REMEMBERING POWERFUL PLACES

From the middle to the late fourth century, Babylas's relics provided a powerful tool by which Antiochenes physically and rhetorically manipulated the physical landscape, and with it the region's historical memory, community identity, and religious topography. In the vocabulary of Andrew Fretter, Antiochene leaders competed with each other to adapt Apollo's temple grounds to appeal to their respective audiences. By narrating the events as a competition between the Christian God and the Greek gods, John Chrysostom identified "a real point of difference" with his opponents, and persuasively memorialized the temple fire and the emperor Julian's death in the context of that competition. Finally, by speaking with one voice about the superiority of Nicene Christianity over traditional religious places, practices, and gods, as well as over other forms of Christianity, Meletius, Flavian, and John Chrysostom succeeded in having Antioch's places remembered as they wished, with the burned temple of Apollo a memorial to the god's impotence, Babylas's empty Daphne shrine a memorial to the strength of the absent saint and a reminder of the power of the Christian God, and Babylas's church in Antioch's *campus martius* a potent new destination in the regional landscape and a marker of Nicene Christian identity.[93]

Antioch's leaders recognized that places could hold power, and that controlling those places could grant authority. Ruth Van Dyke and Susan Alcock write, "As humans create, modify, and move through a spatial milieu, the mediation between spatial experience and perception reflexively creates, legitimates, and reinforces social relationships and ideas."[94] In the midst of intense theological and political conflicts, as emperors supported various Christianities and even traditional temple practices under Julian, and in decades of episcopal schism in the city of Antioch, Gallus, Julian, Libanius, Meletius, and John Chrysostom used the relics of the early Christian martyr Babylas to negotiate religious and political status in the region. Katina Lillios writes, "Memories are not primarily about revisiting the past, but are about defining the present and managing the future of individuals and groups within meaningful, yet shifting, contexts. Thus, the control of memory and objects of memory is an important component of power."[95] Chrysostom's

---

93. Fretter, "Place Marketing," 169–73.

94. Ruth Van Dyke and Susan Alcock, "Archaeologies of Memory: An Introduction," in *Archaeologies of Memory*, ed. Ruth Van Dyke and Susan Alcock (Malden, MA: Blackwell Publishing, 2003), 3.

95. Katina Lillios, "Creating Memory in Prehistory: The Engraved Slate Plaques of Southwest Iberia," in *Archaeologies of Memory*, ed. Ruth Van Dyke and Susan Alcock (Malden, MA: Blackwell Publishing, 2003), 146.

memorial narrations of the events around Babylas's relics participated in legitimat-ing his Christian community as religious orthodoxy. Whether physically moving the saint's relics and constructing a new church building, or rhetorically trying to narrate the significance of the charred Apollo temple, the empty place at the Daphne martyrion, and the new church for Babylas, these leaders recognized "the relationships between spatiality and power,"[96] and did what they could to deploy the authority of these significant local places in their favor in these tumultuous decades.

96. John Allen, "Spatial Assemblages of Power: From Domination to Empowerment," in Massey, Allen, and Sarre, *Human Geography Today*, 212.

3

Being Correctly Christian

John Chrysostom's Rhetoric in 386–87

In fourth-century Antioch religious communities overlapped: Christianity and traditional temple cult sometimes competed for venues, such as at the martyrion of Babylas in Daphne; some Christians shared with Jews a respect for Jewish scripture and local synagogues; and Christians competed among themselves for control over the city's churches. In the face of the multilayered and highly politicized significance of so many local places, Christian leaders such as John Chrysostom, in the vocabulary of modern geographers, named these complex intersections as places of clearly negative or positive value in an attempt to construct and spread a particular religious orthodoxy. Antioch in the 380s was a volatile place, with Bishop Meletius's recent return from exile, an imperial decree that banned "heretics" from meeting in churches, Meletius's death and burial alongside the recently translated relics of Babylas, and John Chrysostom's ordination as deacon and then priest. John Chrysostom's homilies *De incomprehensibili natura dei* and *Adversus Iudaeos* from 386–87 demonstrate the fervor with which he instructed his audience to frequent certain sites, and forbid them from entering others. Locating these exhortations within the context of the political struggles to gain and maintain religious and political authority within the city demonstrates the rhetorical means by which, and the political gains for which, Chrysostom fought to patrol his community's boundaries, identifying where in Antioch his listeners should and should not go. Among the many religious and political factions competing for the allegiance of Antioch's citizens, John Chrysostom required "orthodox" behavior to mirror the "orthodox" theological beliefs that he taught, and through his spatial rhetoric he demonstrated the clear physical and spiritual benefits that his listeners would gain by doing as he recommended.

THE URBAN LANDSCAPE: ANTIOCH IN 386

In 386 Meletius's successor, Bishop Flavian, ordained John Chrysostom as a pres-byter, and John started to preach to church audiences. Since the imperial *cunctos populos* edict of February 380, the Christianity of Meletius, Flavian, and John Chrysostom was the only legally recognized form of Christianity in Antioch, despite the continuing competition between two Nicene bishops and multiple reli-gious communities in the city (*CTh* 16.1.2).[1] When John Chrysostom started to preach, Bishop Flavian's homoian opponents had been forbidden from meeting in church buildings in the city for five years, since an imperial edict of Theodosius in 381, and the much-beloved Meletius had died in the same year and been buried beside Babylas in the church that Meletius had built (*CTh* 16.5.6). Chrysostom explicitly associates two series of homilies that he preached interspersed with each other in 386–87, shortly after his ordination as a presbyter. The *Adversus Iudaeos* homilies and the homilies *De incomprehensibili natura dei* provide significant insight into the manipulation of Antioch's places in Chrysostom's rhetoric, although a comparison will reveal that his spatial rhetoric differed between the two series to reflect their different opponents and audiences.

The dating of both series of homilies reveals their chronological relation to one another, and highlights the value of reading them together. Wendy Pradels, Rudolf Brändle, and Martin Heimgartner have suggested a revised and more specific chro-nology for the *Adversus Iudaeos* homilies based on the new manuscript they pub-lished of the second homily in the series.[2] Their careful analysis dates Discourse 1 in this series to either late August or early September 386, just before the Jewish holidays of Rosh Hashanah and Yom Kippur. They present a persuasive argument that Discourse 4 was the next on this topic to be delivered, and that it dates to the same festival time the following year, August 29, 387, and was followed soon after

---

1. The absence of Antioch's bishop from an imperial list in 381 could signal continued imperial uncertainty about who would succeed Meletius after his death. David Hunt, "Christianising the Roman Empire: The Evidence of the Code," in *The Theodosian Code*, ed. Jill Harries and Ian Wood (Ithaca, NY: Cornell University Press, 1993), 150.

2. Wendy Pradels, Rudolf Brändle, and Martin Heimgartner, "The Sequence and Dating of the Series of John Chrysostom's Eight Discourses *Adversus Iudaeos*," *ZAC* 6 (2002): 90–116. See the text in Pradels, Brändle, and Heimgartner, "Das bisher vermisste Textstück in Johannes Chrysostomus, Ad-versus Judaeos, Oration 2," *ZAC* 5 (2001): 23–49. In light of evidence from their newly uncovered and translated section of Discourse 2, these authors conclude that of these eight sermons, only Discourse 1 dates to 386 (to the days just before Rosh Hashanah), and that Discourses 4, 2, 5, 6, 7, and 8 were preached—in that order—during the autumn Jewish holidays of 387 (106). They also remind readers that Discourse 3 does not appear to be part of this series of sermons, but they date it to January 387, following Discourse 1 and before the remaining Discourses (106). The evidence for this current chapter primarily comes from Discourses 1 and 6, and so is not greatly affected by this new dating. Nonethe-less, this careful alignment of Chrysostom's discourses with the dates of the Jewish holidays makes even clearer the context that these sermons addressed.

by Discourse 2 (September 5), Discourse 5 (September 9), Discourse 6 (Yom Kippur on September 10), Discourse 7 (September 12), and Discourse 8 (September 19). They concur that the homily traditionally identified as the third in this series was presented between Discourse 1 and Discourse 4 on January 31, 387, but note that it addresses a different topic than the other homilies more appropriately collected together in this series.[3] The reference in Discourse 6 in this series to the so-called Statues Riot, which took place in Antioch in late February 387, confirms the date of this homily (*Adv. Iud.* 6.6),[4] and a reference in Discourse 4 to the Jewish fast "again" approaching suggests that it is a full year after the holidays of the first homily (4.1).

Aside from internal evidence about the relation of the *Adversus Iudaeos* homilies to one another, the first of the series reveals its chronological relation to Chrysostom's series of homilies against the Anomean Christians, *De incomprehensibili natura dei.* Chrysostom begins the first homily against the Judaizers with the observation that he is interrupting a series against the Anomeans that he had begun the previous week, but promises that the two subjects are related and that he will return to the Anomeans as soon as the imminent threat of the Jewish festivals has passed (*Adv. Iud.* 1.1). His first homily against the Judaizers thus follows one week after his first homily against the Anomeans, suggesting a date in August 386 for Homily 1 in *De incomprehensibili natura dei.* Scholarship on this anti-Anomean series likewise suggests that the twelve homilies traditionally included in this series were written over a period of time. The name for the series comes primarily from the content of Homilies 1–5, which all seem to stem from the last five months of 386; they share an emphasis on the topic of God's incomprehensibility.[5] Homily 6 dates specifically to December 20, 386, the feast day of Saint Philogonius, who is the subject of the homily. Homilies 7 and 8 appear to have been given by Chrysostom on consecutive days in January 387 and share with Homilies 9 and 10 a focus on the substance of the Son being the same as the substance of God. Homilies 11 and 12, while sharing themes in common with the early homilies in this series, appear to stem from John Chrysostom's time in Constantinople much later, in 398, and thus will not be part of this discussion.

The recent dating revisions of the anti-Judaizing homilies result in a clearer idea of the integrated chronology of these two series of homilies. Chrysostom's first homily against the Anomeans in August 386 was followed a week later by his

---

3. Pradels, Brändle, Heimgartner, "Sequence," 91.

4. Except where noted, all translations from John Chrysostom's *Adversus Iudaeos* are my own from the Greek text in PG 48.843–942, and references are to the paragraph numbering there. See also the English translation by Paul W. Harkins in *St. John Chrysostom: Discourses against Judaizing Christians,* FC 68 (Washington, DC: Catholic University of America Press, 1979).

5. For the dating of these texts, I follow the conclusions of Paul Harkins in his introduction to *St. John Chrysostom: On the Incomprehensible Nature of God,* FC 72 (Washington, DC: Catholic University of America Press, 1984), 23–47.

first homily against the Judaizers. This was followed by Homilies 2–5 against the Anomeans between September and December of that year. Chrysostom preached the homily on Philogonius (traditionally Homily 6 of the anti-Anomean series) on December 20, 386, Homilies 7 and 8 against the Anomeans in January 387, and then concluded January with the homily that has been labeled as the third in the anti-Judaizing series. This explains why Discourse 3 in the *Adversus Iudaeos* series pronounces, like the first *Adversus Iudaeos* homily, that it interrupts Chrysostom's homilies against the Anomeans, since it follows soon after anti-Anomean Homilies 7–8 and precedes 9–10. It seems likely that Chrysostom completed Homilies 9 and 10 against the Anomeans in a timely fashion, perhaps in early February 387 before the Statues Riot. Certainly Homilies 9 and 10 were given well before Chrysostom renewed his anti-Judaizing homilies in August and September 387. Although Chrysostom preached other extant homilies during this time, most notably the series of homilies on the Statues Riot that will be the focus of the following chapter, it is instructive to begin with a discussion of these two series. Chrysostom himself saw a connection between their topics, and spoke explicitly of interspersing the two. Both explicitly addressed the question of how to be correctly Christian; both were concerned with the orthodoxy of people in his church audience and those who should have been there but were not; and both used places to identify correct Christianity, although in interestingly different ways.

JOHN CHRYSOSTOM AND THE THEATER OF ANTIOCH

The previous chapter demonstrated that already as a deacon John Chrysostom was engaged in the struggle to distinguish appropriate Christian practices from those of what he called "Greek superstition," on the one hand, and the worship of impotent *daimones* from the worship of the powerful Christian God, on the other. In 386–87 Chrysostom's arguments against the heteropraxis and heterodoxy of those he called Judaizers and Anomeans built on his polemic against temple practices such as those condemned years earlier in *De sancto Babyla*. A brief survey of his common accusations about the dangers posed by attending venues that he argued would corrupt Christians, such as theaters and sports arenas, demonstrates that they echo his earlier rhetoric against Daphne (e.g., *De s. Babyla* 68), and help to contextualize his polemic against synagogues and gatherings of the Anomeans.

Chrysostom's hostility toward the theater is familiar to ancient as well as modern readers, and Blake Leyerle has elegantly demonstrated not only the pervasiveness of this polemic against the theater, but also the complex role that rhetoric about the theater and spectacle played in Chrysostom's writings.[6] Chrysostom

---

6. Blake Leyerle, *Theatrical Shows and Ascetic Lives: John Chrysostom's Attack on Spiritual Marriage* (Berkeley: University of California Press, 2001).

had inherited a long tradition of understanding the theater to be a place of sexual immorality, and thus of the theater's condemnation by some in Roman society, and his rhetoric fits into a history of educated distaste for what was seen as a place that upended respectable social behaviors, particularly through public displays of sexual acts. According to Leyerle, "Sexual immorality seemed indeed the theater's special study, from which, according to Chrysostom, one could choose a whole curriculum: 'planning for unnatural lust, the study of adultery, practical training for fornication, schooling for wantonness, fostering of filthiness.'"[7] Texts from antiquity are filled with accusations that the theater displayed lewd sexual acts, and with shrill condemnations of the theater and those who attended it.[8] John Chrysostom continues this rhetorical tradition with great fervor, further driven by his own ascetic Christian sense of decorum and virtue.[9]

Chrysostom goes beyond just condemning the acts in the theater, however, by turning his vitriol against the theater structure itself and those who were present there, thus making the theater exemplify his use of spatial rhetoric to attempt to direct proper Christian behavior, including where in the city Christians should and should not go. On March 6, 387, Chrysostom reminds his audience, in the aftermath of the chaos of the riot a week before, "How many words did we release, exhorting many of those who were indifferent, and advising that they give up the theaters and the licentiousness there!" (*De stat.* 15.1/153).[10] Chrysostom, in fact, blames the disaster that befell the city through the riot and its aftermath in part on Antiochenes' unwillingness to heed his warnings: "And they did not cease, but always on this day they gather together at the unlawful spectacles of the dancers, and they set their diabolical assembly against the full measure of the church of God, and their cries from there, being carried by the greatest vehemence, held out against [our] psalmody here" (15.1/153). In Chrysostom's rhetoric the theater became a dangerous and terrible place. Certainly he seems to wish that fear for their physical and spiritual safety would prevent his listeners from attending.

7. Leyerle, *Theatrical Shows*, 43, quoting John Chrysostom, *Hom. in Acta Apost.* 42.4 (PG 60.301); compare a text from Chrysostom's time in Constantinople: *Contra ludos et theatra* 2 (PG 56.267).

8. Soler observes this regarding Libanius, Julian, Ammianus Marcellinus, and John Chrysostom: Emmanuel Soler, *Le sacré et le salut à Antioche au IVe siècle apr. J.-C.: Pratiques festives et comportements religieux dans le processus de christianisation de la cité* (Beirut: Institut français du Proche-Orient, 2006), esp. 29–32.

9. See Leyerle, *Theatrical Shows*, 67–68.

10. All translations from *De statuis* 15 are my own from the Greek text in PG 49.153–62, and I include the PG page number after the PG paragraph number, for ease of reference. I accept the dating conclusions of Frans van de Paverd, *St. John Chrysostom, The Homilies on the Statues: An Introduction*, Orientalia Christiania Analecta 239 (Rome: Pont. Institutum Studiorum Orientalium, 1991), 311–15, 363–64.

Leyerle summarizes one aspect of Chrysostom's substantial rhetoric against the theater by observing, "As a place of deception, the theater is the special province of the devil, who sponsored it."[11] The theater is also, in Chrysostom's rhetoric, "a kind of idolatry" such that those who attend "are forbidden by Chrysostom to receive communion."[12] Demonizing the theater and setting it in sharp contrast to the holy place of "God's church," Chrysostom not only urges Antiochenes to stop attending the theater, but also suggests that attendance there directly opposes the people and places of God. The following analysis will reveal that a similar rhetoric of fear and demonization played a significant and complex role in John Chrysostom's homilies against the Judaizers.

In April 387, Chrysostom reinforced the perception that physical attendance at particular places threatened a congregant's Christian identity. In *Ad finem ieiunii* Chrysostom tells his audience that if they have properly instructed their child in how to live a Christian life, that child "will not be able to go up to a theater, or to enter into a tavern, or to waste time with dice," and that if the child "should ever appear" in those places, he or she would quickly retreat from shame (*Ad finem ieiunii/De stat.* 20.8/210).[13] This demonization of the theater, defining it as morally dangerous as well as suggesting that attendance there constituted an act of aggression against the Christian God, parallels some of the accusations that Chrysostom also leveled against other places in the city that he wanted to prevent Christians from attending, such as Jewish synagogues and gatherings of Anomean Christians.

The theater, while one of the worst offenders of promoting unvirtuous behavior in Chrysostom's eyes, was not alone, and he often associated it with other places of public spectacle of which he disapproved, such as athletic competitions, horse races, public baths, and local taverns. Leyerle observes that Chrysostom "forbade attendance at the theater in the same straightforward way that he condemned visiting fortune-tellers or taverns, gaming with dice, and swearing."[14] In his homily from March 6, 387, Chrysostom levels the accusation that "the past-time in the theaters produces *porneia*, intemperance, and all licentiousness; and the spectacle of horse-racing also brings about fights, abuses, blows, wantonness, and continuing enmities; and the zeal for dice-playing often creates blasphemies, damages, anger, abuses, and myriad other things more fearful than these" (*De stat.* 15.4/159).

11. Leyerle, *Theatrical Shows*, 44.

12. Leyerle, *Theatrical Shows*, 45. See John Chrysostom, *Hom. in Jo.* 1.4 (PG 59.29).

13. All translations from *Ad finem ieiunii/De stat.* 20 are my own from the Greek text in PG 49.197–212, and I include the PG page number after the PG paragraph number, for ease of reference. Although this text is often referred to as *De stat.* 20, van de Paverd notes that this homily is more clearly identified as *Ad finem ieiunii* (van de Paverd, *Chrysostom*, 12). I follow van de Paverd's dating of these texts (*Chrysostom*, 364).

14. Leyerle, *Theatrical Shows*, 43; see *Ad finem ieiunii/De stat.* 20.8 (PG 49.210), 15.4 (PG 49.159); *Ad Theod. laps.* 1.5 (PG 47.282–83); *Hom. in Mt.* 37.7 (PG 57.428).

While this hostility is associated with Chrysostom's overall disapproval of material luxury and ostentation and his ascetic emphasis on the care of the soul rather than the body, he frequently spoke of the ways in which martyrs and other Christian saints curbed inappropriate behavior such as lewdness and drunkenness that he associated with these places he had forbidden and with inappropriate festival celebrations.[15] Although it is clear that Romans did not associate all of these places overtly with particularly religious practice, it is just as clear that Christian leaders like John Chrysostom were attempting to do exactly that. "Indeed," Leyerle concludes, Chrysostom "considers it more sinful to go to the theater than to a pagan temple, precisely because of the former's deceptiveness: at the theater one can pretend that one is not worshipping demons," an argument he will also make for places associated with Judaism.[16] As Isabella Sandwell's book demonstrates, religious identity was becoming a clear and primary category in fourth-century Antioch, and in Chrysostom's view religious orthodoxy required particular behaviors that were mapped onto the city's landscape.[17]

John Chrysostom's rhetoric associated certain urban values and behaviors, such as luxury and ostentation, with worship of the gods, contrasted these values with his version of Christian values, and advocated for new "Christian" behavior that did not include attendance at the theater, pub, and other such places. These examples demonstrate Chrysostom's active use of rhetoric to reshape how those in his audience viewed the places of the city of Antioch. Understanding attendance at particular places to reflect something significant about a person's identity, Chrysostom argued that being correctly Christian required that one attend certain places, such as his church, and abstain from others, some with more overtly religious associations than others. Through such rhetoric Chrysostom remapped the city in an effort to reshape how his audience viewed and interacted with its places.

AGAINST THE JUDAIZERS: JEWISH PLACES AND CHRISTIAN IDENTITY

Given the rich networks and conflicts of fourth-century Antioch, there is no question that when Bishop Flavian ordained John Chrysostom as a presbyter, Chrysostom faced an audience colored by the conflicting religious and political messages of the recent past.[18] Chrysostom's rhetoric in his *Adversus Iudaeos* homilies sug-

---

15. This is the topic of Soler's book *Le sacré et le salut.*

16. Leyerle, *Theatrical Shows,* 45; see John Chrysostom, *Hom. in Jo.* 32.3 (PG 59.188).

17. This is the thesis behind Isabella Sandwell's book, *Religious Identity in Late Antiquity: Greeks, Jews, and Christians in Antioch* (New York: Cambridge University Press, 2007).

18. A version of this section was published as Christine Shepardson, "Controlling Contested Places: John Chrysostom's *Adversus Iudaeos* Homilies and the Spatial Politics of Religious Controversy," *JECS* 15.4 (2007): 483–516.

gests that some in his congregation not only frequented the theater, which he considered to be profane, but also attended Jewish festival celebrations, respected the power of the local synagogues, and associated with "heretical" Anomean Christians. In this highly charged environment, it was the immediate context of the autumn Jewish festivals and fasts associated with Rosh Hashanah, Yom Kippur, and Sukkot that spurred Chrysostom to begin his series of homilies against Judaizing.[19] While the physical map of Antioch is a significant subject in these texts, it is not the physical proximity of Jewish and Christian places that most troubles Chrysostom. Rather, Chrysostom's equal concern about locations as nearby as the old city of Antioch and as distant as the suburb of Daphne suggests that the matter of Jewish and Christian proximity is not to be measured in physical distance, but reflects the threat of a conceptual proximity. That is, it reflects Chrysostom's concern that a perceived overlap of Jewish and Christian places and behaviors could imply an unacceptable blurring of community identities. Chrysostom laments to his church listeners: "You enter into [the Jews'] impure places, set foot into their unclean front doors, and share in the tables of demons!" (*Adv. Iud.* 1.7).[20] His concern to redefine certain Antiochene places to the benefit of his Christianity is explicit in his homilies against the Judaizers, yet most scholars have not recognized the full significance of his spatial rhetoric.[21]

Wendy Mayer persuasively demonstrates that Chrysostom did not have a static audience,[22] and at least two questions regarding Chrysostom's audiences relate

19. Soler usefully describes and contextualizes these festivities within the larger scene of Antiochene festivals (*Le sacré et le salut,* esp. 95–135). Soler's discussion of John Chrysostom's anti-Jewish and anti-Judaizing rhetoric, however, is less persuasive, relying on an outdated notion that such rhetoric most likely responds to the visible local power of Judaism (107–11). Dayna Kalleres has demonstrated the significant ways in which Chrysostom relates illness and martyrdom in Discourse 8 in this series: Kalleres, "Imagining Martyrdom during Theodosian Peace: John Chrysostom and the Problem of Judaizers," in *Contextualising Early Christian Martyrdom,* ed. Jakob Engberg, Uffe Holmsgaard Eriksen, and Anders Klostergaard Petersen (New York: Peter Lang, 2011), 257–75.

20. In this chapter, I consistently and exclusively translate the Greek word τόπος as "place."

21. Two important exceptions to this are Wendy Mayer and Isabella Sandwell. See, for example, Wendy Mayer and Pauline Allen, introduction to *John Chrysostom,* ed. Wendy Mayer and Pauline Allen (New York: Routledge, 2000), 3–52; Isabella Sandwell, "Christian Self-Definition in the Fourth Century AD: John Chrysostom on Christianity, Imperial Rule, and the City," in *Culture and Society in Later Roman Antioch,* ed. Isabella Sandwell and Janet Huskinson (Oxford: Oxbow Books, 2004), 35–58; Sandwell, *Religious Identity,* e.g., 132–43.

22. Wendy Mayer has adeptly highlighted both the significance of questioning the makeup of John Chrysostom's audiences and the challenges involved in doing so (Mayer, "John Chrysostom and His Audiences: Distinguishing Different Congregations at Antioch and Constantinople," *Studia Patristica* 31 [1997], 70–75; Mayer, "John Chrysostom: Extraordinary Preacher, Ordinary Audience," in *Preacher and Audience: Studies in Early Christian and Byzantine Homiletics,* ed. Pauline Allen and Mary Cunningham [Leiden: Brill, 1998], 105–37; Mayer, "Female Participation and the Late Fourth-Century Preacher's Audience," *Augustinianum* 39 [1999]: 139–47; Mayer, "Who Came to Hear John Chrysostom

directly to this current investigation—namely, where in Antioch John Chrysostom preached his homilies, and who made up his audience at each location. J. N. D. Kelly argues that even though after John's ordination to the priesthood in 386 he appears to have been assigned to the Palaia, or Old Church, in practice he regularly preached in the Great Church that was under Bishop Flavian's charge.[23] Chrysostom's reference to returning to the audience of the Old Church after an absence suggests that he preached in different churches, and that the different congregations did not follow the preacher around the city, but rather stayed in their churches (*Hom. in Gal. 2:11* 1).[24] Together these observations complicate our ability to speak of Chrysostom's "audience," or to presume that repetition in Chrysostom's homilies necessarily multiplied the effect of his rhetoric, since any given congregant heard only some of his sermons. Nonetheless, Chrysostom's frequent calls for his audience to share his words with those who are not present (e.g., *Adv. Iud.* 1.8; 2.3; 8.5; 8.9), and the regularity with which he reiterates many of his themes, including his use of spatial rhetoric, suggest that it is still plausible that his sermons noticeably participated in a larger ongoing conversation regarding identity and the naming of Antiochene places. By attempting to identify and sharply define "Jewish" and "Christian" places, these homilies aggressively engaged his listeners in the ongoing competition to control fourth-century Antioch, its places, and the religious orthodoxy and orthopraxy of its citizens.[25]

Preach? Recovering a Late Fourth-Century Preacher's Audience," *Ephemerides Theologicae Lovanienses* 76.1 [2000]: 73–87). Of course, this is also part of a larger conversation not specific to Chrysostom. See, for example, Philip Rousseau, "The Preacher's Audience: A More Optimistic View," in *Ancient History in a Modern University,* vol. 2, ed. T. Hillard, R. A. Kearsley, C. E. V. Nixon, and A. Nobbs (Grand Rapids, MI: William B. Eerdmans, 1998), 391–400; Mary Cunningham and Pauline Allen, eds., *Preacher and Audience: Studies in Early Christian and Byzantine Homiletics* (Leiden: Brill, 1998).

23. J. N. D. Kelly, *Golden Mouth: The Story of John Chrysostom—Ascetic, Preacher, Bishop* (London: Duckworth, 1995), 57; Mayer, "Audiences," 72; Mayer, "Who Came?," 78–79.

24. Compare Mayer, "Audiences," 72–73. On the variety of types of people attending these sermons, as well as the consistency with which any individual might have attended, see the important work of Mayer: "Audiences"; "Extraordinary Preacher"; "Female Participation"; "Who Came?".

25. The complexities of modern vocabulary and of Chrysostom's contexts have caused the very title of these eight homilies to be the subject of considerable scholarly debate. See, for example, Marcel Simon, "La polémique anti-juive de S. Jean Chrysostome et le mouvement judaisant d'Antioche" in *Annuaire de l'Institut de Philologie et d'Histoire Orientales et Slaves* (Brussels, 1936), 4:403–21; A. M. Ritter, "Erwägungen zum Antisemitismus in der Alten Kirche: Acht Reden über die Juden," in *Bleibendes im Wandel der Kirchengeschichte,* ed. B. Moeller and G. Ruhbach (Tübingen: J. C. B. Mohr/Paul Siebeck, 1973), 71–91; Fred A. Grissom, "Chrysostom and the Jews: Studies in Jewish-Christian Relations in Fourth-Century Antioch" (PhD diss., Southern Baptist Theological Seminary, 1978); Robert Wilken, *John Chrysostom and the Jews: Rhetoric and Reality in the Late 4th Century* (Berkeley: University of California Press, 1983); Klaas Smelik, "John Chrysostom's Homilies against the Jews: Some Comments," *Nederlands Theologisch Tijdschrift* 39 (1985): 194–200; A. M. Ritter, "John Chrysostom and the Jews: A Reconsideration," *Ancient Christianity in the Caucasus* (1998): 141–54, 231–32; Pieter W. van der

Imagined Geography, Imagined Community:
Defining and Patrolling Community Boundaries

Chrysostom's rhetoric suggests that his listeners behaved in ways that conflicted with his understanding of the boundaries of Christian orthodoxy by their attendance at places associated with heretics or Jews. Throughout his *Adversus Iudaeos* homilies, Chrysostom chastises those who "run to the synagogue" and those who "celebrate" and "fast with the Jews,"[26] constructing an image of some of his congregants who, in the vocabulary of geographer Yi-Fu Tuan, expressed a strong affinity, or *topophilia,* for "Jewish" places.[27] For Chrysostom, such behavior threatened his definition of Christianity, and his homilies rhetorically patrolled the boundaries of his ideal community. He was adamant that there were "Christians" who would "run" to local synagogues, "respect" them, and sometimes even "drag" other Christians there against their will (*Adv. Iud.* 6.7; 1.3).[28] For Chrysostom, identity was inextricably tied to where a person went, so attendance at Jewish places unacceptably compromised the orthodoxy of his congregation, threatening the individuals who attended the synagogue, and consequently the purity and integrity of the church space and all those who entered it (2.3; 7.6). Chrysostom described what he saw as the problematic blurring of community boundaries, thereby compromising orthodox identity, and tried to enlist his congregants in patrolling vigilantly the behaviors that would preserve his ideal and orthodox "imagined community" in which Christian martyr shrines and churches were prominent features, and from which synagogues were absent altogether.[29]

Horst, "Jews and Christians in Antioch at the End of the Fourth Century," in *Christian-Jewish Relations through the Centuries,* ed. Stanley E. Porter and Brook W. R. Pearson (Sheffield: Sheffield Academic Press, 2000), 228–38; Charlotte Fonrobert, "Jewish Christians, Judaizers, and Christian Anti-Judaism," in *Late Ancient Christianity,* ed. Virginia Burrus (Minneapolis: Fortress Press, 2005), 234–54. Although these texts were earlier identified as Chrysostom's "Homilies against the Jews," scholars such as Harkins and Wilken have argued persuasively that it was not Jews themselves, but rather Judaizing Christians who were the primary subject of these texts.

26. John Chrysostom, *Adv. Iud.* 6.7 (cf. 1.5; 4.3; 4.7; 6.6; 8.6); 4.4; and 1.4 (cf. 8.4). See also the lengthy discussion against joining Jewish fasts and festivals in Pradels, Brändle, Heimgartner, "Das bisher vermisste Textstück," 30–48.

27. Yi-Fu Tuan, *Topophilia: A Study of Environmental Perception, Attitudes, and Values* (Englewood Cliffs, NJ: Prentice-Hall, 1974). Although Libanius (*Or.* 11) uses the Greek word φιλοχωρία to refer to a similar concept, I here adopt Tuan's vocabulary for the purpose of engaging with his modern methodological discussions.

28. While recognizing the complex semiotic challenges involved, I label Chrysostom's audience "Christian" here to reflect Chrysostom's description of his audience.

29. See Gill Valentine, "Imagined Geographies: Geographical Knowledges of Self and Other in Everyday Life," in *Human Geography Today,* ed. Doreen Massey, John Allen, and Philip Sarre (Malden, MA: Polity Press, 1999), 47–48.

Paramount among Chrysostom's concerns in the first of these homilies is his appeal to his congregants neither to join in the imminent celebrations of Jewish festivals, nor to allow anyone else to attend them. Chrysostom describes what he understood to be an unacceptable permeability in his community's boundaries: "Many of those within our ranks claim to think as we do. Yet some will approach the spectacle of the [Jews'] festivals, and others will even join [the Jews] in celebrating and will share in their fasts" (*Adv. Iud.* 1.1).[30] This and other similar passages in these homilies demonstrate that there were people in Chrysostom's congregation whom he considered Christian but who strayed outside the boundaries of Christianity, as he understood it, by participating in local Jewish celebrations. Chrysostom vehemently denounces such boundary-crossing behavior, demanding, "What are you running to see in the synagogue of the Jews who fight against God?" (4.7; cf. 6.6, 6.7; 8.8).[31] Repeatedly he tries to prevent his audience, crying, "Do not run to the synagogue!" (6.7). Chrysostom despairs over what he defined as these Christians' desire to frequent this "Jewish" place, and he promotes instead behavior that would redefine the landscape as he envisioned it.

Chrysostom challenges his audience to monitor their own behavior vigilantly, as well as that of their neighbors. He complains not only that some "Christians" ran to the synagogue, but he also includes an anecdote about a man who considered himself Christian physically forcing a Christian woman into the synagogue so that the power of the place would witness to and protect the oath that they were preparing to swear. Chrysostom describes this scene in the first of these homilies:

> Three days ago—believe me, I am not lying—I saw a certain free woman of good bearing, modest, and faithful, being forced by a certain brutal and unfeeling man who appeared to be a Christian (for I would not call a person who would dare to do such a thing a pure Christian) to enter the [place] of the Hebrews and to offer there an oath about some matters being disputed with him. The woman, coming up, asked for help and demanded that I prevent this lawless act of violence—for it was not allowed to her, who had shared in the divine mysteries, to enter that place. (*Adv. Iud.* 1.3)

Even if Chrysostom created this story to teach a lesson, which Charlotte Fonrobert raises as a possibility, it still emphasizes the respect in which the synagogue was held by some of Chrysostom's congregants, as he relates that the man justified his behavior by explaining, "Many people had told him that oaths sworn there

---

30. Compare also Chrysostom's discussion about the invalidity of Jewish fasts and festivals, and his criticism of those churchgoers who participate in them; see Pradels, Brändle, and Heimgartner, "Das bisher vermisste Textstück," 30–48.

31. Daniel Boyarin discusses examples of fourth-century Christian leaders constructing such boundaries for their audience: Boyarin, *Border Lines: The Partition of Judaeo-Christianity* (Philadelphia: University of Pennsylvania Press, 2004).

were more to be feared" (*Adv. Iud.* 1.3).[32] Chrysostom's rhetoric portrays the synagogue as a powerful place; his commentary on this incident demonstrates some of the means by which he fought to dissuade his audience of such claims, and thus to diminish the attraction of places that he argues compromised the orthodoxy of Antioch's Christians. He chastises listeners who, like the antagonist in the story, might be tempted to attend a synagogue, and he encourages Christians to intervene in what he saw as the inappropriate, and even dangerous, behavior of those around them.[33] Such an obligation strove to strengthen cohesion in an imagined community and attempted to create community pressure to enforce new limits of orthodoxy and orthopraxy.

In the fourth and sixth of these homilies, Chrysostom issues even more insistent pleas for his congregants to patrol the behavior of not only themselves but also of those around them in order to preserve ideal community boundaries. In contrast to the dangers of Jewish synagogues, in these homilies Chrysostom emphasizes the ideal safety of orthodox Christians' homes, which emerged as safe havens where Christians could remain without fear of endangerment. He instructs his congregants to keep anyone under their control at home rather than letting them wander to dangerous places such as the theater or the synagogue (*Adv. Iud.* 4.7).[34] Chrysostom even critically asks the men in his audience about women churchgoers whom he describes attending the synagogue: "Does she know any other site at all other than the church and the way of life here?"[35] Yet, it is not only those who are legally under a zealous Christian's control whom Chrysostom targets for such behavioral correction. The homes of orthodox Christians likewise appear in these homilies as places where those who went astray through "Jewish" fasting could be healed by being persuaded to join a meal.[36] Chrysostom's methods of persuasion in this regard are again anything but gentle: "Dragging our [unwilling brothers and sisters] into our very own homes, let us break the fast, and let us share the table with them today in order that, having ended the fast before our eyes, . . . they may become

---

32. Fonrobert, "Jewish Christians," 238. As Fonrobert notes, however, "Even if the incident is a rhetorical invention, we can safely assume that Chrysostom expected his cautionary anecdote to be an effective means of persuasion" (239).

33. Dayna Kalleres argues that this latter is, in fact, Chrysostom's primary motivation in telling this story: see chapter 3 in Kalleres, *City of Demons: Violence, Ritual, and Christian Power in Late Antiquity* (Berkeley: University of California Press, forthcoming).

34. Compare his similar commands regarding female virgins in John Chrysostom, *De sacerdotio* 314–22.

35. John Chrysostom, *Adv. Iud.* 2 (Pradels, Brändle, Heimgartner 129ra; Pradels, Brändle, and Heimgartner, "Das bisher vermisste Textstück," 46–48). In this chapter I translate the Greek word χωρίον consistently and exclusively as "site."

36. Meals commonly serve to mark the boundaries of community. See Mary Douglas, *Purity and Danger: An Analysis of the Concepts of Pollution and Taboo* (New York: Routledge, 1966); Valentine, "Imagined Geographies," 47–61.

patrons of eternal good fortunes to themselves and to us" (6.7). Both churches and Christians' homes provided safe alternatives to the city's attractive but perilous places. Understanding individual and community identity to be linked inextricably with matters of place, Chrysostom enlists his congregants to monitor carefully their own behavior as well as the behavior of other Antiochene "Christians" in the hope that controlling where Antioch's Christian citizens went would help enforce the boundaries that he wished for his community. Such a place-specific vision for uni-fying his ideal community laid an imaginative geography onto Antioch's cityscape, redefining its places through a lens of Christian orthodoxy.

A Geography of Difference: Identifying Purity and Contagion

Geographers describe the naming, identification, and valuation of a particular location as changing undifferentiated "space" into a distinct "place." Chrysostom's challenge, though, was often to rename and revalue places that already had mean-ing locally, hoping to reduce his congregants' attraction to the synagogue, for example, by replacing positive with negative connotations, much as he worked to impose a new perception of the burned ruins of Apollo's temple at Daphne. Issues of purity and contagion played a significant role in these homilies' portrayal of church and synagogue, as Chrysostom warned his audience to preserve the purity of themselves and their church.[37] By contrasting the church and the synagogue so insistently, Chrysostom constructed a "geography of difference" that he hoped would influence his audience's behavior, sharply differentiating local places as either sacred and pure or else defiling and impure.[38] Chrysostom deployed this geography of difference strategically in efforts to influence his community to see Antioch's urban landscape as filled with potential dangers. By identifying for his congregants pure and impure places, he appealed to them to avoid the contagion of synagogues and other defiling places, and thus to preserve the purity of their own orthodoxy and of the church places that they entered. Positioning himself with the authority to define the true nature of Antioch's value-laden places, Chrys-ostom used a vocabulary of purity and contagion to circumscribe "orthodox" behavior.

In the 386 and 387 homilies in this series, Chrysostom refers explicitly to the respect that some Christians had for the synagogue, and attributes their respect to the allegedly purifying presence in the synagogue of texts that belonged to

---

37. Regarding the significance of purity in ritual distinctions and in constructing communi-ty boundaries, see the seminal work by Douglas, *Purity and Danger;* and the more recent study by Michael Penn: *Kissing Christians: Ritual and Community in the Late Ancient Church* (Philadelphia: University of Pennsylvania Press, 2005).

38. David Sibley, "Creating Geographies of Difference," in Massey, Allen, and Sarre, *Human Geog-raphy Today,* 126.

both Jewish and Christian scripture, that is, the Christian Old Testament.[39] According to Chrysostom, "Since there are some who think that the synagogue is a holy place, it is necessary to say a few words to them" (*Adv. Iud.* 1.5). In Discourse 1 the justification that Chrysostom places in the mouths of those whose behavior he opposes is that they think the synagogue is a holy place because "the Law is stored in it, and the books of the prophets" (1.5).[40] The rhetoric of Chrysostom's response suggests his frustration at this reasoning: "Will anywhere these books are be a holy place? Not at all!" (1.5). Chrysostom's similar reply in Discourse 6 further rejects the argument that sacred books made the place that contained them holy: "Do not say this to me, that the Law and the books of the prophets are there. These do not make it a holy place" (6.6). Such an explicit conversation about whether sacred texts conferred their sacrality on the physical space that contained them highlights the significance of the construction and politicization of Antioch's landscape in these years.[41] By polarizing the possible descriptions of places as either holy or unholy, Chrysostom laid the foundation for a binary geography of difference. By challenging the positive valuation of the synagogue that he attributed to some in his audience, he continued the process of redefining Antioch's urban topography.

Chrysostom furthered these arguments in two separate homilies, presenting a reasoned, scripturally based challenge to claims about the scripture's purifying character in the synagogue (*Adv. Iud.* 1.5; 6.6). In Discourse 1, Chrysostom argues that containing holy texts certainly did not make the synagogue, or any other dangerous place, holy. He compares the holy texts to an honorable man in order to

39. See Fonrobert, "Jewish Christians," 236–43, which likewise notes the significance of this rhetoric in attempting to construct clear boundaries that did not yet exist in Antioch; and Soler, *Le sacré et le salut,* 106–7.

40. Claudia Rapp has demonstrated some of the multiple ways in which scripture was connected with holiness in the imaginations of early Christians, including some examples that echo the thought process Chrysostom attributes to some in his audience in this passage: Rapp, "Holy Texts, Holy Men, and Holy Scribes: Aspects of Scriptural Holiness in Late Antiquity," in *The Early Christian Book,* ed. William Klingshirn and Linda Safran (Washington, DC: Catholic University of America Press, 2007), 194–222. Derek Krueger has traced some of the ways in which not only the material objects of scripture, but also Christian authors themselves, from evangelists to hagiographers, became associated with sanctity: Derek Krueger, *Writing and Holiness: The Practice of Authorship in the Early Christian East* (Philadelphia: University of Pennsylvania Press, 2004); see also Rapp, "Safe-Conducts to Heaven: Holy Men, Mediation and the Role of Writing," in *Transformations of Late Antiquity: Essays for Peter Brown,* ed. Philip Rousseau and Manolis Papoutsakis (Burlington, VT: Ashgate, 2009), 187–203.

41. While this vocabulary necessarily approaches the weighted language of "sacred space" made famous by Mircea Eliade (*The Sacred and the Profane: The Nature of Religion,* trans. Willard Trask [New York: Harcourt Brace Jovanovich, 1959]), in this chapter I intend to refer primarily to local physical places associated with a particular religious tradition. Certainly, though, the concept that once a place has been designated sacred, over time its sacrality can transfer from one religious group to another remains relevant.

intensify his argument, which aggressively conflates a Jewish synagogue with an irreverent tavern and a dangerous den of thieves:

> Tell me this. If you were to see a certain respectable man, illustrious and notable, being dragged off into a tavern or den of thieves, then being outraged there, and beaten, and subjected to the utmost violence, would you admire that tavern or cavern because that admirable and great man was outraged while inside it? I don't think so! Rather, on account of this above all you would have hated and turned away from it. Decide this also about the synagogue. For they brought the [books] of Moses and the prophets with them into the synagogue, not to honor them but to outrage and dishonor them. (*Adv. Iud.* 1.5)

By anthropomorphizing the texts into the character of a respected man, Chrysostom tries to persuade his audience with an example he hopes will resonate more clearly—namely, that a dangerous place is not transformed and does not deserve respect simply because a holy man (or text) enters it. The violence that Chrysostom here attributes to the Jews, comparing them to robbers who assault an innocent man, differentiates clearly between the sanctity of the texts and the dishonorable and dangerous places in which they might be found. Such rhetoric sharply distances the synagogue from the purity of scripture, attempting to dissuade the audience from misguidedly approaching or respecting the synagogue because of a respect for the scriptures.

Three additional stories further support Chrysostom's claim that placing something holy in a profane place does not change the quality of either the item or the place. Two of these stories recount the relocation of something sacred to the Jews (first the scripture, then the ark of the covenant) to a temple dedicated to a powerless god (John Chrysostom, *Adv. Iud.* 1.6; 6.7). In both cases, Chrysostom judges with vigor against the resulting sacrality of the Greek temple. Regarding the sacred scripture relocated there, he cries, "But will the temple of Serapis be holy because of the [holy] books? Heaven forbid! Although these [books] have their own holiness, they do not share a part of it with the place, because of the pollution of those who come there" (1.6). Likewise, Chrysostom explains regarding the ark that it is "so far from making that [temple] a holy place that it even fought against it" (6.7). In these two stories, Chrysostom asks Christians who recognize sacrality in a synagogue to ponder the question of whether the Jewish items that Christians also honor could transform the "profane" places in which they might be stored. Chrysostom's rhetoric here implies that those in his congregation who found scriptural precedent and social support for honoring Jewish places would find no such testimony about temples. By rewriting the confrontation to question the holiness of these temples, Chrysostom aims to persuade his audience that the same applies to the synagogue—that is, it is not made holy by housing sacred texts. The language of pollution that Chrysostom uses heightens the contrast with his descriptions of Christian purity.

In addition to personifying the scriptural texts to demonstrate more vividly the abuse that Chrysostom claims they suffered in the synagogue, and applying his scorn equally to both synagogues and temples, Chrysostom compares the synagogue to the mouths of demons in order to make clear to his audience the synagogue's perpetually unholy state:

> Do not say this to me, that the Law and the books of the prophets are [in the synagogue]. These do not make it a holy place. . . . Tell me then, what about this: the devil spoke from scripture; then did this not make his mouth holy? It is not possible to say so, but he kept on being the devil. What about the demons? Because they spoke out and said, "These men are servants of the highest God, and they proclaim to you a way of salvation," on account of this do we count them among the apostles? By no means! But likewise, we keep turning away from them and hating them. If spoken words do not sanctify that [mouth] that carries them forth, how do the books sanctify where they lie? But how could this be right? (*Adv. Iud.* 6.6)

As with the examples of temples, this story displaces Chrysostom's contemporary conflict with those visiting synagogues by introducing a new comparison that he hopes would persuade his audience—namely, that the devil or demons could never become holy simply by speaking holy words. Chrysostom's conclusion to each of these stories is the same: local temples, demons' mouths, and the Jewish synagogue did not become holy simply by containing sacred scripture. Chrysostom chastises his audience: "Let no one venerate the synagogue because of the books, but rather on account of these let him hate it and turn away, because they outrage the holy ones, because they do not believe their words, because they accuse them of the ultimate impiety" (*Adv. Iud.* 1.5). Such clear efforts to revalue the synagogue as dangerous and polluted instead of as a holy place contributed to Chrysostom's struggle to make his audience see an impermeable distinction between Christian and Jewish places in the city.

This conversation of course recalls the discussion in the previous chapter regarding the reshaping of places through their revaluation and redefinition for a new audience. It is interesting to note that John Chrysostom expresses different attitudes regarding scripture in a synagogue and regarding martyrs' relics in a temple precinct. The previous chapter demonstrated the ways in which Chrysostom argued that martyrs' relics could purify a place, such as at the Apollo temple at Daphne, and the people who came into their presence. It seems that the difference may not be that relics are more powerful than the physical texts of scripture, but that Chrysostom wanted to encourage his audience's presence at martyrs' shrines but not at the synagogues where some books that Jews and Christians shared were housed. This apparent contradiction highlights the highly rhetorical and ideological nature of Chrysostom's constructions regarding power and places. Chrysostom acknowledged that his revaluation of powerful places would surprise those who had believed that the synagogue was a place to be honored (*Adv. Iud.* 1.2). None-theless, this shift in the city's topographical categories insistently provided his audience with both the identities of particular holy and unholy places in the local landscape, and with strong motivation to avoid the dangerous unholy places.[42]

Identifying the danger and pollution of "Jewish" places went hand in hand for Chrysostom with the fear of contagion—for individual Christians, for his ideal reli-gious orthodoxy, and for church buildings themselves. Because Chrysostom claimed that God could dwell in church buildings (*Adv. Iud.* 1.4), he expressed a clear con-cern to maintain the purity of the church, both the congregation and the building. He reminded his congregation of the safety that the church provided (4.1),[43] and attempted to prevent its contamination. He instructs his audience: "If it is a catechu-men who is sick with such a [Judaizing] disease, let him be kept from the front doors. But if [he is] a believer and already initiated, let him be expelled from the holy table" (2.3).[44] In this homily Chrysostom institutes a ritual distinction based on purity/pollution. By refusing to let catechumens who attended a synagogue into the church building, and by forbidding baptized Christians who joined Jewish gather-ings from taking the Eucharist, Chrysostom tried to prevent these "ill" congregants who attended "Jewish" places from contaminating the church building and its other members. In his exhortations he expresses the hope that no one "will dare to flee to [the Jews], but rather the body of the church will be pure" (7.6). In this wish he makes explicit his concern for the purity of the church space, the antithesis of the synagogue in his constructed revaluation of Antiochene landmarks. Chrysostom worked toward his goals, the well-being of his congregants, and the unity and purity of his church,[45] by constructing a "geography of difference," to use geographer David Sibley's phrase, to distinguish which places were holy and which were not.

Topophobia: *Redefining the Synagogue*

The geography of difference that John Chrysostom constructed through his lan-guage of contagion and purity provided a framework for his more elaborate deni-gration of Jewish synagogues. Using the antithesis of Yi-Fu Tuan's concept of *topophilia,* or a particular affinity for a location, I suggest the term *topophobia* to describe a fear of certain places. Chrysostom's anti-Jewish and anti-Judaizing rhet-

42. Compare also Chrysostom's threat that those who run to hear the trumpets of the Jewish fes-tivals will join "with the murderers, with the sorcerers, with the witless and mad Jews" (*Adv. Iud.* 2; Pradels, Brändle, Heimgartner 128rb; in Pradels, Brändle, and Heimgartner, "Das bisher vermisste Textstück," 46). On mapping, see chapter 5 below.

43. Although Discourse 3 is not part of this series of sermons, it was given in the time between Discourse 1 and the rest, and contains some similar rhetoric. See, for example, *Adv. Iud.* 3.1–2.

44. For understanding his view on why such people might be excluded from the Eucharist, see John Chrysostom, *De sacerdotio* 177–81, 519–22.

45. See, for example, John Chrysostom, *Adv. Iud.* 4.1–2; 7.6. Compare also *Adv. Iud.* 3.1 from Janu-ary 387.

oric not only criticized contemporary Christian veneration of Jewish places, but specifically sought to instill in the members of his congregation a deep loathing and fear of the synagogue.[46] With so much at stake politically and religiously in the control of Antiochene places, Chrysostom recognized the significance of controlling the definition and valuation of physical places for gaining authority in the city, and he left nothing to chance.[47] Using reason and insult, and warning of great danger—spiritual and physical—he cultivated a topophobia among his listeners in an attempt to prevent the members of his church from entering the synagogue.

Chrysostom's displeasure at the positive, respected reputation of the synagogues of Antioch and Daphne pervades his first homily in this series. In addition to housing the scripture, the synagogue appears to have gained its positive reputation among some Christians from the respect in which they held the Jews, their ancient traditions, and their powerful God. According to Chrysostom, "Many, I know, respect the Jews and think that their present way of life is a revered one" (*Adv. Iud.* 1.3; cf. 1.5). As a result, he criticizes those who "still hold these [synagogues] to be holy places" (1.3). Further challenging this positive representation, Chrysostom demands to know how any Christian could respect such "disgraceful" places (1.3; cf. 1.4).

Foremost among Chrysostom's efforts to redefine the synagogue was his description of it as among the least respected places in the city. In these homilies Chrysostom repeatedly associates the synagogue with the theater, carrying the negative assertions that he made about the latter into his descriptions of the former: "But these [Jews] are gathering choruses of effeminates and a great rubbish heap of female prostitutes; they drag the whole theater and the actors into the synagogue. For there is no difference between the theater and the synagogue" (*Adv. Iud.* 1.2). Chrysostom acknowledges, "I know that some condemn the boldness of my words because I said there is no difference between the theater and the synagogue; but I condemn their boldness if they think that it is not so" (1.2). Such disagreement, though, only made Chrysostom more adamant, and in the following year he repeats his criticism with another comparison that argues that the synagogue was even

46. The virulence of his anti-Jewish polemic in these homilies is well recognized. See, for example, G. Richter, "Über die älteste Auseinandersetzung der syrischen Christen mit den Juden," *ZNW* 35 (1936): 101–14; Grissom, "Chrysostom"; Wayne Meeks and Robert Wilken, *Jews and Christians in Antioch in the First Four Centuries of the Common Era* (Missoula, MT: Scholars Press, 1978); Wilken, *Chrysostom;* van der Horst, "Jews and Christians in Antioch," 228–38; Christine Shepardson, *Anti-Judaism and Christian Orthodoxy: Ephrem's Hymns in Fourth-Century Syria* (Washington, DC: Catholic University of America Press, 2008), 64–65.

47. In these same sermons Chrysostom also emphasized the priority of place over time in relation to the celebration of the Jewish Passover (*Adv. Iud.* 4.4; cf. 3.3–4). While the topic is different, such arguments further illustrate the significance that he associated with place. Chrysostom is not unique in making this argument regarding the Passover celebration. See the discussion of Chrysostom, Aphrahat, and Ephrem in Christine Shepardson, "Paschal Politics: Deploying the Temple's Destruction against Fourth-Century Judaizers," *Vigiliae Christianae* 62.3 (2008): 233–60.

worse than the theater: "This [going to the synagogue] is a greater transgression than [going to the theater]. What happens there [in the theater] is sin, but here [in the synagogue] is ungodliness" (4.7). Since he recognized that some Christians had a great respect for the synagogue, it is not surprising that they might have taken offense at his disapproving description. It is precisely such respect, however, that he challenges through these homilies.

When Chrysostom compared the synagogue to a theater, his rhetoric degraded the reputation of the synagogue and forced it far from the category of a holy place that Christians should respect and honor. He expressed clearly that his goal in describing the synagogue so negatively was that his congregants would stop attending these places, both the theater and the synagogue, that threatened their well-being. He instructs his listeners: "If you have a female servant or if you have a wife, detain them in the house with great vehemence. For if you do not trust [them] to go into the theater, it is much more necessary to do this concerning the synagogue. . . . But we say these things not so that you let them go into the theater, for that [theater] is wicked, but rather so that you will prevent this [synagogue attendance] much more" (*Adv. Iud.* 4.7). By revaluing the synagogue in such terms, Chrysostom tried to dissuade congregants from threatening their orthodoxy (and that of their families, and even their congregation) by frequenting places associated with Jewish ritual (2.3; 7.6; cf. 3.2).

Chrysostom strengthens his efforts to redefine the synagogue by combining the imagery of the synagogue as a theater with descriptions—often biblically supported—of it also as a den of robbers and thieves, and even the dwelling place of demons: "I said that the synagogue is no better than a theater and I bring forward a prophet as the witness. . . . 'You bore the countenance of a prostitute; you became shameless before all [cf. Jer 3.3].' Where a harlot has set herself up, that place is a brothel. But the synagogue is not only a brothel and a theater, but also is a den of thieves and a lodging for wild beasts" (*Adv. Iud.* 1.3).[48] Chrysostom supports this claim by juxtaposing it with further references to Jeremiah's scriptural prophecy, and concludes: "But when God abandons [someone], what hope of salvation remains? When God abandons [a place], that site becomes the dwelling of demons" (1.3). In this short passage, then, he associates the synagogue not only with the theater, but also with prostitutes, robbers, wild animals, and even demons. The scriptural references that he weaves into his critical descriptions give his claims an authenticity that supersedes even his own ecclesiastical authority. By quoting Jeremiah, scripture for both Jews and Christians, Chrysostom would have suggested to those in his audience who respected Judaism that even the scripture condemned the synagogue in these volatile terms.

Such harsh comparisons emerge throughout these homilies as Chrysostom continually challenges his audience to see the synagogue as an unattractive, hos-

---

48. As Harkins notes (*Discourses against Judaizing Christians,* 10), Chrysostom here quotes the Septuagint.

tile, and dangerous place. In addition to passing references to the synagogue as a "den of thieves" (*Adv. Iud.* 6.7), Jewish festival trumpets as "more unlawful than those in the theaters," Jewish fasts as "more disgraceful than any drinking and festival," and the booths of the Sukkot holiday as "no better than the inns of prostitutes and flute girls" (7.1),[49] Chrysostom repeatedly emphasizes that demons lived in the synagogue—stretching his rhetoric beyond pure insult to invoke an element of danger and fear. On occasion, Chrysostom uses New Testament passages to bolster the authenticity of his arguments, just as he sometimes uses Jeremiah and other biblical prophets. In his first homily in this series, he cites "Christ" as his authority when he undertakes "to show that even demons dwell there [in the synagogue]" (1.6). In 386 he warns his audience: "Indeed the site of the synagogue is less deserving of honor than any inn. For it is not merely the lodging for thieves and peddlers, but also for demons" (1.4). The following year he repeats these descriptions of the "grievous traditions and synagogues of the Jews, those in the city and those in the suburbs; they are the caves of thieves and the lodgings of demons" (5.12). References to robbers and demons and even "the evil power that dwells in the synagogue" move beyond simply insulting the synagogue by comparing it to a theater or brothel, and encourage a fear of the place, suggesting the potential danger that Christians faced if they entered the synagogue (8.8).

Chrysostom several times explicitly highlights his concern for Antiochenes' safety by referring to his congregation as a flock.[50] While the comparison recalls the Christian imagery of Jesus as the "lamb" of God, and the bishop (and Jesus) as a "good shepherd," here it particularly emphasizes the flock's helplessness and the persistent threat that it faces from marauding wild animals (as Chrysostom directly describes Jews) that would attack them. This rhetoric heightens the threat of danger with which he bombards his congregation, assuring them that they will be assaulted should they stray from their shepherd. He describes the Jews collectively as a lion—and elsewhere as wolves—who lie in wait to attack his Christian sheep. Sometimes he claims that the Jews are even more dangerous than these wild animals: "Since today the Jews, who are more difficult than any wolves, are about to surround my sheep, it is necessary to spar with them and fight so that none of us might be conquered by the beasts" (*Adv. Iud.* 4.1). In January 387 he tells his congregation:

> Do you walk outside the herd and not fear the lion that goes around outside? "For your enemy, like a lion, goes around," it is said, "howling and seeking whom he might seize" [cf. 1 Pt 5.8, Ps 21 (22).14]. See the wisdom of a shepherd. He does not let [the

---

49. Compare also 121vb of the Pradels, Brändle, and Heimgartner addition to Discourse 2, which describes the Jewish fast as "cursed," "impure," and "against the Law" (Pradels, Brändle, and Heimgartner, "Das bisher vermisste Textstück," 32).

50. Fonrobert ("Jewish Christians," 241) also notes Chrysostom's use of this imagery in this context.

lion] be in among the sheep, lest it terrify the flock. . . . If you separate yourself from the herd, that one will surely snatch you. (*Adv. Iud.* 3.1)

This last warning carries a stark threat as much as it suggests Chrysostom's concern, much like the threatening prediction in another of his claims: "Nevertheless, he who broke himself off from the assembly, and withdrew from the teachings of the fathers, fleeing from the doctor's office, even if he appears to be healthy, he will quickly fall sick" (*Adv. Iud.* 3.2). Rich in spatial rhetoric, Chrysostom's homilies emphasize his and Bishop Flavian's role as a good shepherd and attempt to make his congregants wary about straying from the safety of his church, trying to replace any respect for the synagogue with fear.

Compounding the potential danger against which this pastoral metaphor warns, Chrysostom also uses scripture to alert his audience to a further physical threat. In his polemic, the synagogue becomes a dangerous place because of the allegedly violent people that it houses. In Discourse 1, Chrysostom alludes to the Levitical sacrifices that scripture traditionally required,[51] and asks his audience, "Do you not shudder to assemble with possessed people, and those who have so many unclean spirits, who were nursed amid slaughter and murder?" (*Adv. Iud.* 1.6). Such a visceral image pointedly identifies the risk that Chrysostom claims Christians accepted by going to the synagogue. Likewise, Chrysostom recalls the New Testament Gospel stories and claims that the Jews killed "the Son of your Lord" (1.7). Chrysostom follows this hostile claim with a pressing question for his congregation: "Do you dare to come together with them into the same [place]?" (1.7). Clearly his rhetoric disallows that any true Christian should do so.

The physical harm against which Chrysostom warned his audience supported his efforts to redefine both Antioch's Jewish places and Antiochene Christians' behavior in his struggle to control the definition and dominance of Christian orthodoxy within the city. He insists, "This [ark that the Jews now have] does great harm daily to those who approach it" (*Adv. Iud.* 6.7). He warns his audience: "In their [synagogue] stands an invisible altar of deceit on which [the Jews] sacrifice not sheep and calves, but rather human souls" (1.6). He speaks of dangers to their bodies and their souls, describing Christians who participate in the Jewish festivals or otherwise enter the synagogue as "being dragged off unjustly and profanely to the pit of destruction, not by the executioner, but by the devil" (1.4). Chrysostom pleads with his audience to rescue themselves and others "from the devil's jaws" (2.3).

Sentence by sentence Chrysostom engages his congregants in a battle, with Christians as soldiers who have to fight against the enemies of Christianity and also heal their comrades who have fallen in the conflict (*Adv. Iud.* 8.1). He warns

51. Like rabbinic texts, Christian arguments such as Chrysostom's here continued to discuss Levitical sacrificial expectations despite the Temple's destruction centuries before. See Shepardson, "Paschal Politics," 233–60.

of the dangers that Jewish people and places present to Christian orthodoxy and purity: Judaizers mingle "with those who cried: 'Crucify; crucify' [Lk 23.21], with those who said: 'His blood be upon us and upon our children' [Mt 27.25]" (1.5). In the face of such danger, Chrysostom calls on his audience to avoid attending Jewish assemblies: "Therefore, I exhort you to flee and turn away from their gatherings. The harm to our weaker brothers is not slight. . . . Therefore, flee both the gatherings and places [of the Jews]" (1.5). Redefining synagogues as not only unappealing but even dangerous foregrounded a seemingly selfless concern for the physical and spiritual safety of Antioch's citizens, obfuscating the role that Chrysostom's rhetoric played in the complex spatial politics of the time. If Christians noticeably stopped attending the synagogue as Chrysostom hoped, their increased physical safety might have been difficult to ascertain, but the authority and power that Chrysostom and his "Meletian" orthodoxy would have garnered would have shone clearly for all to see.

(Re)Mapping Antioch through Christian Eyes

John Chrysostom participated in the religious power struggle in fourth-century Antioch by identifying for his audience particular locations that they should avoid in order to preserve their Christian orthodoxy. By listening carefully to his sermons, Chrysostom's audience would have learned more than a fear of the synagogues in Antioch and Daphne; they would have developed a complex new map of the city and known which places were allegedly dangerous to them, which were safe, and to which they were even encouraged, as Christians, to go.

The clearest target of Chrysostom's polemic against places in these sermons is certainly the synagogue. Chrysostom's rhetoric contains not simply warnings against the dangers that he argues Christians risked by socializing with Jews, and it is not only recapitulation of scriptural and other warnings by those who preceded him. In addition, he describes the specific dangers of particular Antiochene places, identifying not just the synagogue in Antioch, but also one in nearby Daphne. According to Chrysostom, "Even if no idol stands [in the synagogue], still demons inhabit the place. And I say this not only about the synagogue here [in town], but about the one in Daphne as well" (*Adv. Iud.* 1.6; cf. 5.12). The synagogue was not, however, the only target of the rhetorical efforts in these homilies to redefine Antiochene places.

Chrysostom not only warns about the synagogues, but several times mentions that his audience should avoid the less specific locations of all Jewish "festivals" (*Adv. Iud.* 1.1; 1.7). While many of these celebrations took place at the synagogues, Chrysostom also mentions the booths of Sukkot and mixing with Jews in the *agora* as additional physical places that Christians should avoid (7.1; 1.2; 1.4). In the season of Sukkot (15 Tishri), when Jews constructed tents to remember the forty years of wandering in the wilderness after leaving Egypt, Chrysostom warns his audience to avoid "the tents, which at this moment are pitched among [the Jews]" (7.1). The tents of Sukkot thus represent additional, even though temporary, "Jewish" places in the city, and Chrysostom cautions against being tempted to enter them. Chrysostom portrays the *agora* as being fraught with potential danger during Yom Kippur: "Do you fast with the Jews? Then also take off your sandals with the Jews, and walk barefoot in the *agora*, and share with them in their indecency and laughter" (1.4).[52] Libanius, as seen in chapter 1, agrees with Chrysostom that the *agora* represents an important opportunity to perform one's identity for a large audience, and in these homilies Chrysostom expresses his concern that some from his church audience might visibly join in the Jews' celebrations there. For Chrysostom the synagogues were not the only "Jewish" places where Christians' inappropriate attendance threatened the boundaries of his Christian orthodoxy.

In addition, Chrysostom warns his congregation about another Jewish place in the suburb of Daphne—namely, a healing shrine known as the cave of Matrona.[53] This cave in Daphne was apparently quite well known, and very popular among ailing Antiochenes, regardless of their other religious and ritual practices or affiliations.[54] The identity and history of the cave of Matrona, and whether or not it is named for the mother of the Maccabean martyrs, are ongoing academic debates, but the cave's popularity in Chrysostom's lifetime is certain.[55] Martha Vinson dis-

---

52. Compare Mayer and Allen, *John Chrysostom*, 13. Luke Lavan suggests that a person's companions in the *agora* helped construct one's identity: Luke Lavan, "The *agorai* of Antioch and Constantinople as seen by John Chrysostom," in *Wolf Liebeschuetz Reflected: Essays Presented by Colleagues, Friends, and Pupils*, ed. John Drinkwater and Benet Salway (London: Institute of Classical Studies, University of London, 2007), 157–67, esp. 162.

53. Spending the night, or incubating, in a healing shrine was a familiar response to illness in the Mediterranean in late antiquity. While shrines to Asclepius were the best-known healing shrines, others such as this cave in Daphne also dotted the Mediterranean landscape. See Gerald Hart, *Asclepius: The God of Medicine* (Lake Forest, IL: Royal Society of Medicine Press, 2000); Wilbert Gesler, *Healing Places* (Lanham, MD: Rowman & Littlefield Publishers, 2003), 1–41.

54. Mayer and Allen, introduction to Mayer and Allen, *John Chrysostom*, 12; see also Wendy Mayer and Pauline Allen, *The Churches of Syrian Antioch (300–638 C.E.)* (Walpole, MA: Peeters, 2012), 92–93.

55. Raphaëlle Ziadé has rejected the association of the cave with the Maccabees: Ziadé, *Les martyrs Maccabées: De l'histoire juive au culte chrétien, les homélies de Grégoire de Nazianze et de Jean Chrysostome* (Boston: Brill, 2007), 119–20. Discussions of Antiochene shrines to the Maccabees are complex. See Martha Vinson, "Gregory Nazianzen's Homily 15 and the Genesis of the Christian Cult of the Maccabean Martyrs," *Byzantion* 64 (1994): 166–92; Lothar Triebel, "Das angebliche Synagoge der makkabäischen Märtyrer in Antiochia am Orontes," *ZAC* 9 (2005): 464–95; Leonard V. Rutgers, "The Importance of Scripture in the Conflict between Jews and Christians: The Example of Antioch," in *The Use of Sacred Books in the Ancient World*, ed. L. V. Rutgers et al. (Leuven: Peeters, 1998), 287–303. The work of Vinson, Triebel, and Rutgers challenges earlier assumptions, such as those represented in Wilken (*Chrysostom*, 88–89), Harkins (*Discourses*, xlv-xlvi), and Soler (*Le sacré et le salut*, 101, 178–79, 206–7). Mayer and Allen survey the sources for our knowledge about places associated with the Maccabees in Antioch (Mayer and Allen, *Churches*, 90–93; cf. 143).

tinguishes between a place within the southwestern "Kerateion" region of the walled city of Antioch that she associates with a late ancient memorial of the Maccabean martyrs' death, and a cave in nearby Daphne that she identifies as the site of a shrine that contained the relics of the Maccabean martyrs.[56] She links the Antiochene site with a Christian basilica known by John Chrysostom and called "recent" by Augustine (John Chrysostom, *Pan. mart.* 1; Augustine, *Sermo* 300), and the Daphne shrine with a Jewish site (though not the Daphne synagogue that Chrysostom mentions) that housed the martyrs' relics and that Chrysostom calls "Matrona's cave." While these scholarly debates do not alter the fact that the cave of Matrona appears in John Chrysostom's rhetoric as a "Jewish" place that he would like his congregants to stop frequenting, in addition to the synagogues in Antioch and Daphne, it does complicate our reading of these texts as well as our map of the religious landscape that he faced.

Chrysostom refers to this cave in Discourse 1 in this series, as well as in his third homily on the Epistle to Titus. In both these sermons, Chrysostom laments that some Christians frequented this "Jewish" place, and he warns his audience about the dangers they faced in doing so. Chrysostom explains his concern: "For there [at Daphne] is a more wicked pit, which they call Matrona's. For I heard that even many of the faithful go up there and sleep beside the place" (*Adv. Iud.* 1.6; cf. 1.8; *Hom. 3 in Tit.*). According to Chrysostom, Christians were among those who frequented the shrine and spent the night incubating there in the hope of being healed. Chrysostom warns: "To me the shrine of Matrona and the temple of Apollo are equally impure. . . . For tell me, is not where demons dwell a site of impiety even if no [god's] statue stands there?" (*Adv. Iud.* 1.6). As the "dwelling place of demons" and a place "consecrated" by the Jews (*Hom. 3 in Tit.*),[57] the cave of Matrona was particularly dangerous and impure, as it lured in more Christians than did a Greek temple (*Adv. Iud.* 1.6). Chrysostom's rhetoric is particularly sharp in an effort to stop Christian attendance at this dangerously deceptive place.

In these homilies Chrysostom identifies not only "Jewish" locations but also local temples to the gods as dangerous places that Christians should avoid in order to both safeguard and demonstrate their Christian orthodoxy. Chrysostom assumes that his audience is not tempted to enter temples to the same extent that some of them appear to have been tempted by certain "Jewish" places. Nonetheless, with the emperor Julian's escapades only two decades past, Chrysostom's references to temples remind his audience of the less pressing but still significant threat that they pose. Chrysostom describes temples as "profane and unclean" (*Iud. Ind.* 6.7), though he explains, "There [in the temple] the impiety is naked and conspicuous; hence, it would not easily attract or deceive one who has sense and

---

56. Vinson, "Gregory," 179–85.
57. All translations from *Hom. 3 in Tit.* are my own from the Greek in PG 62.

self-control" (1.6). Through his spatial rhetoric, Chrysostom remapped Antioch (and Daphne), constructing a Christian landscape and requiring of his congregation "orthodox" Christian behavior to mirror their "orthodox" beliefs.

A close reading of Chrysostom's homilies against the Judaizers reveals that his rhetoric focused on establishing a binary of safe versus dangerous sites in Antioch. In particular Chrysostom's rhetoric strove to reshape how his listeners would feel about synagogues and other local places. Drawing a sharp dichotomy between Christian places, which he valued positively, and other places, which he sharply devalued, Chrysostom's sermons strove to influence how his congregants saw and interacted with their city's landscape. These clear categories of pure and impure places, however, become complicated when Chrysostom's Christian opponents are involved, as his homilies against the Anomeans reveal.

AGAINST THE ANOMEANS: THE LOCATION OF
CHRISTIAN ORTHOPRAXY AND ORTHODOXY

As noted above, Chrysostom's first anti-Judaizing homily interrupted a series of homilies against those whom Chrysostom called Anomeans. The first six of these homilies were given from August to December 386, with Homilies 7–10 delivered early in 387. In the first five of these homilies, Chrysostom refuted Christians who followed the teachings of leaders such as Antiochene native Aetius and his follower Eunomius, Christians whom their opponents accused of making inappropriate claims about God based on human reason.[58] Although Aetius died in 367 long before John Chrysostom gave these homilies, Aetius's student Eunomius became quite influential in the 360s, and Gregory of Nyssa had published a response to Eunomius's second *Apologia* as recently as the early 380s. Gregory of Nazianzus wrote of the strong and vocal support that Eunomius's views had in the early 380s in Constantinople, and John Chrysostom provides evidence that there were also those in Antioch in 386–87 who supported Eunomius's theology. Homilies 7–10 return to what Chrysostom describes as "another part" of his argument against "Anomeans"—namely, to discuss "if the Son and the Father are of the same power, if they are of the same authority, if they are of the same substance" (*De incomprehensibili natura dei* 7.71–72).[59] Chrysostom's rhetoric against these opponents is as strong as against those he considered Judaizers; he characterizes

---

58. For a history of Eunomius and the controversies in which he was involved, see Richard Vaggione, *Eunomius of Cyzicus and the Nicene Revolution* (New York: Oxford University Press, 2000).

59. All translations from Homily 7 against the Anomeans are my own from the Greek text in SC 396. The citation refers to homily and line number in SC. See the English translation in Paul Harkins, *St. John Chrysostom: On the Incomprehensible Nature of God*, FC 72 (Washington, DC: Catholic University of America Press, 1984).

Anomeans as "mad," considers them "heretics" and "unbelieving," and warns his audience to consider them "ill," as having a "mental illness."[60] Like those against the Judaizers, these homilies also emphasize the importance of correct attendance in forming orthodox Christians, although in significantly different ways than against the Judaizers. Whereas the synagogue was the primary focus of Chrysostom's hostile rhetoric against the Judaizers, his own church is the central point of geographical reference in his sermons against the Anomeans, with the individual Christian's attentiveness becoming a factor in defining the relative safety of the city's places in matters of orthodoxy and heresy.

Anomean and "Orthodox" Christians: Questions of Audience

Chrysostom is explicit in several of his homilies against the Anomeans that his audience is a combination of those he considered part of his and Bishop Flavian's congregation, alongside some he considered to be his opponents, and that the latter were teaching doctrines that could lead his orthodox congregants astray. In the first homily in this series, Chrysostom recounts that he had been hesitant to address the Anomeans' doctrines directly, because he had noticed that some of those who taught the doctrine were attending his sermons, and he wanted first to lull them into feeling comfortable so that his attacks on their teachings would then instruct them rather than chase them away:

> For I have long labored to say these words to you, but I delayed, because I saw that many of the sick were listening to these [words] of ours with pleasure, and not wishing to scare away the prey, for a time I restrained my tongue from these contests, so that only after controlling them completely I might then be stripped and enter into combat. (*De incomp.* 1.334–40)

Nevertheless, Chrysostom claims that his hesitation was brought to an end when the Anomeans themselves allegedly pressed him for a response to their teachings, prompting this series of homilies: "But since, through the grace of God, I heard them summoning and troubling [me] to enter into these contests, hereafter I prepared myself with confidence and took up the weapons" (*De incomp.* 1.340–44). Chrysostom explains that he still began with easy and brief arguments: "Since now is the first time I have come down into these contests, I consider it to be to your advantage to be satisfied for now with what I have said, lest the multitude of the things I intended to say come upon [you] with a rush, sweeping away the memory of these things" (1.329–33). Despite the hostility that Chrysostom projects

---

60. See, for example, John Chrysostom, *De incomp.* 1.188–90, 3.60–63; 1.278; 2.1; 1.336–37, 2.490–93. All translations from Homilies 1–5 against the Anomeans are my own from the Greek text in SC 28. The citation refers to homily and line number in SC. See also the English translation in Harkins, *On the Incomprehensibility*.

toward these opponents, it is clear from his rhetoric that some of them were voluntarily in the congregation of his church.

Other homilies in this series likewise reveal that Chrysostom addressed a congregation that included both those whom he considered to be fundamentally orthodox and those whom he considered to be heretics. He frequently addresses the former by speaking of the heretics in the third person, as those other than his congregants, but periodically he addresses the Anomeans directly in the second person (e.g., *De incomp.* 2.143, 3.70), and he refers to the Anomeans as a wild tree growing in the cultivated land of his church building and threatening the health of the orchard (3.1–5). Chrysostom's metaphors for the struggle against the heretics demonstrate the severity that he granted to the conflict, as he repeatedly describes their theological arguments as military battles that required weapons and drew blood, or as athletic contests that would determine a victor. Likewise, he sometimes positions his opponents as ill and diseased, needing healing from an orthodox teacher in the role of a physician. After 381, Christians who were not considered orthodox by the emperor's standards, including those who adhered to the doctrines that Chrysostom describes his opponents holding in these homilies, could not legally hold meetings in urban church buildings. Whether because they did not have a meeting place of their own, although many such groups continued to hold meetings around the empire outside the formal churches and city walls, or because they had reasons to provoke a discussion on the controversial issues in the "orthodox" churches, or because they disagreed with John Chrysostom that they were not part of his community, it seems that Chrysostom faced a congregation that included some whom he identified as Anomeans, and that he tried to persuade these opponents as well as those more regularly in his audience of the error of the Anomean teachings and the danger of those who taught them.

Valuing Christian Places

John Chrysostom's homilies against the Anomeans confronted a conundrum produced by his place-specific language. On the one hand, Chrysostom argues in these homilies, as in those against the Judaizers, that places have different values and that Christians should patrol their religious identity by carefully regulating their attendance at, and absence from, particular places in Antioch's physical topography. This argument that some places were safer and more appropriate for Christians than others, however, conflicts with Chrysostom's other claim that God is everywhere and cannot be confined to any particular place, an argument that arises particularly in his theological disagreements with the Anomean Christians. As a result, Chrysostom's emphasis differs in different parts of his argument, sometimes stressing the theological claim of God's omnipresence and other times emphasizing the broader concerns facing his congregants as they navigate the city. In these homilies, Chrysostom thus confirms strongly that God is present everywhere, but maintains his claim that Christian attendance is not equal in value or meaning at all places, and that particular places even carry different values for different people.

In these texts Chrysostom's spatial language is not limited to Antioch's local topography, but also touches on the divine presence. One of Chrysostom's primary criticisms against his opponents in these homilies is the knowledge they claim to have about God through their human reason. Countering their claims Chrysostom argues, "I know that God is everywhere and I know that he is wholly everywhere, but I do not know how," thus demonstrating to his opponents the difference he saw between concepts that could be known about God, and the inappropriate investigation of those beliefs by human reason that he associated with his opponents (*De incomp.* 1.157–59; cf. 1.213–18). In the process of this argument, Chrysostom cites passages from Christian scripture to defend his claims, and when some of those passages refer to the location of God, Chrysostom quickly counters that this is only metaphorical, since God cannot be confined to any place, because God is omnipresent (1.315–18). Similarly, Chrysostom explains a quotation from 1 Timothy 6.15–16, which he attributes to Paul, by arguing, "He said these things not in order that you might suspect that there is a house or a place around God, but rather in order that you might learn out of all the abundance [his] inaccessibility" (*De incomp.* 3.121–23). Nevertheless, while Chrysostom had no doubt that God was omnipresent, this did not lead him to value all places equally (2.191).

Just as Chrysostom's homilies against the Judaizers value some places as physically and spiritually dangerous and other places as safe and profitable for Christians to attend, these homilies against the Anomeans also designate places as being significantly of different value. Most notably, Chrysostom denigrates those who show through their attendance that they privilege the chariot races over the church, and he implies that attendance at the church fostered Christian salvation while attendance at the chariot races did not (*De incomp.* 7.1–2). Chrysostom criticizes those who are distracted by chariot races: "Again there are horse races, and again our assembly has become smaller. . . . I grieve on account of the laxity of those [who have fallen away]" (7.1–2, 7). Chrysostom's rhetoric differentiates would-be Christians based in part on where they spend their time, with his church receiving primary importance.

More complex, though, are Chrysostom's references to Christians' homes, which in his anti-Judaizing homilies are so clearly places that would provide a safe refuge for Christians, particularly women, and which could also be the site of enforcing proper Christian behavior, such as forcing would-be Judaizers to break their fast at a meal. Unlike in his homilies against the Judaizers, however, where Christian praxis is the stronger focus of Chrysostom's criticism, in his arguments against the Anomeans Chrysostom focuses more strongly on questions of doctrine as a critical point of distinction between orthodox and heretical Christians.

Perhaps it is in part this different emphasis that leads Chrysostom to value the Christian home differently in his arguments against the Anomeans, where he placed it clearly in a subordinate position to his church building.

Chrysostom ridicules excuses that his audience members allegedly proffer for coming to church only to hear the homily and then leaving before the rest of the service takes place: "But what is the bold defense of most? It is possible, they say, to pray at the house, but at the house it is not possible to hear the homilies and the teachings" (*De incomp.* 3.380–82). Chrysostom counters this reasoning by arguing for the superiority of his church building over their homes:

> Friend, you deceive yourself, for indeed while it is possible to pray at the house, it is impossible to pray there as at the church, where there is such a multitude of fathers, where a cry is sent up to God with one accord. The Lord does not listen to you the same way when you call upon him by yourself, as when you call upon him with your brothers and sisters. (*De incomp.* 3.382–88)

Chrysostom differentiates the church from the home, so that in church his congregants have "something more" than in the home (*De incomp.* 3.388).[61] Thus Christians should not, according to Chrysostom, sit outside the church, including at home, instead of coming together as a group (3.442–44). Despite God being omnipresent, not all places were valued equally, and while the Christian home was safe, unlike the synagogue or the place of the chariot races, Chrysostom identifies his church as the safest and most beneficial place for Christians to spend their time. In the context of intra-Christian controversy in which friendships and socializing with Anomeans could prove harmful to the weaker of Chrysostom's congregants, Chrysostom's church emerged as much more reliably safe than anyone's home.

As in Chrysostom's sermons against the Judaizers, in his anti-Anomean sermons his church building serves as a safe haven of "orthodoxy," but in the latter Chrysostom distinguishes among his church attendees based on their level of participation in the church service itself. Through his rhetoric, Chrysostom demands "correct" doctrine and behavior from his audience, complicating the emphasis that he elsewhere put on place by implying that even a dangerous place could be safe to a strong Christian, while even a safe place could not protect a person who did not attend it with the right mind. In this case, Chrysostom demonstrates more than ever the interaction between people and the places they attend, and how space is turned into meaningful place in the process of their interaction.

In these anti-Anomean homilies Chrysostom intimates that all church attendance is not equally beneficial. Quite the contrary, when congregants are there, and

61. It seems to be the liturgy of the church service as well as the collective gathering as a community that Chrysostom highlights as privileging the place of the church service over the place of a Christian home.

how fully and spiritually present they are at the time, determine to what extent their attendance grants them spiritual benefit. In this respect, Chrysostom is particularly vocal about the importance of attending the celebration of the Eucharist during the church service, as he claims that too many congregants come only to hear his homily and then leave without reaping the benefit of having participated in the Eucharist: "Often during the time of greatest awe, I searched for [the crowd] and was unable to see it" (*De incomp.* 3.360–61). In sharp contrast, while Chrysostom was preaching, he claims, "the zeal [of the crowd] was great, eagerness was rejoicing, with people pressing against one another and remaining until the end" (3.362–64). Much to his dismay, however, "when Christ is about to appear in the holy mysteries, the church becomes empty and deserted" (3.364–66).[62] The church is the place in which Chrysostom most wished his congregants to be, but by their careless abandonment of the Eucharist, many destroyed the benefit they might have gained from hearing the homily. He forcefully explains: "If the things I have said were stored up in your souls, by all means, it would have kept you inside and escorted you toward the things of greatest awe with more piety. But now, just as if you had been listening to some kithara player, when the speech ends you withdraw, devoid of any profit" (3.375–79). Whereas Chrysostom implies that the act of entering the synagogue is itself harmful to Christians, largely because of the misconceptions it could cause for the actor and any observers, the act of entering a church is not in itself deserving of the highest praise. Attending church is beneficial, but it is only fully effective if the attendee participates fully in the Eucharist ceremony.

Chrysostom's rhetoric is complicated, of course, by the requirement that only baptized Christians could receive the Eucharist, and it is unclear whether Anomean Christians would have accepted the Eucharist from Chrysostom, even if they had been baptized into the Anomean Christian community. Likewise, many of Chrysostom's own congregants would have delayed baptism until later in their lives. Chrysostom's exhortations for his entire audience to stay for the Eucharist service are thus aggrandizing rhetoric, but also less explicit calls for the wider Antiochene community to become full members of his particular church.

Since for Chrysostom the nature and value of places are influenced not only by who attends, but in the interaction between attendees, observers, and the place itself, he nuances his discussion of the importance of place by distinguishing in these homilies between physical and spiritual absence and attendance. While Chrysostom praises those who attend church over those who prefer the chariot races, and those who participate in the Eucharist ceremony over those who leave church after the homily, his highest praise is reserved for those who are not only bodily present in his church, but fully spiritually engaged. Likewise, he minimizes

---

62. Wendy Mayer has noted in conversation the similar and contemporaneous comments that Chrysostom made to his congregants in *De Philogonio, In diem natalem,* and *De baptism Christi.*

his praise for those who merely attended but did not comprehend the meaning of what they heard, or gain much benefit from having been present. Thus, he criticizes those who were absent from his services, and those who left before the Eucharist, but he also argues, "Now I wish to accuse those who remain inside, not because you remain inside, but rather because remaining, you are disposed no better than those wasting their time outside" (De incomp. 4.346–48). To explain what he means by such a faulty disposition, he elaborates that they demonstrate this by "talking with one another at that time of greatest awe" (4.348–49).

Chrysostom was certainly not the last public speaker or teacher to express disappointment and frustration at the idle chatter among his distracted audience, those who even when they attend "are not present, but while the body for these is seated here, the mind wanders outside" (De incomp. 7.10–11). Nonetheless, in Chrysostom's rhetoric, such behavior reorganized the very value of the Christians' attendance in the church. Rather than strengthening them, such halfhearted church attendance left their souls unprotected from demons like "a house without a door" (De incomp. 4.359–60; cf. Hom. in Mt. 11).[63] Even in the church building itself, weak Christians must beware lest their careless behavior transform the place from one of safety and edification to one of no benefit or, far worse, one of spiritual danger. This rhetoric is specific to this controversy against Christian Anomeans. Elsewhere Chrysostom notes that simply being in the presence of the martyrs is beneficial, no matter what brought the person there, and he praises the attendance at his church of rural visitors, even though he claims they cannot understand his sermon.[64]

Against the Anomeans, Chrysostom warns the people in his audience that if they chatted with their neighbors during the church service instead of being fully engaged with the ceremony, then their minds would be in danger of demonic occupation, but that they could avoid this danger by attentive attendance. Chrysostom uses those whom he understood to be possessed by demons, who stood at the front of the church at this point in the service, in order to chastise the rest of his audience:

> You see so many prisoners from among your siblings standing nearby and you converse about things which have nothing to do with them. . . . Do you not fear, lest while you are conversing, being indifferent, taking no heed, some daimōn might leap out from there and, finding your soul languishing and having been swept clean, enter in? (De incomp. 4.350–59)

Chrysostom taught, however, that his audience could avoid these dangers and remain safe from demons. He explains that a Christian should remain vigilant,

---

63. The context makes clear that Chrysostom means a house with an open door, not a house without any entrance.

64. See the discussion in chapter 2 above and chapter 5 below.

so that a *daimōn*, seeing that your soul is hot and wide awake, will consider your mind hereafter to be inaccessible to him. For if he sees you yawning and indifferent, he will quickly enter into the deserted inn, but if he sees you straining and wide awake and hanging on the heavens themselves, then thereafter he will not be so bold as to look you in the eyes. So even if you despise your brothers and sisters, at least spare yourself and bar the entrance of your soul from the evil *daimōn*. (*De incomp.* 4.378–87)

These warnings recall those from the homilies against the Judaizers that tried to prevent anyone in Chrysostom's audience from visiting the synagogue or participating in "Jewish" festivals and fasts for fear of the demons that might accost them. While a blunt Christian/Jewish dichotomy led Chrysostom to praise his church building as a safe Christian place in contrast to the dangerous synagogues, the nuances required to fight intra-Christian doctrinal differences led to new ambiguities around Christian places.

As with the warnings about the dangers posed by the demons in the synagogues, however, these warnings also came with Chrysostom's prophylactic protections against demon possession.[65] Whereas the former required avoiding particular places in the city altogether, such as the synagogue, these homilies required particular behavior from those in attendance at church. Chrysostom taught that nothing was as likely to prevent such attacks "as intense prayer and supplication" (*De incomp.* 4.388–89). In a clever use of liturgical ritual, Chrysostom comments,

For this same exhortation that the deacon says to everyone, "Let us stand up straight," was established as law not simply or randomly, but rather in order that we might restore the thoughts that were dragging on the ground, so that, throwing away the feebleness that comes to us from the things of life, we might be able to raise up our soul to be straight before God. (*De incomp.* 4.389–95)

The command was, in Chrysostom's interpretation, "extended not to the body but to the soul" (*De incomp.* 4.396–97). This interpretation allowed Chrysostom to provide those in his congregation with a clear path of correct behavior that could allow them to reap the full benefits of their attendance at the church.

For the spiritually weaker or less mature in his audience, Chrysostom's anti-Anomean warnings echo those against Jews and Judaizers: "If someone is weaker, let him flee their company, let him leap away from their assemblies, lest the pretext of friendship become a starting point for impiety" (*De incomp.* 2.511–13; cf. *Cat.* 1.24).[66] Chrysostom specifically recognizes that Anomean Christians could be expected to be mixed with orthodox Christians in Antioch, including as friends and

---

65. On fourth-century Christian demonology, see Kalleres, *City of Demons*; David Brakke, *Demons and the Making of the Monk: Spiritual Combat in Early Christianity* (Cambridge, MA: Harvard University Press, 2006).

66. Compare Dayna Kalleres's contextualization of this passage (*City of Demons*, chap. 3).

family, and he warns against the possible dangers that such relationships might raise: "If, therefore, the friendships hurt and drag you toward sharing in the impiety, even if they are your parents, leap away!" (*De incomp.* 1.360–62). Similarly, he warns, "Therefore if, the very thing that I said, friendships hurt, let us flee and leap away" (1.373–74). Just as he did with Jews and Judaizers, Chrysostom warns his congregants about the dangers inherent in associating with those he calls Anomean Christians: "I exhort you, then, to flee their madness. For I, at least, say that it is the utmost madness to struggle to know what God is in substance. . . . How mad it is for them to think that they are able to subject this substance itself to their own reasoning!" (1.188–98). While Chrysostom is not explicit about where in Antioch these interactions between Anomeans and Chrysostom's congregants might take place, he is clear that such contact endangered many orthodox Christians, who should flee.

Chrysostom also describes the weaker members of his audience, in contrast to the stronger Christians, as in danger of being contaminated by the illness, or "madness," of the Anomeans, which is why they should avoid any contact with them. Chrysostom uses a metaphor to explain the situation to his audience: "If a doctor comes to one who is sick, he often helps both that one and himself. But one who is weaker hurts both himself and the one who is sick by mixing with the ill. For it will not be possible for that one to help anyone, and he will draw upon himself great harm from the sickness" (*De incomp.* 2.521–25). That these ill patients were Anomean Christians is explicit from Chrysostom's address of the homilies against "the unbelieving Anomeans" (2.1). While Chrysostom does not mention specific Antiochene locations with regard to the Anomeans, he assumes that his audience knows of their "gatherings" and could distinguish them from healthy ("orthodox") Christians, and concludes, "Therefore, in order that we not hurt ourselves the most, let us flee their company" (2.531–32). In this case, there was not one clear location that bore the brunt of Chrysostom's polemic, such as with the synagogue, but in these sermons he nonetheless attempted to shape where in the city his Christian congregants should and should not go in order to maintain their Christian orthodoxy.

The corollary, however, is Chrysostom's praise for strong Christians, those who not only benefited from their fully engaged participation in regular church services, but who even when they left this safest environment also had the ability to heal the "ill" Anomeans. In the case of strong Christians, Chrysostom actually encourages them to develop friendships with Anomeans in order to heal them of their illness: "But if they do us no wrong in the matter of impiety, let us pursue and drag them to ourselves" (*De incomp.* 1.374–76).[67] As with Judaizers, Chrysostom treated the Anomean "heresy" as a disease. As a result, he advocated different behaviors for Christians of different

---

67. This analysis echoes that of Dayna Kalleres in her discussion of John Chrysostom's *Adversus Iudaeos* homilies in *City of Demons*, chap. 3.

abilities. Strong Christians, that is, those whom Chrysostom felt were not at risk of being persuaded away from "orthodoxy," Chrysostom encourages to act as a physician to the Anomeans, taking a "soft sponge" that was wet with soothing water, that is, Chrysostom's own orthodox teachings, and bathing the "burning wound" that the Anomeans have in their souls (2.490–97). In this instance, Chrysostom ironically advocates close proximity between the two groups: "Even if they mistreat you, even if they kick, even if they spit, even if they do whatsoever, my beloved, do not abandon the treatment" (2.502–4). A strong Christian could, Chrysostom claims, like a physician visiting the sick, help both the patient and himself (2.521–22). These words, however, were only for "the stronger" among his church congregants, "those who are able to exhibit no harm from being together with them," a warning that served to highlight the danger inherent in such associations (2.509–11).

Far from being in danger in places that should be safe, strong Christians' security allowed them to transform their experiences of dangerous places, so that even when they were not physically in a church building, they nonetheless remained spiritually present there. Chrysostom praises these pillars of orthodoxy: "As long as you are present, [our assembly] will not become smaller. For just as if a tiller should see his grain in bloom and ready, he takes little account of the falling leaves" (*De incomp.* 7.2–5). Unlike the weak Christians who even when they attended were "not present," the strong Christians are described in glowing terms: "Even if you are ever absent, even then you are present; your body might be outside, but the mind is here" (7.11–13).[68]

The church thus remained the focus of Chrysostom's praise in these homilies, but it was "church" as a constructed place and not just the geographical space of a building.[69] The church building has the greatest potential to contain and support Christian orthodoxy, but it became an "orthodox" place that performed that function only when Christians themselves participated in its construction as such. On its own, it remained a place with a lot of positive potential, but still with the danger of housing "ill" people whose inner demons might "leap" into a weak congregant, as through an open door. Strong Christians, on the other hand, not only prospered within the place of the church building, but they remained safe elsewhere with their minds focused on the church. Chrysostom's rhetoric against the Anomeans thus maintained a focus on the spatial, continuing to associate Christian attendance and Christian orthodoxy, even as the realities of an intra-Christian dispute

68. Chrysostom makes a similar distinction in another homily when he notes that even though Bishop Flavian is not present in the flesh at the church that day, he is nevertheless there in spirit (John Chrysostom, *In kalendas* 1).

69. This concept appears in other writings of John Chrysostom, particularly as discussed in chapter 5 below regarding Christian processions to and from the martyrs' shrines, and the ways in which attendance at the martyrs' relics physically transforms visitors.

produced new complexities in the rhetoric far beyond the clearer distinctions of his anti-Judaizing homilies.

CONCLUSION: CHRISTIAN AND
NON-CHRISTIAN PLACES

Comparison of these two series of homilies, *Adversus Iudaeos* and *De incomprehensibili natura dei,* given by the same preacher in the same city within the same thirteen-month period, reveals interesting points of similarity and difference. Both series include rhetoric that advocates Christian attendance at certain places and avoidance of others, and shapes the connotations associated with certain places in the city. The rhetoric against Jewish people and places is, however, significantly different from the rhetoric against heretical Christian people and places. With the former, Chrysostom is more particular about which physical locations and buildings his congregants should avoid, such as synagogues, temples, and theaters, and he speaks without qualification about the goodness of Christian homes and church buildings, and about the physical and spiritual safety that one gains by attendance there. His spatial rhetoric against those he calls Anomean heretics, however, presents a new challenge to his efforts to distinguish clearly safe and beneficial Christian places. Rather than forbid attendance at particular buildings, Chrysostom instead forbids his congregants more generally from associating with the heretics, and he qualifies the benefits to be gained from attendance at Christian homes and churches by requiring particular behaviors while there, claiming that in fact one could still be endangered even in these places. Both the similarities and the differences in the spatial rhetoric of these two series of homilies reflect the context in which Chrysostom spoke, and suggest that there was a qualitative difference between his efforts to address the topographical dangers related to Christian heretics and those related to Jews.

Chrysostom suggests throughout his writings that there are two possibilities for places that were not yet associated with Christianity: like the Apollo temple precinct in Daphne, they could be made into Christian places, or like the synagogues and the theater, they could remain outside the Christian community. The places that become Christian, Chrysostom suggest, become beneficial for Christians to visit, as they are sites of Christian power and victory; Chrysostom aggressively demonizes and condemns, however, the places that remain apart from Christianity. Thus in his rhetoric the synagogue becomes the dwelling place of demons and a threat to Christians' physical and spiritual safety. The theater similarly becomes a den of sexual and spiritual immorality that would jeopardize a Christian's identity and salvation. Martyrs' shrines, however, and most especially the shrine for Babylas in the temple precinct in Daphne, are places Chrysostom encourages everyone to attend, because, whether by their intention or not, he claims, the saint would heal them and bring them into the Christian fold.

The places of Christian heretics, however, posed a series of different challenges for Chrysostom and his efforts to remap the city for his congregants. Perhaps the greatest historical influence in creating this rhetorical difference was that church buildings in Antioch switched hands among the various Christian communities in the city in the decades preceding Chrysostom's homilies. In such an environment, it would have been unhelpful for Meletius's group, for example, to demonize the place of the Great Church simply because it was in the hands of his Christian opponents at the time. Other places, such as at least some of the region's martyr shrines, appear to have remained places that opposing Christian groups shared. This complex history of ownership and control over the places in and around Antioch that were associated with Christianity created a context in which it was not in the best interest of Christian leaders to identify particular physical places with their Christian opponents, since those very places were often ones that the leaders themselves hoped one day to control.

Two significant results of this historical context have already emerged from the comparison of these homilies. First, while still interested in places that Christians should and should not go, Chrysostom's rhetoric was less topographically specific in relation to places of Christian heretics than it was in relation to places that he considered more dangerous. While he warned his congregants away from synagogue and theater buildings, he instead warned them not to join in any gatherings of the Anomeans, and to avoid relationships with heretics that could cause them spiritual harm. Second, rather than monolithically describing places as beneficial or harmful, as he did in his homilies against Jewish places, in his anti-Anomean homilies Chrysostom introduced a new nuance—namely, that those he termed weaker Christians experienced places differently from those he termed stronger Christians. Thus, weaker Christians should flee from any contact with heretics, no matter where it occurred, even in the safety of their own home, while stronger Christians should seek contact with heretical Christians so that they might persuade them to accept Christian orthodoxy. Likewise, weaker Christians could be in danger even in the church building itself if they did not engage with the church service and found themselves open to demonic possession, while stronger Christians were safe even in otherwise dangerous places (John Chrysostom, *De incomp.* 7.1). This rhetoric is still distinctly focused on the significance of place and Christian attendance, and its relation to religious identity, even though the historical context of Antioch has forced Chrysostom to add nuances to his rhetoric against his heretical opponents that were different from the nuances he employed against those whom he felt were inappropriately attending what he understood to be places associated with practices that were not Christian. Comparing these homilies thus provides insight not only into the significant role that spatial rhetoric played in Chrysostom's sermons, but also into the distinctions that Antioch's fourth-century religious and political history created in how Chrysostom approached issues of religious identity with respect to those he called heretics versus those whom he considered to be outside the bounds of Christianity altogether.

In the vocabulary of modern geographers, Chrysostom's spatial rhetoric constitutes an "imaginative geography." Such geographies often unite an "imagined community," a term that Gillian Rose defines as "a group of people bound together by some kind of belief stemming from particular historical and geographical circumstances in their own solidarity."[70] In this case, Chrysostom used spatial rhetoric in an attempt to unite Christians as a coherent and "orthodox" self within the complex communities that made up fourth-century Antioch. According to Gill Valentine, "The importance of these imaginative geographies is not only, as [Jon] May argues, that they 'overlay a more tangible geography and help shape our attitudes to other places and people,' but more importantly, that they are fundamental to our understanding of space itself and how we construct our sense of self and other."[71] In 386–87, politicized religious groups competed for both places and loyalties in Antioch. John Chrysostom entered this competition by recognizing the significant connection between identity and place, and by using his ecclesiastical authority to redraw the map of Antioch in such a way that promoted and preserved his Christianity. Phil Hubbard, Rob Kitchin, and Gill Valentine comment, "Places are complex entities situated within and shaped by forces from well beyond their own notional boundaries. . . . Places should not be romanticized as pre-political entities but are shaped by often oppressive institutional forces and social relationships."[72] Places are socially and rhetorically constructed, and they in turn shape the politics that take place in and around them. John Allen has noted that successful imaginative geographies "make it difficult to see or make sense of things in ways other than that represented. There is an apparent obviousness about the way in which, for example, a distant landscape, or the peoples of a close territory, or a particular culinary culture are represented which makes it difficult to contest."[73] In a context of rich religious complexity, Chrysostom's rhetoric strove for this kind of success, which would make the city, and eventually the empire, "orthodox" Christian—not only in beliefs and behavior, but in the very geographical landscape that its citizens saw.

70. Benedict Anderson's "imagined community" and Rose's definition are cited in Valentine, "Imagined Geographies," 47–48. See also Benedict Anderson, *Imagined Communities: Reflections on the Origin and Spread of Nationalism* (London: Verso, 1983); Gillian Rose, "Contested Concepts of Community," *Journal of Historical Geography* 16.4 (1990): 425–37.

71. Valentine, "Imagined Geographies," 48.

72. Phil Hubbard, Rob Kitchin, and Gill Valentine, "Editors' Introduction," in *Key Thinkers on Space and Place*, ed. Phil Hubbard, Rob Kitchin, and Gill Valentine (Thousand Oaks, CA: Sage Publications, 2004), 6.

73. John Allen, introduction to Massey, Allen, and Sarre, *Human Geography Today*, 44.

4

Transformative Transgressions

Exploiting the Urban/Rural Divide

John Chrysostom strongly tied religious identity to Antioch's physical places, and this is true also of the distinction that he made between the rural space around the city and the urban space within its walls. Although scholars have demonstrated that geographical boundaries are often more permeable than rhetorical descriptions of them allow,[1] boundaries nevertheless ideologically separate places from one another, distinguishing one side from the other in ways that accumulate cultural significance.[2] It should, therefore, come as no surprise when rhetorical descriptions of mass boundary crossings depict them as transforming the places on either side, as those who are seen to represent the culture of one side move to the other, which had initially been understood to differ in some significant way from the first.[3] Cultural geographer Tim Cresswell's discussion of contemporary

1. Roman scholars have noted this particularly for the border regions of the empire. See, for example, C. R. Whittaker, *Frontiers of the Roman Empire: A Social and Economic Study* (Baltimore: Johns Hopkins University Press, 1994), 130–31. This is also, of course, a topic that has been addressed in other contexts; see Gloria Anzaldúa, *Borderlands/La Frontera: The New Mestiza* (San Francisco: Spinsters/Aunt Lute Press, 1987).

2. Tim Cresswell discusses the ideological construction of geographical boundaries, and the meanings associated with placement on either side, as well as transgressions across boundaries, in his book *In Place/Out of Place: Geography, Ideology, and Transgression* (Minneapolis: University of Minnesota Press, 1996).

3. This becomes acutely evident in the case of modern national boundaries, such as the boundary between the United States and Mexico. Stephen Castles and Alastair Davidson agree: "Western European countries have . . . tended to write immigration out of their histories, because it contradicted myths of national homogeneity" (Castles and Davidson, *Citizenship and Migration: Globalization and the Politics of Belonging* [New York: Routledge, 2000], 60).

borders provides a useful model for thinking about Roman Antioch as well. Cresswell argues that boundaries often become more rigidly defined and defended at moments of transgression, and that such boundaries are not inherently self-evident or "natural" in their location, but that they are actively naturalized through the ideologically motivated narratives of the people who wield the power to define them.[4] He writes, "Value and meaning are not inherent in any space or place—indeed they must be created, reproduced, and defended from heresy."[5] In this sense, normative societal forces create narratives that certain people are "out of place" when they move beyond locations socially defined as their appropriate domain.[6] The transgression of socially constructed spatial expectations frequently leads to the transformation of the places themselves.[7] The writings of Libanius and of his student and later Christian leader John Chrysostom are rich resources for studying such spatial constructions in Roman Antioch. Like the actors in Cresswell's twentieth-century examples, John Chrysostom and his teacher Libanius participated in boundary construction and maintenance, albeit toward quite different ends. John Chrysostom, in particular, also explicitly narrated the transformation that he perceived taking place when the boundaries drawn by his sharp rhetoric were crossed.

By rhetorically manipulating traditional Roman stereotypes of urban and rural places and privileging the ideals of Christian asceticism, John Chrysostom contributed to shifting local power dynamics and perceptions of Antioch's topography, elevating the prestige and authority of his Christian community in the process. Despite a common assumption that urban life and urban dwellers were far superior to their ostensibly uneducated and less advantaged rural counterparts, the status quo in Chrysostom's rhetoric is that the city, represented by such places as the *agora* and theater, calls to mind a populated and corrupt place whose citizens do not embody Christian orthodoxy, while the space outside the city, represented by such places as ascetics' caves and martyrs' shrines, calls to mind a sparsely populated good and safe place whose inhabitants reflect true Christian orthodoxy and orthopraxy.[8] In John Chrysostom's rhetoric, the inverting civic

---

4. Cresswell, *In Place/Out of Place*, 3–27.

5. Cresswell, *In Place/Out of Place*, 9.

6. Cresswell gives an example of three young black men eating at a pizzeria in an affluent all-white neighborhood who were perceived by the neighborhood's inhabitants to be threateningly out of place (*In Place/Out of Place*, 3, 5–6). This also calls to mind the 2012 shooting death of Trayvon Martin in Florida.

7. Cresswell, *In Place/Out of Place*, 8–10, 23, 60.

8. For the centrality of the *agora* in Chrysostom's rhetoric, and his suggestion that it is at the heart of the city, see Luke Lavan, "The *agorai* of Antioch and Constantinople as seen by John Chrysostom," in *Wolf Liebeschuetz Reflected: Essays Presented by Colleagues, Friends, and Pupils*, ed. John Drinkwater and Benet Salway (London: Institute of Classical Studies, University of London, 2007), 157–67.

chaos of the urban riot of 387, in which numerous Antiochenes fled to the mountains and mountain ascetics flocked to the city, and in which Antioch's public baths and theater were emptied and Chrysostom's church building was filled, allowed a significant momentary transformation—in this case, Christianization—of Antioch's people and places.

THE NORMATIVE LANDSCAPE:
URBAN AND RURAL IN ROMAN RHETORIC

As with any spatial boundaries, Roman society's expectations for urban and rural people were socially constructed and tied to the ideological motivations of the educated Roman elites, producing "a normative landscape."[9] The influences on John Chrysostom's rhetorical presentation of urban people and places in fourth-century Antioch, and of those outside the city walls, are predictably numerous. From praises of urban culture to laments of urban decay, from laudatory pastoral traditions that praised the countryside to elite disdain for life outside of urban civilization, Chrysostom inherited a variety of Greek and Roman traditions, including through his education under Libanius, as well as Christian traditions.[10] A brief overview of some of the rhetorical models available to Chrysostom reveals that he presumed that his audience privileged the city and urban living and scorned the countryside and its inhabitants, even though he argued that rural living produced better Christians than life in the metropolis of Antioch did. Inheriting a common cultural perception that urban and rural were significantly distinct from one another, Chrysostom—like Libanius—selected for his orations particular depictions of each from a variety of possible models in an effort to reshape how members of his audience perceived the local landscape.

Aesop's long-lived fable about the country mouse and the city mouse testifies that the perception of a sharp distinction between city and country was ancient and culturally ingrained in the eastern Mediterranean by the time of the Roman Empire:

> A city mouse once happened to pay a visit to the house of a country mouse where he was served a humble meal of acorns. The city mouse . . . persuaded the country mouse to pay him a visit. The city mouse then brought the country mouse into a room that was overflowing with food. As they were feasting on various delicacies, a butler opened the door. The city mouse quickly concealed himself in a familiar

---

9. Cresswell, *In Place/Out of Place*, 8.

10. For Libanius as John Chrysostom's teacher, see, for example, Jorit Wintjes, *Das Leben des Libanius* (Rahden/Westf.: Marie Leidorf Press, 2005), 177–79; Raffaella Cribiore, *The School of Libanius in Late Antique Antioch* (Princeton, NJ: Princeton University Press, 2007), 2.

mouse-hole, but the poor country mouse was not acquainted with the house and frantically scurried around the floorboards, frightened out of his wits.[11]

The story of the country mouse and the city mouse attributed to Aesop survives in many forms in Greek and Latin. One version is even attributed to Aphthonius, a fourth-century Antiochene who knew Libanius. At least rhetorically, then, the distinctions that Chrysostom drew between those in the city and those outside were well established in his culture. There were, however, different possibilities for how the two were valued, and the relation that they were seen to have to each other.[12]

On the one hand, perhaps the most prevalent cultural norm in the Roman period portrayed urban culture, people, and places as the epitome of all that was cultured, as what distinguished the civilized Romans from the so-called barbarians, who, at least rhetorically, lived outside the empire's boundaries.[13] In this sense, cities were the center of education and *paideia;* they were the site of government, sophistication, knowledge, and law. In this model, the countryside suffered in comparison, appearing as a place without luxury and sophistication, without the games and laws that made life civilized, and as home to people who were uncultured and uneducated.

Some of the writings of Libanius provide a useful example of this model and a comparison for Chrysostom's rhetoric, since Libanius was Chrysostom's teacher for a time and they cohabited in the same city for decades. Like many authors, Libanius did not hold only one view on urban/rural characteristics consistently throughout his writings. Perhaps predictably, though, for a man who had devoted his life to the sophisticated intellectual pursuits of formal education and who was quite vocal about his displeasure at the discomfort of his physical ailments, Libanius often had disdainful words for the country and those who preferred it to the sophistication and luxury of urban living. In 364, for example, Libanius complained in a letter to the governor of Isauria concerning Libanius's student Dionysius, who had been accused of abduction (or rape): "I have regarded Dionysius as ill-starred since that day when you called him, but he chose his trees and the birds

11. *Aesop's Fables,* trans. Laura Gibbs (New York: Oxford University Press, 2008), 190–91.

12. In their introduction to the edited volume "Mondes ruraux en Orient et en Occident," Gisella Cantino Wataghin and Hervé Inglebert note the idealized positive and stereotypically negative images that emerge from Roman descriptions of rural people and places (Wataghin and Inglebert, "Introduction," *Antiquité Tardive* 20 [2012]: 14). They warn readers about adopting late medieval vocabulary and perceptions of a dichotomous countryside versus city when speaking about a premedieval context (21), and suggest that the phase "mondes ruraux" better captures the diverse and vast landscapes of the parts of the Roman Empire that were not urban (22). My current discussion attempts to trace rhetorical representations of urban and rural places rather than providing a concrete description of the physical topography.

13. Liebeschuetz highlights this view of the Roman city in his study "The End of the Ancient City," in *The City in Late Antiquity,* ed. John Rich (New York: Routledge, 1992), esp. 1–3.

in them over becoming powerful in your retinue. If he had listened and had welcomed Fortune when she approached, he would have fame and wealth as an advocate and would not have had the leisure for the abduction" (*Ep.* 1168).[14] In this letter Libanius was clearly critical of Dionysius's choice of the trees and birds over a career as an advocate and lay some of the blame for Dionysius's current legal predicament on his rejection of a successful urban career. Libanius reiterated these sentiments to the governor the following year when he again described Dionysius as "the one who chose to tend goats rather than to practice rhetoric" (*Ep.* 1470). Given Libanius's own career, and his reference to Dionysius as one who "does not know the good that he has in his hands and will recognize it only when it is gone" (*Ep.* 1470), it is clear that Libanius did not think well of Dionysius's decision to leave a career in rhetoric to be in the countryside.[15]

Certain Christian traditions, too, adopted this narrative preference for the virtues of the city. As Christianity spread, more educated Romans sometimes flinched at the rather pedestrian nature of many of the teachings, texts, and company of early Christian congregations. While some humbled themselves by praising this very aspect of Christianity, others began to raise the status of the tradition, creating a complex Christian theology, reading scripture allegorically to demonstrate its sophistication, and writing Christian treatises that could compete with texts by the empire's other educated citizens as examples of elite learning and piety.[16] Constantine offered bishops financial backing and urban land, increasing political strength and episcopal structure, and the emperor Theodosius showed his strong support by legislating a particular Christian orthodoxy as the religion of the empire. Thus, Christianity became, by the time of John Chrysostom's ordination in 386, part of the empire's elite culture, and much of the empire's wealth, power, and learning was in the hands of Christian churches, congregants, and leaders. Such Christians, like many whom Chrysostom described among his congregants, could in good conscience join those Roman forebears who praised the "civility" of city life and disdained the "unlearned" and "uncivilized" countryside.

There was, however, an opposite value system that pervaded Christianity as well as the pastoral Greek and Roman textual traditions. From the early Greek writings of Aristophanes, Hesiod, Theocritus, Bion, and Moschus to the Latin pastoral poet Virgil, fourth-century elites like John Chrysostom inherited a long tradition that praised the countryside as an idyllic place of honest, sincere, and wise

14. Cribiore, *School,* 257. Cribiore has recently produced a translation of these letters about Dionysius from the Greek text in Richard Foerster, *Libanii Opera,* 12 vols. (Leipzig: Teubner, 1903–27). All translations from Libanius's *Epp.* 1168 and 1470 are Cribiore's (*School*), with my consultation of Foerster's Greek text, and Foerster's epistolary number.

15. Cribiore, *School,* 259.

16. See, for example, the discussion in Catherine Chin, *Grammar and Christianity in the Late Roman World* (Philadelphia: University of Pennsylvania Press, 2008).

people living in tune with nature as they had in an earlier idealized golden age.[17] Similarly, Plato narrated, through the character of Socrates, that true philosophers were those who were aloof from and ignorant of the things of the city (Plato, *Theaetetus* 173c–e). The city, in this case, was depicted as a place of corruption, evidence of a lost ideal, while those outside, and especially farmers or philosophers, were praised as the epitome of a happy human life.

Despite the sentiments that Libanius expressed in personal letters, as a successful professional teacher of rhetoric he was also familiar with the literary traditions that praised the idyllic countryside and the farmers who lived there. He wrote an encomium on farming, which was among the models that he used to teach his students, and this text is a rhetorical display of praise for rural life (*Encomium* 7).[18] He harkened back to Hesiod and noted the role that the gods played in the development of farming, thereby signifying its importance (7.1–2). Libanius praised farming as the best of all possible human pursuits, and one that made the farmers themselves good people; a farmer was serious and stayed far from "the quarreling in the *agora,* the courts and false accusations in the courts, the assembly and uproars in the assembly, neither indicting, nor lying, nor acting as a defendant, nor giving false testimony, nor demanding fair restitution, nor working for money with which to overwhelm another with disasters" (7.4). Libanius alleged that the gods were particularly responsive to farmers, who showed an unusual measure of self-control, "for no prostitutes or revelers or pimps or bouts of drunkenness provoke them toward Aphrodite; for these are not native to the countryside, but they devote attention to their wives and attend only to rightful intercourse for the production of children" (7.5). Farmers were courageous, wise, and escaped "the wide variety of diseases that luxurious living engenders" because they were "too strong to be defeated" by illness (7.6, 7, 8). Thus despite the disdain of his epistles, Libanius could also praise the countryside and those who lived there.[19]

---

17. See, for example, the idealized golden age and the high value placed on labor in Hesiod, *Works and Days,* and the portrayal of urban and rural dwellers in Aristophanes, *Acharnians.* See Carol Steer, "City Slicker versus Country Bumpkin: Farmers in the *Acharnians* of Aristophanes and the *Dyskolos* of Menander," in *Daimonopylai: Essays in Classics and the Classical Tradition presented to Edmund G. Berry,* ed. Rory Egan, Mark Joyal, and Edmund Grindlay Berry (Winnipeg: University of Manitoba, 2004), 383–96.

18. Craig Gibson has recently published the Greek text with a new English translation: *Libanius's Progymnasmata: Model Exercises in Greek Prose Composition and Rhetoric,* Writings from the Greco-Roman World 10 (Atlanta: Society of Biblical Literature, 2008). Gibson based his text on the Greek text in Richard Foerster, *Libanii Opera* (Leipzig: Teubner, 1915), 8:1–571. All translations from Libanius's *Encomium* 7 are Gibson's, with my consultation of Gibson's Greek text.

19. Even in this encomium on farming, however, Libanius's preference for city life is still visible. He claims that farming was what distinguished humankind from other animals, suggesting that a distinction from the naturalistic world was positive progress (Libanius, *Encomium* 7.3).

Christianity, meanwhile, developed its own complex responses to the question of the relative value of those people and places perceived as uneducated and unsophisticated. While some Christians worked to raise the status of Christian texts and congregants, early Christian apologists pointed positively to the humble origins of Jesus's first followers, illiterate fishermen and those whom Jesus cured of demon possession.[20] Likewise, the simple Greek of the New Testament texts became for many early Christians further evidence of the greatness of the texts' teachings, which were so self-evidently true that even the simplest people could understand them. Furthermore, Christian asceticism emerged alongside the increasing wealth and other trappings of power and prestige of many Christians around the empire. Thus, as some Christians reconciled their worldly success with Christian teachings, or even saw the former as evidence of Christianity's power and truth, other Christians rejected the material world and its priorities and privileges.[21] Such ascetics often saw material wealth, possessions, and luxury as detrimental to true Christianity, warning that they would lead to laziness and sexual immorality and would turn a person's attention away from God. These Christians echoed the values praised by Virgil, Moschus, and Theocritus when they lauded the virtues of a simple life of rural hard work, and understood such a life to cultivate a "natural" wisdom that was superior to the structured learning of an urban classroom.

As a student in Libanius's classroom in Antioch, it is possible that John Chrysostom learned Libanius's encomium on farming. Regardless, Chrysostom's formal education would have introduced him to the pastoral traditions of ancient literature at the same time that he would have been living among Antiochenes who were famous for their love of distinctly urban luxuries—baths, games, the theater, extravagant feasts, ostentatious clothes, and other physical signs of wealth.[22] It is

20. See, for example, Origen, *Contra Celsum* 1.62. Compare Peter Brown, *Power and Persuasion in Late Antiquity: Towards a Christian Empire* (Madison: University of Wisconsin Press, 1992), 73–74.

21. These efforts of course began long before the fourth century. See, for example, Clement of Alexandria, *Quis dives salvetur,* and the many verses in the books that became canonical in the New Testament, such as Acts 5.1–11, 1 Cor. 7.32–35, and James 5.1–9. Peter Brown long ago commented on the role that Christian ascetics played as "true philosophers" and in relation to traditional forms of Roman authority (Brown, *Power and Persuasion,* 4, 71–117). See also Helen Rhee, *Loving the Poor, Saving the Rich: Wealth, Poverty, and Early Christian Formation* (Grand Rapids, MI: Baker Academic, 2013); and Peter Brown, *Through the Eye of a Needle: Wealth, the Fall of Rome, and the Making of Christianity in the West, 350–550 AD* (Princeton, NJ: Princeton University Press, 2012).

22. Soler notes that Libanius, Julian, Ammianus Marcellinus, and John Chrysostom all characterize Antioch's citizens as inappropriately tied to luxury and frivolity: see Emmanuel Soler, *Le sacré et le salut à Antioche au IVe siècle apr. J.-C.: Pratiques festives et comportements religieux dans le processus de christianisation de la cité* (Beirut: Institut français du Proche-Orient, 2006), esp. 29–32; Soler, "Sacralité et partage du temps et de l'espace festifs à Antioche au IVe siècle," in *Les frontières du profane dans l'antiquité tardive,* Collection de l'École Française de Rome 428, ed. Éric Rebillard and Claire Sotinel (Rome: École française de Rome, 2010), 273–86.

no surprise, then, that Chrysostom recognized a clear rhetorical distinction between urban and rural; as he noted in one homily, "City and countryside are distinct from one another in day-to-day matters" (*De sanctis martyribus* [*De ss. martyr.*] 1).[23] At the same time, his respect for Christian asceticism led him to draw more heavily in his own writings on traditions that valorized the simplicity and goodness of the countryside and the natural wisdom of those who lived there, and to condemn all signs of luxury that he associated with urban living.[24] When Libanius and Chrysostom's audience praised the city over the country, it was to emphasize the civilized nature of urban life, whereas when Libanius and Chrysostom praised the countryside their emphasis was on the virtue of the more austere living it encouraged. This characterization might help to explain Libanius's preference for the (civilized) city life and Chrysostom's opposite preference for the (virtuous) country life. In addition, Libanius's primary goal was to educate and therefore urbanize his students, whereas Chrysostom's primary goal was to mold his students into good Christians. For Libanius, a rural background was thus more often something to be overcome, while for Chrysostom the austerity of rural life was something to be imitated.[25] Choosing carefully from among various traditional representations of city and country, John Chrysostom took advantage of connotations of urban and rural places and their inhabitants to construct a new "normative landscape" for his church congregants.

23. For all translations from *De ss. martyr.* I consulted the Greek text in PG 50.645–54 but follow the recent English translation in Johan Leemans, Wendy Mayer, Pauline Allen, and Boudewijn Dehandschutter, *"Let Us Die That We May Live": Greek Homilies on Christian Martyrs from Asia Minor, Palestine, and Syria (c. AD 350–AD 450)* (New York: Routledge, 2003), 115–26. In this chapter I consistently and exclusively translate the Greek word πόλις as "city" and the Greek word χώρα as "countryside." Isabella Sandwell has also observed the complex rhetorical relationship that John Chrysostom constructs between the city and the church: Sandwell, "Christian Self-Definition in the Fourth Century AD: John Chrysostom on Christianity, Imperial Rule, and the City," in *Culture and Society in Later Roman Antioch*, ed. Isabella Sandwell and Janet Huskinson (Oxford: Oxbow Books, 2004), 35–58.

24. Although Derwas Chitty's famous study is now outdated, not least for its tendency to take primary sources at face value without recognizing sufficiently their rhetorical nature, it discussed the perceived distinction between "the desert" and "the city" in early Christian ascetic literature: Chitty, *The Desert a City: An Introduction to the Study of Egyptian and Palestinian Monasticism under the Christian Empire* (Oxford: Blackwell Press, 1966). More recent scholars have continued the conversation by noting that the rhetorical construction of a sharp dichotomy between "the desert" and "the city" provided a means through which urban bishops could distance and control influential Christian ascetics, and that scholars should not interpret the sharp narrative distinction as representing a clear historical reality: see, for example, James Goehring, *Ascetics, Society, and the Desert: Studies in Early Egyptian Monasticism* (Harrisburg, PA: Trinity Press International, 1999), esp. 89–109, 110–33. John Chrysostom echoes this rhetorical distinction in *Hom. in Matt.* 68.3, as well as in the homilies discussed below, even though some Christians practiced their asceticism within cities, including Antioch during Chrysostom's lifetime.

25. I am grateful to Wendy Mayer and Gregor Kalas for these observations.

SIMPLY ORTHODOX: CONSTRUCTING URBAN
AND RURAL IDENTITIES

One effect of a normative geography is that it participates in constructing the identities of those who live within its landscape, whether or not they are part of the powerful elite who benefit from its ideological narrative. As Pierre Bourdieu writes, "Spatial structures structure not only the group's representation of the world but the group itself, which orders itself in accordance with this representation."[26] Chrysostom's *Catechesis* 8, *De sanctis martyribus,* and *Epulis sanctorum martyrum* (*De statuis* 19),[27] all preached in Antioch in the decade between 386 and 397, provide three examples of Chrysostom taking advantage of the presence of rural Christians to construct a new norm that he attributes to his urban congregants.[28] While he presumes that his audience values urban life and education much more highly than the life and teachings found in the countryside, Chrysostom attempts to shame his urban audience into abandoning the spiritual corruption that he believes is encouraged by urban living in favor of the allegedly simple and pure Christianity of their rural compatriots. Although the nature of the extant evidence makes it difficult to draw too many specific conclusions, it is worth noting that John Chrysostom's choice to highlight rural Christianity came at a time (the late fourth and early fifth centuries) when the rural land on the Limestone Massif east of Antioch was becoming noticeably more populated, and its population more visibly associated with Christianity.[29] By praising the work ethic of the thriving rural settlements in the region around Antioch, Chrysostom again connected religious

26. Pierre Bourdieu, *Outline of a Theory of Practice* (New York: Cambridge University Press, 1977), 163; cited in Cresswell, *In Place/Out of Place,* 8–9.

27. Frans van de Paverd duly notes in his book on Chrysostom's *De statuis* homilies that scholars might better refer to *De statuis* 19 as *Epul. ss. mart.,* and he dates the first delivery of this homily to April 12, 387: van de Paverd, *St. John Chrysostom: The Homilies on the Statues, An Introduction* (Rome: Pontifical Institute, 1991), xxvi–xxvii, 241–46, 364.

28. A version of this section is included in Christine Shepardson, "Meaningful Meetings: Constructing Linguistic Difference in Late Antique Antioch," in *Syriac Encounters* (Leuven: Peeters, forthcoming).

29. See Catherine Duvette, Bertrand Riba, and Marion Rivoal, "Évolution démographique et modes d'occupation du sol en Syrie du Nord: Les cas du Ğebel Waṣṭāni, du Ğebel Zāwiye et des marges arides (IIe-VIIe s.)," *Antiquité Tardive* 20 (2012): 92–94; Georges Tchalenko, *Villages antiques de la Syrie du Nord, le massif du Bélus à l'époque romaine, I-III,* Bibliothèque Archéologique et Historique 50 (Paris: P. Geuthner, 1953–58); and Georges Tate, *Les campagnes de la Syrie du Nord du IIe au VIIe siècle,* Bibliothèque Archéologique et Historique 133 (Paris: P. Geuthner, 1992). For the settlement and religious affiliations of the rural population closer to the city of Antioch, see Jesse Casana, "The Archaeological Landscape of Late Roman Antioch," in Sandwell and Huskinson, *Culture and Society,* 121; Tashe Vorderstrasse, "The Romanization and Christianization of the Antiochene Region: The Material Evidence from Three Sites," ibid., 94–95; Frank Trombley, "Christian Demography in the *territorium* of Antioch (4th–5th c.): Observations on the Epigraphy," ibid., 59.

orthodoxy, orthopraxy, and physical place, rhetorically deploying a normative geography to construct his ideal Christian identity. Inverting the cultural trope that he attributed to his audience, as shown below, he tried to persuade his city congregants to forgo the luxuries and excesses available in the city in order to live according to his asceticized ideal of orthodox Christianity.[30]

In all three of these texts it is clear that Chrysostom addresses Greek-speaking urban Christians about their rural Christian visitors and presumes that the former scorn the latter. His eighth baptismal homily addresses a congregation within the city of Antioch on the Saturday before Easter's baptismal ceremony, welcoming those he knows well, as well as those who "flowed into us from the countryside" (*Cat.* 8.1).[31] In this context, John Chrysostom chastises his urban listeners not to judge the visitors negatively because of their "barbarous language (*barbaron tēn glōttan*)" (8.2).[32] While many within Antioch who were well educated spoke a sophisticated Greek that displayed their status and education, Chrysostom here associates speech that he understood to be less civilized—almost certainly more "barbarous" Greek as well as the local Aramaic dialect, which was closely related to Edessene Syriac—with rural inhabitants. Chrysostom further encourages his urban congregants, "Let's overlook the fact that they have a way of speaking distinct from our own" (8.2). The linguistic and cultural differences of some of the rural visitors must have appeared striking to the urban residents, as he quickly reiterates, "Let's not simply look at their outward appearance and their mode of speech" (8.4).[33] In *Epulis sanctorum martyrum* Chrysostom addresses a mixed audience of Christians during a festival celebration within the city in April 387, again describes the rural visitors as "a people other to us in language" (*Epul. ss. mart.* 1/188),[34] and asks that his urban audience "not think less of them" (2/190).

---

30. Wendy Mayer has demonstrated that in such instances, John Chrysostom drew on his ideal of asceticism to redefine the value of material wealth for his Christian community, praising the "voluntary poverty" of the ascetics as the morally superior Christian life. See Mayer, "John Chrysostom on Poverty," in *Preaching Poverty in Late Antiquity: Perceptions and Realities*, ed. Pauline Allen, Bronwen Neil, and Wendy Mayer (Leipzig: Evangelische Verlagsanstalt, 2009), esp. 78–81, 96–111; and Mayer, "Poverty and Generosity toward the Poor in the Time of John Chrysostom," in *Wealth and Poverty in Early Church and Society*, ed. Susan Holman (Grand Rapids, MI: Baker Academic, 2008), 140–58.

31. For translations from Chrysostom's baptismal instructions I consulted the Greek text edited and translated into French by Antoine Wenger, *Jean Chrysostome: Huit catechèses baptismales inédites*, SC 50, 3rd ed. (Paris: Editions du Cerf, 1985), 247–60; unless otherwise indicated, however, I follow the recent English translation in Wendy Mayer and Pauline Allen, *John Chrysostom*, The Early Church Fathers (New York: Routledge, 2000), 126–31. For an English translation of the full set of baptismal homilies, see Paul Harkins, *St. John Chrysostom: Baptismal Instructions*, ACW 31 (New York: Newman Press, 1963).

32. In this chapter I consistently translate the Greek word γλῶττα as "language."

33. Chrysostom made similar comments in *De sanctis martyribus*, which he likewise presented at a church within the city walls (*De ss. martyr.* 1).

34. All translations from *Epul. ss. mart.* are my own from the Greek in PG 49.187–98; I include the PG page number after the PG paragraph number, for ease of reference.

His comments in these texts suggest that at least many of the visitors from the countryside were noticeably visually and aurally distinct from John's urban congregants, who generally greeted them with some disdain.

There is no question that there was significant linguistic diversity among the people who lived in and around the metropolis of Antioch in the fourth and early fifth centuries.[35] In addition to Chrysostom's comments that those from the countryside were "a people different from us in language" (*Epul. ss. mart.* 1/188),[36] in the fifth century Theodoret refers to "the few phrases" that the ascetic Aphrahat, who settled outside of Antioch, "had learned of Greek speech," claiming that Aphrahat spoke in "a semi-barbarous language" (*HR* 8.2; cf. 13.4, 7; 14.2; 17.9).[37] While it is important to note the possibility that someone who spoke a rural, uneducated dialect of Greek might be said by an educated urban Greek-speaker not to be able to speak "Greek," Theodoret's specific references to "the Syrian language (*tēi syrai glōttēi*)," and the evidence that Theodoret himself understood at least some Aramaic, suggest that he here refers to rural Aramaic and not rural Greek speech, although the details of what forms of Greek and Aramaic were spoken when, where,

35. While David Taylor and Fergus Millar note that the overwhelming majority of extant inscriptions in northern Roman Syria are in Greek up through the early fifth century, there is still some epigraphic evidence of local Aramaic dialects. See the discussion in David Taylor, "Bilingualism and Diglossia in Late Antique Syria and Mesopotamia," in *Bilingualism in Ancient Society: Language Contact and the Written Text*, ed. J. N. Adams, Mark Janse, and Simon Swain (New York: Oxford University Press, 2002), 298–331. See also Fergus Millar, *A Greek Roman Empire: Power and Belief under Theodosius II (408–450)* (Berkeley: University of California Press, 2006), 107; Fergus Millar, "Theodoret of Cyrrhus: A Syrian in Greek Dress?" in *From Rome to Constantinople: Studies in Honour of Averil Cameron*, ed. Hagit Amirav and R. B. ter Haar Romeny (Leuven: Peeters, 2007), 105–26; Frank Trombley, *Hellenic Religion and Christianization c. 370–529* (Leiden: E. J. Brill, 1994), 2:134–204; Trombley, "Christian Demography," 59–85; Tate, *Les campagnes*. Although Liebeschuetz wrote in an era when overly strong linguistic and social boundaries were presumed between "city and country dwellers," he nevertheless notes the complexities of these relations: J. H. W. G. Liebeschuetz, *Antioch: City and Imperial Administration in the Later Roman Empire* (Oxford: Clarendon Press, 1972), 61–73.

36. Compare John Chrysostom, *De ss. martyr.* 1 (PG 50.646).

37. In this chapter I consistently and exclusively translate the Greek word φωνή as "speech." All translations from Theodoret's *Historia religiosa* are my own from the Greek text edited by Pierre Canivet and Alice Leroy-Molinghen in *Théodoret de Cyr, Histoire des moines de Syrie (I-XIII)*, vol. 1, SC 234 (1977; repr., Paris: Les Editions du Cerf, 2006); and *Théodoret de Cyr, Histoire des moines de Syrie*, vol. 2, SC 257 (Paris: Les Editions du Cerf, 1979). There is an English translation in Richard Price, *A History of the Monks of Syria, by Theodoret of Cyrrhus* (Kalamazoo, MI: Cistercian Publications, 1985). Theresa Urbainczyk has noted some of the political advantages that Theodoret would have gained through his presentation of these monks as Syriac-speakers and of himself as an able translator: Urbainczyk, "'The Devil Spoke Syriac to Me': Theodoret in Syria," in *Ethnicity and Culture in Late Antiquity*, ed. Stephen Mitchell and Geoffrey Greatrex (London: Duckworth and The Classical Press of Wales, 2000), 253–65.

and by whom are complex.[38] Scholars have recently addressed two influential mis-representations: the simple categorization of the languages as "Greek" and "Syriac,"[39] and the sharp distinction between urban dwellers speaking the former and rural residents speaking the latter.[40] Sebastian Brock and David Taylor agree that there was a significant degree of bilingualism, and perhaps diglossia (using each language in particular contexts), in late antique Syria—a conclusion whose consequences have yet to be fully reflected in scholarship on Antioch. While formal Greek was most prevalent in the city, there were clearly also some people in the city whose first language was Aramaic, some in the countryside who spoke Greek, and some in both contexts who were functionally bilingual.[41]

Even if two particular individuals struggled to communicate with each other, it is unlikely that they were ever far from someone who could facilitate their conversation, as noted by Theodoret: the ascetic Macedonius spoke "in the Syrian lan-

38. Fergus Millar offers a conservative analysis of how much Aramaic (which he calls "Syriac") Theodoret knew, yet even he acknowledges that Theodoret's "comprehension of spoken Syriac went beyond grasping the meaning of individual words" ("Theodoret," 119; cf. 121, 124). See also J.-N. Guinot, *L'exégèse de Théodoret de Cyr,* Théologie Historique 100 (Paris: Beauchesne, 1995), 183–97. Theodoret also distinguished the dialects "of the Osrhoenoi, Syroi, Euphratesioi, Palestinoi, and Phoinikes" (*Quaestiones in librum Judicum* 19) and relates a dream in which he understood the Syrian language (*HR* 21.15). See Urbainczyk, "'The Devil Spoke Syriac,'" 253–65.

39. David Taylor rightly warns, "Some care should be taken to distinguish between different Aramaic dialects and not to presume that they are identical, or to label them all as, for example, 'Syriac,'" the specific Aramaic dialect of Edessa that seems to have remained primarily east of the Euphrates through the end of the fourth century ("Bilingualism," 303); cf. Millar, *A Greek Roman Empire,* 109. Likewise, we should distinguish the varieties of Greek that would have been spoken in various urban and rural settings. Pedro Gainzarain notes that Libanius's formal written Greek is itself influenced both by traditional Attic Greek and in some cases by the later, Koine Greek (Gainzarain, "La lengua de Libanio," *Veleia* 4 [1987]: 229–53); and Taylor adopts the vocabulary of "High" and "Low" languages, which could differentiate the public profile of Greek from the local use of Aramaic, as well as distinguish the "High" Greek of the educated elite from a variety of "Low" forms of Greek spoken by others in and around Antioch ("Bilingualism," 298 n. 2; 301). Brock and Taylor document, for example, Syrians who spoke Greek with a distinctively Syrian accent (Taylor, "Bilingualism," 308, citing Socrates, *HE* 6.11; Sebastian Brock, "Greek and Syriac in Late Antique Syria," in *Literacy and Power in the Ancient World,* ed. Alan Bowman and Greg Woolf [Cambridge: Cambridge University Press, 1994], 150); Taylor notes Aramaic grammar and vocabulary influences on Greek inscriptions ("Bilingualism," 308ff.), and Georges Tate earlier noted the imperfect Greek of some of the inscriptions from the neighboring Limestone Massif (Tate, "Les relations villes-campagnes dans le nord de la Syrie entre le IVe et le VIe siècle," in *Antioche de Syrie: Histoire, images et traces de la ville antique; Colloque de Lyon [octobre 2001],* ed. B. Cabouret, P.-L. Gatier, and C. Saliou, Topoi Suppl. 5 [Lyon: Maison de l'Orient et de la Méditerranée, 2004], 314).

40. Brock, "Greek and Syriac," 150, 153; Libanius, *Or.* 42.31; Taylor, "Bilingualism," 305, 314–15.

41. Although Edward Schoolman downplays the presence of "Syriac" in fourth-century Antioch, along the lines of earlier scholarship, he incorporates some of the evidence for linguistic variation in his study of the city: Schoolman, "Civic Transformation of the Mediterranean City: Antioch and Ravenna, 300–800 C.E." (PhD diss., University of California, Los Angeles, 2010), esp. 56–57, 71–74.

guage" in the center of Antioch, and an interpreter translated it "into Greek speech" for the military generals who were his audience (*HR* 13.7; cf. 13.4). There were daily interactions among those buying and selling in Antioch's markets, those participating in martyrs' festivals or baptism and ordination rituals, and those who interacted with the various mountain ascetics in the region. Thus, while Antiochenes were certainly aware of linguistic differences of all shades in their surroundings, there were probably few situations where communication across these linguistic differences was not possible. To be taken seriously, then, scholarship that presents the linguistic nuances of this region must also provide a thorough evaluation of the social interactions that took place there. It is now important to ask not only what the linguistic differences of late antique Antioch were, but also what rhetorical benefit a leader such as John Chrysostom gained by highlighting the differences.

All three of John Chrysostom's texts discussed above expect the audience to privilege urban over rural life, but encourage urban Christians to see their rural visitors as part of the one true Christian community. Thus, in the mixed congregation of his baptismal homily, Chrysostom reminds the urban congregants that the rural visitors "are our brothers [and sisters] and members of the body of the church" (*Cat.* 8.2),[42] and encourages the urban congregants, "Let's show genuine love towards them as if embracing our own members" (8.2). In *De sanctis martyribus,* Chrysostom reminds his audience, "Although city and countryside are distinct from one another in day-to-day matters, they share and are one in the reckoning of piety" (*De ss. martyr.* 1; cf. *Epul. ss. mart.* 1/188), just as they are one body, all of the true church. Chrysostom notes that Bishop Flavian had left the city for the day in order to celebrate at a martyr's shrine in the country. At first imitating the dichotomous language that he attributes to his Greek audience, Chrysostom claims that Flavian has "left us" and "run off to them" (*De ss. martyr.* 1). Only then does he model the change that he encourages from his congregation, quickly restating, "Rather, in going off to them he hasn't left us, for he has gone off to our brothers [and sisters]" (*De ss. martyr.* 1).

Speaking to a mixed congregation in *Catechesis* 8 and *Epulis sanctorum martyrum,* John directly addresses without any hesitation the equality of rural Christians with his urban congregants. In *De sanctis martyribus,* however, when he claims that the rural Christians are back in the countryside with Bishop Flavian,

---

42. Chrysostom's use of pronouns in this homily further emphasizes that he primarily addresses those who were part of his Greek-speaking congregation, for whom he uses first-person and sometimes second-person pronouns, in contrast to the third-person pronouns that he uses to speak of the visitors. In reality, Chrysostom's congregation undoubtedly consisted of people with widely varying language skills, from those who were highly educated in formal Greek rhetoric and oratory to those who struggled to understand any Greek at all.

Chrysostom allows a rhetorical sympathy with his urban listeners, acknowledging the divide between urban and rural that his listeners expect, and only then replacing the separation with a shared Christian unity. Beyond the distinction between "us" and "them," he here refers to the countryside as "weaker" and "inferior" to the city, temporarily upending the value system that he advocates in the other homilies. Explaining why "God planted martyrs . . . more in the countryside than in the city," he claims, "God has given more abundant honor to the inferior, because that's the weaker part [cf. 1 Cor 12.23], which is why it has enjoyed greater attention" (*De ss. martyr.* 1). While the thrust of all three of these texts is to encourage Greek-speaking Antiochene Christians to look beyond linguistic and visual differences to appreciate their rural Christian counterparts, Chrysostom tailors his rhetorical style to his audience, iterating in greater detail the stereotypes that he assumes his Greek audience holds only in the absence of the rural visitors. In each context, however, the listener is made aware of perceived differences between rural and urban Christians.

Having highlighted the differences, real and imagined, between rural and urban Christians while ostensibly trying to discourage drawing such distinctions, Chrysostom revalues the characteristics of each. Chrysostom differentiates the rural visitors from his urban congregants in order to define ideal Christian behavior for the latter. Overturning the assumptions of urban superiority and rural inferiority that he attributes to his audience, Chrysostom not only advocates for the equality of all Christians but even describes the people in the countryside as better Christians than his urban followers.[43]

Adopting an image available from Greek philosophy and early Christian asceticism, Chrysostom argues that the unlearned simplicity of the rural Christians actually reflects a deeper wisdom than his urban congregants assume.[44] He preaches to the mixed audience of his baptismal homily, "Let's overlook the fact that they have a barbarous language; instead let's get to know their inner thoughts," suggesting that while the urban Christians may mistake language that they do not understand for ignorance, in fact the rural Christians "demonstrate in practice the

---

43. Compare Sandwell, "Christian Self-Definition," 49.

44. Compare, for example, Athanasius's mid-fourth-century portrayal of the ascetic Antony, whom scholars such as David Brakke have shown was educated, but whom Athanasius portrayed as "unlearned yet wise" (Brakke, *Athanasius and Asceticism* [Baltimore: Johns Hopkins University Press, 1995], 203). Twenty years ago Peter Brown influentially demonstrated the ways in Christian ascetics, and sometimes bishops, began to supplant the roles of philosophers and became seen as representing the true philosophy in the later Roman Empire: Brown, *Power and Persuasion*, esp. 71–117. See also Athanasius, *Vita Antonii*; and Niketas Siniossoglou's analysis of Theodoret's description of asceticism as the true philosophy: Siniossoglou, *Plato and Theodoret: The Christian Appropriation of Platonic Philosophy and the Hellenic Intellectual Resistance* (New York: Cambridge University Press, 2008).

philosophy that we make an effort to learn" (*Cat.* 8.2).[45] Chrysostom reiterates, "This common person, who's of a rural background and knows no more than the details of farming and how to care for the land" in fact knows "precisely those truths which the philosophers who base their reputation on their beard and staff couldn't begin to imagine" (8.6). The visitors "have been educated in the true wisdom," and their "great wisdom about virtue" is, Chrysostom argues, "a clear demonstration of God's power" (8.5; 8.6). In *Epulis sanctorum martyrum* Chrysostom contrasts these rural Christians with a caricature of an urban philosopher. He describes the rural Christians as having "adorned their souls with the doctrines of the true philosophy," and even without formal learning any one of them would be able to give an accurate reply from his wisdom (*Epul. ss. mart.* 1/189–90).[46] Superior to educated Greeks who are not Christian, they are also, he claims, better Christians than his Greek urban congregants (*Epul. ss. mart.* 1/190; *De ss. martyr.* 1). Such comments are quite clearly for the benefit of his urban audience in both cases. The rural Christians themselves become a cipher through which Chrysostom can challenge his urban audience by arguing for the "illiterate" Christians' superiority over the educated city congregants.

In all three of these texts, Chrysostom demonstrates this superiority by emphasizing that actions are more powerful than spoken words. In the two homilies to a mixed congregation, he praises the deeds of the visitors, and in *De sanctis martyribus* the deeds of the martyrs themselves, located in the presence of the rural inhabitants. In so doing, Chrysostom spatially locates ideal religious piety in the rural outskirts, in sharp contrast to the corrupt urban center of Antioch.

The actions of the rural Christians in traveling into the city are but one part of John Chrysostom's praise of their Christian orthopraxy (*Cat.* 8.1). He challenges his mixed audience at the baptismal celebration: "Let's recognize that they demonstrate in practice (*dia tōn pragmatōn*) the philosophy that we make an effort to learn though discourse (*en logois*) (*Cat.* 8.2). That is, these "*idiōtes*" from the country demonstrate through their behavior the very same religious wisdom that Chrysostom and other Christian preachers attempt to convey through their sermons. He uses Paul's words from 1 Corinthians (4.12) and words attributed to Paul in Acts (20.34) to laud physical labor as the work of saints (*Cat.* 8.3), and praises the visitors in their presence, though in the third person, perhaps implying that he addresses anyone who understands, and speaks about only those who do not (8.3). Chrysostom's admiration for the rural life that he envisions these visitors leading

45. Jaclyn Maxwell examines the apparent levels of education of John Chrysostom's congregants, and the rhetorical sophistication of his sermons: Maxwell, *Christianization and Communication in Late Antiquity: John Chrysostom and His Congregation in Antioch* (New York: Cambridge University Press, 2006), esp. 65–117.

46. Maxwell analyzes this rhetorical trope (*Christianization*, 32–33).

is clear, as he describes their "angelic way of life" (8.4). Highlighting the power of the rural Christians' actions, Chrysostom claims that they have "demonstrated that they've fulfilled through their labors that saying of the apostle: 'That God's foolishness is wiser than human wisdom [1 Cor 1.25]'" (8.5).

Chrysostom's *Epulis sanctorum martyrum* similarly praises the actions of the rural visitors in the congregation that day, including praise that they "hurried to us" for the martyr's festival in the city (*Epul. ss. mart.* 1/190).[47] Although some of them could be found "ascending the holy *bēma* and cultivating the souls of those who listen," it was "the labor of the land" that was "a school of virtue and self-control" for them (1/188–89).[48] These visitors who "live in the country . . . confirm through actions the faith that comes through doctrines," through which they "surpassed all worldly imagination" (1/189). Thus echoing the classical pastoral genre as well as early Christian praise for the meek and lowly, Chrysostom uses the behaviors of the rural visitors to argue that life in the countryside promotes better Christian living, and better Christians, than the urban life of Antioch.[49]

Chrysostom spares no detail in his frequent criticisms of his urban church congregants, and these texts are no exception, as he works to distance his Greek audience members from their preference for urban living. In each of these homilies, he laments the physical laziness and wealthy ostentation of urban Christians, especially in contrast to the praiseworthy behavior of the rural Christians whom these wealthier urbanites scorn. Chrysostom criticizes the "extravagance and gluttony" that he claims only the rural Christians avoid: "They take only as much food as they need to stay alive" (*Cat.* 8.4). In *Epulis sanctorum martyrum,* Chrysostom conjures idealized pastoral images when he argues that unlike the urban Christians, the rural Christians have none of the "disorder of the city," and "they are not ashamed of work" like those who live in the city; they "gaped after none of the things that seem to be magnificent" (*Epul. ss. mart.* 1/188–89). The image that Chrysostom paints is one of the city as a hotbed of wealthy hedonism and the country as a paragon of virtuous sobriety; there is no question that Chrysostom's rhetoric constructs the urban landscape as presenting perpetual challenges to living as a Christian.

---

47. Chrysostom draws on earlier Christian images to associate the rural farmers with the apostles and other early followers of Jesus, suggesting a simple purity in their religiosity that came with their physical labor (*Epul. ss. mart.* 1/190).

48. Chrysostom here appears to suggest that some of these rural Christians served as preachers, as well as being farmers like those who listened to them. See van de Paverd, who argues that these men were rural priests (*Chrysostom,* 255–93, esp. 292).

49. Chrysostom's *De sanctis martyribus* similarly lauds actions over speech, in this case using the examples of martyrs housed at rural shrines (*De ss. martyr.* 1–2). In the absence of visible role models in their midst in the form of rural Christians, Chrysostom in this homily highlights the powerful actions of the martyrs associated with the rural shrines at which Bishop Flavian was preaching that very day.

In his baptismal homily, Chrysostom extends this discussion to the theological realm, emphasizing the distinction between "visible" and "spiritual" goods in order to stress the contrast between urban and rural Christians. Unlike the rural Christians who "received the promise of visible goods but kept their desire on the spiritual," Chrysostom claims about those in the city, "We who have received the promise of spiritual goods become excited about visible things" (*Cat.* 8.11). He insists, "We gape after the goods of this world, wealth, the glory of this life, luxury, and the honors that men can offer," which in fact are "nothing but shadows and dreams," dissipating quickly, the opposite of spiritual wealth (8.11). Having described the situation in such dichotomous terms, Chrysostom creates an easy springboard for his advocacy of imitating the rural Christians who have forgone luxury and ostentation in order to live a simple Christian life.[50]

The rural Christians who visited Antioch's church service emerge as carefully sculpted role models for Chrysostom's urban congregants.[51] Chrysostom criticizes his audience because whereas the countryside "poured" into the city for the urban festival, "the whole city should have gone off to them while the festival of the martyrs there is under way" (*De ss. martyr.* 1). That they did not do so is clear from the context of the sermon itself in an Antiochene church. He exhorts his audience, "Whenever we go away from [the church] let's not immediately surrender ourselves to inappropriate company or senseless conversations and fruitless pastimes" (4). He wishes his congregants would learn to "despise the money you have now," rather than flaunt it in competitive ostentatious displays (4). While Chrysostom elsewhere differentiates the "poor" from the "wealthy" in his urban congregation,[52]

---

50. Regarding Chrysostom's complex rhetoric regarding poverty, see Mayer, "John Chrysostom on Poverty"; Mayer, "Poverty and Generosity."

51. Although focusing on John Chrysostom's preaching in Constantinople more than in Antioch, Aideen Hartney has examined Chrysostom's propensity to offer role models to his audience through his preaching: Hartney, *John Chrysostom and the Transformation of the City* (London: Duckworth, 2004), 67–83.

52. In her research on John Chrysostom's audiences in Antioch and Constantinople Wendy Mayer notes the variety of people who would likely have heard him speak, as well as pointing out that when Chrysostom distinguishes between the "rich" and the "poor" among his listeners, he "usually means the very wealthy and the not quite so wealthy" (Mayer, "Who Came to Hear John Chrysostom Preach?" *Ephemerides Theologicae Lovanienses* 76.1 [2000]: 81). Brown (*Power and Persuasion*, esp. 91–103) notes that the abjectly poor were largely excluded from such church activities. Mayer observes that John Chrysostom's texts suggest that these poor remained outside the church building during his homilies ("Who Came?" 83). See also Wendy Mayer, "John Chrysostom and His Audiences: Distinguishing Different Congregations at Antioch and Constantinople," *Studia Patristica* 31 (1997): 70–75; Mayer, "John Chrysostom: Extraordinary Preacher, Ordinary Audience," in *Preacher and Audience: Studies in Early Christian and Byzantine Homiletics,* ed. Mary Cunningham and Pauline Allen (Boston: Brill, 1998), 105–37; Maxwell, *Christianization*, which addresses questions of Chrysostom's audience; and Isabella Sandwell, *Religious Identity in Late Antiquity: Greeks, Jews, and Christians in Antioch* (New York: Cambridge University Press, 2007), 14–15, 188–90, 205–8.

146 TRANSFORMATIVE TRANSGRESSIONS

in these texts he implies that all of his urban congregants are well off and able to be accused of laziness and hedonism in comparison to the Christians of the country-side.

In his baptismal homily, Chrysostom more vigorously calls on his urban audience to imitate the admirable lives of the rural Christians. He reiterates: "We said that, although they received a promise of what they could perceive, they sought out what they could imagine. . . . We, on the other hand, practice the opposite to them, and although we have a promise of what we can imagine, we lust after what we can perceive" (*Cat.* 8.20). Chrysostom thus urges his audience: "Let us imitate those who . . . were able to arrive first at such a height of vir-tue. . . . Let us transpose all our zeal to the care of the soul" (8.21).[53] This homily's baptismal context leads Chrysostom to strengthen his exhortations, urging eve-ryone who would be baptized to start their new life on the best possible path and never slip: "Let us strain our whole purpose to the desire for spiritual things. . . . Do not again let the whole day be used up in laziness and useless pastimes and in destructive gatherings and *symposia* and daily drink" (8.24). Inverting a tradi-tional Roman valuation of manual labor as appropriate only for those of lower status, Chrysostom discourages what he calls laziness but others might more generously associate with the Roman ideal of *otium*. More than merely an object for praise on the occasion of their visit, the rural Christians become a forceful means of disgracing the proud and wealthy urban congregants whom Chrysos-tom addresses in his effort to recalibrate their perceptions and consequently their behavior.

Antiochene leaders gained historical advantages by manipulating the rhetorical connotations of Antioch's physical places in order to define a new normative geog-raphy with expectations of orthopraxy that benefited their community. In these texts, John Chrysostom exploits classical and Christian tropes regarding urban and rural life (and people), highlighting the pastoral and Gospel images that ideal-ize the rural, and roundly criticizing the stereotypes of the urban excesses that he claims his Antiochene audience value so highly. Chrysostom took advantage of popular connotations of physical places (and their inhabitants) to construct his vision of Christianity as the true philosophy, exploiting the allegedly simple and pure orthodoxy of Christians outside the city—especially ascetic rural Chris-tians—to encourage his version of ideal behavior among his urban congregants. Such rhetoric had the added benefit of enabling his claims to control the charis-matic authority of the rural Christian ascetics who dotted the landscape outside Antioch's city walls.

---

53. The translation of this passage and the next are my own, since the excerpts in Mayer and Allen, *John Chrysostom,* do not include this chapter of the homily.

FROM MOUNTAINTOP TO MARKETPLACE:
THE TOPOGRAPHY OF TRANSGRESSION

Antioch's urban/rural divide was transgressed in significant ways in the aftermath of the so-called Statues Riot in 387 C.E.[54] Early in that year the city erupted in a chaotic riot that saw the statues of the imperial family dragged through the streets, and buildings set ablaze by an unruly mob. A heavy tax announced by the emperor Theodosius seemed unbearable to Antioch's citizens, who undoubtedly still had in mind the famines their city had suffered in recent years, and the city erupted in a violent outcry at the new imperial imposition. Such abuse of the images of the imperial family, however, and hostility toward the emperor's wishes could not be overlooked, and as the heat of the riot subsided, Antiochenes of every status were filled with fear about how violent the emperor's response would be to the citizens and structures of their city. Those of lower status who were found to have participated in the riot were quickly put to death, while the city's baths, theater, and hippodrome were closed by imperial decree. In the days immediately following the riot, many citizens fled the walls of the city, fearful of the looming additional imperial punishment that seemed certain. Officials came from Constantinople to hold trials and ultimately held Antioch's leading members of the *boulē* responsible. The great city of Antioch, one of the stars of the empire, feared for its very existence, let alone its renown, and it was only an imperial pardon, engineered according to John Chrysostom by Bishop Flavian and several Christian ascetics, that saved the condemned city and its civic leaders.

---

54. For more on the riot, including rhetorical constructions of it, see Dorothea French, "Rhetoric and the Rebellion of A.D. 387 in Antioch," *Historia: Zeitschrift für alte Geschichte* 47.4 (1998): 468–84; Hartmut Leppin, "Steuern, Aufstand und Rhetoren: Der Antiochener Steueraufstand von 387 in christlicher und heidnischer Deutung," in *Gedeutete Realität: Krisen, Wirklichkeiten, Interpretationen (3.-6. Jh. n. Chr.)*, ed. Hartwin Brandt (Stuttgart: Franz Steiner Press, 1999), 103–23. On the riot and this series of homilies more generally, see van de Paverd, *Chrysostom*; Robert Browning, "The Riot of A.D. 387 in Antioch: The Role of the Theatrical Claques in the Later Empire," *Journal of Roman Studies* 42.1–2 (1952): 13–20; J. Volk, "Die Predigten des Johannes Chrysostomus über die Statuen," *Zeitschrift für praktische Theologie* 8 (1886): 128–51; Laurence Brauttier, "L'image d'Antioche dans les homélies *Sur les statues* de Jean Chrysostome," *Revue des Études Grecques* 106 (1993): 619–35; J.-M. Leroux, "Saint Jean Chrysostome: Les Homélies sur les statues," *Studia Patristica* 3 (1961): 232–39; Alberto Quiroga Puertas, *La retórica de Libanio y de Juan Crisóstomo en la Revuelta de las Estatuas* (Salerno: Helios Editrice, 2007); Emmanuel Soler, "Evêque et pasteurs à Antioche sous l'empereur Théodose: L'engagement chrétien dans la défense de la cité après la sédition des statues (387)," in *Vescovi e pastori in epoca teodosiana*, Incontro di Studiosi dell'Antichità 25, Studia Ephemeridis Augustinianum 58 (Rome: Roma Inst. Patristicum Augustinianum, 1997), 461–67; J. H. W. G. Liebeschuetz, *Ambrose and John Chrysostom: Clerics between Desert and Empire* (New York: Oxford University Press, 2011), 209–15; Kirsten Gross-Albenhausen, *Imperator christianissimus: Der christliche Kaiser bei Ambrosius und Johannes Chrysostomus* (Frankfurt am Main: Marthe Clauss Press, 1999), 170–83.

John Chrysostom's *De statuis* homilies, which stem from the days immediately following the riot, not surprisingly tell us as much about his own interest in reshaping the image of the city as they tell us about the riot.[55] With his interest in Antioch's physical topography, Chrysostom highlights the significant ways in which the city was transformed in the aftermath of the riot. Numerous urban citizens fled to the mountains outside the city, while others took refuge in Chrysostom's church. The *agora* and other public civic areas of the city became silent and deserted.[56] On the other hand, Chrysostom narrates that the crisis was resolved and the city restored thanks in large part to a group of mountain ascetics leaving their places of withdrawal and entering the very center of the city's public space in order to negotiate a peaceful resolution to the crisis.[57] As Chrysostom relates, "Those living in the cities flew away to the mountains and the deserted areas, but those of the deserted area rushed into the city" (*De statuis* 17.2/174).[58] In these homilies Chrysostom's rhetoric about transgression locates his church building as a safe refuge in an otherwise dangerous urban environment, and highlights the authority of the rural ascetics.[59]

55. See the useful comparison of Chrysostom's and Libanius's narrations of these events in Alberto Quiroga Puertas, "Juan Crisóstomo *De Statuis* XVIII, 2 y Libanio *Or.* XXII, 22: Variaciones sobre un mismo hecho," *Florentia Iliberritana* 16 (2005): 285–95. See also Leppin, "Steuern," 103–23.

56. Lavan notes, "Chrysostom's view of the *agora* was decidedly negative," and observes that for Chrysostom "the Church was now the new focus" of the city (*"Agorai,"* 167). This claim is perhaps best illustrated through Chrysostom's writings about the Statues Riot.

57. In this case, the ascetics acted on behalf of the city much as Andrea Pellizzari describes that the *curia* traditionally did. Pellizzari notes that Libanius frequently uses the words σωτήρ and σωτηρία to train his students to consider intervening on behalf of the city or "saving" the city as one of the highest virtues, a virtue that he hoped they would demonstrate when many of them grew up to be local officials themselves: Pellizzari, "'Salvare le città': Lessico e ideologia nell'opera di Libanio," *KOINΩNIA: Revista dell'Associazione di Studi Tardoantichi* 35 (2011): 45–61. Leppin ("Steuern," 103–23) has persuasively shown the ways in which John Chrysostom and Libanius each constructed a particular narrative of the riot and its aftermath that reflected well on its author. Soler (*Le sacré et le salut*, 216–18) discusses the entry of the ascetics during the crisis; cf. Alberto Quiroga Puertas, "'Como ángeles venidos del cielo': Los monjes en la homilía XVII (*De Statuis*) de Juan Crisóstomo," *Euphrosyne* 36 (2008): 327–32. Peter Brown (*Power and Persuasion*, 105–6) notes regarding this incident that Theodosius chose to credit "the bishop and the monks" instead of "the civic notables" with persuading him to act leniently toward the city.

58. All translations from *De statuis* 17 are my own from the Greek in PG 49.171–80 and include the PG page number after the PG paragraph number. An English translation of this text can be found in Mayer and Allen, *John Chrysostom*, 105–17.

59. Here, as elsewhere, Chrysostom presents himself as the powerful mediator of the ascetics. See also Puertas, "Como ángeles venidos del cielo." Compare also *De incomp.* 6.19, in which Chrysostom reminds the ascetics that they should support the episcopal leadership in the city. Peter Brown's influential essay, "The Rise and Function of the Holy Man in Late Antiquity," *Journal of Roman Studies* 61 (1971): 80–101, has made this a standard element of understanding the power dynamics of Christianity in late antiquity. Decades of scholars have used Brown's ideas since the publication of this article to give

In the sermons given in the days and weeks following the riot, Chrysostom repeatedly refers to the large number of Antioch's citizens, many of them wealthy, who fled to the mountains and what Chrysostom calls the deserted areas (*erēmia*) outside the city walls, seeking refuge from the tribunal that had been called to investigate the riot and punish those who had participated. While Chrysostom refers to the flight in the midst of the crisis as well as after the crisis had been resolved, his criticism of those who fled the city is understandably sharper in retrospect, after their pardon, than it was while the outcome was still pending.

In Homily 2, the first that Chrysostom preached after the riot, he refers to the flight of Antioch's citizens in order to lament the city's loss and desolation. He describes the contrast before and after the riot: "Before there was nothing more blessed than our city; nothing more melancholy than it has now become. Just as bees buzzing around the honeycomb, so every day those living in the city flew about the *agora* . . . but look now, this 'honeycomb' has become deserted. For just as smoke [drives away] those bees, so fear drove away these 'bees'" (*De statuis* 2.1/34–35).[60] Chrysostom reiterates that Antioch "stands deserted, stripped of nearly all her inhabitants," suggesting that large numbers had fled outside the city walls: "All flee the [place that] bore them as they would a snare; they leave it behind as they would a ruin; they leap away as from a fire. And just as when a house is set on fire not only those living in the house but all nearby leap away with great haste . . . so . . . each hurries to go forth" out of fear that the emperor might destroy the city; the city suffered "a flight without enemies; a migration without a battle," and now others receive Antioch's exiles (2.1/35). The large crowds that usually bustled in the city's public places "have now been driven away" (2.2/36). In the most immediate aftermath, Chrysostom laments the flight from the city without the chastisement that would follow as the days progressed.

With a few more days to adjust to the situation, Chrysostom imagines the future and predicts, "The multitude will return again to our city; and now we will teach the fugitives to entrust our hopes of salvation (*sōtēria*) not to the safety of place nor to flight and withdrawal, but to reverence of soul and to virtue of

---

this conversation more depth and nuance. See, for example, Peter Brown, "The Rise and Function of the Holy Man in Late Antiquity, 1971–1997," *JECS* 6.3 (1998): 353–76; the collection of essays published by other scholars on the twenty-fifth anniversary of Brown's initial essay, collected as a special issue in *JECS* 6.3 (1998); and the essays in James Howard-Johnston and Paul Antony Hayward, eds., *The Cult of Saints in Late Antiquity and the Middle Ages: Essays on the Contribution of Peter Brown* (New York: Oxford University Press, 1999). For an analysis of John Chrysostom's personal construction of priestly power in *De sacerdotio*, see Chris de Wet, "The Priestly Body: Power-Discourse and Identity in John Chrysostom's *De Sacerdotio*," *Religion & Theology* 18 (2011): 351–79.

60. All translations from *De statuis* 2 are my own from the Greek in PG 49.33–48 and include the PG page number after the PG paragraph number.

manners" (De statuis 4.6/68).[61] Already his lament for his city's desolation has turned to a warning about the spiritual safety and welfare of its inhabitants, and the following day he uses the story of Jonah and the Ninevites to show that in contrast to Antioch's citizens, the Ninevites "did not flee the city as we do now, but remaining they caused it to stand. . . . They did not withdraw, each from his house, as we do now, but they withdrew, each from his evil way" (5.5/76).[62] Chrysostom chastises the Antiochenes for their behavior: "We wheel around the things of our house and go around seeking where we might lay down the property, but it is necessary to seek where we might entrust our soul" (5.6/77). Chrysostom ridicules those who have fled, or who wish to flee, for misinterpreting the situation: "Is it because you remain in the city that God is provoked, that you flee? It is because you sin that God is irritated" (5.6/78). Chrysostom echoes this expression of ridicule the following day, claiming that he does not do so "to accuse those who fled," but nevertheless asking his audience to reconsider their response to the crisis: "Let us not entrust our salvation to flight, but let us flee from sins and let us depart from the evil way" (6.4/87).[63] In the initial aftermath of the riot, Chrysostom mourned that the citizens had fled the city; as the days passed, he used their flight as a lesson for spiritual growth; but weeks later, after the danger had passed and the city had escaped serious punishment, he reflected anew on the initial flight from the city.

In hindsight after the peaceful resolution of the crisis, Chrysostom again refers to the mass exodus from the city in the days following the riot, but in that context he recalls the flight in order to contrast the cowardly and useless behavior with the productive behavior of others who did not flee the city. Chrysostom remembers with his audience the time "when the majority of the city had moved from the fear and threats, . . . fear setting them everywhere" (De statuis 13.6/136).[64] Days later he criticizes specifically the philosophers who "abandoned the city; they all leapt away"; and he censures the high-ranked administrators "who were in power, who were surrounded with extraordinary wealth, who had great freedom of speech toward the emperor" because "leaving their houses deserted, they all considered

---

61. All translations from De statuis 4 are my own from the Greek in PG 49.59–68 and include the PG page number after the PG paragraph number. In this chapter I consistently and exclusively translate the Greek word τόπος as "place." In addition, the Greek term σωτηρία meant more mundanely "safety," but in Christianity it came to have the connotations of the English term "salvation," so I use "salvation" in these texts to suggest this dual connotation of physical safety and spiritual salvation for Chrysostom's church audience, as he plays with both meanings of this term in these homilies.

62. All translations from De statuis 5 are my own from the Greek in PG 49.67–82 and include the PG page number after the PG paragraph number.

63. All translations from De statuis 6 are my own from the Greek in PG 49.81–92 and include the PG page number after the PG paragraph number.

64. All translations from De statuis 13 are my own from the Greek in PG 49.135–44 and include the PG page number after the PG paragraph number.

their own safety" (17.2/174). The following day he adds to that another sharp criticism of the wealthy and powerful of the city: "Our city was in danger of being utterly destroyed, and none of the rich and famous and notable men dared to appear in the [city's] center, but all fled and leapt away" (18.4/186).[65] Over the weeks following the riot, Chrysostom's homilies make clear that noticeably large numbers of people left the city seeking safety elsewhere. While some Antiochenes fled to the church, those whom Chrysostom describes above fled farther, leaving the city gates and entering the areas outside.

Chrysostom is explicit in several homilies that large numbers of refugees fled the city altogether, crossing the urban/rural boundary for the specific purpose of seeking safety in the mountains and deserted places of the surrounding countryside. He describes them rushing to the allegedly deserted area (*De statuis* 2.5/41), saying that those who left the city "hid themselves in caves" (17.2/174). He later addresses those who had returned by referring to the time of crisis "when you fled into the deserted areas, and ran to the tops of the mountains" (18.4/188).[66] He recounts the large number of Antioch's inhabitants who took refuge "in the deserts, in the ravines, and in unseen places" (13.6/136; cf. *De statuis* 11.1/119).[67] Chrysostom's rhetoric is complicated by the fact that he not only describes the rhetorical binaries of the dangerous city and the safe countryside, but he also recognizes that the deserted places outside the city walls could pose dangers to the city's fleeing inhabitants. Thus he describes some of the refugees falling prey to wild animals (*De statuis* 21; cf. Libanius, *Or.* 23). These stories do not, however, deter Chrysostom from his general characterizations. In fact, the dangers that the refugees discovered in the wilderness in the aftermath of the riot, as well as the increased purity of the city, parallel a much broader narrative of inversion that Chrysostom attributes to this liminal time.

In addition to those who fled the city's public spaces for the refuge of the surrounding countryside, others who stayed within the city walls nevertheless removed themselves from the public areas such as the *agora* and the streets, and from the temporarily closed theater, hippodrome, and public baths, taking refuge, according to Chrysostom, in their homes and in the Christian church in which he presented these homilies. Chrysostom describes many of the city's public spaces as deserted and closed, saying that the emperor "closed up the orchestra, that he made the hippodrome inaccessible, that he has shut up and checked the streams of wickedness. . . . Our baths have been shut up" (*De statuis* 17.2/176).[68] According to

65. All translations from *De statuis* 18 are my own from the Greek in PG 49.179–88 and include the PG page number after the PG paragraph number.

66. Compare also John Chrysostom, *De statuis* 6.

67. All translations from *De statuis* 11 are my own from the Greek in PG 49.119–28 and include the PG page number after the PG paragraph number.

68. See Edward Schoolman's detailed analysis of Antioch's baths, including this incident of their closure after the riot: Schoolman, "Civic Transformation," 211–70.

Chrysostom, "Even the *agora* has become impassable to us, and each person is shut up within the walls of his own house. . . . For many of those who inhabit this city it is not safe to go out or to appear in the [city's] center" (2.2/35). In fact, Chrysostom claims, even "if someone who is free of this fear and anguish wishes to rush into the *agora*, he is immediately driven into his own house by the joyless sight" (2.2/36). While many fled outside the city, even those who remained within the city walls vacated the public spaces.

There is no question that the riot of 387 was an urban crisis, and in fact Chrysostom describes the upheaval as inherent to the urban context, home to lascivious theaters, immoral behavior, and rowdy, impious people. Given Chrysostom's emphasis on urban corruption and the superior piety of those in the countryside, it is little surprise that the city walls, far from offering protection to the wealthy and educated who lived therein, in this case delimited the troubled area of chaos and danger, and that endangered city-dwellers sought refuge by transgressing the urban/rural divide and fleeing for the presumed safety of the surrounding countryside, the rhetorical antithesis of the urban center.

In the aftermath of the riot, however, movement went not only from the city to the mountains, but from the mountains to the city, as the Christian ascetics who had withdrawn from urban living entered the very center of the city, bringing with them, in Chrysostom's retelling, an authority that overcame the urban government authorities and brought peace and reconciliation to the troubled city.[69] Despite their physical location outside the city walls, the Christian ascetics who lived near Antioch were quite present to Antioch's citizens and Chrysostom's congregation. Chrysostom refers in passing to these ascetics two weeks after the riot, suggesting that if his audience wanted to test the truth of his claims, they should "go up to the tops of the mountains and examine the monks there, those in sackcloth, those in bonds, those in fasting, those shut up in darkness" (*De statuis* 6.3/85).[70] After the

69. Chrysostom describes the ascetics' entry into the city to those who were present during the events, but Libanius does not mention these ascetics in his descriptions of the events (*Or.* 19–21). It is possible that Chrysostom rhetorically increases the significance and numbers of these ascetics, though Libanius would have had strong ideological reasons to remain silent about the ascetics' participation (cf. Libanius, *Or.* 30; *Or.* 2), as Leppin suggests ("Steuern," 103–23). Theodoret mentions that Macedonius was one ascetic who intervened (*HR* 13), and that this was not a unique occurrence (*HR* 2). See also the discussion of the ascetics' authority and John Chrysostom's construction of their entry in Puertas, "Como ángeles venidos del cielo."

70. A visit to present-day Antakya, Turkey, recalls that the physical distance between these ascetics and the city could be quite different from the conceptual distance, as argued in Wendy Mayer, "Monasticism at Antioch and Constantinople in the Late Fourth Century: A Case of Exclusivity or Diversity?" in *Prayer and Spirituality in the Early Church,* ed. Pauline Allen and Raymond Canning, with Janelle Caiger (Brisbane: Centre for Early Christian Studies, Australian Catholic University, 1998), 1:275–88. While Chrysostom and others portray these ascetics as removed from city life, they remained an integral part of the life of many in the city. Antioch was nestled partway up the foot of the series of

crisis of the riot has passed, Chrysostom remembers in retrospect the critical role that some of the mountain ascetics played in negotiating a peaceful conclusion to the troubles. Chrysostom proudly remembers the ascetics' behavior, writing, "Those who feared God, those who spent time in monasteries, these ran down with great boldness and set all free" (18.4/186). Chrysostom assures his audience that the ascetics' behavior stemmed from the strength that they had gained through their religious practice and devotion, since they did not fear death, noting that although they were "far from" the trouble, they "willingly cast themselves into the middle of the fire, and delivered all" (18.4/186). Their withdrawal contributed to their authority, but they nevertheless remained proximate to the city and in many ways integral to the lives of its inhabitants.

Chrysostom describes in great detail the ascetics' migration from mountaintop to marketplace, and the benefit that their voluntary reentry into the urban center brought to the city's inhabitants, claiming that large numbers of ascetics arrived en masse in the city: "Then the monks who lived on the ridges of the mountains . . . left behind their tents and caves and ran together from every direction . . . while those saints appeared everywhere" (*De statuis* 17.1/172–73). While historically implausible, there is a rhetorical strength to Chrysostom's further claim that the ascetics left the mountains at "no one's exhortation, no one's advice when they saw such a cloud encircling the city" (17.1/172). With the city's citizens noticeably flee- ing to the mountain caves and areas around the city where the ascetics themselves lived, with the established habit of urban dwellers of visiting the mountain ascetics with entreaties for prayers and aid at other times, and with Chrysostom's com- ments that Antiochenes had flocked to the church in surprising numbers hoping that the Christian God could help in this time of crisis, it is implausible to imagine that no one had approached any of the ascetics about the city's current crisis or asked for their assistance. Nevertheless, by suggesting that the ascetics came to the city unbidden, Chrysostom highlights the selflessness of their actions as well as implying that knowledge of the need for their aid and prompting for their entry came from divine, not human, suggestion. The ascetics "ran from the mountains

small mountains called Silpius (and today also Staurin), where many of these fourth-century ascet- ics lived. The mountains sheltering Antakya still contain small caves, some of which were originally tombs and most of which show signs of habitation at some point in their long history. See Hatice Pamir, "Preliminary Results of the Recent Archaeological Researches in Antioch on the Orontes and Its Vicinity," in *Les sources de l'histoire du paysage urbain d'Antioche sur l'Oronte* (Paris: Université Paris 8, Vincennes-Saint-Denis, 2012), 259–70. Many of these face the city, giving the ascetics a view over the city and giving the city's inhabitants a view of the caves from the city streets. Chrysostom comments that the ascetics made the trip from their caves into the center of the city in one day (*De statuis* 17), spent most of the day, it seems, petitioning the magistrates, and then returned to their caves. As a young child, Theodoret also accompanied his mother to visit some of these ascetics on a day trip from the city, and he mentions ascetics who come into the city more regularly, such as Zeno's weekly visit (*HR* 12).

to the court" and in fact came in such large numbers and to such a sober and quiet city that Chrysostom says, "Our city has suddenly become a monastery" (17.2/173, 175).[71] Emphasizing that these ascetics had previously "been enclosed in their cells so many years," Chrysostom stresses the significance of their urban visit (17.1/172).

Chrysostom likewise highlights the authority that the ascetics held in the city, ironically granted to them in part from the recognition that they had withdrawn from urban life for their ascetic life in the mountains. Sight of them, alone, was enough to console the mourning population, and fearing nothing, including death, they addressed the leaders with boldness and would not leave until the judges agreed either to spare the people of the city or to send the ascetics to the emperor with the accused (*De statuis* 17.1/173).[72] They "appeared fearlessly in the *agora*" to address those who sat in judgment over the city; Chrysostom suggests that there were some who underestimated the ascetics, judging them only as poor, "having nothing more than a cheap cloak, living rustically (*agroikia*), formerly appearing to be nobodies, being in mountains and wooded areas" (17.2/174). Yet their behavior demonstrated that they were too powerful for anyone to resist, and they overcame the dangers that threatened the city as if they had been great warriors or lions, rescuing the inhabitants who cowered in fear (17.2/174). As unusual as the urban citizens fleeing en masse to the countryside was this mass entry of mountain ascetics to the city's center—and as Cresswell predicts from his research on twentieth-century culture, such topographical transgressions could transform the city.

CHRISTIANIZATION AND THE RHETORIC OF INVERSION

John Chrysostom's *De statuis* homilies narrate the turmoil that ensued after the riot, with many urban citizens fleeing to the mountains for safety, while the ascetics who had withdrawn from the city to the mountains entered the town center to negotiate a peaceful end to the conflict. In addition, Bishop Flavian traveled to Constantinople to speak to Emperor Theodosius, while officials from Constantinople traveled to Antioch to oversee the trials; wealthy and educated people in the city abandoned their wealth, while those who were physically poor and uneducated are described as the ones possessing true (spiritual) wealth and wisdom; and men abandoned Antioch's public spaces to be confined to prisons, homes, and caves, while women, forced from the privacy of their homes, are portrayed as wandering the wilds outside the city walls and roving the streets of the city looking for

71. John Chrysostom was apparently fond of drawing analogies to the city's self-presentation (cf. *In Kalends* 1).

72. Like the visiting Christians from the countryside, the ascetics emerge from Chrysostom's descriptions as visually distinct from the urban-dwelling Antiochenes.

shelter. Chrysostom's rhetoric raises theoretical issues of transgression that Cresswell has addressed in a different context. In a discussion of acts that are interpreted by normative culture as spatial transgressions, in this case, graffiti artists painting on public property without permission, Cresswell writes, "Along with this transgression is an alleged transformation (or threatened transformation) of the meaning of a place."[73] He concludes that a dominant culture often interprets what it understands to be spatial transgressions as disorder, which in turn can redefine the place that has been transgressed.[74] In Chrysostom's narration, the inversion of place that followed the riot of 387, with city dwellers fleeing out of the city and mountain ascetics entering the city's center, transformed the usually corrupt and theater-centered city into a pure Christian place, with his church at its center, thus Christianizing the very city itself and its structures of authority.[75] By highlighting such geographical and social inversions, John Chrysostom's *De statuis* homilies emphasize the severity of the civic chaos that the riot caused, chaos that, in turn, uniquely facilitated his narrative of the city's temporary Christianization.[76]

The depiction of the behavior of men and women in the city during the riot is particularly revealing, as the typical public/private (male/female) roles were reversed in the riot's aftermath. Whereas it was a commonplace that the public sphere in the ancient world was narratively the place of men, whose gender roles and expectations were often tied to their public role and visibility, *De statuis* 13 portrays Antioch's men as unusually cloistered, hidden from view in the days following the riot. The urban/rural rhetoric above addressed one way in which Antioch's men were no longer visible in the city, as they had fled the city altogether, leaving the *agora* deserted and the city silent. Antioch's public places were no longer the domain of its orators, shopkeepers, and leading men; the city streets were deserted, and the public baths and theaters were closed: "The *agora* was empty of men (*andrōn*)" (*De statuis* 13.6/136).[77] As discussed above, some of these men fled outside the city walls, and Chrysostom portrays them not as wandering in public view, but rather as having moved to "the deserted areas, ravines, and

73. Cresswell, *In Place/Out of Place*, 59.

74. See, for example, Cresswell, *In Place/Out of Place*, 37–50.

75. Hartmut Leppin has highlighted several particular ways in which John Chrysostom and Bishop Flavian took advantage of the riot in order to try to further Christianize the city and its citizens ("Steuern," 107–12). Liebeschuetz, on the other hand, has demonstrated some of the ways in which Roman cities, including Antioch, underwent slow administrative and population transformations in late antiquity ("End of the Ancient City," 6–36).

76. Claire Sotinel similarly noted that in these homilies Chrysostom describes an idealized Christian city: "Sotinel, La sphère profane dans l'espace urbain," in Rebillard and Sotinel, *Les frontières du profane*, 325.

77. Lavan has commented, "Chrysostom conceived of the market place primarily as a place for men," though he notes that Chrysostom's texts refer to women who are in the *agora* ("*Agorai*," 163).

unseen places" (13.6/136). Indeed, Chrysostom portrays these men as not only out of the public eye, but hidden out of sight in secret places.

Other men, some of Antioch's public officials among them, stayed within the city walls but nevertheless found themselves confined out of sight. Some were "snatched away from the house and held within, as if in a net or a snare" as prisoners while the tribunal sent from Constantinople held their trial to determine who was responsible for the riot and what their punishment should be (*De statuis* 13.2/138). Chrysostom describes residents silent from fear, "since many already, against all expectation, having been dragged away from the middle of the *agora*, were restrained within" (13.1/137). These prisoners included many of Antioch's city leaders, typically visible and freely mobile in the city's public places (13.2/138). These were "those who bred horses, who had judged the games, who could count a thousand more distinct duties they had," but who now lost their property and had seals placed on the doors of their homes; the riot's aftermath caused these public men to be sent away to the prison, where they were confined out of view (13.2/139). Whether in caves outside the city's walls or waiting out of sight for their trial, Antioch's prominent men are not publicly visible in Chrysostom's descriptions of the chaos that followed the riot.

The women of Antioch's great families, on the other hand, found themselves forced from their privacy and their homes and unusually on full and humiliatingly public display. Just as Chrysostom depicts the *agora* as "empty of men," he also claims, "The houses were empty of women," thus echoing the expectation that the *agora* was where men should be found, and houses were the places of women (*De statuis* 13.1/136). As with the men of the city, some of those women fled the city walls into the area outside. Chrysostom tells his audience, "Many also fell in with wild animals, while seeking deserted areas . . . not only men, but also small children and free and noble women" (21.3/218).[78] Other women stayed inside the city, but like the men, they fared scarcely better than those who fled. In fact, the wives of those imprisoned leading men of the city were cast into the public eye just as their husbands were confined out of view. Chrysostom noted that the wives of these men, "having been thrown out of their family house, . . . went around from house to house and from place to place" seeking a place to stay (13.2/139). Not only were these women publicly on display, but they did not even have a house to which they could retreat and were left wandering the streets without anywhere to go.

Still other women from the city went down to the *agora* and became a public spectacle in the city's center while their male relatives were walled up inside during the trial. "A mother and a sister of a certain person among those under trial within sat before the very vestibule of the judges, rolling themselves on the pavement and

---

78. All translations from *De statuis* 21 are my own from the Greek in PG 49.211–22 and include the PG page number after the PG paragraph number.

becoming a common spectacle to all the bystanders" (*De statuis* 13.1/137). They were not alone. Chrysostom speaks of the situation more broadly: "Wives and virgins who had been living in inner chambers now became a common spectacle to all; and those women who had been lying on a soft couch had the pavement instead of a bed" (13.1/138). There is, no doubt, an element of exaggeration in these homilies, though Libanius's retrospective descriptions of women wandering and endangered outside the city walls in *Oratio* 23 suggest that Chrysostom's texts must in some sense also reflect the events themselves. In Chrysostom's rhetoric, the city had been turned on its head, with its leading men confined out of sight and its well-born women wandering outside the city walls being eaten by wild animals. Nevertheless, in highlighting the ways in which the riot disrupted, and in fact upended, the behavior of Antioch's citizens, Chrysostom recreates the civic chaos that the riot caused in a way that echoes a not uncommon Christian inversion of traditional values.

The inversions caused by the riot coincide in these homilies with other Christian rhetoric, such as the revaluation of material wealth and the redefinition of "true" wisdom.[79] Christians like Chrysostom frequently valued spiritual Christian wisdom more highly than Greek education, and voluntary poverty (and an emphasis on spiritual wealth) more highly than material wealth, confronting, at least in an ideal sense, some of Antioch's cultural norms. In these texts, this Christian rhetoric complements the atypical behaviors described above and facilitates Chrysostom's narration of the Christianization of the city as a side effect, if only temporarily, of the riot.

Chrysostom regularly criticized his church congregants, as he does in *De statuis*. In these homilies he challenges his wealthier congregants' pride in their material possessions, lamenting the ostentation of Antioch's urban Christians, especially in contrast to the rural Christians, who "have no indecent spectacle, nor horse races, nor female prostitutes, nor any remaining disorder of the city, but rather every kind of licentiousness is driven out" (*Epul. ss. mart.* 1/188–89). Among the rural Christians, he claims, "there are no coquettish women, nor adorned clothes, nor makeup. . . . They have driven away all luxury and thrown out the evil floods of drunkenness, and they eat as much as they need to live" (1/190). Antioch, one of the largest cities in the fourth-century empire, was renowned in late antiquity for its luxury; it was home to a palace for the emperor, host of Olympic competitions, and site of the famed golden-domed church started under Constantine. Criticizing material wealth as well as gluttony and licentiousness, Chrysostom advocated moderation and asceticism. It seems clear from Chrysostom's sermons that this message was not easy to sell to Antioch's more prominent citizens, and that Chrysostom's ascetic values went against the grain for some in his congregation.

---

79. As Cresswell puts it, "Transgression, and the reaction to it, underlines those values that are considered correct and appropriate" (*In Place/Out of Place*, 21).

Chrysostom likewise revalued knowledge in a way that reversed the cultural expectations of many of Antioch's elite and educated residents. Adopting an image available from some Greek philosophers and early Christian ascetics, Chrysostom argued that the unlearned simplicity of the rural Christians actually reflected a deeper and truer wisdom that could not be gained through traditional Greek education or even from those "lovers of wisdom," Greek philosophers. The description of rural, uneducated Christians as skilled philosophers appears, for example, in *Epulis sanctorum martyrum,* as discussed above.[80]

According to Cresswell, "Social transformation usually implies an end state—a utopian dream"; and this is true in the case of Chrysostom's *De statuis* homilies.[81] In the context of such inversions, Chrysostom took advantage of the riot's aftermath to portray his church as a new center for the city of Antioch, whose earlier order had come undone. When the citizens fled, leaving the city deserted and silent, some locked themselves in their homes, but many others ran to Chrysostom's church building. In these homilies, Chrysostom's church becomes at least rhetorically the new focal point of the city, harboring Antioch's citizens within its walls and being the only bustling and crowded "urban" place, while Antioch's other public places lay silent and abandoned.[82] Chrysostom narrates this temporary response to the crisis as the Christianization of his city, as the city's focal point and center of social interaction changed from the *agora,* baths, and theater to his church. Add to this the silence and (at least temporary) end to the debaucheries that Chrysostom portrays as having taken place regularly in the baths and the theater, as well as the flocking of ascetics into the city's center, and Chrysostom easily depicts the whole of the city as transformed. In Chrysostom's words, the ascetics came into the silent city in such numbers that "our city has suddenly become a monastery" (*De statuis* 17.2/175).

According to Chrysostom, the post-riot exodus left the once-bustling city lifeless and silent. After the resolution of the conflict, Chrysostom recalls, "On account of this we also kept silent in those former days, because our whole city had been emptied and all had migrated to the deserted areas, and because those who were left behind were darkened by the cloud of hopelessness" (*De statuis* 11.1/119). In the first days after the riot, Chrysostom describes this silence with greater rhetorical flourish: "Silence is everywhere, full of shuddering, and solitude, and that longed-

---

80. Gilles Dorival also notes that Chrysostom's rhetoric in *De statuis* 17 and 19 contrasts the value and expected locations of Greek philosophers and Christian ascetics, with the former typically inhabiting the city and the latter the mountains and desert, though the aftermath of the riots temporarily turned this expectation on its head: Dorival, "Cyniques et chrétiens au temps des pères grecs," in *Valeurs dans le stoicism: Du portique à nos jours,* ed. M. Soetard (Lille: Presses Universitaires de Lille, 1993), 63–65.

81. Cresswell, *In Place/Out of Place,* 176.

82. Leppin also analyzes Chrysostom's rhetoric around this issue ("Steuern," 107–12).

for clamor of the crowd is stifled; and just as if all had sunk into the earth, so speechlessness now occupies the city, and all live as stones . . . and maintain the most severe stillness" (2.2/36). A few days removed from the violence of the riot, however, Chrysostom sees the silence in a more positive light: "Our city is being purified every day, and the lanes and streets and *agorai* are freed from lascivious and enervating songs . . . and our whole city has become a church, the workshops being shut, and all passing the day in these public prayers" (15.1–2/154–55).[83] So great, to Chrysostom, was the city's transformation, that the whole city of Antioch had "become a church," and during this time of transformation, he preaches to the city's inhabitants that they should transform their values to align with this newly Christianized city.[84]

Although Chrysostom notes that Christian leaders in Antioch had long counseled the city's inhabitants "to give up the theaters, and the licentiousness there," their preaching alone did not persuade them to desist, but the riot brought about these very things: "They voluntarily blocked off the orchestra, and the hippodrome has become inaccessible. Before this many among us ran to those, but now they all fled from there into the church, and all sing hymns to our God" (*De statuis* 15.2/153–54). Not only could Chrysostom rejoice that the theater was empty and closed, but even more, that his church was at the same time filled. He preaches in wonder that those very people "who never saw a church, but regularly attended the theater, now pass the whole day in church" (4.2/62). Chrysostom in fact reiterates this observation several times. He thanks God: "The *agora* has been emptied, but the church has been filled. . . . When therefore, beloved, you rush into the *agora* and you groan when you see the desolation, flee to the mother [the church] for refuge and immediately she will console you with the multitude of her own children" (4.1/59). Chrysostom continues by saying: "In the city we long to see people, just as those who live in the deserted areas. But when we flee into the church for refuge, we are pressed for room by the crowd. And just as when the sea rises up . . . fear compels all to flee from without into the harbor for refuge, so now also the waves of the *agora* and the storm of the city drive all together from everywhere into the church" (4.1/59). Through the crisis the city was transformed. Antioch's civic spaces became like the deserted areas outside the city, with their connotation as Christian space, home to ascetics and martyr shrines, and Chrysostom describes his church building as the center of this newly Christianized Antioch.

83. All translations from *De statuis* 15 are my own from the Greek in PG 49.153–62 and include the PG page number after the PG paragraph number. Compare also *De statuis* 2, in which Chrysostom differentiates the church from the theater. Emmanuel Soler also highlights the force of this image (*Le sacré et le salut,* 6).

84. Compare Sandwell, "Christian Self-Definition," 47–49.

Weeks later, in retrospect, Chrysostom reminds his audience of their flight to his church, and tries to encourage continued church attendance even in the absence of an impending threat. He recalls the difficulties for his audience, remembering, "The city has gained esteem because when such a danger seized her, neglecting all those in power . . . it fled for refuge to the church and to the priest of God, and with much faith clung to the hope from above" (*De statuis* 21.1/211); and he reminds his listeners that when Antioch's citizens were "cowering and dying first from fear they moved quickly to [God's] feet" (21.3/217). In his first homily after the reconciliation, he cries, "Blessed be God, that we no longer run here [to the church] together fleeing the danger without, but rather desiring to hear; that we no longer meet one another with agony, trembling, and concern, but with great freedom from fear, having shaken off all fear" (11.1/119). And the following day he promises the spiritual rewards of continued attendance: "Let us run to the church, from which we reaped the aid. For you know where you first fled, where you ran together, and from where our salvation came. Let us then hold this sacred anchor and as in the time of danger it did not betray us, so let us not leave it in the time of relief" (12.1/128).[85]

The chaos that followed the riot transformed, in John Chrysostom's eyes, the city of Antioch from corrupt to pious and Christian, with his church at its center.[86] There was a danger, though, that this Christianization of the city would be fleeting. As the physical danger subsided, the ascetics returned to their mountain caves, the citizens returned to the city, the baths and the theaters reopened, and all of the city's public spaces once again bustled with noisy life, John Chrysostom struggled to hold onto the lessons he had culled from the recent chaos, and to the Christianization of the city that the upheaval had allowed.[87] As the urban citizens who had flocked to the church in fear of physical danger drifted away, he chastised them that they should remember that the Christian God had saved them from physical destruction, and he encouraged them to save themselves from spiritual destruction as well. The transgression of places that followed the riot, with the urban citizens fleeing the city's public places that they usually inhabited, and the ascetics leaving their mountain caves to enter this newly silenced city center, allowed his city to be transformed, and having once become Christian, as he portrayed the liminal lands outside the city walls, it might, he could hope, be so again.

85. All translations from *De statuis* 12 are my own from the Greek in PG 49.127–36 and include the PG page number after the PG paragraph number.

86. Soler notes that the Statues Riot provided an excellent opportunity for Bishop Flavian and his followers to defend and attempt to Christianize the city (*Le sacré et le salut,* 215). Sotinel observes that the transformation that John Chrysostom describes, leaving no "profane" place in the city, was necessarily fleeting and possible only in such moments of acute crisis ("La sphère profane," 348–49).

87. Compare also John Chrysostom, *In Acts apost. hom.* 7, 41, 46, which also refer to the temporary effects a natural disaster could have in turning people's attention toward Christian practice. I am grateful to Wendy Mayer for bringing these references to my attention.

CONCLUSION: TRANSFORMING THE CITY

Given Greek and Roman traditions that privileged the learned *paideia* of the class-room, and Antioch's renown as a city whose citizens loved urban luxuries such as the baths, games, and theaters, it is little surprise that John Chrysostom attributes to his urban audience the perception that the city's educated elite were not only more sophisticated and well-to-do than their rural Christian compatriots, but far superior to the people who lived in the countryside outside Antioch's walls. These views represent some of the normative traditions of social and topographical boundaries that exist in any society, although Roman and Greek traditions and Christianity offered an alternative positive evaluation of the countryside as well.

Both Libanius and John Chrysostom demonstrate their rhetorical strengths through their choices of narrative models of urban and rural caricatures for differ-ent audiences, constructing new boundaries and participating in their mainte-nance in ways that furthered their own ideals. While Libanius was clearly familiar with the pastoral rhetorical traditions that praised the virtues of life in the coun-tryside, he still found strong support for his own preference for the relative com-fort of urban living. Chrysostom, on the other hand, knew the pastoral traditions but preferred the language of Christian asceticism as a means of valuing those whose lives were allegedly spiritually richer than their sparse material assets might have suggested to a stereotypical city-dweller. Both authors manipulated the pos-sible depictions of urban and rural people in their rich repertoire to be effective in their individual rhetorical projects. Chrysostom's *Catechesis* 8, *De sanctis martyri-bus,* and *Epulis sanctorum martyrum* demonstrate, for example, how the gifted preacher led his audience from their presumed preference for urban luxury toward Chrysostom's own ascetic Christian values on the occasions of rural guests' visits to his urban sanctuary.

When people cross a normative boundary they are perceived to be "out of place," and such transgressions transform how people see the places and the peo-ple in question. The Statues Riot of 387 produced severe transgressions, which in turn transformed the city of Antioch in John Chrysostom's descriptions. Chrysos-tom narrates the chaos of spring 387 by highlighting how it turned the city upside down—the residents of the city fled to the mountains, and the mountain ascetics came into the city; Antioch's leading men were locked up out of sight, and the lead-ing women became public spectacles in the *agora*. This language has noteworthy parallels with one of John Chrysostom's undated Antiochene homilies, *De terrae motu,*[88] in which Chrysostom notes that a serious earthquake terrified Antioch's

---

88. On the dating, see Wendy Mayer, *The Homilies of St John Chrysostom—Provenance: Reshaping the Foundations* (Rome: Pontificio Istituto Orientale, 2005), 27, 83. Soler notes the similarity of these texts, although he suggests without significant evidence that *De terrae motu* might be about the earth-quake mentioned in *De statuis* 2 (Soler, *Le sacré et le salut,* 237–38, 242).

citizens, and as a result "all" the people of Antioch flowed into the church.[89] As in his homilies *De statuis,* Chrysostom claims that in the aftermath of the earthquake "the houses are cleansed, the *agora* has been wiped clean," and Antioch's citizens sing psalms to God (*De terrae motu*). Most notably, Chrysostom observes to his audience in this homily, "You sanctified the foundation, the *agora;* you made our city [into] a church" (*De terrae motu*).[90]

Within the *De statuis* homilies, such rhetoric of inversion becomes the means through which the audience relives the severity of the chaos. Perhaps not coincidentally, the more typical Christian rhetoric that Chrysostom concurrently used, valuing Christian wisdom above Greek education or philosophy, and voluntary poverty and spiritual wealth over material luxury and ostentation, coincides well with his descriptions of such topsy-turvy times. Sculpted through this rhetoric, the turmoil of the Statues Riot—the spatial transgression and the disintegration of civic order that followed in its wake—offered Chrysostom a unique opportunity publicly to imagine a reordered, Christianized Antioch, transformed into an ideal version of itself. Chrysostom and his Christian community would have benefited from the identification of his church building as a powerful center in Antioch, as he again exploited narratives regarding place in an effort to reshape local performances of religious orthodoxy.

89. All translations from *De terrae motu* are my own from the Greek in PG 50.713–16.

90. Compare also John Chrysostom, *De Lazaro* 6, in which he also claims that during a local earthquake "all ran to the church." All translations of *De Lazaro* are my own from the Greek text in PG 48.963–1044; on the dating of Chrysostom's series of homilies on Lazarus, see Mayer, *Homilies of St John Chrysostom,* 74–75, 80. For an English translation of John Chrysostom's *De Lazaro* 1–7, see Catharine Roth, trans., *St. John Chrysostom: On Wealth and Poverty* (Crestwood, NY: St. Vladimir's Seminary Press, 1984).

5

Mapping a Textured Landscape

Temples, Martyrs, and Ascetics

Beyond church buildings and synagogues, Antioch's urban and rural landscape was populated by a variety of smaller places of religious ritual, from a host of temples of all sizes to a growing number of Christian martyr shrines scattered across the landscape. Also, Christian ascetics increasingly settled in the surrounding region, their live bodies drawing pilgrims to them in ways similar to the relics of earlier saints.[1] Like Libanius's classrooms, the locations of Babylas's relics, churches, and synagogues, these temples, shrines, and saints (living and dead) also shaped topography and identity within Antioch's *territorium,* particularly through the ways in which Libanius, John Chrysostom, and later Theodoret, church historian and a fifth-century bishop in Cyrrhus, mapped these extramural sites in their presentation of the region.

Maps, whether "graphic representation" or literary construction,[2] are, according to geographers, subject to influence by their creators, and as such "maps themselves often involve politics."[3] Phillip and Juliana Muehrcke describe cartography as "an

---

1. The work of Brouria Bitton-Ashkelony is particularly apt on this point, as it traces the rise of a Christian sacred geography through the fourth and fifth centuries: Bitton-Ashkelony, *Encountering the Sacred: The Debate on Christian Pilgrimage in Late Antiquity* (Berkeley: University of California Press, 2005).

2. Denis Cosgrove, "Mapping New Worlds: Culture and Cartography in Sixteenth-Century Venice," *Imago Mundi* 44 (1992): 65.

3. Gregory Knapp and Peter Herlihy, "Mapping the Landscape of Identity," *Yearbook: Conference of Latin Americanist Geographers* 27 (2002): 252. Compare Mark Monmonier, *How to Lie with Maps,* 2nd ed. (Chicago: University of Chicago Press, 1996). On the "rejection of the neutrality of maps" and the power "exercised with cartography," see J. B. Harley, "Deconstructing the Map," *Cartographica* 26.2 (1989): 8, 12.

intricate, controlled fiction,"[4] and according to Angèle Smith, "Maps, as representations of landscape, are political tools for controlling the sense and meaning of that landscape by claiming authority in the presentation of one perspective and heralding it as 'real' and 'true.'"[5] Libanius, John Chrysostom, and Theodoret painted narrative maps that advocated for their views of religious orthodoxy and orthopraxy. Superimposed on one another, their texts provide a richly textured topography.[6] By mapping the same area in different voices, they provide depth as well as diversity to the image of the region around Antioch. As Smith writes, "Representations of landscape are culturally determined, dependent on who is doing the 'seeing,'" and thus are sites of "cultural negotiations."[7] Just as a physical map might highlight waterways but exclude state borders, so Libanius highlighted places of the gods, while John Chrysostom and Theodoret privileged sites associated with Christianity.

After providing an overview of some of the places of religious piety in and around Antioch, this chapter will examine the individual pictures of extramural sites of religious ritual in the texts of Libanius, John Chrysostom, and Theodoret, and the benefits of comparing the perspectives and focal points of the three authors. The texts of these authors provide contrasting idealized visions of the landscape, whether they emphasize temples, martyrs, or ascetics. In addition, these authors describe active contests between representatives of different religious communities over particular extramural temples and saints' shrines, and these narratives add depth and nuance to the authors' initial idealized portrayals. Indeed, the depictions in these ideologically disparate sources reveal a complex and religiously charged landscape outside Antioch's city walls, and the roles that Christian martyrs and ascetics increasingly played in the shifting perceptions of its character.[8]

PLACES OF PIETY: ANTIOCH'S
RELIGIOUS LANDSCAPE

Temples and shrines to the gods, and the festivals and processions associated with them, played an important role in the lives of most Greeks and Romans, and their

4. Phillip Muehrcke with Juliana Muehrcke, *Map Use: Reading, Analysis, and Interpretation* (Madison, WI: JP Publications, 1978), 295.

5. Angèle Smith, "Landscape Representation: Place and Identity in Nineteenth-Century Ordnance Survey Maps of Ireland," in *Landscape, Memory, and History: Anthropological Perspectives,* ed. Pamela Stewart and Andrew Strathern (Sterling, VA: Pluto, 2003), 71.

6. This phrase echoes a book title on the academic study of place: Paul Adams, Steven Hoelscher, and Karen Till, eds., *Textures of Place: Exploring Humanist Geographies* (Minneapolis: University of Minnesota Press, 2001).

7. Smith, "Landscape Representation," 72.

8. Ramsay MacMullen has recently highlighted the significance of rural martyr shrines in the Christianization of the empire: MacMullen, *The Second Church: Popular Christianity, A.D. 200–400* (Atlanta: Society of Biblical Literature, 2009), esp. 104–11.

influence could still be felt in fourth-century Antioch.[9] Urban centers, for example, would often have large and well-funded temples, usually dedicated to some of the Olympian gods who were worshipped around the empire, such as Zeus, Athena, and Apollo. Temples for these Olympian gods, or at least the local versions of them (since the Olympian gods might be conflated with local gods that predated the Romans' occupation of the region), served to strengthen the Roman (or earlier Greek) identity of the city and its population. The more famous of these temples, such as Athena's Parthenon in Athens, Apollo's oracular temple at Delphi, or the large Asclepeion in Pergamon, drew visitors from all over the empire because they were seen as particularly powerful sites, ones at which visitors would have the best chance of connecting directly with the deity they wished to supplicate or honor. The oracular temple of Apollo in Daphne was a prominent site that drew supplicants from around the empire. In addition, an ancient temple of Artemis in the village of Meroë, five miles east of Antioch, appears also to have been viewed with great respect.[10] Such prominent temples marked powerful and highly visible places of traditional religious ritual around Antioch.[11] Combined with the numerous other temples and shrines in the city and outside its walls, some to gods known around the empire and others to local deities, these places reveal that the fourth-century map of the region still strongly reflected its historical connections with the gods.

Festival processions, while not permanent or always clearly defined places, also visibly transformed parts of the city into places associated with the gods, and affected the identities of those who participated, at least in the minds of leaders who wished to draw clear boundaries around religious orthopraxy.[12] As Ray Laurence

9. Emmanuel Soler's work is invaluable in this regard: Soler, *Le sacré et le salut à Antioche au IVe siècle apr. J.-C.: Pratiques festives et comportements religieux dans le processus de christianisation de la cité* (Beirut: Institut français du Proche-Orient, 2006). For an overview of Roman religion, see Mary Beard, John North, and Simon Price, *Religions of Rome*, vol. 1, *A History* (New York: Cambridge University Press, 1998); John North, *Roman Religion*, Greece & Rome: New Surveys in the Classics 30 (New York: Oxford University Press, 2000); Valerie Warrior, *Roman Religion*, Cambridge Introduction to Roman Civilization (New York: Cambridge University Press, 2006); Clifford Ando, *Roman Religion*, Edinburgh Readings on the Ancient World (Edinburgh: Edinburgh University Press, 2003); James Rives, *Religion in the Roman Empire*, Blackwell Ancient Religions (Malden, MA: Blackwell Publishers, 2007).

10. This prominent temple was originally dedicated to the regional goddess Anat (Anaitis), but by the Greek period she became associated with Artemis, and Libanius refers to the temple simply as a temple to Artemis (see Libanius, *Or.* 11.59 and *Or.* 5.42; Glanville Downey, *A History of Antioch in Syria: From Seleucus to the Arab Conquest* [Princeton, NJ: Princeton University Press, 1961], 48).

11. The emperor Julian writes at some length about his efforts to restore the temples in Antioch and Daphne, and Ammianus confirms his claims. See Julian, *Misopōgōn* 344–46, 361–63; Ammianus Marcellinus, *Res gest.* 22.12.6–8, 22.14.2. Ammianus also mentions Julian's religious rituals in Seleucia Pieria, Antioch's port city (Ammianus Marcellinus, *Res gest.* 22.14.4).

12. Maud Gleason and Timothy O'Sullivan have demonstrated the significance of public personal performance for identity, and O'Sullivan focused in particular on how the ways in which Romans walked through the city affected others' perceptions of them. Maud Gleason, *Making Men: Sophists*

and David Newsome observe in the preface to their edited volume on movement
and space in ancient Rome, Ostia, and Pompeii, "Movement did not simply occupy
space, it shaped and redefined it."[13] Emmanuel Soler notes that three Antiochene
regions were central to such celebrations: the city itself, the plateau of Daphne, and
Mount Silpius, the mountain abutting Antioch's southwestern edge.[14] The great
number of festival days celebrated around the empire, in addition to local festivals,
meant that processions through the streets in honor of a god, sometimes carrying
the god's image, and gatherings at the temples, would have transformed Antioch's
streets and *agorai*. While Julian made efforts to renew the funding in Antioch for
the traditional priesthoods during his time as emperor, Libanius's later claim (*Or.*
30.17–19) that people would still gather for celebratory meals in the temple precincts
on festival days, even though they were no longer allowed to offer sacrifices at the
altars, suggests that many traditional ritual practices continued through the late
fourth century. John Chrysostom also mentions visible community celebrations
devoted to the gods that transformed the city's streets, making the accusation that
during such festivities the participants became drunk, loud, and boisterous (e.g., *In
martyres*, PG 50.663).[15] While not stationary and permanent places, these festivals
and their processions are local points in addition to the temples that provided visible reminders and ritual celebrations of the gods.[16]

The region around Antioch was also home to numerous small temples and
shrines that do not appear in extant literary sources, but remain significant for a

---

and *Self-Presentation in Ancient Rome* (Princeton, NJ: Princeton University Press, 1995); Timothy
O'Sullivan, *Walking in Roman Culture* (New York: Cambridge University Press, 2011).

13. Ray Laurence and David Newsome, eds., *Rome, Ostia, Pompeii: Movement and Space* (New
York: Oxford University Press, 2011), vii.

14. Soler, *Le sacré et le salut*, 7; Soler also delineates some of the region's major festival celebrations
(*Le sacré et le salut*, 9–10). Some of the most recent critical work on Roman processions is on the city of
Rome. See, for example, Jacob Latham, "The Ritual Construction of Rome: Processions, Subjectivities,
and the City from the Late Republic to Late Antiquity" (PhD diss., University of California, Santa Barbara, 2007). See also James Skedros, "Shrines, Festivals, and the 'Undistinguished Mob,'" in *A People's
History of Christianity*, vol. 3, *Byzantine Christianity*, ed. Derek Krueger (Minneapolis: Fortress Press,
2006), 81–101.

15. All translations from *In martyres* are my own from the Greek text in PG 50.661–66; I have
noted the page number, since the homily is not broken into chapters. An English translation of this text
can be found in Wendy Mayer and Pauline Allen, *John Chrysostom*, The Early Church Fathers (New
York: Routledge, 2000), 93–97. See Soler, *Le sacré et le salut*, esp. 29–32; Soler, "Sacralité et partage du
temps et de l'espace festifs à Antioche au IVe siècle," in *Les frontières du profane dans l'antiquité tardive*, Collection de l'École Française de Rome 428, ed. Éric Rebillard and Claire Sotinel (Rome: École
française de Rome, 2010), 273–86.

16. Peter Brown notes the role that processions to the martyrs' shrines played, and their continued
competition with traditional festival celebrations around the empire (Brown, *The Cult of the Saints: Its
Rise and Function in Latin Christianity* [Chicago: University of Chicago Press, 1981], 42–43).

discussion of the Christian transformation of the landscape.[17] There are examples around the empire of a special hill or spring or tree that was associated with a local story about a god, much like the springs at Daphne or the mountain described by Theodoret (*HR* 4) at Teleda (Tel ʿAdeh), an ascetic settlement roughly thirty-five miles east of Antioch and just over five miles southwest of Qalʿat Simʿān, the site of the ascetic Symeon the Stylite's famous pillar.[18] The textual and archaeological evidence, including the numerous late Roman and early Byzantine remains of small towns on the Limestone Massif east of Antioch and the agricultural region of the ʿAmuq Valley, the so-called plain of Antioch that stretches east and north from the city, provide ample testimony regarding widespread villages and temples to the gods outside Antioch in late antiquity.[19] Likewise, travelers would have encountered shrines by the roadside during their journeys from one town to the next, especially shrines dedicated to Hermes, the messenger god, who was thought to protect travelers. Since Antioch was a major intersection between northern Mesopotamia and the sea, and for land travel between Jerusalem (and places south) and Constantinople (and places west), the roads in and out of the great city were both numerous and well traveled.[20] Libanius provides evidence that there were many temples dotting the landscape outside the city (*Or.* 30). While not usually part of conversations about the Christianization of Antioch or the religious conflicts that

17. See, for example, Jesse Casana, "The Archaeological Landscape of Late Roman Antioch," in *Culture and Society in Later Roman Antioch,* ed. Isabella Sandwell and Janet Huskinson (Oxford: Oxbow Books, 2004), 102–25.

18. See also, for example, Martin Henig and Anthony King, eds., *Pagan Gods and Shrines of the Roman Empire* (Oxford: Oxford University Committee for Archaeology, 1986). As Wendy Mayer has noted in conversation, the cave currently identified for tourists in Antakya as the first-century cave church of St. Peter could easily have been a pre-Christian site of worship, since it contains a spring and has an early Roman mosaic floor.

19. Kim Bowes's recent work provides an important reminder that many shrines in the western empire would have been located on (and kept up by) the rural estates of wealthy landowners: Bowes, *Private Worship, Public Values, and Religious Change in Late Antiquity* (New York: Cambridge University Press, 2008). Unlike the rural estates that were common in Italy and parts of North Africa, however, northern Roman Syria was primarily settled in villages. See, for example, Casana, "Archaeological Landscape," 102–25; and Kevin Butcher, *Roman Syria and the Near East* (London: The British Museum Press, 2003), 137–40. In fact, Georges Tate has challenged Georges Tchalenko's claim that there were significant large property-owners on the Limestone Massif: Georges Tate, *Les campagnes de la Syrie du Nord du IIe au VIIe siècle,* Bibliothèque Archéologique et Historique 133 (Paris: P. Geuthner, 1992), 289–95. Some of the work of the ʿAmuq Valley Regional Project of the Oriental Institute at the University of Chicago is also relevant to the Roman history of the region, such as Andrea De Giorgi, "The Formation of a Roman Landscape: The Case of Antioch," *Journal of Roman Archaeology* 20 (2007): 283–98. Liebeschuetz has also discussed the role that these and other rural villages played in late antiquity: J. H. W. G. Liebeschuetz: *The Decline and Fall of the Roman City* (New York: Oxford University Press, 2001), 63–74.

20. See, for example, Theophanes' early fourth-century travels to Antioch, as discussed in John Matthews, *The Journey of Theophanes: Travel, Business, and Daily Life in the Roman East* (New Haven, CT: Yale University Press, 2006).

took place there, these temples and shrines, and the festivals associated with them, played a significant role in these events.

Outside the city walls the burial sites of the deceased offered yet another place relevant to the transformation of religious orthopraxy and community identity.[21] While cemeteries had a different relation to the gods than the temples and shrines, they were likewise places of traditional ritual practices that later Christian leaders understood to be in competition with Christian praxes and sought to transform for reasons related to religious identity.[22] Because Romans understood dead bodies to be polluting, they were buried outside the walls of a city in the early Roman Empire. Typically a person leaving a city would immediately pass through a cemetery, with tombs visible on either side.[23] Romans would usually visit their departed family members on the birthday of the deceased, sharing a meal at the tomb in their honor.[24] Archaeological evidence has confirmed the existence of a substantial cemetery on either side of the main road leading out of Antioch to Daphne. There are also literary references to other extramural Antiochene burial sites, and some corroboration has been found through archaeological excavations, such as at

21. See Ann Marie Yasin, *Saints and Church Spaces in the Late Antique Mediterranean: Architecture, Cult, and Community* (New York: Cambridge University Press, 2009), esp. 46–100. For the most recent archaeological evidence regarding burial sites in Roman Antioch, see Hatice Pamir, "Preliminary Results of the Recent Archaeological Researches in Antioch on the Orontes and Its Vicinity," in *Les sources de l'histoire du paysage urbain d'Antioche sur l'Oronte* (Paris: Université Paris 8, Vincennes-Saint-Denis, 2012), 259–70.

22. For a recent study of death and its ritual practices in the first centuries of Christianity, see Ulrich Volp, *Tod und Ritual in den christlichen Gemeinden der Antike* (Boston: Brill, 2002). Volp not only provides a context for Christian rituals by examining Egyptian, Jewish, Greek, and Roman practices, but demonstrates the wide variety of Christian practices in late antiquity. See also Éric Rebillard's discussion of the continuities between early Christian traditions surrounding death, and earlier Roman traditions: Rebillard, *Religion et sepulture: L'Église, les vivants et les morts dans l'Antiquité tardive (IIIe-Ve siècles)* (Paris: Éditions de l'École des hautes études en sciences socials, 2003); and the English translation: Éric Rebillard, *The Care of the Dead in Late Antiquity,* trans. Elizabeth Trapnell Rawlings and Jeanine Routier-Pucci, Cornell Studies in Classical Philology 59 (Ithaca, NY: Cornell University Press, 2009).

23. The city of Rome was atypical in having a system of underground catacombs, but like typical Roman cemeteries, they were located not far outside the city walls.

24. There is some evidence that the deceased was thought to be sharing in the remembrance feast, and there are even examples of sarcophagi with holes in them that may have been used to share the feast more literally with the dead. MacMullen discusses this evidence in *Second Church,* 25–26. For an overview of Roman burial practices, see Valerie Hope, *Roman Death: Dying and the Dead in Ancient Rome* (New York: Continuum, 2009); J. M. C. Toynbee, *Death and Burial in the Roman World* (Ithaca, NY: Cornell University Press, 1971); Keith Hopkins, *Death and Renewal* (New York: Cambridge University Press, 1983); Franz Cumont, *After Life in Roman Paganism* (New Haven, CT: Yale University Press, 1922). Juana Torres addresses traditional views of corpses in her essay on the emperor Julian's response to burials and martyrs' relics: Torres, "Emperor Julian and the Veneration of Relics," *Antiquité Tardive* 17 (2009): 205–14, esp. 206.

the church discovered in the suburb of Kaoussie (Qausīyeh), which has been identified with the church that Bishop Meletius built for Babylas's relics. Chrysostom once commented that his city was protectively walled all around by martyrs' tombs (*De coemeterio et de cruce* 1; cf. John Chrysostom, *In martyres Aegyptios*).[25]

As Romans, Christians inherited these burial traditions, and integrated them into their Christian lives.[26] Early Christian burials, therefore, took place outside the city walls, with families visiting them at least annually. These traditions expanded in relation to Christian martyrs and other saints.[27] As early Christian communities understood themselves to be a new family that was superior to a person's biological family, it became customary for Christians to visit the tombs of the saints as a biological family would visit a relative who had died.[28] Like other Romans, Christians made these visits typically on the birthday of the deceased, though in the case of Christian saints this was understood to be the day of their death, or their rebirth in heaven. Christians thus transformed the traditional birthday memorial celebration at the tomb of a departed family member into a ritual community celebration of a saint's death, with a Eucharist meal sometimes substituting for, and sometimes complementing, the more traditional meal at the gravesite. This practice was familiar in Antioch during John Chrysostom's time, and he encouraged his audience to visit the burial places of the martyrs frequently, not just once a year on the day of their death, and to rest there and share a meal with the saint (e.g., *In Iuventinum et Maximum* 10; *In s. Ignatium* 18; *De ss. Bernice et Prosdoce* 24; *In martyres*, PG 50.663). Predictably, of course, John Chrysostom and other Christian leaders concurrently tried to reshape this familiar familial

25. Although Wendy Mayer raises the possibility that *De coemeterio et de cruce* originated in Constantinople, she notes that the reference to the city being surrounded by martyrs is one reason to think it might have originated in Antioch. See Wendy Mayer with Bronwen Neil, *St. John Chrysostom: The Cult of the Saints* (Crestwood, NY: St. Vladimir's Seminary Press, 2006), 209. The Greek text of John Chrysostom, *De coemeterio et de cruce* is in PG 49.393–98. The Greek text of John Chrysostom, *In martyres Aegyptios* is in PG 50.693–98.

26. Christians inherited funerary and burial traditions from their local region, Roman and Greek practices more generally, and biblically from earlier Jewish traditions. For an overview, see Volp, *Tod und Ritual*; Geoffrey Rowell, *The Liturgy of Christian Burial: An Introductory Survey of the Historical Development of Christian Burial Rites* (London: Alcuin Club/S.P.C.K., 1977); and Robin Jensen, "Dining with the Dead: From the *Mensa* to the Altar in Christian Late Antiquity," in *Commemorating the Dead: Texts and Artifacts in Context—Studies of Roman, Jewish, and Christian Burials,* ed. Laurie Brink and Deborah Green (New York: Walter de Gruyter, 2008), 107–43. See also John Baldovin, "Relics, Martyrs, and the Eucharist," *Liturgical Ministry* 12 (2003): 9–19. Éric Rebillard's work *The Care of the Dead* (e.g., 176–78) is an important reminder that Christians often had more practices in common with their non-Christian neighbors than their church leaders liked.

27. Compare Yasin, *Saints and Church Spaces,* 61–69.

28. Vasiliki Limberis has recently discussed the rhetoric of kinship that developed around martyrs: Limberis, *Architects of Piety: The Cappadocian Fathers and the Cult of the Martyrs* (New York: Oxford University Press, 2011), 97–156.

tradition by discouraging alcohol and frivolity at the Christian memorials, drawing these burial places into the growing number of places that they hoped to make
distinctively Christian.[29]

For Christians these celebrations of past saints often provided an opportunity
for processions to and from their tombs that offer interesting comparisons with
the processions associated with the traditional ritual celebrations of the gods.[30] On
the rare occasion that new relics arrived in a city, there was another festive public
celebration and procession of the relics to the site of their interment. This happened in Antioch with the relics of Babylas, first as they went from the cemetery
up to Daphne, then when they returned to Antioch from Daphne, and then as they
moved to the church that Meletius had built for them. In the fifth century, the relics of the famous ascetic Symeon the Stylite also received a formal procession into
Antioch. In addition, each annual commemoration of a local martyr provided
another opportunity for a public procession; John Chrysostom's congregation, for
example, gathered at a martyr's shrine outside the wall and then returned to the
city after the service was finished. These processions became opportunities for the
performance of religious identity, as seen in John Chrysostom's instructions to his
audience about how they should (and should not) behave, and the implications of
their behavior (e.g., *In martyres*, PG 50.663–64; *De ss. martyr.*; *De s. Pelagia* 4).[31]

One innovation of Christian late antiquity in this respect was that through the
"cult of the saints" that developed around the martyrs, saints' burials slowly moved
inside the city walls, and into churches.[32] As Christians came to venerate relics

29. For comparison, see the Roman example discussed in Gregor Kalas, "Topographical Transitions: The Oratory of the Forty Martyrs and Exhibition Practices in the Early Medieval Roman Forum,"
in *Santa Maria Antiqua al Foro Romano: Cento anni dopo*, ed. John Osborne, J. Rasmus Brandt, and
Giuseppe Morganti (Rome: Campisano Editore, 2004), 201–13.

30. Scholars have studied the development of Christian processions, and their relation to earlier
funerary practices and festival celebrations of the gods, as well as the tradition of an imperial *adventus*.
See, for example, Soler, *Le sacré et le salut*, esp. 165–214; Franz Alto Bauer, "Urban Space and Ritual:
Constantinople in Late Antiquity," *Acta ad Archaeologiam et Atrium Historiam Pertinentia* 15, n.s. 1
(2001): 27–61; Wendy Mayer, "The Sea Made Holy: The Liturgical Function of the Waters surrounding Constantinople," *Ephemerides Liturgicae* 112 (1998): 459–68; John Baldovin, *The Urban Character
of Christian Worship: The Origins, Development, and Meaning of Stational Liturgy* (Rome: Pontificium
Institutum Studiorum Orientalium, 1987).

31. See also the discussion in Wendy Mayer and Pauline Allen, *The Churches of Syrian Antioch
(300–638 C.E.)* (Walpole, MA: Peeters, 2012), 182–99.

32. Peter Brown's work, especially his book *The Cult of the Saints*, has been foundational in the
early study of this subject. In *The Cult of the Saints*, Brown speaks about Christian trends in late antiquity, including occasional examples from Roman Syria. Brown notes explicitly in some cases the ways
in which the cult of the saints facilitated the Christianization of the local places around the empire.
See also the developments traced by Yvette Duval, *Auprès des saints, corps et âme: L'inhumantion "ad
sanctos" dans la chrétienité d'Orient et d'Occident du IIIe au VIIe siècle* (Paris: Études Augustiniennes,
1988); and Volp, *Tod und Ritual*, esp. 247–68.

more and more, the saints' bodies changed from being seen as polluting corpses to being honored as sacred relics. This transition not only affected the saints' physical remains, but the new sacrality could in fact sanctify the places in which the relics lay, a far remove from the pollution associated with corpses that had pervaded the Roman Empire before this period and that continued in late antiquity in other contexts. This sanctifying use of saints' bodies took place at Antioch with, for example, Babylas and Meletius, although they remained outside the city walls; Saint Julian, whose relics were moved into the city from the cemetery by the sixth century (John Chrysostom, *In s. Iulianum martyrem* and *De s. Droside*);[33] Ignatius, whose relics Theodosius II (r. 408–50) translated into a former Tychaeum in Antioch;[34] and other saints who were buried in the floor of the martyrion at the Romanesian Gate, outside the city walls, as discussed below.

In mapping fourth-century Antioch's landscape, church buildings are some of the places most obviously associated with Christianity, and they have understandably received the most attention in the past. Wendy Mayer and Pauline Allen's recent study, however, rightly goes beyond the major church buildings, examining all manner of martyria—in cemeteries, in churches, and elsewhere.[35] As much as the church buildings, these places that housed saints' bodies were powerful markers of Christian space, at which Christian leaders increasingly required distinctly Christian practices and behaviors.[36] These smaller Christian loci were scattered all over the region, inside the city and out, and, with their attendant processions and festivals, competed with traditional temples and shrines to define the religious landscape in and around Antioch.

MAPPING WHAT MATTERS:
REAL-AND-IMAGINED ANTIOCH

Libanius's *Oratio* 11 (the *Antiochikos*), John Chrysostom's homilies on Christian martyrs, and Theodoret's *Historia religiosa* all include descriptions of the landscape of Antioch and its surroundings. Given that maps reflect the interests and politics of their creators, it is no surprise that the representations by these diverse authors present quite varied images of the city and the territory around it. As Geoff King writes, "Every map offers only its own perspective on the world, however

---

33. Mayer and Allen, *Churches*, 83–85.

34. Mayer and Allen, *Churches*, 81.

35. Mayer and Allen, *Churches*.

36. Dennis Trout has clearly demonstrated this for late Roman Italy: Trout, "Saints, Identity, and the City," in *A People's History of Christianity*, vol. 2, *Late Ancient Christianity*, ed. Virginia Burrus (Minneapolis: Fortress Press, 2005), 165–87. Ramsay MacMullen's recent study (*Second Church*, 22–31, 104–11) stresses the significance of martyria as places of early Christian gatherings, ritual, and community definition.

objective it may appear or claim to be, a perspective that implies a particular assertion of reality."[37] Noticing not only what Libanius, John Chrysostom, and Theodoret each include and the meaning each associates with those places, but also what
each excludes, reveals the ways in which these authors mapped for their audiences
the places that they considered to be most meaningful.

"We are becoming increasingly aware," according to Edward Soja, "that we are,
and always have been, intrinsically spatial beings, active participants in the social
construction of our embracing spatialities"; Soja offers the term Thirdspace to
describe places that are "real-and-imagined" as a way around the typical binary of
identifying a place as only one or the other.[38] Analysis of texts by Libanius, John
Chrysostom, and Theodoret demonstrates that their narratives present a variety of
real-and-imagined maps of Antioch, each of which constructively shaped the ways
its audience would perceive, and act in, the world around them.[39] Angèle Smith
reminds readers, "The competing perceptions of the landscape shape the artifact
of the map as the site of social interaction, contestation and cultural negotiation of
identity and place within the landscape."[40] Such narrative maps, therefore, not
only present different views of the physical landscape, but also promote distinct
ideals of behavior and identity.

Libanius's Map: A Land of Temples

In *Oratio* 11, his famous speech in honor of his native city, Libanius eloquently
describes Antioch's topography and beauty, as well as its wealth of places devoted
to the gods.[41] Libanius's description provides a literary model of the landscape that

37. Geoff King, *Mapping Reality: An Exploration of Cultural Cartographies* (New York: Macmillan
Press, 1996), 175.

38. Edward Soja, *Thirdspace: Journeys to Los Angeles and Other Real-and-Imagined Places* (Malden, MA: Blackwell Publishing, 1996), 1, 6.

39. Catherine Saliou notes the rhetorical nature of Libanius's description of Antioch in *Oratio*
11: Saliou, "Antioche décrite par Libanios: La rhétorique de l'espace urbain et ses enjeux au milieu du
quatrième siècle," in *Approches de la Troisième Sophistique: Hommages à Jacques Schamp*, ed. Eugenio
Amato (Brussels: Editions Latomus, 2006), 274.

40. Smith, "Landscape Representation," 86.

41. A.-J. Festugière also used Libanius's text to extrapolate a view of the city of Antioch, and the
relations of Libanius, John Chrysostom, and the ascetics described by Theodoret, in Festugière, *Antioche païenne et chrétienne: Libanius, Chrysostome et les moines de Syrie* (Paris: Éditions E. de Boccard,
1959); cf. Downey, *History*; Downey, *Antioch in the Age of Theodosius the Great* (Norman, OK: University of Oklahoma Press, 1962). Many scholars have begun updating this older scholarship, including Tate,
Les campagnes; Grégoire Poccardi, "Antioche de Syrie: Pour un nouveau plan urbain de l'île de l'Oronte
(ville neuve) du IIIe au Ve siècle," *Mélanges de l'École Française de Rome* 106 (1994): 993–1023; Poccardi,
"L'île d'Antioche à la fin de l'Antiquité: Histoire et problem de topographie urbaine," in *Recent Research
in Late-Antique Urbanism*, ed. Luke Lavan, Journal of Roman Archaeology Supplementary Series 42
(Portsmouth, RI: Journal of Roman Archaeology, 2001), 155–72; Casana, "Archaeological Landscape,"
102–25; Catherine Saliou, "Le palais imperial d'Antioche et son contexts à l'époque de Julien: Réflexions

Meletius, Flavian, and John Chrysostom worked to Christianize. Written in 356, shortly after his return to the city after years away, this speech by Libanius may well have been delivered as part of the ceremonies surrounding the beginning of the Olympic games that were primarily held in a large arena in the suburb of Daphne.[42] In it Libanius offers an overview of the layout of the city, a view of the surrounding mountains and villages, and a sense of how city, suburbs, and countryside interacted. While his descriptions are embellished with the highest praise, they nevertheless coincide in some cases with modern archaeological findings, and provide at least a taste of how fourth-century visitors might have experienced the city,[43] with a notable exception: the absence in Libanius's descriptions of any evidence of Judaism or Christianity in Antioch.[44] "Maps," Angèle Smith writes, "can be understood

---

sur l'apport des sources littéraires à l'histoire d'un espace urbain," *Antiquité Tardive* 17 (2009): 235–50. From a literary perspective, see Maria Francesio, *L'idea di città in Libanio* (Stuttgart: Franz Steiner Press, 2004), esp. 77, 137; Jorit Wintjes, *Das Leben des Libanius* (Rahden/Westf.: Marie Leidorf Press, 2005), 29–41; and Soler, *Le sacré et le salut,* esp. 14–15.

42. See A. F. Norman, *Antioch as a Centre of Hellenic Culture as Observed by Libanius,* Translated Texts for Historians 34 (Liverpool: Liverpool University Press, 2000), 3. Norman accepts the dating presented by Paul Petit, "Sur la date du 'Pro Templis' de Libanius," *Byzantion* 21 (1951): 285–309. See also Catherine Saliou's study of this text as a rhetorical presentation of the topography of fourth-century Antioch ("Antioche décrite par Libanios," 273–85).

43. Libanius's descriptions of the colonnaded streets, the hippodrome, and the city's walls, gates, and aqueducts, for example, can be compared with John Chrysostom's descriptions, as well as with archaeological surveys. See, for example, the early work gathered in Downey, *History,* as well as that noted more recently in Wintjes, *Das Leben,* 33–36. See also the publications of the Princeton archaeological surveys: *Antioch-on-the-Orontes, Publications of the Committee for the Excavation of Antioch and Its Vicinity,* vol. 1, *The Excavations of 1932,* ed. George W. Elderkin (Princeton, NJ: Princeton University Press, 1934); *Antioch-on-the-Orontes,* vol. 2, *The Excavations, 1933–1936,* ed. Richard Stillwell (Princeton, NJ: Princeton University Press, 1938); *Antioch-on-the-Orontes,* vol. 3, *The Excavations, 1937–1939,* ed. Richard Stillwell (Princeton, NJ: Princeton University Press, 1941); Christine Kondoleon, ed., *Antioch: The Lost Ancient City* (Princeton, NJ: Princeton University Press, 2000), published in conjunction with the exhibition of the same name, shown at Worcester Art Museum, October 7, 2000–February 4, 2001; The Cleveland Museum of Art, March 18–June 3, 2001; The Baltimore Museum of Art, September 16–December 30, 2001. Blake Leyerle has also studied the physical and rhetorical evidence for Antioch's sewer systems: Leyerle, "Refuse, Filth, and Excrement in the Homilies of John Chrysostom," *Journal of Late Antiquity* 2.2 (2009): 337–56.

44. Andrew Jacobs provides a sophisticated study of such selective views of a landscape in his description of Christian pilgrims' narratives of Jerusalem: Jacobs, *Remains of the Jews: The Holy Land and Christian Empire in Late Antiquity* (Stanford, CA: Stanford University Press, 2004). See also Catherine Saliou's discussion of Libanius's portrayal of Antioch (Saliou, "Antioche décrit par Libanios," 179–81). Johannes Hahn refers to an anonymous text that described Alexandria in 360 C.E., or just before, and offers an interesting comparison to Libanius's oration in its exclusive focus on temples and its silence regarding Christianity (and Judaism): Hahn, "The Conversion of the Cult Statues: The Destruction of the Serapeum 392 A.D. and the Transformation of Alexandria into the 'Christ-Loving' City," in *From Temple to Church: Destruction and Renewal of Local Cultic Topography in Late Antiquity,* ed. Johannes Hahn, Stephen Emmel, and Ulrich Gotter (Boston: Brill, 2008), 336.

as sites of negotiation of multiple meanings of landscape, place, and identity at the local level,"[45] and Libanius's representation of Antioch reveals his involvement in such negotiations, in contrast to the later Christian presentations of John Chrysostom and Theodoret. Presented in 356, Libanius's *Oratio* 11 followed the first translation of Babylas's relics under Caesar Gallus (351–54) and preceded by only six years the emperor Julian's lament that temple cult in Antioch was pathetically malnourished (e.g., Julian, *Misopōgōn* 363–64). As will become clear in the discussion below, Libanius's silence regarding Antioch's otherwise well-attested Jewish and Christian communities, and the synagogues, churches, and martyr shrines associated with them, reinforces that while maps "may appear to be objective, neutral, and scientific," they are often "tools" in the process of groups trying to "create boundaries between themselves and other groups."[46]

In presenting his glowing view of his city, Libanius highlights Antioch's ideal location (*Or.* 11.34–117) and the unrivaled comfort of its climate (*Or.* 11.29–33). He describes the layout of the city, some of the major buildings, and the ornate colonnaded and paved streets;[47] a variety of houses and shops along the main streets and the smaller streets that go out from them, including houses nestled at the base of the mountain that overlooks the town; and beautiful gardens along the river (11.196–202, 209–29, 249–50). He distinguishes this older part of the city from the new city that he describes as being on an island in the river, which was connected to the old city by five bridges and was home to the expansive grounds of the imperial palace (11.203–8).[48] He further expounds on the advantages of the Orontes River, which flowed through the city, the lake that fed the river, and the rich marketplaces that abounded throughout the city, providing ready access to anything from near or far that anyone might wish to find (11.260–62, 251–59). Beyond the city walls, he praises the pleasurable and healing springs of Daphne, as well as the unparalleled fertility of the region's land, both that of "the mountain districts" and that of "the plains" (11.230–48, 13–28, 174–75, 22–24). Catherine Saliou has demonstrated the ways in which Libanius constructed a history and memory of Antioch in this oration that proved useful in his contemporary context, by highlighting its Hellenistic heritage and its strong association with the gods.[49] Within this land-

---

45. Smith, "Landscape Representation," 85.

46. Knapp and Herlihy, "Mapping the Landscape of Identity," 252.

47. Kurtuluş Caddesi is still a main street in Antakya today, following the course of one of the main Roman roads through Antioch, although the street today is narrower than it was in the Roman period. Parts of the Roman road have been uncovered in digging projects, such as for sewer lines, in the modern city. See also Catherine Saliou, "Bains d'été et bains d'hiver: Antioche dans l'empire romain," *Topoi* Supplement 5 (2004): 289–309.

48. See Saliou, "Le palais imperial," 235–50, on the layout of the island during the reign of Julian.

49. Catherine Saliou, "Les fondations d'Antioche dans l'*Antiochikos* (*Oratio* XI) de Libanios," *ARAM* 11–12 (1999–2000): 357–88.

scape, Libanius specifically describes places associated with a variety of gods.[50] The insistent absence of Christianity in his vision of the city is striking. Even if this speech was delivered on the occasion of the Olympic games in Daphne, with their attendant rituals invoking the gods, it was nevertheless given after two decades of Christian imperial rule, fifteen years after the dedication of the Great Church in Antioch, and not long after Gallus's translation of Babylas's relics to the precinct of Apollo's temple in Daphne—clear evidence that Libanius's Antioch in this text is real-and-imagined Thirdspace.

Speaking generally of the land's fertility, Libanius recounts that the gods Dionysus, Athena, and Demeter love the region and bless it with their gifts of grapes and wine, olives and olive oil, and corn, respectively (*Or.* 11.20–21). He claims that in addition to numerous Greek gods and heroes, even Persian gods respect the place where Antioch was established (11.59). "The region," he insists, "was loved by the gods from the beginning" (11.64). More specifically, Libanius mentions a temple of Artemis outside Antioch's walls in Meroë and the long-standing worship of Zeus Bottiaeus in the region (11.59, 76, 88), and claims that Seleucus "granted the region" of Daphne to the god Apollo (11.94–99, 236). Libanius provides several examples to demonstrate not only the variety of gods who were worshipped in Antioch throughout its history, but also that gods from all over desired to dwell in such a wonderful city (11.110–14). "The city," he concludes, "was a dwelling-place of the powerful ones [the gods], so that it was possible, if we wished, to rival even Olympus, for the residence of the gods at that spot is a rumor of poets, but on the other hand here we are persuaded by our eyes" (11.115). Although Libanius claims that the Romans tried to remove Zeus Cassius from Antioch when they took control of the Greek region, he notes that Zeus's wrathful lightning bolts persuaded the Romans to return the god to the city (11.116). According to Libanius,

> Therefore those [gods] from elsewhere revealed that they wished to come to us, and those [gods] among us will not be removed elsewhere. . . . They were drawn by their lovers, and in turn they held onto the land they loved. Such was the love for the region (*philochōria*) that possessed our *daimones,* and the desire of foreign ones to become ours. (11.117)[51]

Libanius thus praises his city while also highlighting the plethora of different gods who were worshipped in the area, introducing the term *philochōria* to express explicitly the gods' affinity for the *place* of the local region.

---

50. Catherine Saliou interprets Libanius's representation of the city as his effort to present a unified front of a city that was in reality fractured by religious divisions; she also notes that the rhetorical tradition of which Libanius's oration is a part may have constrained his portrayal of his city on the occasion of the celebration of the Olympic games ("Antioche décrit par Libanios," 279–81).

51. Note that when Libanius uses the word *daimones* it does not carry the negative connotations that it clearly has in John Chrysostom's usage of the word.

In Libanius's glowing rhetoric, Antioch appears replete with ancient temples.[52] Of the city's early benefactors, Libanius says: "One built a temple of Minos, another of Demeter, another of Heracles, and so on. . . . Temple after temple was built, and the majority of the city was among the temples. . . . The adornment and protection for the city were the temples of the gods" (*Or.* 11.125). He added to this that Antiochenes built many temples for the Muses, both as places for students to study and as gifts for the goddesses (11.188). He reiterates elsewhere in the oration that in Antioch public buildings such as temples and baths were intermingled "everywhere" among the houses (11.212). More specifically, Libanius identifies "the towering temple of the Nymphs" in the center of Antioch, a temple that "turns every eye with its gleaming stones, and colored pillars, and radiant paintings, and wealth of streams" (11.202),[53] and "the temple of [Apollo] Pythius," which Libanius claims was the fourth such temple on the same site (11.228). Libanius's rhetorical efforts to tie the land, city, people, and history of Daphne and Antioch so strongly to the gods would have had particular significance in the context of Apollo's contested Daphne precinct, particularly at the time of the festivals surrounding the Olympic games. Geoff King writes, "Maps inevitably distort reality."[54] Looking through Libanius's eyes, the necessarily distorted landscape vividly reminds its visitors of the gods, and encourages them, as they wend their way through the city streets, to attend the temples, in Antioch and its popular suburb of Daphne. Contrary to other evidence that survives, in this rhetorical description from 356, the Christianization of the region's landscape would appear not even to have been visible on the horizon.

John Chrysostom's Map: Martyrs and the Christianization of the In-Between Places

While Chrysostom's homilies from 386–97 on the many martyrs celebrated by late fourth-century Antiochene Christians acknowledge that there were places associated with the gods as well as those associated with martyrs, he narratively highlights the latter as superior to the former, encouraging his audience to draw their mental maps of the region to look less like the map encouraged by Libanius's texts and more like Chrysostom's idealized Christian world.[55] As geographer Mark

---

52. Downey's collection of references to Greek and Roman temples in the city confirms Libanius's claims that there were numerous temples to a variety of gods throughout Antioch's Greek and Roman history (Downey, *History;* references to temples are scattered throughout this work by Downey).

53. It is interesting to consider whether Libanius's description of the temple of the Nymphs in 356 was an effort to compete with the impressive architecture of the relatively new Great Church, which by all accounts dazzled visitors with its wealth and architecture. Mayer and Allen have recently translated the comparable passages from Eusebius's descriptions of the Great Church (Mayer and Allen, *Churches,* 69).

54. King, *Mapping Reality,* 18.

55. Dayna Kalleres notes the spatial significance of martyrs' shrines in John Chrysostom's *Adversus Iudaeos* homilies; she raises the broader question "of the degree to which martyr cult served

Monmonier notes, "A single map is but one of an indefinitely large number of maps that might be produced . . . from the same data."[56] It is, therefore, little surprise that Libanius's and John Chrysostom's presentations of their region differ. In these texts Chrysostom encourages attendance at the Christian sites, hoping to modify the behavior and the very character of the visitors to the martyrs' tombs, making those individuals additional points of Christianity as they move across the landscape between the city and the extramural martyrs' shrines.[57] Through such rhetoric Chrysostom presents a map that highlights Christian locations but also fills the spaces in between with processions of people who had been (re)formed by their time with the martyrs to become individual loci of Christianity.

Although saints' relics more and more frequently found their way into churches in the late fourth and early fifth centuries, many remained outside city walls and were powerful agents in shifting the religious topography of the countryside from a landscape that primarily called to mind the gods toward one that was increasingly associated with Christianity.[58] While it is more difficult to demonstrate that this shift in topography was influenced by a self-conscious plan on the part of early Christian leaders, the textual evidence from Antioch suggests that Meletius, Flavian, and John Chrysostom actively encouraged attendance at rural shrines, where they constructed clear narratives of the martyrs' power, and defined appropriate "Christian" behavior

---

as a crucial point of reference when crafting Christian identity in a post-persecution era of empire" (Kalleres, "Imagining Martyrdom during Theodosian Peace: John Chrysostom and the Problem of Judaizers," in *Contextualising Early Christian Martyrdom*, ed. Jakob Engberg, Uffe Holmsgaard Eriksen, and Anders Klostergaard Petersen [New York: Peter Lang, 2011], 259).

56. Monmonier, *How to Lie with Maps*, 2.

57. Dayna Kalleres's engaging study of John Chrysostom's narrative use of demons also discusses the fourth-century preacher's efforts to modify his congregants' behavior in ways similar to those discussed in this chapter. See chapter 2 in Dayna Kalleres, *City of Demons: Violence, Ritual, and Christian Power in Late Antiquity* (Berkeley: University of California Press, forthcoming). I am grateful to her for sharing this manuscript with me.

58. For a detailed study of Roman martyria, see André Grabar, *Martyrium: Recherches sur le culte des reliques et l'art chrétien antique*, vols. 1–2 (Paris: Collège de France, 1946). See also the more recent critique of the overly rigid category distinctions used by Grabar, in J. B. Ward-Perkins, "Memoria, Martyr's Tomb, and Martyr's Church" in *Studies in Roman and Early Christian Architecture*, ed. J. B. Ward-Perkins (London: The Pindar Press, 1994), 495–516. See especially Ann Marie Yasin's study, *Saints and Church Spaces*, which discusses the ways in which Christian saints affected church spaces in late antiquity. Although Yasin's work focuses on "sacred space" in the tradition of Mircea Eliade, tailored through the criticisms of Jonathan Z. Smith, her work usefully demonstrates the ways in which individuals shaped church spaces in late antiquity to affect community memories and family status, and the significant role that images and relics played in shaping late antique places around the Roman Empire. More recently Ramsay MacMullen (*Second Church*) has discussed the role of martyria in the development and lived practice of early Christianity. Although his focus on the significant role that the martyria played is useful in reconstructing third- and fourth-century Christianity, his work must be used with some caution; see, for example, the criticisms in Mayer and Allen, *Churches*, 85–86, 209.

for those in attendance. Thus while scholars have demonstrated many ways in which behavior at rural saints' shrines perpetuated behaviors and traditions that predated Christianity, Christian leaders' manipulation of those traditions, and self-awareness of the role that the shrines and Christians' behavior at them (and en route to and from them) played in shaping perceptions of individual and community identity, helped make the empire's landscape more visibly Christian.[59]

In *Oratio* 30 Libanius presents the emperor Theodosius with a picture of continuing local celebrations despite the banned ritual sacrifice. Libanius relates that on occasion people from the countryside would slaughter a bull "for a banquet, and a meal, and a feast," but they did so legally: "No altar received the blood, no part was burned, no offering of meal preceded, nor libations followed" (*Or.* 30.17). Through such descriptions, Libanius depicts what continued of traditional practices. "If certain people come together in some bright spot," Libanius explains to Theodosius, and "slaughter a calf or a sheep, or both, and boil and roast it, and then lie down on the ground and eat it, I do not see that they have broken any of the laws" (30.17). Libanius, in fact, goes further to include the use of incense, which was strongly associated with temple sacrifice, saying that even if people drank together amid every kind of incense or sang songs and called on the gods, they would have broken no law since they had not offered a sacrifice to the gods (30.18).[60] Libanius would have been well aware of the fine line that distinguished legal from illegal practices, and he suggests that despite a ban on sacrifice, the accompanying festivities continued legally in Antioch and its surrounding countryside during Theodosius's reign.

It is little surprise that John Chrysostom went to great effort, also during Theodosius's reign, to differentiate Christian celebrations from their traditional counterparts, and to encourage the former among Antioch's inhabitants.[61] Chrysostom explicitly attempted to distinguish Christian places and practices, among other things, in the shared traditions of visiting the graves of loved ones, and of celebrating with festive processions. In addition to the expectation that Christians would regularly visit the saints' graves, by the late fourth century many of the saints' festival days included a procession to and from the saint's resting place. As Christians'

59. Peter Brown comments that as Christianity spread in late antiquity "it lay around the shrines of the saints like pools of water on a drying surface" (*Cult*, 124). See also the description of overlapping festival days and spaces, in Soler, "Sacralité et partage," 273–86; and the ways in which the martyrs' celebrations Christianized the city, in Isabella Sandwell, *Religious Identity in Late Antiquity: Greeks, Jews, and Christians in Antioch* (New York: Cambridge University Press, 2007), 132–43.

60. See Susan Ashbrook Harvey, *Scenting Salvation: Ancient Christianity and the Olfactory Imagination* (Berkeley: University of California Press, 2006), e.g., 34-40, which demonstrates the strong association that incense often had with temple cult.

61. See also Jaclyn Maxwell, "Lay Piety in the Sermons of John Chrysostom," in *A People's History of Christianity*, vol. 3, *Byzantine Christianity*, ed. Derek Krueger (Minneapolis: Fortress Press, 2006), 19–38; Sandwell, *Religious Identity*, 132–43.

neighbors also visited their deceased relatives' graves, often bringing with them food and drink, and had a long tradition of ritual processions in relation to the gods throughout the year, neither the cemetery nor the public streets could be uniquely "Christian" places, and leaders like Chrysostom were at pains to distinguish clearly what appropriately Christian behaviors should take place in those religiously mutable places.

On more than one occasion, Chrysostom mentions the large number of tombs in the area of that day's martyr celebration, suggesting a location in one of Antioch's extramural cemeteries. For example, at a memorial celebration for Saint Drosis, he refers to going outside the walls of the city to a place with "a multitude of tombs on every side" (*De s. Droside* 1);[62] he comments happily, "Whenever we run past the other coffins and come to the chests of the martyrs, our mind becomes more elevated, our soul more vigorous, our eagerness greater, our faith more heated" (*De s. Droside* 2; cf. *De s. Pelagia* 3). It would not have been uncommon if on the festival day his audience was larger than usual, as the crowds made "an exodus to these saints" (*De s. Droside* 1; cf. *In s. Iulianum martyrem* 1).[63] On one occasion Chrysostom says that "nearly the whole city" had gathered for a night of vigils for the martyrs—slaves and free, poor and rich, elderly and young, women and men, and even the governor himself (*In martyres*, PG 50.663). Given the power that saints were thought to have had, it is little surprise that they could draw a large crowd on the annual occasion of their feast day. For Chrysostom, however, people would benefit from their attendance at the martyrs' tombs "not only today, but also every day" (*In s. Ignatium* 5);[64] and he encourages their regular attendance at these powerful Christian places (e.g., *In Iuventinum et Maximum* 3; *De ss. Bernice et Prosdoce* 7; *In*

62. All translations of *De s. Droside* are my own from the Greek text in PG 50.683–94. An English translation of this homily can be found in Mayer with Neil, *Cult of the Saints,* 191–207.

63. Ramsay MacMullen discusses Chrysostom's claims that his audience increases in size for festival days: MacMullen, "The Preacher's Audience (AD 350–400)," *JTS* 40.2 (1989): 506–7. MacMullen's essay also claims, however, that only the educated elite of John Chrysostom's audience would have understood his educated rhetoric (508–11), a claim that Wendy Mayer, Philip Rousseau, and Jaclyn Maxwell have persuasively critiqued: Jaclyn Maxwell, *Christianization and Communication in Late Antiquity: John Chrysostom and His Congregation in Antioch* (New York: Cambridge University Press, 2006), 65–87; Wendy Mayer, "John Chrysostom: Extraordinary Preacher, Ordinary Audience," in *Preacher and Audience: Studies in Early Christian and Byzantine Homiletics,* ed. Pauline Allen and Mary Cunningham (Leiden: Brill, 1998), 105–37; Mayer, "Female Participation and the Late Fourth-Century Preacher's Audience," *Augustinianum* 39 (1999): 139–47; Mayer, "Who Came to Hear John Chrysostom Preach? Recovering a Late Fourth-Century Preacher's Audience," *Ephemerides Theologicae Lovanienses* 76.1 (2000): 73–87; Philip Rousseau, "The Preacher's Audience: A More Optimistic View," in *Ancient History in a Modern University,* ed. T. Hillard, R. A. Kearsley, C. E. V. Nixon, and A. Nobbs (Grand Rapids, MI: William B. Eerdmans, 1998), 2:391–400.

64. All translations from *In s. Ignatium* are my own from the Greek text in PG 50.587–96. An English translation of this homily can be found in Mayer with Neil, *Cult of the Saints,* 101–17.

martyres, PG 50.663). Through such exhortations, Chrysostom seeks to distinguish Christians from other Antiochenes through their visible and frequent attendance at the martyrs' shrines.

The question of who attended John Chrysostom's and Bishop Flavian's martyr celebrations is a thorny one. In one homily, Chrysostom notes, "Many of the heretics are mixed among us" (*De s. Pelagia* 4), suggesting that at least by the reign of Theodosius it was possible for Christians from more than one of Antioch's theologically distinct Christian communities to celebrate together at the shrines.[65] While this may have been true of some celebrations, however, Wendy Mayer notes that it is unlikely to have been true for all of them, and particularly the celebration of Bishop Meletius, who was so closely tied to a particular community.[66] While attendance at the celebrations that could be shared among Christian communities could help to construct a Christian identity for those in the audience, attendance at more community-specific celebrations like those for Meletius could help to associate a person with a particular Christian "orthodoxy" (in this case, Meletian Christianity) more specifically.

Such attendance would, Chrysostom claims, reveal itself both in the benefits the attendees received, as well as in their physical appearance, as seen in Chrysostom's discussion of Babylas's relics above (e.g., *De s. Babyla* 70–72), and as discussed below. Chrysostom describes the martyr's coffin as a safe harbor that would protect and heal those in need; like a ship entering a harbor, souls arrive overwhelmed with daily affairs but are calmed by the martyrs (*De ss. martyr.* 2).[67] The martyrs were also able, Chrysostom claims, to conquer demons (*In s. Iulianum martyrem* 2). At the festival of the martyr Lucian, Chrysostom notes the power of the saint to moderate the listeners' behavior: "We go home from the *agora* and the theater and the other outside gatherings dragging numerous cares and faintheartedness and sicknesses of the soul. If you continuously spend your time here [with the martyr], you will completely escape the evils that you received outside" (*In s. Lucianum* 1).[68] These benefits were, of course, in addition to the rich spiritual

---

65. All translations from *De s. Pelagia* are my own from the Greek text in PG 50.579–84. An English translation of this homily can be found in Johan Leemans, Wendy Mayer, Pauline Allen, and Boudewijn Dehandschutter, *"Let Us Die That We May Live": Greek Homilies on Christian Martyrs from Asia Minor, Palestine, and Syria (c. AD 350-AD 450)* (New York: Routledge, 2003), 148–61.

66. Mayer with Neil, *Cult of Saints,* 40; see also Mayer and Allen, *Churches,* 191–99.

67. All translations from *De ss. martyr.* are my own from the Greek text in PG 50.645–54. An English translation of this homily can be found in Leemans et al., *"Let Us Die,"* 115–26.

68. All translations from *In s. Lucianum* are my own from the Greek text in PG 50.519–26. An English translation of this homily can be found in Mayer with Neil, *Cult of the Saints,* 63–73. Christian writers had long criticized the theater and the culture they associated with it. See Tertullian, *De spectaculis;* and Blake Leyerle, *Theatrical Shows and Ascetic Lives: John Chrysostom's Attack on Spiritual Marriage* (Berkeley: University of California Press, 2001).

rewards that Chrysostom taught his audience they would gain through participation in the saints' festivals.

Beyond the benefits in their lives, Chrysostom notes that when the celebrants left the martyr's shrine, they would be different in their appearance and their demeanor from those who had not attended. He tells his listeners, "When you go back from here, try to see those who were absent today, and you will see how great is the separation between your tranquility and their faintheartedness" (*In s. Lucianum* 1). Elsewhere he exhorts his audience, "Gather together the profits of the soul and thus go home, indicating to all by your appearance that you are returning from viewing the martyrs" (*In martyres,* PG 50.665). Just like those who attended the theater, "the person returning from viewing the martyrs should be known to all," preaches Chrysostom (PG 50.665). Nevertheless, whereas the people leaving the theater will "reveal to all that they have been disturbed, confused, weakened, bearing the images of everything that happened there," the person leaving the martyrs will, according to Chrysostom, be identifiable "through their glance, their appearance, their walk, their contrition, their collected thoughts. [They should be] breathing fire, humbled, beaten, sober, vigilant, proclaiming the internal pursuit of wisdom through the movements of the body" (PG 50.665–66). As Timothy O'Sullivan has written with regard to Romans more generally, "There is a persistent belief in Roman literature (and in Roman culture more broadly) that we might call the rule of the gait: how you walk defines who you are. Such a principle, moreover, quite obviously depends upon the participation of an audience trained in the art of watching others walk."[69] John Chrysostom was immersed in this culture, and hoped that he and the martyrs could train his congregants to perform a particular Christian identity as they moved through the city. The saints' tombs were so powerful, he taught, that attendance at their tombs made people visually distinct, and in his view visibly Christian, even after they had returned to the city.

Chrysostom notes the superior benefits that Christian places and practices provided, remapping the city for his audience in the process.[70] Speaking of the saints' tombs, he comments, "Let us prefer spending time here over every enjoyment, every pleasure" (*In s. Ignatium* 5). More specifically, he offers a series of contrasts between Christian places and others:

> If those who are crazy about the theater and who gape after the horse races never have their fill of those inappropriate spectacles, much more should we be insatiable for the festivals of the saints. There, there is devilish conduct; here, Christian celebration;

69. O'Sullivan, *Walking,* 13.

70. Maxwell (*Christianization,* 144–68) provides a useful discussion, using Pierre Bourdieu's vocabulary of *habitus,* of Chrysostom's efforts to reshape and distinctly "Christianize" the behaviors of those who hear him.

there, *daimones* bound; here, angels dance; there, the destruction of souls; here, the salvation of all who are gathered. (*De ss. martyr.* 1; cf. *In s. Barlaam* 4)[71]

Like his efforts to encourage *topophobia* for the synagogue, this passage explicitly contrasts ideal Christian places and practices, especially visiting the martyrs' burial sites, with places and practices that Chrysostom distances from Christianity and condemns in no uncertain terms. Laura Nasrallah has demonstrated that early Christian apologists did not define Christianity "against paganism or Judaism as much as they define Christianity against certain *kinds* of other ethnic and religious practices, practices they usually attribute to the 'many' or the crowd."[72] Educated Christians continued to draw such distinctions into the fourth century, as demonstrated by John Chrysostom's homilies that criticize the behavior of the crowds at the theater or the hippodrome. "Chrysostom," according to Jaclyn Maxwell, "hoped to eclipse the distinctions of class or culture, by making religious identity the primary marker of difference in society."[73] The Antiochene preacher thus carefully used martyrs' shrines in an effort to encourage behavior that he considered appropriate for the members of his audience, distinguishing them through their behavior from their Antiochene neighbors.

At least two of Chrysostom's homilies, in fact, respond to direct competition for attendees, and reflect Chrysostom's privileging of Christian places in his narrative presentation of the landscape. In remembering a Christian martyr named Julian, Chrysostom laments to his audience, "Some of those gathered here today (for heaven forbid that I accuse the whole church of such a thing!), leaving us behind tomorrow under a certain laziness and simplemindedness, will leap off to Daphne" (*In s. Iulianum martyrem* 4).[74] Praising the virtues of attendance at the martyria

---

71. Sandwell (*Religious Identity,* esp. 63–90) also analyzes John Chrysostom's construction of Christian and non-Christian categories of behavior and identity.

72. Laura Nasrallah, *Christian Responses to Roman Art and Architecture: The Second-Century Church amid the Spaces of Empire* (New York: Cambridge University Press, 2010), 6–7.

73. Maxwell, *Christianization,* 147.

74. All translations from *In s. Iulianum martyrem* are my own from the Greek text in PG 50.665–76. An English translation of this homily can be found in Leemans et al., "*Let Us Die,*" 126–40. Soler describes in detail the festival days of fourth-century Antioch, and their "Dionysian" character, particularly of the Maioumas festival, but also the Kalends festival for the new year (Soler, *Le sacré et le salut,* esp. 38–40, 89–90), as well as John Chrysostom's preaching against participation in them (Soler, esp. 165–87). See also Soler's article devoted to this topic: Soler, "Sacralité et partage," 273–86. Edward Schoolman also discusses Antioch's festivals, including the Maioumas festival: "Civic Transformation of the Mediterranean City: Antioch and Ravenna, 300–800 C.E." (PhD diss., University of California, Los Angeles, 2010), 107–9; as does N. Belayche, "Une panégyrie antiochéenne: Le maïouma," in *Antioche de Syrie: Histoire, images et traces de la ville antique; Colloque de Lyon (octobre 2001),* ed. B. Cabouret, P.-L. Gatier, and C. Saliou, Topoi Suppl. 5 (Lyon: Maison de l'Orient et de la Méditerranée, 2004), 401–15; and Maxwell discusses Antiochenes' celebration of the New Year festival (*Christianization,* 154–57).

while critiquing the luxuries of the suburb on a festival day, Chrysostom exhorts his audience, "I am not preventing you [in general] from going off to the suburb, but I prevent it [only] tomorrow . . . so that the enjoyment might not hold condemnation" (4). Similarly in another of Chrysostom's homilies on the martyrs, he argues that the heavy drinking associated with the celebrations in Daphne "is always bad, but especially on a day of the martyrs" (*In martyres*, PG 50.664). The martyr's shrine, by contrast, brought different pleasures—namely, a spiritual theater and a quiet and chaste meal that Chrysostom lauds in comparison (*In s. Iulianum martyrem* 4).[75]

For Chrysostom, Christians' attendance at Daphne was not inherently problematic. Chrysostom exhorts his audience that if they wished to spend time in "gardens and meadows and parks," such as are associated with Daphne, however, they should not do it now, "while there is such a crowd, but on another day" (*In martyres*, PG 50.665). Attendance at Daphne during a traditional festival became particularly problematic if it came at the cost of being absent from a Christian celebration on the same day. During another competing holiday, Chrysostom incites the members of his audience to prioritize the region's Christian places, and praises the congregants who had chosen to attend his church service rather than "the Satanic festival" (*tēn heortēn satanikēn*), presumably, given this sermon's delivery at the beginning of the year, the lively Kalends celebrations (*De Lazaro* 1).[76]

In his usual fashion, Chrysostom encourages those in his audience to be vigilant not only about their own behavior, but about their neighbors' as well. He marshals his followers with these words: "Tomorrow, let us occupy the gates ahead of time; let us watch over the streets; let us pull them down from the carts, men [pulling] men, women [pulling] women. Let us bring them up here . . . to the holy martyr!" (*In s. Iulianum martyrem* 5). In his exuberance, Chrysostom even suggests: "If you wish, let us also take the martyr with us. . . . Let us set him before their very eyes, make them fear his presence, feel ashamed as he summons and

75. John Chrysostom's specific contrast of "a chaste meal" with Libanius's description of meals to celebrate the gods in the meadows of Daphne (e.g., Libanius, *Or.* 30.17), as well as the traditional meals at the grave of a deceased family member, both of which typically included celebration and wine. See Volp, *Tod und Ritual*, 60–63, 77–86, 214–24.

76. All translations of the series of homilies *De Lazaro* are my own from the Greek in PG 48.963–1044. The series of homilies on Lazarus most likely comes from early January, since the festival of the martyr Babylas (January 24) takes place between the third and fourth sermon (*De Lazaro* 4). See also Wendy Mayer's discussion of the dating: Mayer, *The Homilies of St John Chrysostom—Provenance: Reshaping the Foundations* (Rome: Pontificio Istituto Orientale, 2005), 74–75, 80. Compare John Chrysostom's rhetoric in his homily *In Kalendas,* about which Maxwell writes: "The traditional festivities also included night choruses, gift exchanges, and the careful observation of omens to learn the luck of the New Year. While systematically condemning all these practices, Chrysostom suggested substitutions" (Maxwell, *Christianization,* 155).

begs" (5). The aggressive nature of Chrysostom's suggestions only increases as the homily continues, as he tells his audience:

> If you are present there the one hour during which the person, leaving the house, sets out on the road, and you redirect them to arriving here, there will not be any discontent remaining. . . . Therefore, considering the profit that comes to us from this, let us all pour out in front of the city, and grabbing our brothers and sisters, let us bring them back here so that tomorrow, too, our theater might be full and the festival thus completed. (5)

Such texts leave no doubt that Chrysostom understood himself to be in a struggle to gain attendance at Christian martyrs' shrines and churches in place of other celebrations in Daphne, and that in his view what places people chose to attend in these times of competition clearly impinged on their religious identity.

Not only does Chrysostom attempt to require attendance at the martyrs' burial sites, but he also discusses appropriate conduct there, and suggests that the martyr would prevent any untoward behavior at his or her shrine. In speaking at the memorial of the martyr Julian, Chrysostom warns his audience: "The martyr, watching from nearby and being close and standing next to the table itself, does not allow the pleasure to spread over into sin. Rather, like a certain *paidagōgos* or an excellent father, watching with the eyes of faith he represses the laughter, circumscribes the enjoyments that are out of place, takes away all the leaping of the flesh" (*In s. Iulianum martyrem* 4). In another homily on the martyrs, Chrysostom similarly pleads with his audience that if they are tempted to indulge and leave for the pubs and brothels, they should instead

> stay beside the tomb of the martyr; pour out streams of tears there; restrain your mind; raise a blessing from the tomb. Taking her as an advocate in your prayers, spend time always with the descriptions of his contests. Encircle the coffin; nail yourself to the funerary chest. . . . Take holy oil and anoint your whole body, the tongue, the lips, the neck, the eyes, and you will never fall into the wreck of drunkenness. (*In martyres*, PG 50.664; cf. *De ss. martyr.* 3)

Such "Christian" places come with expectations for how those who attend them will behave, but this image of appropriate Christian behavior carried, for Chrysostom, beyond the martyrs' shrines themselves.

Such contrasts are also explicit in Chrysostom's commands regarding the behavior of his attendees as they depart from the martyrs' tombs. Chrysostom, in fact, focuses most of a short homily on the distinction that he wished to see in Christians' behavior as they left the martyrion (*In martyres*, PG 50.661–66). The request was driven, it seems, by Chrysostom's interest in making the people and places associated with Christianity respectable and sober, and thus (ostensibly) clearly distinguishable from their counterparts who were not Christian. Chrysostom presents this homily at one of the martyr shrines outside Antioch's city walls. He expresses pleasure at the "brilliant spectacle" of the large crowd gathered for the martyrs (PG 50.663), but teaches that they would be judged not only on their attendance, but also on their behavior (PG 50.661–62). "Let us return home," Chrysostom pleads, "with the same reverence when this spiritual spectacle is finished," and he clarifies his very particular concerns, clearly based on tradition and past experience: "not releasing ourselves into taverns and brothels and drinking and village festivals" (PG 50.663).[77] It is apparent from the ferocity and specificity of John's rhetoric that he was trying to prevent behavior that was long ingrained in this Antiochene crowd, as he continues to warn at length about the dangers and embarrassments that such behavior would cause.

He urges his audience to keep their good behavior: "You made the night become day through the holy vigils. Do not in turn make the day become night through the drinking, and the hangover, and the harlots' songs" (In martyres, PG 50.663). The fact that most of the homily warns and chastises against the joint dangers of drunkenness and indulgence demonstrates the depth of Chrysostom's concern. Daphne would, Chrysostom claims, be taken over the next day by "choruses of men," the sight of whom often leads even the most well-behaved person to imitate "the same indecency," especially when "even the devil is in the middle of them. For he certainly is present, called by the harlots' songs, by the shameless words, by the demonic procession" (In s. Iulianum martyrem 4).[78] In fact, his sharp rhetoric suggests that the behavior that he dreaded was the very behavior that could be expected of Antiochenes returning on a festival day along this road back into the city, so that he appears to address not particularly troubled individuals from the city who were unusually guilty of such displays, but rather the city's (and empire's) traditional ways of celebrating. What he feared was not aberrant behavior, but typical behavior to which he wanted to contrast idealized and notably different Christian actions. Soler concludes that the Meletian clergy wanted to reshape Antiochene festival practices and to construct in their Christian community "a new festival geography" that privileged extramural martyr shrines.[79]

John Chrysostom is explicit that his efforts aimed to make Christians distinctive through their behavior. He warns those gathered for the martyrs: "You honored the martyrs with your presence, your attention, your zeal. Honor them also with your orderly departure, lest someone seeing you behaving disgracefully in a tavern say that you came not on account of the martyrs, but so that you might increase your passion, so that you might gratify your base desire" (In martyres, PG

---

77. Note that this type of behavior is condemned by a variety of Antiochene authors in these decades (Soler, Le sacré et le salut, esp. 29–32).

78. See Dayna Kalleres's productive reading of this text (City of Demons, chap. 1).

79. Soler, Le sacré et le salut, 187; cf. 165–214.

50.663). He repeats his warning that those in his audience should take care so that they did not become "a public spectacle," and were not seen "spending the day in a tavern" (PG 50.664), and reiterates his reason, that those who saw them en route should be able to associate them with the place of the Christian martyrs. He encourages his audience, "Therefore in this way let us go back to the city, with the proper discipline, with orderly walking, with intelligence and self-control, with a subdued and calm glance . . . so that we ourselves may enjoy much contentedness and become envoys of liberty for others (*eleutherias proxenoi*)" (PG 50.666; cf. *De ss. martyr.* 4; *De s. Pelagia* 3).[80] In his homily on the martyr Pelagia, Chrysostom clarifies what behaviors he hoped to prevent: "I am not simply saying these things now, but because I see many running to drinking and the taverns and the tables in inns and the other indecencies after this spiritual spectacle is let out" (*De s. Pelagia* 3). Here he also comments, "For this crowd that is present now, if it were present with discipline, it would be a great ornament for us" unlike the "disgrace and accusation" that an unruly gathering would garner (3). He urges those in attendance, "Let us go back home with the same discipline with which it is right for those who have met with this martyr to depart" (4). "The length of the road is great," Chrysostom says of the return trip from Pelagia's martyrion back to the city's walls, and he urges his listeners to turn the road itself into Christian space, filling it with sober, orthodox Christians filled with the utmost decorum (4).

Chrysostom's concern in these cases was explicitly that others would see what he understood to be the un-Christian behavior of those who attended the celebration of the Christian martyrs, and might associate the people and the places that he considered Christian with this unruly behavior rather than with the ideal behavior that Chrysostom wished would be associated with Christianity. Again, Chrysostom calls on his followers to regulate their own behavior as well as that of their neighbors: "If you see disorderly laughter, and unseemly running, and uncivilized walking and unbecoming manners, approach and give a piercing and formidable look to those doing these things" (*De s. Pelagia* 4). If that failed to interrupt the behavior, Chrysostom suggests going as a group to try to correct the behavior; and if even that failed, he suggests telling the priests so that they can address the problem (4). His fear was explicitly that if any of his opponents "see us dancing, laughing, shouting, drinking like this, they will go away condemning us completely" (4).

In these texts, Chrysostom portrays each person who attended the Christian celebration as a microcosm of the martyr's place. The saints' shrines became more visible as Christian places on Chrysostom's map of the region's landscape during the festival celebrations; and as the Christians left the shrine, their chaste procession became an additional site of Christianity. Finally, Chrysostom encourages the attendees to consider themselves additional loci of Christianity after they had

---

80. I have adopted the translation of "envoys" from Mayer and Allen, *John Chrysostom*, 97.

returned to the city, revealing their Christianity through their sober practices and their demeanor, and thus making momentarily Christian the landscape through which they passed.

Theodoret's Map: Ascetics and the Christianization of the Countryside

Theodoret in his *Historia religiosa,* like John Chrysostom in his homilies, privileged Christian places over those associated with the gods. Whereas John Chrysostom focused on the places associated with Christian martyrs, however, in mapping the region outside of Antioch, Theodoret devoted his fifth-century text to the role that Christian ascetics played in defining the religious identity of the landscape. "In the course of the fourth and fifth centuries, especially the latter," Brouria Bitton-Ashkelony writes, "a sacred Christian topography had come into being in the East and the West that owed its existence, inter alia, to the rise of the holy man in late-antique Christian society."[81] Without authors to narrate their stories and the significance that should be seen in their actions, however, these "holy men" who populated the landscape would not have had as far-reaching an effect on the landscape. Like Libanius and John Chrysostom, Theodoret presented a narrative map of the region that reflected his own religious, social, and political interests, and encouraged his audience to see the world through his Christian lens. Studying the texts of Libanius, John Chrysostom, and Theodoret in relation to one another reveals some of the complex processes by which fourth- and fifth-century authors created the saint-populated "sacred Christian topography" that Bitton-Ashkelony describes.

Theodoret claimed that like martyrs, and the congregants who had been visibly marked by their visits to the martyrs, Christian ascetics could change the religious topography of a region by settling in a new place, since through their ascetic practice they became a visible locus of Christianity. Ascetics who became well known during their lifetime reshaped the region even more dramatically by becoming a site of pilgrimage, at least locally, and sometimes, like Symeon the Stylite (d. 459), attracting visitors from all over the empire.[82] Writing in the fifth century, Theodoret

---

81. Bitton-Ashkelony, *Encountering the Sacred,* 187.

82. Numerous scholars have written on the development of Christian pilgrimage, and some of the ways in which it helped to reshape and "Christianize" the landscape of the Roman Empire in late antiquity. Pierre Maraval describes the creation "d'une géographie sacrée chrétienne" in his book *Lieux saints et pèlerinages d'Orient: Histoire et géographie des origines à la conquête arabe* (Paris: Les Éditions du Cerf, 2004), 60. See also David Frankfurter, ed., *Pilgrimage and Holy Space in Late Antique Egypt* (Boston: Brill, 1998); Georgia Frank, *The Memory of the Eyes: Pilgrims to Living Saints in Christian Late Antiquity* (Berkeley: University of California Press, 2000); Jaś Elsner and Ian Rutherford, eds., *Pilgrimage in Graeco-Roman & Early Christian Antiquity: Seeing the Gods* (New York: Oxford University Press, 2005); Frank, "Pilgrimage," in *The Oxford Handbook of Early Christian Studies,* ed. Susan Ashbrook Harvey and David Hunter (New York: Oxford University Press, 2008), 826–41; Bitton-Ashkelony, *Encountering the Sacred;* as well as Joan Taylor's work on the fourth-century development of Christian holy places: Taylor, *Christians and the Holy Places: The Myth of Jewish-Christian Origins* (New York:

famously describes the transformation of the once isolated hilltop north of Beroea where the ascetic Symeon finally settled, marked today by the remains of the monastic complex at Qal'at Sim'ān that grew up around Symeon's pillar. Theodoret claims that Symeon was known by all the subjects of the Roman Empire and had also been heard of "by the Persians, the Medes, the Ethiopians" and that his fame spread quickly "as far as the nomadic Scythians" (*HR* 26.1).[83] Theodoret paints a vivid picture:

> As his fame spread in all directions, everyone came together, not only those in the neighborhood, but also many days' journey removed. . . . Thus with everyone arriving in every direction, and every road like a river, a sea of people can be seen coming together in that region, receiving rivers from every direction. For not only do those who inhabit our part of the world stream together, but also Ishmaelites, and Persians, and Armenians who are subject to them, and Iberians, and Homerites, and those who are further inland than these. And many arrived who inhabited the farthest west, Spaniards, and Britons, and the Gauls who occupy the area between them. Of Italy it is superfluous to speak. (26.11)

The growth of this pilgrimage reveals that Symeon reshaped the landscape, creating a place newly identified with Christianity on a hill outside the small village of Telanissus that drew visitors from all over the region (26.7, 10).

As told by Theodoret, however, Symeon's narrative reveals additional forces that flowed from Symeon's occupation of this hilltop. Theodoret writes that Symeon, who stood on a broad stone pillar for almost forty years, until his death in 450, "enlightened the Ishmaelites, who were enslaved in their many tens of thousands to the darkness of impiety"; he further claims that it was possible "to see Iberians, and Armenians, and Persians arriving and benefitting from the divine baptism"; and that "the Ishmaelites, arriving in companies, two and three hundred at once, sometimes even a thousand, deny with a shout their ancestral deceit, and crushing before that great luminary the idols worshipped by those people, and bidding farewell to the secret rites of Aphrodite—for they had originally accepted the worship of this *daimōn*—they benefit from the divine mysteries" (*HR* 26.13). Frank Trombley's overview of the physical remains of this region suggests that the villages in the area around Symeon's pillar were largely Christian already by the

---

Clarendon Press, 1993). For a history of pre-Christian and Christian stylites, see David Frankfurter, "Stylites and *Phallobatēs:* Pillar Religions in Late Antique Syria," *VC* 44 (1990): 168–98.

83. All translations from Theodoret's *Historia religiosa* are my own from the Greek texts edited by Pierre Canivet and Alice Leroy-Molinghen in *Théodoret de Cyr, Histoire des moines de Syrie (I-XIII)*, vol. 1, SC 234 (1977; repr., Paris: Les Éditions du Cerf, 72006); and *Théodoret de Cyr, Histoire des moines de Syrie*, vol. 2, SC 257 (Paris: Les Éditions du Cerf, 1979). There is an English translation in Richard Price, *A History of the Monks of Syria, by Theodoret of Cyrrhus* (Kalamazoo, MI: Cistercian Publications, 1985).

time that Symeon started his ascetic practice in the area, which may help to explain why the biographies about Symeon describe primarily his conversion of pilgrims from elsewhere to Christianity and do not have similar stories about his conversion of local communities.[84] Regardless, Theodoret's stories show his understanding that these ascetics were engaged in creating new Christian pilgrimage sites and communities.

The bodies of these living saints drew crowds to their location, and were thought to bring divine protection and favor, and as such there were many who wished to be near them, both while the saints were living and after they had died. Theodoret relates the story of the ascetic Maron who settled in the region of Cyrrhus where Theodoret became bishop (HR 16.3). Theodoret claims that when the ascetic died, "a violent fight arose among his neighbors concerning the body. One of the neighboring villages that was well-populated came out en masse, scattered the others, and snatched that much-desired treasure" (16.4).[85] As for the ascetic Salamanes who lived in Capersana, on the west bank of the Euphrates River, east of present-day Gaziantep (Turkey), Theodoret claims that he acted as if he were dead even while he was still living, and that people from his hometown carried him from his ascetic cell back to their village, from which he was then taken back to his cell by villagers from that region (19.3). As if already dead, his body was abducted first by one community and then another in what appears to have been a mutual desire among the people to have him near them, presumably because of the sanctity that they associated with his body.[86]

Theodoret's story about James of Cyrrhestica embodies the complexities among the bodies of living saints, the relics of dead saints, and the villagers who hoped to benefit from their proximity to them. Theodoret recounts that when James was once near death from illness, "many came together from all sides to snatch the body," no doubt hoping to acquire a sacred relic at his apparently imminent death; many rushed to protect him and chased off the crowd, but even so, Theodoret claims, "the people from the countryside" were plucking out his hair (HR 21.9). After his recovery, however, the James of Theodoret's memory revealed a deep respect for the relics of earlier saints, going from being the object of others' honor to honoring the relics of saints who had died before him, most particularly John the Baptist (21.19–21). Theodoret recounts that toward the end of his life James asked the bishop to make preparations so that the ascetic would be buried near the

---

84. Frank Trombley, *Hellenic Religion and Christianization, c. 370–529* (Leiden: E. J. Brill, 1993), 2:249.

85. Compare also the Syriac life of Symeon the Stylite, which says that at his death his disciples feared that people would want to steal his body, so they kept him in a coffin on top of his pillar until his remains could be carried to Antioch in a formal procession.

86. Duval (*Auprès des saints*, 73–82) also discusses Theodoret's descriptions of the efforts of people to be near the bodies of saints in northern Syria.

relics of earlier martyrs, not wanting to become an object of devotion himself, but wishing to honor others. Theodoret notes that James accomplished the latter: "Gathering together many prophets, and many apostles, and as many martyrs as possible from everywhere, he placed them in a single coffin, wishing to reside with the population of the saints" (21.30). Of course, regardless of James's wishes, Theodoret's stories imply that James's body was likely to become an object of piety itself (cf. 10.8). Christian ascetics appear to have had a strong influence on making the places and people of the countryside more visibly Christian.

In these writings, Libanius, John Chrysostom, and Theodoret each present a picture of the places around Antioch, offering a map of the region to the people in their audience. While these maps engage with the physical landscape that the audiences could see around them, each presentation also asks the audience to imagine the landscape in a particular way. Libanius asks his audience to see only the places associated with the gods, as if his silence regarding Antioch's synagogues, churches, and martyr shrines might hide those other places from view. As J. B. Harley writes, maps are "actions" that teach through their "emphatic utterances" as well as their "equally emphatic silences";[87] maps "exert a social influence through their omissions as much as by the features they depict."[88] John Chrysostom and Theodoret, in contrast to Libanius, reveal their Christian bias in their emphasis on the significance of Christian landmarks, and their clear superiority to places associated negatively with *daimones*. Superimposing these authors' representations on each other demonstrates the extent to which they are real-and-imagined, the advantages that each of these competing perspectives offered to its author, and the significant role of Christian martyrs and ascetics in how the region around Antioch was perceived in the late fourth and early fifth centuries.

UNDER NEW MANAGEMENT:
COMMUNITIES IN CONFLICT

Presenting an ideologically useful map of Antioch and its surroundings was not, however, only a matter of filtering the important places from those that were less

87. J. B. Harley, "Silences and Secrecy: The Hidden Agenda of Cartography in Early Modern Europe," *Imago Mundi* 40 (1988): 71. Despite the early concerns about Harley's critical approach to geography raised by John Andrews, Harley's work was at the forefront of a significant shift in the study of geography that became more acceptable with the growing multidisciplinary familiarity with work by Foucault and other such theorists. See Andrews, *Meaning, Knowledge, and Power in the Map Philosophy of J. B. Harley*, Trinity Papers in Geography 6 (Dublin: Department of Geography, Trinity College, 1994).

88. J. B. Harley, "Maps, Knowledge, and Power," in *The Iconography of Landscape: Essays on the Symbolic Representation, Design, and Use of Past Environments*, ed. Denis Cosgrove and Stephen Daniels (New York: Cambridge University Press, 1988), 277–311.

significant; it also required the author to assert the correct interpretation of places that were contested. That is, in addition to exhorting church attendees to frequent a martyr's shrine instead of a temple, Christian leaders recorded examples of saints making "Christian" a place that had previously been associated with the gods, what David Frankfurter refers to as holy places that served "as theaters of contestation between new religious ideologies and traditional religious formulations."[89] The texts of Libanius, John Chrysostom, and Theodoret agree that some Christians went beyond homiletic efforts to change the landscape and engaged in physical acts that they hoped would transform the meaning of a religiously charged place. In turn, the texts that narrate these alleged actions continued these leaders' efforts to insure their community's dominance. Examining three texts that narrate physical competition over some of these extramural places of religious ritual reveals the complexity of these topographical negotiations.

While Christian martyrs' shrines coexisted with non-Christian burial sites, often with relative ease, in Roman cemeteries, much of the extant literary evidence describes moments of competition between places of different religious ritual.[90] In some cases, Christians were accused of destroying altars to the gods; in other cases, Christians seem to have tried to co-opt the sanctity already associated with an older place of religious cult; and in still other cases, such as at Daphne's Apollo temple, the conflict was more prolonged and complicated. Peter Brown refers to the role that Christian martyrs and ascetics played outside the walls of the empire's cities when he writes, "Christianity had a genius for impinging with gusto on the late-Roman landscape";[91] and David Frankfurter has persuasively demonstrated through his study of spirit-possession that in the fourth and fifth centuries saints' shrines "were the axes of Christianity's power in an evolving supernatural landscape."[92] Libanius's *Oratio* 30 (*Pro templis*) and Theodoret's *Historia religiosa* provide a compelling narrative of Christian ascetics' participation in "Christianizing" the region around Antioch in the late fourth and early fifth centuries, as well as of Libanius's efforts to impede such developments. Finally, John Chrysostom's homily *In ascensionem* reveals that Christian leaders sometimes targeted

89. David Frankfurter, "Where the Spirits Dwell: Possession, Christianization, and Saints' Shrines in Late Antiquity," *Harvard Theological Review* 103.1 (2010), 28. Frankfurter's discussion of possession confirms that in the late fourth and early fifth centuries, "much attention came to be directed to the locations and powers of holy places as sites that embraced local experience and that situated the new pantheon of Christian 'spirits' in the landscape" (37).

90. Jitse Dijkstra reminds scholars that rhetorical descriptions of hostility are sometimes at odds with the evidence provided by material culture: Dijkstra, "The Fate of the Temples in Late Antique Egypt," in *The Archaeology of Late Antique "Paganism,"* ed. Luke Lavan and Michael Mulryan (Boston: Brill, 2011), 389–436.

91. Brown, *Cult*, 8.

92. Frankfurter, "Where the Spirits Dwell," 46.

"heretical" as well as "pagan" people and places in such efforts at topographical transformation.

Libanius's and Theodoret's rhetorical descriptions of ascetics attacking temples are ideologically motivated and should not be mistaken for straightforward descriptions of "reality"; material evidence from elsewhere in the empire facilitates a more nuanced reading of their texts. Garth Fowden has investigated the relationship between imperial and episcopal efforts to end ritual practices at temples and to destroy temples around the eastern empire, particularly highlighting the role of the praetorian prefect Cynegius.[93] Helen Saradi-Mendelovici has also noted this destructive tendency, although she usefully tempers these examples with other examples of Christians using and sometimes even respecting temples.[94] As the evidence in chapter 6 shows, Antioch fits easily with examples from elsewhere in the empire. While Jason Moralee makes a strong argument for a few examples of intentional Christian use of "pagan" *spolia* in Gerasa,[95] the archaeological critique offered by Jitse Dijkstra persuasively argues that these cases of explicit Christian hostility to "pagan" architecture were more textually supported than archaeologically, and seem to have been a minority.[96]

Dijkstra warns against relying solely on rhetorical textual narratives to presume that in the late fourth century large numbers of temples were being destroyed or converted to churches, and the additional information she provides through the study of material culture supports the need for such caution.[97] This scholarship provides an important reminder to read Libanius's and Theodoret's texts with an eye toward the rhetorical training of these authors; each narrative reflects the perspective of the author, and undoubtedly an exaggerated version of the events

93. For a survey of the evidence for legal and episcopal hostility against temples in the fourth and early fifth centuries, see Garth Fowden, "Bishops and Temples in the Eastern Roman Empire, A.D. 320–435," *JThSt* 29.1 (1978): 53–78. See also the discussion on the Christian "conversion" and destruction of temples in Trombley, *Hellenic Religion*, 1:108–47.

94. Helen Saradi-Mendelovici, "Christian Attitudes toward Pagan Monuments in Late Antiquity and Their Legacy in Later Byzantine Churches," *Dumbarton Oaks Papers* 44 (1990): 47–61.

95. Jason Moralee, "The Stones of St. Theodore: Disfiguring the Pagan Past in Christian Gerasa," *JECS* 14.2 (2006): 183–215.

96. Dijkstra, "Fate of the Temples."

97. In addition to Dijkstra's essay, see also Lavan and Mulryan, *Archaeology of Late Antique "Paganism"*; Hahn, Emmel, and Gotter, *From Temple to Church*, esp. 1–14; Ortwin Dally, "'Pflege' und Umnutzung heidnischer Tempel in der Spätantike," in *Die spätantike Stadt und ihre Christianisierung: Symposion vom 14. bis 16. Februar 2000 in Halle/Saale,* ed. Gunnar Brands and Hans-Georg Severin (Wiesbaden: Reichert Press, 2003), 98–114; Bryan Ward-Perkins, "Re-using the Architectural Legacy of the Past, *entre idéologie et pragmatisme,*" in *The Idea and Ideal of the Town between Late Antiquity and the Early Middle Ages,* ed. G. P. Brogiolo and Bryan Ward-Perkins (Boston: Brill, 1999), 225–44; and Ward-Perkins, "Reconfiguring Sacred Space: From Pagan Shrines to Christian Churches," in Brands and Severin, *Die spätantike Stadt,* 285–90; the last highlights the importance of regional variation, although the argument relies on textual rather than archaeological evidence.

around late fourth-century Antioch. Nonetheless, this need not suggest that no ascetics vandalized any temples or shrines associated with the gods. Libanius's accounts of marauding ascetics destroying temples, side by side with Theodoret's and Chrysostom's Christian descriptions, still plausibly suggest that there may have been some incidents of intentional Christian violence against places associated with the gods outside Antioch, even if the number and severity of the attacks have certainly been exaggerated.

Libanius's oration *Pro templis* reveals that Antioch's ordained Christian leaders were not alone in trying to shape the religious and ritual contours of Antioch's topography; Libanius himself and unnamed Christian ascetics also participated in the process, the former working to reinvigorate the temples and attendance at them, and the latter apparently contributing to their erasure. Between 385 and 390, Libanius produced *Pro templis*,[98] which asked the emperor Theodosius to address an alleged Christian threat to the region's temples. This oration bears witness to Libanius's efforts to preserve places dedicated to the gods, and to put an end to Christian violence that he said threatened to radically reshape the landscape.[99]

In this much-referenced oration, Libanius accuses Christian ascetics, whom he insults by describing them as "those black-garbed people who eat more than elephants and, by the quantities of drink they consume, weary those that accompany their drinking with songs, who hide these excesses under an artificially contrived pallor," of destroying temples (*Or.* 30.8; cf. 30.11).[100] Libanius writes that the ascetics "run to the temples, carrying firewood, and stones, and iron, and when they do not have these they use hands and feet. Then follows . . . the stripping of the roofs, demolition of the walls, the tearing down of statues and the overthrowing of altars"; and then, according to Libanius, they threaten the priests of the temples during the

98. Although Otto Seeck dated this oration to the later side, certainly after 388 and likely in the summer of 390 (Seeck, *Die Briefe des Libanius zeitlich geordnet* [Leipzig: J. C. Hinrichs, 1906]), Paul Petit influenced most later scholarship with his argument for a date of 386: Petit, "Sur la date du 'Pro Templis' de Libanius," *Byzantion* 21 (1951): 285–309. More recently, Wiemer demonstrated some of the weaknesses of assumptions that led to Seeck's and Petit's dating, and argued that the oration could come either from 385–87 or from 389–90, although he expresses a preference for the former over the latter: Hans-Ulrich Wiemer, "Die Rangstellung des Sophisten Libanios unter den Kaisern Julian, Valens und Theodosius: Mit einem Anhang über Abfassung und Verbreitung von Libanios' Rede Für die Tempel (Or 30)," *Chiron* 25 (1995): 89–130, esp. 124–26.

99. See Ellen Perry's discussion of Libanius's defense of the temples' statues in relation to their legal status under Theodosius: Perry, "Divine Statues in the Works of Libanius of Antioch: The Actual and Rhetorical Desacralization of Pagan Cult Furniture in the Late Fourth Century C.E.," in *The Sculptural Environment of the Roman Near East: Reflections on Culture, Ideology, and Power*, ed. Y. Eliav, E. Friedland, and S. Herbert (Leuven: Peeters, 2008), 437–48. See also Soler's discussion of this oration (*Le sacré et le salut*, 18–21).

100. All translations from Libanius's *Oratio* 30 are from the English translation in A. F. Norman, ed. and trans., *Libanius: Selected Orations*, vol. 2 (Cambridge, MA: Harvard University Press, 1977), with my own small emendations from the Greek in the same volume.

attacks, so that the priests "must either keep quiet or die" (30.8). This happened not only at one temple, according to Libanius, but at temples all over the region (30.8–9). Throughout this oration, Libanius reiterates explicitly, "Such outrages occur even in the cities, but they are most common in the country" (30.9). According to Libanius, "one after another the temples of the country" suffered this fate through the "insolence, violence, greed and deliberate lack of self-control" of the ascetics (30.21). Libanius claims that Christian ascetics were programmatically committing acts of violence in an effort to destroy the numerous temples in and around Antioch.

Libanius pleads with Theodosius to put an end to such violence, arguing that the temples were fundamental not only to the history of the region, but also to its identity, safety, and prosperity (*Or.* 30.4).[101] Libanius attributes the Romans' past military successes to their respectful relationship with the gods (30.5). Such a history, Libanius argues, made the temples indispensable to the empire. He describes the ascetics who "flow through the countryside like torrents, ravaging the lands by means of the temples, for wherever they cut down the temple of the land, that land is blinded and lies dead"; such colorful imagery highlights the significance that Libanius attributes to the temples, which he portrays as "the soul of the countryside" (30.9). He elaborates that those who lived in the country rested their hopes for everything in their temples, and their relation to the gods who protected their family, their livestock, and their crops (30.10). The Christians, however, Libanius accuses of every sort of abuse. He accuses the ascetics of not only destroying the temples, but also stealing the produce and livestock from the people who lived on the rural land, and sometimes of going even further, claiming private land for their church under the pretense that it was property that had belonged to a temple (30.11). He writes that more than once Christian ascetics illegally appropriated private land, and that local Christian pastors allowed this behavior to continue and did nothing for the victims who came to them seeking retribution. Furthermore, Libanius adds that if the ascetics learned of land that had something of value, immediately they claimed that it was involved in sacrifices and other such crimes, and acting as a rural police force, they confiscated whatever was of value on the land (30.12). Through such descriptions Libanius presents a map that contrasts sharply with that of the contemporary Christian leaders of Antioch, as Libanius here, as in his *Oratio* 11, describes a city and region that was fundamentally defined through its long-standing, highly visible temples.

In this oration Libanius addresses Christian claims regarding the conversion of many of the local citizens, commenting to the emperor Theodosius that he should

---

101. Vasiliki Limberis also observes Libanius's interest in the temples' civilizing role: Limberis, "'Religion' as the Cipher for Identity: The Cases of Emperor Julian, Libanius, and Gregory Nazianzus," *HTR* 93.4 (2000): 389. In this oration, Libanius further argues that the statues in the temples are culturally important as art, as noted also by Saradi-Mendelovici ("Christian Attitudes," 52).

be cautious about accepting at face value the claims made by marauding ascetics that their destructive behavior caused some people to adopt their beliefs about God. Libanius scoffs that these changes were in appearance only and had not actually taken place: "For no one of them has turned away, but they only say [they have]" (*Or.* 30.28). The people had not actually, Libanius argues, exchanged one form of worship for another, but the ascetics had been deceived by the peoples' words to think that this was the case. Competing claims about these alleged new Christians cannot confirm whether their professions were "genuine" in any way that might have been meaningful to the Christian leaders. It does, however, reveal a great deal about the competition over religious practices, identities, and places.

Libanius does not, after all, deny that such people newly attend Christian ceremonies, and in fact he firmly connects their performance of Christianity with their attendance at particular places, writing, "These join [Christians'] events and crowds, and go with the others" (Libanius, *Or.* 30.28). Libanius denies, however, that this performance and appearance of Christian prayer reflected a change in their worship from the gods to the Christian God, thus removing any theoretical justification for the violent behavior that he attributes to the Christian ascetics. He narrates that when these rural people followed Christians and prayed with them, "either they call upon no one, or else they invoke the gods"; Libanius acknowledges that certain gods should be invoked only at particular places, however, as he allows that invocations of the gods during the appearance of Christian prayer in a Christian place were not proper because they were done "from such a place" (30.28). For Libanius, too, then, religious practices were place-oriented, and he seems to recognize that Christians were in those years competing over the religious identity of the people who lived in Antioch's *territorium* through the manipulation of the physical landscape, and especially of the places associated with ritual praxes.

One of Libanius's goals in this oration seems to have been to facilitate the continuation of traditional cult, and to stop Christian ascetics from redefining the local landscape to their advantage. In an effort to accomplish this, he calls on imperial law as well as human reason to try to persuade the emperor Theodosius to put an end to Christians' alleged destruction of temples around Antioch. He points to historical examples of how the gods had preserved the empire and helped it and its heroes to thrive; and he places Theodosius in the context of recent emperors, suggesting that an intelligent, reasonable, and kind emperor like Theodosius would necessarily imitate those who supported the gods, or at least did not prevent their worship. If Hans-Ulrich Wiemer's preference for dating the oration to 385–87 is correct, it is noteworthy that Libanius produced *Pro templis* at roughly the same time that John Chrysostom presented his series of sermons against those who admired the power of the Jewish synagogue, and his series of sermons against the Anomeans. Although Libanius found himself on the opposite side from his former student John Chrysostom in this conflict, like the Christian leaders, Libanius nevertheless recognized the strong association of places with religious practices and identity.

Libanius's late fourth-century claims about the efforts of ascetics in the region around Antioch find some general support in the fifth-century writings of Theodoret. After growing up in Antioch, Theodoret became bishop of Cyrrhus, a small city approximately seventy miles northeast of Antioch and forty miles northwest of Beroea on a tributary of the Orontes River.[102] Theodoret maintained close associations with many of the ascetics in his region, as witnessed not only through some of the stories in his *Historia ecclesiastica* but most specifically through his *Historia religiosa,* which provides numerous examples of Christian ascetics taking over places that had been associated with the gods.[103]

The region of Teleda (Tel ʿAdeh) is one significant locus of Theodoret's stories about the Christianization of places formerly associated with the gods.[104] While we cannot know if the worship of the gods that Theodoret describes was active when the ascetics began living in these places (in fact, in the case of the ascetic Eusebius, Theodoret specifies that the worship had taken place long ago), Theodoret's description of these activities is itself important, and given Theodoret's audience, it seems plausible that he presents a recognizable portrait of ascetic activity. Frank Trombley's study of this region concludes from the archaeological and epigraphical evidence that "the main period of Christianization for the villages of the Limestone Massif was . . . c. 363–425, with a trickle of conversions continuing thereafter until down to c. 500."[105] The region was integrated with the larger Antioch region economically, religiously, and politically, as seen, for example, in the stories of several ascetics who traveled from Teleda to Antioch at the behest of Antiochene Christian leaders in order to engage with the theological schisms in the city. This

102. Theodoret notes that Cyrrhus was two days' travel from Antioch (*HR* 2.21). For more about Theodoret's life, context, and role in the theological controversies of his day, see Theresa Urbainczyk, *Theodoret of Cyrrhus: The Bishop and the Holy Man* (Ann Arbor: University of Michigan Press, 2002); Adam Schor, *Theodoret's People: Social Networks and Religious Conflict in Late Roman Syria* (Berkeley: University of California Press, 2011).

103. See also Festugière, *Antioche,* 245–346; and the unpublished doctoral thesis by Daniel Hull, "The Archaeology of Monasticism: Landscape, Politics, and Social Organisation in Late Antique Syria" (York University, 2006). It goes without saying that these academic conversations about the role of ascetics' engagement with the people of the country and surrounding villages are still shaped all these decades later by the foundational work of Peter Brown, especially his influential article "The Rise and Function of the Holy Man in Late Antiquity," *Journal of Roman Studies* 61 (1971): 80–101.

104. Ross Burns's guide to the Roman ruins of the Limestone Massif was extremely useful in locating these places on my research trip to Syria with Dayna Kalleres (Burns, *The Monuments of Syria: A Guide* [New York: I. B. Tauris, 2009]). Even so, we would not have been able to see these places without the professional and knowledgeable aid of Aleppo native Muhammad Moubarak.

105. Trombley, *Hellenic Religion,* 2:247.

region is, therefore, a productive addition to conversations about the area's changing religious topography.[106]

Theodoret describes this region of ascetic habitation with great topographical detail in his narrative about the ascetic Eusebius of Teleda:

> There is a high mountain lying to the east of Antioch and to the west of Beroea, sitting above the mountains lying around it, imitating the shape of a cone at the highest summit. . . . To the south a curved plain stretches out, encompassed on either side by not very high hills. These extend as far as the road for horses, receiving footpaths on either side that cut from south to north. In this plain people settled in sites (*chōria*) both small and large, bordered by the mountains on either side. At the very skirts of the high mountain there is a certain large and well-populated village, which they call Teleda in the rural speech. Above the foot of the mountain there is a certain glen, not very steep but sloping moderately toward that plain and facing the south wind. In this glen a certain Ammianus built a place for philosophical meditation. (*HR* 4.2)

While these ascetics did not settle directly on the peak of the highest mountain, but rather just up from its base, Theodoret mentions that the mountain had been a site associated with local gods: "Long ago at its peak there was a precinct of *daimones* much honored by those in the neighborhood" (4.2). It is not difficult to see the ascetics' settlement on the slope of this mountain as a way of contesting this site in an effort to transform it from the place of the local *daimones* to a place that demonstrated the power of the Christian God.[107]

Theodoret is even more explicit about the intentional transformation of places in his narratives of the ascetics Maron, Abraham, and Symeon. Theodoret informs his readers that Maron "occupied a certain peak [near Cyrrhus] that had long ago been honored by the impious, and dedicating the precinct of *daimones* on it to God, he spent time there, constructing a small hut" (*HR* 16.1). Abraham, on the other hand, was a native of Cyrrhus who, according to Theodoret, traveled to Lebanon, where he had heard that "a large village was held fast in the darkness of impiety"; having won over the population after a series of challenges, they "exhorted him to become their patron" (17.2–3). Abraham accepted on the condition that they would build a church, which they encouraged him to begin at once,

---

106. While Antioch's port city of Seleucia Pieria would also be of interest, and Wendy Mayer and Pauline Allen include its churches in their recent research (*Churches*, 58–67), the lack of narrative descriptions about the construction of its topography limits the types of conversations that are possible for that region.

107. Peter Brown notes similar examples from the western empire, including Saint Hilarius's relics, which were housed on the edge of a marsh "formed in the volcanic crater within a mountain top" that had previously been the site of local polytheistic cult (*Cult*, 125); Brown comments that the site had been redefined through the ascetic's inhabiting and redefining the place so that "seen in this way, the rise of Christianity in Western Europe is a chapter in the 'hominization' of the natural world" (126). Compare also the discussion in Trombley, *Hellenic Religion*, 2:143–73, 184–204.

and together they chose the best site for it in the village, presumably causing a new church building to become a prominent Christian place in the landscape (17.4, 6). Theodoret claims that after this success, Abraham went as far east as Carrhae (present-day Harran, Turkey), located twenty-five miles south of Edessa (present-day Şanliurfa, Turkey). Theodoret caricatures Carrhae as "a city that was enveloped in the drunkenness of impiety and that had given itself up to the frenzy of the *daimones*," but he rejoices that the people of this city also became Christian under Aphrahat's care (17.5). Theodoret's narrative of another ascetic named Symeon (not to be confused with Symeon Stylites) likewise notes that Symeon worked miracles that were so impressive to those around him that he even "attracted many of the neighboring barbarians" from the surrounding desert; Symeon eventually settled on Mount Amanus, a mountain just north of the Lake of Antioch, about which Theodoret notes, "This mountain, formerly full of much polytheist madness, he cultivated with many miracles of all kinds and planted the piety that now governs on it" (6.4).[108] These examples suggest that Theodoret portrays Christian ascetics as particularly effective agents for causing places and people formerly associated with the gods to become affiliated with Christianity.

While Libanius and Theodoret highlight the role that they claim ascetics played in reshaping the region around Antioch, John Chrysostom provides evidence that Christian martyrs could prove useful in making a place religiously orthodox in competition with Christian "heretics."[109] By far the most intriguing example is the striking physical manipulation of saints' remains by Bishop Flavian in the martyrion that John Chrysostom and Palladius describe at the Romanesian Gate.[110] In his homily *In ascensionem*, which must date from after 381 and before 398, John

---

108. Symeon later moved farther south to Mount Sinai (Theodoret, *HR* 6.7), another mountain whose peak had long been associated with a deity, in this case the God of Moses. Other Christian ascetics had already settled on this mountain before Symeon's arrival (Egeria mentions them in her account of her travels there, *Peregrinatio* 1–5). See also Reyhan Durmaz's work on Tur ʾAbdin (Turkey), including her paper, "Reconstructing the Mount Athos of the East: Christian Hierotopy of Tur ʾAbdin in Late Antiquity," delivered at the Sixth North American Syriac Symposium, at Duke University, June 2011; and her master's thesis completed at Koç University in Turkey: "Tur Abdin at Close: The Church Complex at Zaz, Mardin: Its Architecture, History and Contemporary Revitalization Process" (2010). See also Andrew Palmer's unpublished essay, "The Mountain of the Seventy Monasteries: The Monastic Geography of Tur ʾAbdin." I am grateful to these scholars for sharing their work with me.

109. See the discussion on control of martyria and churches in Antioch in Mayer and Allen, *Churches*, 167–74, 191–99.

110. For mention of this martyrion, see Palladius, *Dialogus de vita Ioannis Chrysostomi* 5; John Chrysostom, *In ascensionem*. Catherine Saliou's thorough study of the region surrounding the imperial palace at Antioch locates the Romanesian Gate on the island with a bridge leading to the less populated side of the Orontes River ("Le palais imperial," 244–46). I am grateful to Wendy Mayer for first bringing John Chrysostom's description of this martyrion to my attention; see also Mayer and Allen, *Churches*, 94–95, 141–42.

Chrysostom claims that saints' relics had been buried "under the floor" of the martyrion at the Romanesian Gate (*In ascensionem* 1).[111] The previous decades had seen control of Antioch's church buildings shift dramatically among the city's different Christian factions, and it appears from this homily that some of the relics in this martyrion had been buried by Bishop Meletius's group, while others had been buried by his opponents. Chrysostom comments that the true saints had "a shared burial" with "heretics" (1). Although some early Antiochene saints who preceded the city's episcopal split, such as Ignatius, could have been defined as orthodox by all of Antioch's Christians, others such as Meletius were associated particularly with one faction. With control of many of the city's publicly Christian places changing hands under each new emperor, it is easy to see how a single martyrion might have accumulated relics buried by leaders of more than one of Antioch's competing Christian communities. This also highlights, however, the complex challenges that bishops such as Flavian inherited from the city's checkered past.

Chrysostom suggests in this homily that Flavian understood there to be a danger that those attending the martyrion could not accurately distinguish the relics authorized by his church from those that were laid with them by bishops from another Christian faction. Chrysostom assures his audience that the orthodox saints' relics did not suffer any harm in body, soul, or spirit from being buried with the heretics (*In ascensionem* 1). Nevertheless, the Christians who remained alive were being harmed, Chrysostom claims, because when they ran to the martyrs to pray, they were filled with uncertainty because they could not recognize "the tombs of the saints, and where the true storehouses lay" (1). One might, of course, wonder if as much as the danger of praying to someone who was not as powerful or saintly, Chrysostom might not also have worried about the contemporary political effects of having Christians in Antioch visibly honoring relics that had been interred by his theological opponents. One might guess that it was the local political and religious authority of Bishop Flavian and John Chrysostom that was at stake as much as the efficacy of attendees' prayers and their future salvation.

John Chrysostom claims that Flavian physically rearranged the relics in this martyrion in ways that reveal his interest in using the locus of the saints' relics as an opportunity for defining orthodox Christian practices, people, and places. Concerned about attendees' possible confusion, Flavian "restrained and barred the passage" of the "foul and reeking" odors that allegedly came from the buried heretics by placing them "under," presumably further under the floor; on the other hand, "the pure fonts of the martyrs he set in a clean region," though Chrysostom comments that Flavian "did not disturb their bones, but let them remain in the

111. All translations from *In ascensionem* are my own from the Greek text in PG 50.441–52. See also Soler, *Le sacré et le salut*, 203–5.

place" where they had been (*In ascensionem* 1).[112] Wendy Mayer reasonably interprets this description in light of the modern archaeological excavations outside of
Antioch, and suggests that it is possible that Chrysostom meant that Flavian "had
the unapproved tombs sunk lower into the floor and covered over completely by
the flooring in such a way that they were no longer visible, leaving the covers to the
approved tombs exposed."[113] The visibility of the approved martyrs is at the center
of Chrysostom's praise of Flavian's actions, and Chrysostom urges that as people
ran to visit the martyrs earlier when they had been less clearly distinguished,
"much more now is it necessary to do this, when the pearls are by themselves,
when the flocks are released from the wolves, when the living have withdrawn
from the dead"—that is, now that the saints have been separated from the "heretics" (1). It is noteworthy that Flavian did not remove the other relics from the
martyrion altogether, but it is equally significant that he separated them and
moved them out of sight, attempting to censure them in the community's memory.
While Antioch's Christians appear to have been visiting this martyrion for years,
under various factions' leadership, Flavian emended the martyrion to remove
the ambiguity of the type of Christianity that the martyrion represented by
making it more visibly a place that was clearly associated with his Nicene Christian
community.

Cultural geographers have demonstrated that maps reflect the interests of their
authors, and the narrative maps of Libanius, John Chrysostom, and Theodoret are
no exception. In addition to presenting the views of these three men, however,
their texts also claim to memorialize transformative actions by others, including
Christian ascetics, and Christian leaders who relocated martyrs' relics. From
mountaintops to rural temples, from martyria to villages on the Limestone Massif,
Christians appear in these texts engaged with the world around them, suggesting
that some Christians physically altered their landscape in ways that encouraged
what they perceived to be religious orthodoxy and orthopraxy.

CONCLUSION: BODIES ON THE LANDSCAPE

This investigation of fourth-century Antioch has demonstrated that the places
inhabited by saints played a role in Christian leaders' efforts to reshape local
behavior and religious identity through places outside the city walls. Temples like-

---

112. Given Susan Ashbrook Harvey's work on smells in late antiquity, and their strong associations
with the divine, it is no surprise that a foul stench is understood by Roman Antiochenes to be evidence
of heretical bodies, since true saints' bodies would smell sweet and pleasant. See Harvey, *Scenting Salvation*, e.g., 11–21.

113. Mayer and Allen, *Churches*, 95. It is also possible that mosaics in the floor helped to distinguish (and obscure) the saints' tombs, as they did elsewhere in the empire. On the roles of mosaic
inscriptions in churches, see Yasin, *Saints and Church Spaces*, esp. 101–50, 189–209.

wise served as loci of religious practice that marked the landscape, particularly in the country, and apparently became a target, even if only rarely, for some Christian ascetics, and thus the subject of Libanius's efforts to preserve the traditional landscape of the city and its surrounding region. As geographer J. B. Harley writes, "Maps . . . are regarded as refracted images contributing to dialogue in a socially constructed world."[114] The map of Antioch was being redrawn in late antiquity, and there is no doubt that the competing depictions of the landscape offered by Libanius, John Chrysostom, and Theodoret hoped to reify their vision for the region's future. Highlighting the agency of these local actors reveals that the transformations, and resistance to them, were not exclusively by-products of imperial machinery, but included physical and rhetorical choices made by individuals who had a stake in their city's future.

While different from each other in significant ways, Libanius and the emperor Julian acted in the second half of the fourth century to try to prevent the erasure of temples and the practices associated with them. Julian, with his imperial authority, initiated changes to Antioch's landscape as part of his larger efforts to restore ritual temple practices across the empire. He quickly became notorious for the unseemly (by the aesthetics of late antiquity) amount of blood that he appears to have spilled in animal sacrifices at temples' altars, including those in Antioch and Daphne (see, e.g., Ammianus Marcellinus, *Res gest.* 22.12.6–8).[115] He likewise legislated the restoration of temples that had fallen into disrepair and their cultic objects, such as altars and statues of the gods, and enforced that restoration in person when he traveled to Antioch. Julian likewise reinstated imperial funding for the running of the temples, the festivals for the gods, and the priests who were responsible for their oversight; in Daphne he removed Babylas's relics from the precinct of Apollo's temple in an effort to restore the temple's oracle. It was with a very self-conscious and heavy hand that Julian tried in his short time as emperor to make Antioch's and Daphne's temples newly prominent, powerful places, attendance at which would associate the city's inhabitants with the newly coherent sense of being a Hellene.[116] While Libanius did not work to restore ritual sacrifice, he too tried to prevent the destruction, whether by force or by neglect, of the temples that remained in the region, and, with the exception of sacrifice, to encourage the continuation of traditions that honored the gods.

114. Harley, "Maps, Knowledge, and Power," 278.

115. Scott Bradbury, "Julian's Pagan Revival and the Decline of Blood Sacrifice," *Phoenix* 49.4 (1995): 331–56.

116. Susanna Elm's recent book discusses Julian's relation to Hellenism, and the connotations of that term, in detail: Elm, *Sons of Hellenism, Fathers of the Church: Emperor Julian, Gregory of Nazianzus, and the Vision of Rome* (Berkeley: University of California Press, 2012). Compare also Alan Cameron's analysis of "paganism" in this period: Cameron, *The Last Pagans of Rome* (New York: Oxford University Press, 2011).

On the Christian side, there were numerous actors, not even considering those whose actions are not visible to us through the texts and material evidence that survive.[117] Meletius, Flavian, John Chrysostom, Theodoret, and the Christian ascetics described above all reshaped the places in and around Antioch, and how people interacted with those places. Meletius actively fostered the Christianization of Antioch's landscape by building a new church across the Orontes River, thereby creating a new Christian building that belonged to his community. By moving Babylas's relics from the cemetery to this new church, and by having his own body buried in the church at his death, he amplified the site as the locus of two beloved and powerful saints and assured that as long as his tomb remained visible, this newly Christian place would bring authority to those Nicene Christians who had been under his leadership. Despite long and frequent exiles that would have appeared to challenge his ability physically to control the places of the city, Meletius actively and successfully furthered the Christianization of Antioch's landscape, even leaving his body as a legacy for the generations that followed.

It was, though, with Flavian's episcopacy under the emperor Theodosius that the Meletian strain of Antiochene Christianity gained its fullest power to control the places in and around the city. Theodosius granted Bishop Flavian control of Antioch's churches in 381, after which Flavian led regular services not only in the city's most prominent churches but also in the cemeteries and at other martyria scattered outside the city's walls on the occasions of the martyrs' festivals. Flavian thus gained control of places that were already Christian, and in addition Libanius accused him of turning a blind eye to ascetics' destruction of temples, especially outside the city (*Or.* 30.11).

Bishop Flavian was not only, though, leading Christian processions through the streets, cemeteries, and countryside and allegedly allowing Christian ascetics to attack temples—all of which would actively make the landscape visibly more Christian; he also seems to have been engaged in making sure that the martyrs supported his particular version of Christianity. The floor of the cruciform church discovered at Kaoussie (Qausīyeh), most likely Babylas's church, is tiled with mosaics that include inscriptions from 387. Three of these floor inscriptions, donated by a priest named Dorys, explicitly mention the "most holy bishop Flavian," showing one method of claiming the church for this community.[118] In the same vein, Flavian rearranged "heretical" and orthodox bodies in the martyrion outside the Romanesian Gate, shaping formerly more ambiguous places to be not just Christian, but "orthodox" by his definition, and newly by the definition of the emperor.

---

117. Hanns Christof Brennecke has, however, tried to recover some of the homoian activities: see Brennecke, *Studien zur Geschichte der Homöer: Der Osten bis zum Ende der homöischen Reichskirche* (Tübingen: J. C. B. Mohr/Paul Siebeck, 1988), esp. 87–157.

118. Mayer and Allen, *Churches,* 41–42.

John Chrysostom, though not himself a bishop of Antioch, was also one of the influential voices through which we hear the city's fourth-century history. Without episcopal authority, Chrysostom did not demonstrate Meletius's and Flavian's ability physically to manipulate church buildings and martyrs' relics. There is no question, though, that his deft and vast rhetorical skills effected at least as great a change in how people experienced and saw the topography as any of his ecclesiastical superiors. We hear in his rhetoric the support for the bishops' physical manipulations, advocating that his listeners go always to the martyrs' shrines, that they spend time and return from there solemnly and not like those celebrating festivals associated with the gods. Chrysostom's homilies rhetorically reshaped Antioch's places, including the places associated with the bodies of the saints, as he worked to create a recognizable difference in Christian cemetery rituals, festivals, burial places, and processions.

The Christian ascetics who lived outside of Antioch also reshaped the religious landscape. Certainly Libanius's exaggerated accusation that bands of roving ascetics wreaked destruction on temples in the region reveals one way in which ascetics as a group might have become a force for topographical change. The ascetics themselves, however, as living saints became in Theodoret's narratives additional Christian loci similar to the martyrs' tombs. Gerard Rouwhorst observes that in the first of John Chrysostom's two homilies on the Maccabean martyrs, Chrysostom has a tendency "to spiritualize the ideal of martyrdom."[119] Chrysostom thus connected the heroism and fortitude demonstrated by the martyrs with that of the ascetics who likewise dotted the landscape. We know from Theodoret and John Chrysostom that many Antiochenes regularly visited the ascetics who lived on the mountains outside of Antioch, traveling there and back in a day to visit those nearby as they also would do for the martyrs' shrines.

Harley writes: "Maps are never value-free images. . . . Both in the selectivity of their content and in their signs and styles of representation maps are a way of conceiving, articulating, and structuring the human world which is biased towards, promoted by, and exerts influence upon particular sets of social relations."[120] Interpreting the narrative maps of Libanius, John Chrysostom, and Theodoret, using Harley's vocabulary, "as reciprocal images used to mediate different views of the world" reveals the force of their narratives on the perceptions and behaviors of their audiences.[121] Examining rural temples and extramural saints' shrines side by side demonstrates that they were similarly significant places in a local landscape whose meaning was being renegotiated in the late fourth and early fifth centuries.

119. Gerard Rouwhorst, "The Emergence of the Cult of the Maccabean Martyrs in Late Antique Christianity," in *More Than a Memory: The Discourse of Martyrdom and the Construction of Christian Identity in the History of Christianity,* ed. Johan Leemans (Leuven: Peeters, 2006), 91.

120. Harley, "Maps, Knowledge, and Power," 278.

121. Harley, "Maps, Knowledge, and Power," 278.

6

Elsewhere in the Empire

The investigation of fourth-century Antioch has revealed that the manipulation, and particularly the narrative construction, of topography played a significant role in shaping the increasing visibility of Christianity in urban and rural contexts, as well as in establishing the type of Christianity that became most prominent. The transference of relics, especially the final transfers of Babylas and the saints buried in the floor of the martyrion at the Romanesian Gate, granted more authority to Bishop Meletius's community in Antioch, while diminishing the authority of the temple of Apollo and of local homoian Christians. John Chrysostom's numerous rhetorical efforts further shaped the ways in which Antioch's Christians saw, and behaved in, the region's landscape. Not only Antioch's ordained church leaders but ascetics and saints' relics (and narratives about them) also took part in this topographical restructuring, and the bids for power that accompanied it. This chapter will survey imperial legislation and data from elsewhere in the empire—namely, Milan, Jerusalem, North Africa, Alexandria, and Minorca—to demonstrate that while Antioch is unique in its wealth of relevant extant sources from this period and in the particular details of its examples, this study points to much broader phenomena in the late fourth-century empire in terms of the role that physical places and control over them played in the complex and variegated processes of defining religious orthodoxy and orthopraxy.

LEGISLATING RELIGION

Church leaders were not alone in their efforts to put the empire's churches into the hands of only those whom they considered to be orthodox; the late fourth century—especially under the emperor Theodosius I—was also a time when imperial legislation began to dictate this very thing. It is often difficult to determine how broadly any particular piece of legislation was applied, how carefully it was enforced, or how much legislation was not included in the *Codex Theodosianus*, collected under the emperor Theodosius II between 429 and 437.[1] Caroline Humfress notes that perhaps it is better to ask what the laws reveal about their creators than to speculate on the unknown extent to which they were applied in practice.[2] Scott Bradbury also notes the significant distinction between the laws issued by an emperor and the emperor's intention to have the law enforced (or not).[3] He observes, along with Paul Veyne, that Roman laws appear sometimes to have set forth an ideal that was not intended to be put fully into practice.[4] Nevertheless, the Code provides intriguing evidence of, according to Harry Maier, the emperors "increasingly defining orthodoxy spatially."[5] The topographical efforts that we have seen in fourth-century Antioch thus saw their fruition under Theodosius in the 380s, when emperors not only continued to exile and reinstate bishops according to which form of Christianity they chose to patronize, but also began legally to require a particular definition of orthodoxy and to legislate it spatially. Perhaps nowhere is the self-conscious social construction of space highlighted by contemporary cultural geographers so bluntly apparent as in this imperial legislation.

The early fourth-century legislation attributed to Constantine that is preserved in the Theodosian Code reflects the newly protected status of Christian leaders, and primarily focuses on the exemptions that Christian clergy have the right to receive from burdensome obligations, especially from nonecclesial service that would require their time and money to fulfill. Although Constantine tried to

1. See, for example, the discussion in John Matthews, *Laying Down the Law: A Study of the Theodosian Code* (New Haven, CT: Yale University Press, 2000), 168–99, 280–93; Jill Harries, *Law and Empire in Late Antiquity* (New York: Cambridge University Press, 1999), 77–98; David Hunt, "Christianising the Roman Empire: The Evidence of the Code," in *The Theodosian Code*, ed. Jill Harries and Ian Wood (Ithaca, NY: Cornell University Press, 1993), 143–60; Tony Honoré, *Law in the Crisis of Empire, 379–455 AD: The Theodosian Dynasty and Its Quaestors* (New York: Clarendon Press, 1998), esp. 123–53; John Curran, *Pagan City and Christian Capital: Rome in the Fourth Century* (Oxford: Clarendon Press, 2000), 161–217. A forthcoming edited collection should also prove useful on this subject: *Law and Empire*, ed. Jeroen Duindam, Jill Harries, Caroline Humfress, and Nimrod Hurvitz (Boston: Brill, forthcoming).

2. Caroline Humfress, *Orthodoxy and the Courts in Late Antiquity* (New York: Oxford University Press, 2007), 233.

3. Scott Bradbury, "Constantine and the Problem of Anti-Pagan Legislation in the Fourth Century," *Classical Philology* 89.2 (1994): 120–39.

4. Bradbury, "Constantine," 133–35.

5. Harry Maier, "Private Spaces as the Social Context of Arianism in Ambrose's Milan," *JTS* 45 (1994): 86.

prevent abuse of this rule,[6] he legislated, "Those who are called clerics shall be exempt from all compulsory public offices whatever" (*CTh* 16.2.2).[7] Constantine also forbade "heretics and schismatics" (*haereticos atque schismaticos*) from receiving any privileges allowed to Christian clergy, and specifically required such people to "be bound and subjected to various compulsory public offices" (16.5.1).[8] Constantine's legislation further assured that people would be allowed to leave their money and possessions to a bishop's church (16.2.4); that Christians could not be forced to perform sacrifices or other acts that might compromise their Christianity (16.2.5); and that those called "heretics" could not remove lectors, subdeacons, and other clerics from their positions (16.2.7). Constantine was certainly elsewhere quite involved with changing the physical topography of the empire by funding large Christian building projects around the empire, including the Great Church in Antioch. Nevertheless, with the exception of one ruling, which allowed Novatians to keep "their own church buildings (*ecclesiae suae domos*) and places (*loca*) suitable for burial" that they have "held for a long time" (16.5.2),[9] Constantine's early fourth-century legislation protected Christian clergy, and differentiated generally between "heretics" and catholic Christians, but did not specifically address the physical topography of Christianity that became so critical in later decades.

The laws of the emperors Constans and Constantius II that were preserved in the Theodosian Code suggest that under their rule the legislation concerning Christians remained primarily focused on the rights and exemptions of clergy. Rules issued under these emperors repeated some of the legislation from Constantine that exempted Christian clergy, and in this case also some members of their families, from onerous public offices (*CTh* 16.2.9), as well as from certain taxes (16.2.8; 16.2.10–11). In addition, bishops were at this time exempted from accusations in secular courts of law (16.2.12). Similar laws were issued again after Julian was elevated to caesar (e.g., 16.2.13–16), but in these decades, legislation about Christianity remained about exemptions and protections more than about places.

---

6. See, for example, *CTh* 16.2.3 and 16.2.6, which warn against joining the clergy in order to escape other duties.

7. All translations from the Theodosian Code are from the English translation in Clyde Pharr, *The Theodosian Code and Novels and the Sirmondia Constitutions: A Translation with Commentary, Glossary, and Bibliography* (Union, NJ: The Lawbook Exchange, Ltd., 2001), with reference to, and my own occasional emendations from, the Latin text in *Codex Theodosianus*, vol. 1, *Theodosiani libri XVI cum constitutionibus Sirmondianis*, ed. Paul Krueger and Theodor Mommsen (Hildesheim: Weidmann, 2000). Unless otherwise noted, I have relied on the dating provided in Pharr.

8. Caroline Humfress has demonstrated the ways in which the legislation's deployment of the categories of "orthodoxy" and "heresy" called into being the theological binary that it purported to describe (*Orthodoxy*, 234–42).

9. Given the discussion in chapter 5, the significance of cemeteries should come as no surprise, especially with the fourth-century rise in community remembrances of their deceased saints.

There was in this period, however, a new legislative interest in temples.[10] Constantius II and Constans, for example, not only echoed their father Constantine's prohibition of sacrifice (*CTh* 16.10.2),[11] and forbid *superstitio* (16.10.2–3),[12] but also addressed the temple buildings themselves, as preserved in two separate pieces of legislation. In the earlier case sent to Catullinus, the prefect of the city of Rome, the emperors ruled:

> It is our will that the buildings of the temples (*aedes templorum*) situated outside the walls shall remain untouched and uninjured. For since certain games or things of the circus or contests derive their origin from some of these [buildings], it is not appropriate to tear them down. (16.10.3)

This complements the information from Antioch that numerous temples continued to exist into the fifth century even though ritual sacrifices were forbidden to take place there.[13] This law evidences a growing awareness in the legislation about the importance of physical places in Roman contests about religion, but it is here as yet still confined to temples, and specifically temples outside city walls. While the law implies that some extramural temples have suffered in these years, whether through violence or neglect, the emperors chose to prohibit their destruction; so while the law acknowledges that religious places are contested, in this ruling the emperors helped to preserve places associated with the worship of the gods.

Another law from Constans and Constantius II, however, likewise acknowledges the significance of controlling physical places, and focuses on temples, but in this case forbids access to them: "It is our pleasure that the temples (*templa*) shall be immediately closed in all places (*omnibus locis*) and in all cities (*urbibus universis*), and access to them forbidden" (*CTh* 16.10.4). Although this legislation was sent, at least initially, to Taurus, the praetorian prefect of Italy and Africa, the reference to "all places" and "all cities" is much broader than the earlier legislation sent to the city of Rome. Bradbury comments on these two apparently contradictory pieces of legislation as evidence of the lack of imperial clarity in this period about the legal status of traditional religious practices and the places associated

10. See Michele Salzman, "*Superstitio* in the *Codex Theodosianus* and the Persecution of Pagans," *VC* 41 (1987): 172–88.

11. Bradbury argues persuasively that Constantine issued legislation that outlawed blood sacrifices, even if the legislation was not enforced at that time ("Constantine," 120–39). See also Frank Trombley's discussion in *Hellenic Religion and Christianization, c. 370–529* (Leiden: E. J. Brill, 1993), 1:1–97.

12. For a discussion of the complex history of the term *superstitio,* especially in relation to Christianity, see Dale Martin, *Inventing Superstition: From the Hippocratics to the Christians* (Cambridge, MA: Harvard University Press, 2004).

13. Compare also the evidence collected by Frank Trombley for the continuing use of temples around the eastern empire in this period (*Hellenic Religion,* vols. 1–2).

with them.[14] Regardless of how broadly these laws were applied, however, these developments under Constans and Constantius II show the legislation moving toward a concern for the places of religious practice, beginning with rulings about temples, much of which was reversed by the emperor Julian during his brief reign.

While the legislation about religion from Julian's time as emperor is not preserved in the Theodosian Code, we know that he worked hard to rebuild temples, having a particular interest in the Jewish Temple in Jerusalem, and to aggravate the chaos already present among Christians by recalling all exiled bishops. It was not until after his successor Jovian that emperors Valens and Valentinian renewed Christian efforts to legislate religion in our extant sources. Valens and Valentinian undid much of Julian's legislation, and renewed exemptions and protections for the clergy (and sometimes others, such as consecrated virgins) and distinctions for legal cases involving clergy (*CTh* 16.2.18–19, 21–24). Another of their laws protected Christians from being appointed as a "custodian of the temples (*templorum*)" (16.1.1). Like the early fourth-century Christian legislation under the emperor Constantine, these laws primarily protected the clergy but did not address issues regarding places of religious practice.

Valens and Valentinian also, however, issued other types of legislation that acknowledged the significance of physical places for the practice of religion—not only temples, as under Constantius II, but Christian places as well. While the law prohibiting male ascetics from visiting "the homes (*domos*) of widows and female wards" was arguably as much about maintaining the appearance of chastity as it was about the places of proper religious practice (*CTh* 16.2.20), the 370s saw the legal prohibition of Manichaean assembly and the assembly of "heretics" (16.5.3).[15] Referring to an earlier piece of legislation that is not extant, a law issued from Trier to Hesperius, the praetorian prefect of Africa, states,

> Previously . . . in order that the practice of heretical assembly should cease, we commanded that whether such assemblies were held in towns (*in oppidis*) or in the countryside outside the churches (*in agris extra ecclesias*), where our peace prevails, all places (*loca omnia*) should be confiscated in which their altars were located under the false pretext of religion (*religionis*). (16.5.4)

14. Bradbury, "Constantine," 120–39.

15. For discussion, see also Harry O. Maier, "Heresy, Households, and the Disciplining of Diversity," in *A People's History of Christianity*, vol. 2, *Late Ancient Christianity*, ed. Virginia Burrus (Minneapolis: Fortress Press, 2005), 213–33; Maier, "The Topography of Heresy and Dissent in Late-Fourth-Century Rome," *Historia: Zeitschrift für alte Geschichte* 44.2 (1995): 232–49. See also Hunt's observation that to read through this particular legislation from this period "is to be struck by the regularity of the language of separation and segregation used against condemned groups" ("Christianising the Roman Empire," 156).

This was issued in close proximity to a law of uncertain provenance against Christians who would rebaptize adherents from other Christian groups:[16]

> The churches (*ecclesiis*), which they retain contrary to good faith, shall be restored to the catholics.[17] . . . Very many people who have been expelled from the churches (*ecclesiis*) nevertheless go about with secret madness, frequenting unlawfully the places (*loca*) of great houses or estates. Such [estates] shall be included in the fiscal confiscation if they should provide hiding places (*secreta*) for the sinful doctrine. . . . But if they love their error, they shall cherish the poison of their impious teachings to their own hurt, in domestic secrecy and alone. (16.6.2)

This law expresses an explicit concern that "heretics" not have public places for worship, and requires that those churches that were in the hands of "heretics" must be given to "catholic" Christians. Nevertheless, despite (or perhaps because of) the so-called Arian conflict, the primary schism that was consuming the empire in these decades, these laws focused on denying property to those more on the political fringes and in the religious minority, the Manichaeans and those who rebaptized. The emperors of the late fourth and early fifth centuries also addressed the right to assemble of Manichees and others deemed heretical. A fifth-century law prevents Donatists from assembling (16.6.4), and a law issued in 379 against those who rebaptized prevents the assembly of those who teach "this perverse superstition" (16.5.5). In 381 Manichees were forbidden from leaving property to others and were not allowed to establish meeting places in towns or in cities (16.5.7). It was not, though, until the reign of Theodosius that emperors began to legislate more explicitly the control of property and buildings in the homoian/Nicene controversy.

The number of laws issued regarding religious places, who was allowed to use them, and in which ways grew exponentially in the late fourth and early fifth centuries under Gratian, Theodosius, Arcadius, and Honorius. The earlier prohibitions against ritual sacrifice were repeated numerous times in these decades (*CTh* 16.10.7; 16.10.9–12). While a certain temple in the region of Osrhoene, east of Antioch, was reopened so that its statues could be admired as works of art, visitors are warned in a decree issued from Constantinople in 382 against the use of the place for religious ritual (16.10.8),[18] and a law issued from Constantinople in 395 to

16. Although the precise date of these two pieces of legislation is contested, the range of years in question is relatively small (ca. 376–78), and does not jeopardize their significance here. The place of issue and the recipient of *CTh* 16.6.2 are debated. See Pharr, *Theodosian Code*, 450, 463.

17. I translate the Latin term "catholic," lowercase, in the sense of the "universal" church that received the empire's support at this time, out of concern that Pharr's choice to translate the Latin into English as "the Catholic Church" might anachronistically be taken as a reference to a distinctly Roman Catholic church (Pharr, *Theodosian Code*, 464).

18. See the discussion in Helen Saradi-Mendelovici, "Christian Attitudes toward Pagan Monuments in Late Antiquity and Their Legacy in Later Byzantine Centuries," *Dumbarton Oaks Papers* 44 (1990): 47–61; Luke Lavan, "Political Talismans? Residual 'Pagan' Statues in Late Antique Public Space,"

Flavius Rufinus, the praetorian prefect of the East, altogether forbids "the right to approach any shrine (*fanum*) or temple (*templum*) whatsoever" (16.10.13).

Similarly there are multiple laws regarding the destruction of temples and the reuse of their building materials, with the laws issued from and to the eastern empire generally more hostile to temples than the laws issued in the West. A law from Ravenna to regions in the West in 399 requires that "the ornaments of public works" should be preserved (*CTh* 16.10.15), which would have included many elements of temples and the statues that they contained, and a consonant law from the same year to the proconsul of Africa states that "no one by the benefit of our sanctions shall attempt to destroy temples (*aedes*) that are empty of illicit things" (16.10.18). On the other hand, a law also issued in 399 but posted in Damascus and addressed to Eutychianus, the praetorian prefect of the East, declares, "If there should be any temples (*templa*) in the country (*agris*), they shall be demolished without disturbance or tumult" (*CTh* 16.10.16). Later laws continued to try to delineate which artifacts (statues, altars) were illegal and should be removed, and which should be left standing and could even be reused (e.g., 16.10.19).[19] The diversity in this series of laws recalls the discussion above in chapter 5 that contrasted the literary evidence for Christian temple-destruction with the archaeological evidence that temples often continued to exist later than the literary texts suggest, falling into disrepair over time more often than being aggressively destroyed. These laws from the later fourth and early fifth centuries demonstrate the legal concern that first emerged under Valens and Valentinian and that spread across the empire regarding places associated with the gods, and particularly how best to remove any authority that their relation to the gods had granted them.

Jewish places, too, became the subject of legislation in these decades more than they had been previously, although in this case legislation was primarily imperial statements preventing the illegal destruction of synagogues. While anti-Jewish legislation under Constantine concerned primarily issues of the conversion of people to and away from Judaism, later laws directly addressed the places of Judaism—namely, the status of Jewish synagogues. A law from 393 expresses imperial concern that some Christians had taken matters into their own hands by attempting to "destroy and to despoil the synagogues," and a law from 397 likewise insists that people should desist from attacking "the Jews" and that Jews' "synagogues shall remain in their accustomed quietude" (*CTh* 16.8.9, 12). Similar laws were issued

---

in *The Archaeology of Late Antique "Paganism,"* ed. Luke Lavan and Michael Mulryan (Boston: Brill, 2011), 439–77; Béatrice Caseau, "Religious Intolerance and Pagan Statuary," ibid., 479–502.

19. See also Saradi-Mendelovici, "Christian Attitudes," 47–61; and Gregor Kalas, *Transforming Public Space in Rome: The Late Antique Revision of the Roman Forum* (Austin: University of Texas Press, forthcoming), chaps. 5 and 6.

again in the early fifth century, although these were accompanied by other laws that forbid the construction of new synagogues (16.8.20–22, 25–27). While synagogues thus fared better than temples in the legislation, in that they were legally allowed to remain places of religious ritual, the legislation suggests a concern that some Christians were taking matters into their own hands at this time and actively destroying these visibly Jewish places. The examples below of the Christian destruction of synagogues in Rome and Callinicum, addressed by Bishop Ambrose of Milan in 388, and on the island of Minorca, described by Bishop Severus of Minorca in 418, speak to the type of problems that this legislation addressed.

With the *cunctos populos* edict that supported Nicene orthodoxy around the empire in 380, however, came new legislation that engaged in the decades-long debates that had split many of the empire's episcopacies (*CTh* 16.1.2). In this later period, legislation forbid the name "catholic Christian" to those called Arians and followers of Aetius and Eunomius, and the name "church" to their places of assembly (16.1.2; 16.5.6).[20] Legislation from Constantinople in January 381 required church buildings that these "heretics" controlled to be given to their Nicene opponents, and the "heretics" were not even allowed to enter their opponents' church buildings:

> They shall be removed and completely barred from the threshold of all churches, since we forbid all heretics to hold unlawful assemblies within the towns. If factions should attempt to do anything, we order that their madness shall be banished and that they shall be driven away from the very walls of the cities (*urbium moenibus*), in order that catholic churches throughout the whole world may be restored to all orthodox bishops who hold the Nicene faith. (16.5.6)

The enforcement of this legislation is of course called into question by examples such as John Chrysostom's homilies from 386–97 that addressed those he called "Anomean" Christians among his own church congregants (e.g., *De s. Pelagia* 4; *De incomp.* 1.334–40). Nonetheless, a similar order was issued months later to the proconsul of Asia, emphasizing the regulations that would govern this long-standing conflict from this point forward:

> We command that all churches (*ecclesias*) shall immediately be surrendered to those bishops who confess that the Father, the Son, and the Holy Spirit are of one majesty and virtue. . . . These bishops who are of the communion and fellowship of such acceptable priests must be permitted to obtain the catholic churches. All, however, who dissent . . . shall be expelled from their churches as manifest heretics and hereafter shall be altogether denied the right and power to obtain churches. (*CTh* 16.1.3)

---

20. These efforts to control public narratives, vocabulary, and memory recall the discussion of erasure, silence, and memory in Charles Hedrick's work *History and Silence: The Purge and Rehabilitation of Memory in Late Antiquity* (Austin: University of Texas Press, 2000), especially his overview of the *damnatio memoriae* (xii-xiv, 89–130).

In fact, not only were places of assembly that Christian "heretics" had controlled before Theodosius's succession removed from them, but so were any new places that might be built illegally, according to a law issued in the East in 381:

> We direct that none of the Eunomians and the Arians or the adherents of the dogma of Aetius shall have the right to build churches in the community (*civitate*) or in the countryside (*agris*). But if this right should be rashly presumed by anyone, the afore-said house (*domus*), wherever such forbidden constructions have been made, and also the estate (*fundus*) or private holding (*private possessio*) shall immediately be vindicated to the resources of our fisc. All places (*omnia loca*) also that have received either the settlement or the ministers of this sacrilegious dogma shall immediately become fiscal property. (*CTh* 16.5.8)

Theodosius's accession to the throne clearly worked to the advantage of Nicene Christians, and the control of church buildings was one way that the emperors in this period demonstrated their patronage.

That the laws became more detailed, including specifically rural places and private estates as well as urban places, is clear from a piece of legislation from Constantinople late in 383:

> The vicious instruction hateful to God and people alike, namely the Eunomian, the Arian, the Macedonian, the Apollinarian, and all other sects that are condemned by the sincere faith of the true religion, according to the venerable cult of the catholic observance shall not presume the ability to assemble in congregations or to establish churches, either by public or private undertakings, within the places (*loca*) of the cities (*urbium*) and of the country (*agrorum*) and of the villas (*vilarum*). (*CTh* 16.5.12)[21]

The Theodosian Code records a great number of such laws, varying sometimes in the names of the groups who are prevented from assembling or controlling church buildings. By later that decade, some expelled groups seem to have been meeting outside the city walls. A law issued in Milan in 389 states that heretics "shall by all means be driven from their pernicious meeting places (*funestis conciliabulis*), whether they appear to be within the city (*urbem*) or in the suburbs (*suburbanis*)" (16.5.19). The places to which this law refers are not entirely clear, but whether *funestis conciliabulis* is best understood in this context as funeral places or more generally as harmful or deadly places, the allusions inherent in the vocabulary suggest an association between Christian "heresy" and the burial places of Christian saints. A later law issued in Milan finds deplorable "the fact that Jovinianus holds sacrilegious meetings outside the walls of the most sacred city" (16.5.53); and an early fifth-century law orders "that the nefarious assemblies and the pernicious

---

21. Compare Kim Bowes's work on the role that religious practices at villas played in the late Roman Empire: Bowes, *Private Worship, Public Values, and Religious Change in Late Antiquity* (New York: Cambridge University Press, 2008); Bowes, "'Christianization' and the Rural Home," *JECS* 15.2 (2007): 143–70.

associations (*funesta conventicula*) of the Eunomians shall be entirely prevented" (16.6.7; cf. 16.4.6).[22] Much as early Christians met in the catacombs outside Rome's walls, later Christians whom the empire deemed heretical also seem to have sought meeting places outside the city walls, just as Bishop Meletius's community met in Antioch's military exercise field during part of his time in exile.[23]

The Theodosian Code reveals that the examples of topographical manipulations and heavy-handed redefinition of places in Antioch were not unique during the heated controversies of the fourth century. The rhetorical and physical efforts of Antioch's Christian leaders in the 380s did not occur in a vacuum, but in the context of imperial legislation that aided Bishop Meletius's and Bishop Flavian's plans by designating sites of Christian orthodoxy throughout the Mediterranean. While on one level the Antiochene dynamics were local, this legislation suggests that they were concurrently part of a much larger story that requires an understanding of site-specific dynamics and the broader movements in the late Roman Empire. Nevertheless, Antioch is not the only example of the local conflicts that these imperial rulings both responded to and affected. Examples from Jerusalem, Milan, Alexandria, and elsewhere reveal that the late fourth and early fifth centuries, and particularly the 380s in Milan, witnessed similar topographical struggles around the Mediterranean.

AMBROSE AND "ARIANS" IN MILAN

Like John Chrysostom in Antioch, other powerful Christian actors around the empire were involved in multiple and complex ways in the transformation of their local topography. Dennis Trout has skillfully demonstrated that Damasus, in addition to his struggle in 366–67 with Ursinus to control Rome's church buildings, later used the martyrs buried inside and outside the city to change the way in which people saw the city's places.[24] Maura Lafferty has likewise revealed the ways in which Damasus's inscriptions and liturgical changes reshaped Roman Christianity along with the city of Rome.[25] She notes that besides improving Peter's basil-

22. Harry Maier examines the evidence for meetings at martyrs' shrines and cemeteries outside Rome's city walls ("Topography of Heresy," 232–49).

23. According to Sozomen (*HE* 8.8) and Socrates (*HE* 6.8), homoian Christians similarly met outside the city walls in Constantinople during John Chrysostom's episcopacy. As Wendy Mayer noted in conversation, these church historians suggest that Constantinopolitans demonstrated an interest in reclaiming the places given to the Nicene Christians by the homoian Christians' nocturnal processions through the city.

24. Dennis Trout, "Damasus and the Invention of Early Christian Rome," *Journal of Medieval and Early Modern Studies* 33.3 (2003): 517–36; Trout, "Saints, Identity, and the City," in *A People's History of Christianity*, vol. 2, *Late Ancient Christianity*, ed. Virginia Burrus (Minneapolis: Fortress Press, 2005), 165–87.

25. Maura Lafferty, "Translating Faith from Greek to Latin: *Romanitas* and *Christianitas* in Late Fourth-Century Rome and Milan," *JECS* 11.1 (2003): 21–62. See also Alan Thacker, "Rome of the Martyrs: Saints, Cults, and Relics, Fourth to Seventh Centuries," in *Roma Felix: Formation and Reflections*

ica and building a basilica for Paul, Damasus also appropriated the city's most famous martyrs as citizens of Rome through their rebirth there in martyrdom, and visually added Christian markers to the landscape through the monumental inscriptions that he erected to them. There are numerous other relevant examples from around the empire; for example, conflicts against the Donatists in North Africa and later skirmishes with Miaphysite Christians in the eastern empire often contained significant topographical elements. Likewise, some stories from Constantinople, including the earlier conflicts over control of church buildings during the episcopacy of Paul I in the 340s, reveal that Antioch was not unique in the empire, as the examples below will further reveal.

A nuanced discussion of the multifaceted efforts of Ambrose in Milan, however, provides some of the most conspicuous evidence that Antioch was not the only site of such topographical religious struggles in the political and theological conflicts of the late fourth century. Ambrose may, in fact, be the first bishop to come to mind for most scholars with regard to the subject of episcopal struggles over controlling church buildings during the last decades of the fourth century, and for good reason. Not only has Ambrose remained among the most well-known leaders of the early Western church, but his high-profile conflicts with imperial authority were relatively well documented and offer striking examples of the success of episcopal over imperial authority and of the tipping of the scales in favor of Nicene Christianity at this critical juncture in the empire's history.[26] Although the events surrounding Ambrose's conflicts over church buildings in Milan, the altar of Victory in Rome, and the synagogue building in Callinicum will be familiar to many, they here demonstrate that Antioch's fourth-century history was anything but unique. While bishops Meletius and Flavian did not receive the same lasting renown as Ambrose, who even outshines John Chrysostom in Western (though not Eastern) Christian histories, from Valens's death in 378 through the end of the fourth century these leaders were engaged in similar projects across the breadth of the empire.[27]

When Ambrose was hastily ordained bishop in the context of civil unrest in Milan in 374, he entered into at least three ongoing conversations that would dra-

---

of Medieval Rome, ed. Éamonn Ó Carragáin and Carol L. Neuman de Vegvar (Aldershot, UK: Ashgate, 2007), 13–49; Curran, *Pagan City,* 116–57.

26. See Harry Maier's conversation about the topographical focus of Ambrose's Milanese struggles ("Private Spaces," 72–93). Most recently Dayna Kalleres has made a nuanced and rich contribution to the discussion of Ambrose's rhetorical and physical manipulation of Milan's topography (see chapter 7 of *City of Demons: Violence, Ritual, and Christian Power in Late Antiquity* (Berkeley: University of California Press, forthcoming).

27. J. H. W. G. Liebeschuetz has also found a comparison between John Chrysostom and Ambrose productive, although his comparison focuses on the theme of asceticism (Liebeschuetz, *Ambrose and John Chrysostom: Clerics between Desert and Empire* [New York: Oxford University Press, 2011]).

matically shape not only his personal life and career, but the history of Christianity as well.[28] One of these conversations was the empire-wide controversy over Christian theology, particularly with respect to the Council of Nicaea in 325. In this sense, Ambrose became part of the controversies that were concurrently shaping events in Antioch in these decades, although as a Western city, Milan was often under the authority of emperors who had different religious leanings than those who governed Antioch. When Constantine died in 337, for example, Milan spent the following years under the authority of the emperor Constans, who supported the Council of Nicaea, rather than under Constantius II, who rejected the council's outcomes; of course, upon Constans's death in 350, Milanese Christians found themselves also under Constantius II's authority. Nicene Christians in both Antioch and Milan suffered under the emperor Julian, had better support under the emperor Jovian, and then again had opposite fortunes, with Valentinian supporting Nicene Christianity in Milan and the West, while his brother supported their homoian opponents in Antioch and the East. In 374 Ambrose became bishop on the eve of the emperor Valentinian's death in 375 and the election of the four-year-old Valentinian II under the influence of his homoian Christian mother, Justina. Both Valentinian II and Justina would loom large in Ambrose's future, although he would live to see Theodosius gain control of the entire empire, East and West, and make illegal the assembly of his Christian opponents.

A second stream of events into which Ambrose's election placed him were the church-building enterprises that had been taking place around the empire since the time of the emperor Constantine.[29] Certainly some church buildings were in existence at Milan when Ambrose became bishop, including the "old church" and the "new church, Basilica Nova," which Richard Krautheimer speculates were actually at most only a few decades apart from each other in age, both having been built between 313 and 350.[30] Likewise an extramural church known as the Portiana existed by early in Ambrose's episcopacy. In the midst of intense theological and

28. For a recent account of Ambrose's life and career that is particularly sensitive to the nature of our extant sources, which prevent any unmediated access to Ambrose, see Neil McLynn, *Ambrose of Milan: Church and Court in a Christian Capital* (Berkeley: University of California Press, 1994). Liebeschuetz, *Ambrose and John Chrysostom,* 57–94, also provides a brief overview; see also John Moorhead, *Ambrose: Church and Society in the Late Roman World* (London: Longman Press, 1999). Warren Smith's recent book provides an in-depth analysis of Ambrose's theology and ethics, and a useful up-to-date bibliography, although he is not as interested in the historical events discussed here: Smith, *Christian Grace and Pagan Virtue: The Theological Foundation of Ambrose's Ethics* (New York: Oxford University Press, 2011); see also Marcia Colish, *Ambrose's Patriarchs: Ethics for the Common Man* (Notre Dame, IN: University of Notre Dame Press, 2005).

29. Dayna Kalleres provides a recent overview of the scholarship on Milan's fourth-century church buildings (*City of Demons,* chap. 7).

30. See Richard Krautheimer, *Three Christian Capitals: Topography and Politics* (Berkeley: University of California Press, 1983), 69–92, esp. 74–77.

political conflicts with his Milanese Christian opponents who were supported by Justina and Valentinian II, Ambrose consecrated two new churches in 386: the Basilica Ambrosiana (at the site of the current S. Ambrogio) and the Basilica Apostolorum (at the site of the current S. Nazaro). Krautheimer suggests that Ambrose may also have planned the Basilica Virginum (at the site of the S. Simpliciano), though it was not started until just after his death.[31] Ambrose, like Meletius and numerous other fourth-century emperors and bishops, took advantage of political and financial resources to claim territory physically through the construction of new church buildings that he then controlled, changing perceptions of the local landscape through means reminiscent of the strategies related to the relics of Babylas in Antioch, discussed above in chapter 2.

A third ongoing conversation in which the new bishop of Milan participated quite aggressively was the debate over the altar of Victory, which had long been a focal point in the Senate house in Rome, and which some Christians had successfully had removed, and some other senators had successfully restored.[32] While this controversy focused on events and places in Rome rather than Milan, the centrality and significance of the city of Rome for the empire was not lost on fourth-century leaders, and Ambrose's entanglement in this controversy is one more way in which he proactively manipulated Italy's physical topography in favor of his Nicene orthodoxy.[33] The altar of Victory had been established in the first century B.C.E. under Octavian, and remained in the Senate until it was removed by the emperor Constantius II in 357.[34] The emperor Julian restored the altar during his brief reign (361–63) as part of his patronage of the Roman gods and the ritual practices and traditions that surrounded them.[35] By 382, when the emperor Gratian again removed the altar, Ambrose was bishop in Milan and became involved in the debate, and in 384 he ostensibly persuaded the young emperor Valentinian II, then living in Milan, to reject a request from the Roman senator Symmachus to restore the altar.[36] Ambrose clearly was intimately familiar with the importance of con-

---

31. Krautheimer, *Three Christian Capitals*, 77, 79, 81.

32. Alan Cameron presents a persuasive new analysis of these events in *The Last Pagans of Rome* (New York: Oxford University Press, 2011), 33–51.

33. Ambrose's topographical manipulations reached farther afield than those of Antioch's leaders. Neil McLynn likewise comments on Ambrose asserting his Western authority into the East, such as in response to the Antiochene schism between Bishops Meletius (and then Flavian) and Paulinus (*Ambrose of Milan*, 145).

34. John Curran discusses Constantius II's removal of the altar in *Pagan City*, 191.

35. A survey of this history can be found in the first chapter of Fabrizio Canfora, *Simmaco e Ambrogio, o di un' antica controversia sulla tolleranza e sull' intolleranza* (Bari: Adriatica Editrice, 1970); and in J. J. Sheridan, "The Altar of Victory: Paganism's Last Battle," *L'Antiquité Classique* 35 (1966): 186–206.

36. Regarding the politics of these negotiations, see McLynn, *Ambrose of Milan*, 151–52, 166–67. Jennifer Ebbeler and Cristiana Sogno agree with McLynn's assessment, and further demonstrate that Symmachus's appointment of the Manichaean *auditor* Augustine is unlikely to have been "revenge" for

trolling the shape of significant, powerful places, as he was equally familiar with ongoing contests over them.[37]

Although this is not a complete list of the relevant examples from Ambrose's career, these three topics are sufficient to demonstrate the comparison to some of the examples from Antioch. Neil McLynn refers, for example, to an accusation from Ambrose's Christian opponents that he was spending church treasure to build "cemetery basilicas" that concurrently reshaped Milan's landscape and strengthened Ambrose's visibility and authority.[38] Ambrose likewise arranged for his brother Satyrus to be buried "in the *martyrium* of Victor, one of Milan's prized collection of imported martyrs; his sarcophagus was placed directly adjacent to the saint's"; Ambrose's sister Daedalia was buried "adjacent to the twin graves of Victor and Satyrus"; and Ambrose translated several relics into Milan, including to the Basilica Apostolorum.[39] J. H. W. G. Liebeschuetz summarizes some of Ambrose's activities as follows: "Ambrose built three great churches outside the walls of Milan, at least partly at his own expense, and furnished them with the relics of martyrs. On three occasions he found graves of martyrs and had the relics reburied in his churches with great ceremony."[40]

The political and theological controversies in Milan, a city that like Antioch by this time sometimes housed an imperial retinue in its palace, came to a head between 378 and 381 under Ambrose's episcopacy, and then again most spectacularly in 385 and 386;[41] all of these events echo the topographical manipulations in

---

the "catholic" Christian success in refusing the return of the altar of Victory, as scholars once thought. See Ebbeler and Sogno, "Religious Identity and the Politics of Patronage: Symmachus and Augustine," *Historia: Zeitschrift für alte Geschichte* 56.2 (2007): 240. Liebeschuetz also mentions these events in *Ambrose and John Chrysostom,* 91–94. Kirsten Gross-Albenhausen discusses Ambrose's role in this confrontation, focusing more on the bishop's engagement with Symmachus than with the emperor: Gross-Albenhausen, *Imperator christianissimus: Der christliche Kaiser bei Ambrosius und Johannes Chrysostomus* (Frankfurt am Main: Marthe Clauss Press, 1999), 63–78. See also Daniel Williams, "Ambrose, Emperors, and Homoians in Milan: The First Conflict over a Basilica," in *Arianism after Arius: Essays on the Development of the Fourth-Century Trinitarian Conflicts,* ed. Michel Barnes and Daniel Williams (Edinburgh: T&T Clark, 1993), 127–46; Williams, *Ambrose of Milan and the End of the Nicene-Arian Conflicts* (New York: Oxford University Press, 1995), esp. 210–17.

37. See Ambrose, *Epp.* 72–73 (Maurist *Epp.* 17–18), in which Ambrose warns that if Valentinian II restores the altar to the Senate, the whole building will become a place of traditional sacrifice, suffused by smoke and incense. All translations from Ambrose's epistles are my own from the Latin in CSEL 82, pt. 10, vol. 3. The citation refers to the CSEL epistle and paragraph, followed by the comparable reference in the earlier Maurist edition in PL 16, which numbered the epistles differently.

38. McLynn, *Ambrose of Milan,* 56.

39. McLynn, *Ambrose of Milan,* 78, 221, 234–36.

40. Liebeschuetz, *Ambrose and John Chrysostom,* 74.

41. McLynn traces much of this history throughout his book on Ambrose, including specifically "the establishment of the court at Milan" under the emperor Gratian (*Ambrose of Milan,* 157). See also G. Nauroy, "Le fouet et le miel: Le combat d'Ambroise en 386 contre l'arianisme milanais," *Recherches augustiniennes* 23 (1988): 3–86; Liebeschuetz, *Ambrose and John Chrysostom,* 84–94. Barnes has argued that while scholars have historically read the events of Valentinian II's conflict with Ambrose over control of

Antioch in significant ways. The first series of events, under the emperor Gratian, is difficult to recreate with any precision, although it reveals Ambrose's struggle over controlling Milanese church buildings.[42] Ambrose's *De spiritu sancto* from 381 claims that Gratian had earlier sequestered a church in Milan, a building that he eventually presented to Ambrose (*De spir. sancto* 1.19–21).[43] Although it is unclear which church this was, when it had been built, and if it had already been in the hands of one of the Christian factions in Milan, Daniel Williams and Neil McLynn speculate that a powerful homoian supporter, such as Julianus Valens or Valentinian II's mother, Justina, could have challenged Ambrose for control of the church, leading to Gratian's intervention by sequestering the church until he could determine who should rightfully control it.[44] While some scholars understand that Gratian gave this sequestered church to Ambrose as early as 379, Williams makes a persuasive argument that the church did not come under Ambrose's control until 381, once Theodosius and Gratian had coissued *Codex Theodosianus* 16.1.3, which forbid Ambrose's opponents from controlling any church buildings.[45] The precise dates are not necessary, however, in order to show persuasively that church buildings were politically and religiously contested places in Milan in these years, that Ambrose was deeply involved in the conflicts, and that by 381 he succeeded in gaining control of this church, most likely the Portiana, as well as the others in the city.[46]

The most well-known physical and ideological struggles for control of Milan's powerful Christian buildings, however, reached their height in 385 and 386, and show more fully the lengths to which Ambrose proactively went in order to gain control of existing churches, and build and consecrate new ones that would add to the authority of his community in Milan.[47] While the complicated chronology of these events is

---

Milan's basilicas as a single series of events in 386, in fact the data support the conclusion that there were two distinct conflicts, both including the emperor's use of soldiers: the first in 385 and the second in 386. See Timothy D. Barnes, "Ambrose and the Basilicas of Milan in 385 and 386: The Primary Documents and Their Implications," *Zeitschrift für antikes Christentum* 4 (2000): 289–99.

42. McLynn notes the difficulty of reconstructing these events (*Ambrose of Milan*, 121–23).

43. Regarding the presentation to Ambrose, see Daniel Williams, "When Did the Emperor Gratian Return the Basilica to the Pro-Nicenes in Milan?" *Studia Patristica* 24 (1993): 208–15.

44. Williams, "Ambrose," 140–43; cf. McLynn, *Ambrose of Milan*, 122.

45. Williams, "Ambrose," 143–45; for a discussion of the earlier scholarship, see 131.

46. McLynn, *Ambrose of Milan*, 174–75.

47. For an insightful and well-contextualized analysis of these events, see McLynn, *Ambrose of Milan*, esp. 181–96. Kirsten Gross-Albenhausen also analyzes this struggle, focusing on the bishop's effort to gain the upper hand over the young emperor in terms of authority, at least in Milan: Gross-Albenhausen, *Imperator christianissimus*, 79–93. Timothy D. Barnes, however, suggests a significant reordering of the events, locating Ambrose's letter to his sister (*Ep.* 76 [20]) in 385 and thus arguing that scholars such as McLynn have conflated two separate basilica conflicts: Barnes, "Ambrose and the Basilicas," 289–99. See also the contextualization of these events by Catherine Chin, "The Bishop's Two Bodies: Ambrose and the Basilicas of Milan," *CH* 79.3 (2010): 531–55, esp. 548–53.

difficult to ascertain precisely, Ambrose's writings provide more than enough evidence to grasp the events' significant implications regarding Milan's physical topography and the latter's relation to local and imperial authority and religious orthodoxy.[48]

Ambrose describes the heart of one crisis over Milanese church possession, dated by Timothy Barnes to 385 and by Neil McLynn to 386, in a plaintive plea from the young emperor Valentinian II: "I also ought to have one basilica!" (*Ep.* 76.19 [20.19]).[49] With the Nicene Christians in charge of the city's church buildings, the homoian Christians of Milan, including Valentinian II and his mother, had no public church buildings that they could use for their services.[50] It seems that in 385, in a clearly spatial exercise of power that recalls Libanius's manipulations in Antioch discussed above in chapter 1, Ambrose had refused a request from Valentinian II to hand over the Portiana basilica.[51] An imperial law issued in Milan in January 386, however, gives "the right of assembly" to a wider collection of Christians, including those who agreed to the outcome of the Council of Ariminum.[52] It specifies, against those like Ambrose, "If those persons who suppose that the right of assembly has been granted to them alone should attempt to provoke any agitation against the regulation of our tranquility, they shall know that as authors of sedition and as disturbers of the peace of the church, they shall also pay the penalty of high treason with their life and blood" (*CTh* 16.1.4). In light of this new law, in 386 Valentinian seems to have issued an invitation for Ambrose to meet him at the palace and discuss again church ownership in Milan.[53]

48. See McLynn, *Ambrose of Milan,* 173–96; Williams, "Ambrose," 127–46; Andrew Lenox-Conyngham, "The Topography of the Basilica Conflict of A.D. 385/6 in Milan," *Historia* 31 (1982): 353–63; Barnes, "Ambrose and the Basilicas," 289–99.

49. Barnes, "Ambrose and the Basilicas," 288–92; McLynn, *Ambrose of Milan,* 170–208.

50. Barnes suggests, "Justina attempted to obtain one church in the city for the emperor's Gothic troops to use for 'Arian' worship in both 385 and 386, and in both years Ambrose and the catholics of Milan resisted with pertinacity" ("Ambrose and the Basilicas," 298).

51. Ambrose refers to this conflict in *Ep.* 75a.29 (21a.29), sometimes called *Sermo contra Auxentium.* Barnes and McLynn agree that these events took place in 385 and were described by Ambrose in *Ep.* 75a (21a) in 386. See the narrative reconstructed in McLynn, *Ambrose of Milan,* 170–80; Barnes, "Ambrose and the Basilicas," 287–92. See also Lenox-Conyngham ("Topography," 353–63) and Moorhead (*Ambrose,* 137–40), although they do not agree that the church initially under dispute was the Portiana.

52. Also called the Council of Rimini, this Western council took place in 359 and attempted to resolve the impasse between those who supported and those who rejected the creed that resulted from the first Council of Nicaea.

53. This is according to the chronology established in Lenox-Conyngham, "Topography," 353–63. Barnes agrees in principle: "Valentinian's summons . . . was based either on a constitution which Valentinian issued at Milan to his praetorian prefect Eusignius on 23 January 386 or on a subsequent imperial ruling dependent on it" ("Ambrose and the Basilicas," 287).

Echoing the power dynamics of Libanius's alleged refusal to attend the emperor Julian's daily sacrifices in Antioch, Ambrose makes much of his refusal to obey the emperor's summons and of his motivating concern: "Would that it were clearly certain to me that the church would definitely not be given to the Arians! Then I would willingly offer myself to the wish of your piety" (*Ep.* 75.19 [21.19]). Ambrose's epistle against Auxentius from 386 also notes this concern: "Would that I were sure that the church would never be given to heretics! I would gladly go to the emperor's palace, if this were suitable for the office of a priest, and thus have our discussion in the palace rather than the church" (*Ep.* 75a.3 [21a.3]).[54] Despite his traditional rhetoric of humility, Ambrose demonstrates his clear intentions, first to refuse to attend the emperor at the place of his request, inviting him instead to meet him in the church that Ambrose controls (a bid for power over the emperor that recalls Libanius's negotiations with the praetorian prefect Strategius), and second to maintain control of Milan's church buildings for Nicene Christianity at any cost.[55]

As for the physical struggle for control, Ambrose provides evidence for a complex series of events, some of which took place in the days leading up to Easter in March 386, and some of which Barnes argues occurred earlier in 385.[56] Ambrose's letter to his sister Marcellina (*Ep.* 76 [20]) provides the most detail about the use of church buildings in the power struggle between the bishop and the emperor. Ambrose's observation that "this time it was not the Portiana, that is the basilica outside the walls, that was demanded, but the new basilica" harkens back to the earlier imperial request of 385, and suggests that Valentinian II next requested the Basilica Nova inside the city, perhaps with the hope of compromising on the Basilica Portiana (*Ep.* 76.1 [20.1]).[57] Ambrose records that he refused to relinquish any church buildings, ostensibly because the churches were not his to relinquish but belonged to God (e.g., *Ep.* 76.2, 8, 19 [20.2, 8, 19]). Whether *Epistle* 75a (21a) refers to the same struggle or a new conflict, in 386 Ambrose claims that he refused to relinquish a church building to Valentinian II "when throughout the catholic church priests are being expelled, being put to the sword if they resist," suggesting that Ambrose ostensibly risked martyrdom by his refusal (*Ep.* 75a.16 [21a.16]). In his rhetorical remembrance, Ambrose insists to his swelling crowd of supporters that he would stand firm and not relinquish the church under any circumstance

---

54. On the dating of this text to 386, see Barnes, "Ambrose and the Basilicas," 287–88; McLynn, *Ambrose of Milan*, 186; for further discussion of the events surrounding this text, see McLynn, 196–208.

55. Kalleres vividly demonstrates that what is at stake for Ambrose is more than only the control over the place of the church buildings when she teases out Ambrose's complex demonology and understanding of ritual in her excellent study of these events (*City of Demons*, chap. 7).

56. Dayna Kalleres has collected a thorough survey of the recent literature surrounding these events and the controversies over their precise chronology (*City of Demons*, chap. 7).

57. For McLynn's reconstruction, see *Ambrose of Milan*, 181–96.

(*Ep.* 75a.1 [21a.1]). It is clear that Ambrose is acutely aware of the power at stake in the physical occupation of Milan's church buildings.

Although Ambrose benefited from the conflicts with Valentinian II, the emperor went so far as to engage military troops against Ambrose and his supporters.[58] In the first of these conflicts, referenced in Ambrose, *Epistle* 76 (20), Valentinian II asked Ambrose for the new basilica, was refused, occupied the Portiana, and eventually withdrew, a conflict that Ambrose managed largely from the older basilica. A later military action mentioned by Ambrose (*Ep.* 75a [21a] and *Ep.* 75 [21]) suggests that the conflict continued. Ambrose reports that while he was teaching catechumens in the baptistery of what he called "the basilica" (likely the old basilica), people told him that officials were hanging royal banners at another of the basilicas (most likely the Portiana) as a way of marking Valentinian II's ownership of the building (*Ep.* 76.4 [20.4]).[59] Just as the *temenos* of Apollo's Daphne temple continued to be redefined through the addition of a shrine to Babylas, the burning of Apollo's temple, and then the visible absence of Babylas's remains, so too the hanging of the emperor's banners represents Valentinian II's efforts to redefine and lay claim to the place of the basilica. These extant descriptions of the conflicts over the control of church buildings in Milan heighten the regret that no contemporary descriptions exist of the frequent exchange of control of the Great Church in Antioch, where emperors were also sometimes in residence.

Furthermore, "armed men," Ambrose narrates, "had been sent to the basilica to occupy the church" (*Ep.* 76.9 [20.9]).[60] Although Ambrose suggests that "none of the Arians," whom he claims consisted of no more than "a few of the royal family and some of the Goths," dared to go about the city during this tense time, his own supporters were out in great numbers to claim the church buildings as their own: "the basilica was surrounded" and "the new basilica also was full of people" (*Ep.* 76.12–13 [20.12–13]). With the crowd vocally in Ambrose's favor and Ambrose apparently taking little action to stem their demonstrations, Valentinian II eventually withdrew the soldiers; Ambrose was told that the royal banners were taken down, and "the basilica was crowded with people" who were calling for him (Ambrose, *Ep.* 76.20 [20.20]).[61] Continuing imperial pressure was met by Ambrose's continued resistance, and the conflict concluded with Ambrose and his Nicene

---

58. See the reconstruction of these events in Lenox-Conyngham, "Topography," 353–63, in which he outlines at least two conflicts in 386. Barnes agrees that the emperor deployed troops against the bishop on at least two separate occasions; he disagrees with Lenox-Conyngham that the events of *Ep.* 76 (20) must be dated to 386, preferring instead 385 (Barnes, "Ambrose and the Basilicas," 288–92).

59. Williams supposed that the second church mentioned is the Portiana ("Ambrose," 128); cf. McLynn, *Ambrose of Milan*, 188. See also Marcia Colish, "Why the Portiana? Reflections on the Milanese Basilica Crisis of 386," *JECS* 10.3 (2002): 361–72.

60. See McLynn, *Ambrose of Milan*, 188–92.

61. McLynn narrates and analyzes these events in much greater detail (*Ambrose of Milan*, 181–96).

Christians maintaining control of all the church buildings in Milan.[62] Significantly, Ambrose claims that soldiers who had participated in the events joined as congregants of his church as soon as his victory was clear, reinforcing that Ambrose saw his control over the church buildings as a powerful tool in making "correctly" Christian not only the city's places but also its people, and that the former could easily precede—and perhaps even effect—the latter (*Ep*. 76.21, 26 [20.21, 26]).[63]

During this time, Ambrose seems to have been constructing two new extramural church buildings at Milan, the Basilica Ambrosiana and the Basilica Apostolorum, both of which were consecrated in 386. Much as Meletius's new building for Babylas's relics could claim to rival the prestige of the Great Church, Krautheimer points out the ways in which Ambrose's new church buildings not only participated in local struggles, but also were the bishop's efforts to rival the structure (and importance) of Rome with the Milanese Basilica Ambrosiana, and to compete with the Constantinopolitan Church of the Holy Apostles with the Basilica Apostolorum in Milan, which housed the relics of numerous famous Christian saints, including the apostles Andrew and Thomas, and John the Evangelist.[64] Like the church that Meletius built for Babylas's relics in Antioch, both of these Milanese churches helped Ambrose to establish architectural language of the dominance of Nicene Christians over places in the landscape, and used relics to heighten the power of the place and assure their permanent association with the bishop who had secured them.

The events surrounding the Basilica Ambrosiana most closely parallel Bishop Meletius's efforts with Babylas in Antioch. Following the political turmoil caused by Valentinian II's efforts to control at least one of Milan's churches, in June 386 Ambrose initiated an excavation in the cemetery church of Saints Nabor and Felix outside Milan's city wall. Ostensibly prompted by "prophetic ardor," this excavation unearthed what Ambrose claimed were the remains of two early Christian brothers, Protasius and Gervasius, who had been martyred (*Ep*. 77.1 [22.1]). These relics were quickly and widely accepted as authentic by Ambrose's supporters (though not by their homoian opponents, including the emperor and his mother), thanks to their prophetic discovery and the miracles that they were consequently said to have worked, and shortly after their discovery Ambrose translated them to the new Basilica Ambrosiana as part of the church's consecration ceremony (*Ep*. 77.1–2 [22.1–2]).[65] Ambrose emphasizes their physical loca-

---

62. Augustine also mentions these events in *Conf*. 9.7.15.

63. McLynn concludes that the soldiers' desertion was not spontaneous, but was spurred by Ambrose's threat to exclude them from taking the Eucharist (*Ambrose of Milan*, 192).

64. Krautheimer, *Three Christian Capitals*, 79–80.

65. For a critical analysis of Ambrose's description of these events, and their political implications, see McLynn, *Ambrose of Milan*, 209–15. See also V. Zangara, "L'*inventio* dei martiri Gervasio e Protasio," *Augustinianum* 21 (1981): 119–33; E. Dassmann, "Ambrosius und die Märtyrer," *JAC* 18 (1975):

tion "at my right hand and at my left," "underneath the altar" where Ambrose himself intended to be buried (*Ep.* 77.4, 13 [22.4, 13]). At the same time, he highlights his role in bringing these martyrs to light ("I [acquired] these martyrs for you"), and the power of miracles that the relics brought to him personally, his church, and his form of Christianity (*Ep.* 77.12 [22.12]; *Ep.* 77.9 [22.9]): "These I acquired for you. . . . Let them come, then, and see my attendants. I do not deny that I am surrounded by such arms" (*Ep.* 77.10 [22.10]). The many miracles testified (for Ambrose's trusting followers) to the relics' strength, and Ambrose's sharp anti-Arian polemic in this epistle makes clear against whom he most wished to wield the authority of these saints (*Ep.* 77.19–22 [22.19–22]).[66] McLynn observes that with the transference of the relics of Milanese saints Gervasius and Protasius to the church that already held the relics of Victor and Ambrose's brother, Satyrus, "the church was transformed into a point of reference for the whole city," and not just for Ambrose's supporters.[67] Like Bishop Meletius, Ambrose was ultimately successful in using relics to redefine the city's places through his aggressive and persuasive strategies.

A final but not insignificant parallel with Meletius in Antioch came a decade later, in 397, when Ambrose was buried in the Basilica Ambrosiana near the relics of Gervasius and Protasius, becoming himself a saint whose remains helped to solidify control of that building and Nicene orthodoxy more generally in Milan, just as Meletius's own body did as it rested with Babylas's relics in the church that he had built to house them. McLynn notes the parallels between the burial locations of Meletius in Antioch and Ambrose in Milan, although he highlights the difference that Ambrose prepared a burial place for himself beneath the very altar of the church.[68] Although Ambrose did not die until 397, he made his intention to be buried near these martyrs clear a decade earlier, coincidentally very close in time to John Chrysostom's presentation of his homily *De s. Meletio.* As in Antioch, this use of martyrs' relics demonstrates the bishop's understanding of the significance of the city's landscape in the religious and political struggles, particularly in this case between homoian and Nicene Christians, a conflict whose final outcome could not yet have been certain to Ambrose. Bishops Meletius and Ambrose recognized the power of persuasion in their culture, and put their skills to good use,

---

49–68. Dayna Kalleres beautifully situates this story in Ambrose's larger understanding of theological difference and the demonic, shedding new light on the significance of the retelling and its relation to the process of making the inhabitants and locations of Milan Christian by Ambrose's Nicene definition (*City of Demons*, chap. 7).

66. On the unusual process of the discovery of these relics, and Ambrose's opponents' skepticism about their legitimacy, see McLynn, *Ambrose of Milan*, 212–15. See also Kalleres's clear demonstration that the discovery of these relics served a distinctly anti-Arian agenda (*City of Demons*, chap. 7).

67. McLynn, *Ambrose of Milan*, 229.

68. McLynn, *Ambrose of Milan*, 209.

gaining a large audience and visible, tangible connections with their local martyrs that accorded legitimacy to these contested bishops.

As Ambrose's episcopal power increased, his awareness of, and attention to, the authority associated with topography led to his negotiations with those outside as well as inside his see. Valentinian II did not retain control of Milan long after the church conflict of 386, as Maximus's armies soon threatened the young emperor, who fled to the emperor Theodosius in Thessalonica for protection; and it was not long thereafter that Theodosius defeated Maximus in the late summer of 388 and took control of Milan. In August 388, Ambrose addressed Theodosius in a strongly worded letter that discussed two examples of Christians who were allegedly responsible for the destruction of a local synagogue, one in Rome and one in Callinicum in Mesopotamia near the eastern bank of the Euphrates River (*Ep.* 1a [40]). As with the controversy over the altar of Victory in Rome in the years preceding his Milanese conflict with Valentinian II, Ambrose used his episcopal authority to reach beyond Milan in an effort to impose Christianity more visibly on the landscape of the empire.

In the cases of the destroyed synagogues, Ambrose sharply criticizes Emperor Theodosius's initial response to the situation in Callinicum, which was apparently to condemn the destruction and require that the local bishop repair the building (*Ep.* 1a.6 [40.6]).[69] Ambrose explains to Theodosius that this ruling placed the bishop in Callinicum in the unpleasant position of needing to act either against his religious convictions or against imperial orders—a conflict that should not arise, Ambrose argues, when the emperor claimed to uphold the same religious truths as the bishop himself (*Ep.* 1a.7 [40.7]). Ambrose defends the destruction of the synagogue with the hypothetical justification "I declare that I burned the synagogue, at least that I ordered them [to burn it], so that there might not be a place (*locus*) in which Christ was denied" (*Ep.* 1a.8 [40.8]). Further, Ambrose counters, "Shall, then, a place (*locus*) for the faithlessness of the Jews be made out of the spoils of the church?" (*Ep.* 1a.10 [40.10]). Finally, touching directly on the power associated with such spatial manipulations, Ambrose asks Theodosius what Ambrose should do if he should discover that Christians had been killed "by the authority given" from these events (*Ep.* 1a.29 [40.29]).[70] Through such rhetoric Ambrose explicitly addresses the crux of the concern, which was that the message that Theodosius gave through requiring the Christian vandals to restore the synagogue was that the Callinicum synagogue represented a powerful place that harmed Christianity

69. For a critical discussion of these texts and events, see McLynn, *Ambrose of Milan*, 298–315; (briefly) Liebeschuetz, *Ambrose and John Chrysostom*, 91–94; and Gross-Albenhausen, *Imperator christianissimus*, 99–112.

70. McLynn discusses Ambrose's rhetoric, and the possibility that Ambrose was trying to overcome his own shortcomings in addressing local Judaism in northern Italy (*Ambrose of Milan*, 299).

both through the teachings taught within it, and even more so through its visible existence despite Christian efforts toward its destruction. Much like the charred remains of Apollo's temple in Daphne, the destroyed synagogue in Callinicum would be a valuable witness to passersby of Christianity's conquest of Judaism. On the other hand, if the synagogue that Christians destroyed were rebuilt by imperial order at the expense of Callinicum's Christian community, the refurbished building would signify the weakness of Christianity against Judaism; the synagogue would become a powerful and embarrassing memorial to a Christian defeat.

Ambrose places the example of the synagogue in Callinicum into the context of other buildings' destructions, including attacks on various Christian places under the emperor Julian, as well as Christians' vandalism of other places. In the case of the former, Ambrose laments that Christians and Christianity suffered greatly through such destructions, and argues that just as Christians did not receive imperial support under the emperor Julian, neither did those who were not correctly Christian deserve imperial support under the emperor Theodosius (*Ep.* 1a.15, 18 [40.15, 18]). In the case of the latter, Ambrose asks if even "the burning of the sanctuary (*fanum*) of the Valentinians [i.e., Gnostics]" would also "be avenged" by Theodosius (*Ep.* 1a.16 [40.16]). As warning, Ambrose raises the example of Maximus, so recently defeated in battle, noting:

> Is it not because of this that Maximus was forsaken, who before the days of the expedition, hearing that a synagogue of Rome had been burned, sent an edict to Rome, as if he were the defender of public discipline? At which point the Christian people said, "Nothing good is coming soon for this one. That king has been made a Jew. . . . " And then immediately he was conquered by the Franks and the Saxons, in Sicily, at Siscia, at Petavio . . . everywhere. (*Ep.* 1a.23 [40.23])

Ambrose's message to the emperor Theodosius is clear; if Theodosius hopes to retain divine support and military success, he cannot follow Maximus's example by condemning the destruction of a synagogue. In case that argument were not strong enough, Ambrose later records that when he soon afterward saw Theodosius in person, the bishop withheld the Eucharist from the emperor until Theodosius gave his word that he would "amend the rescript" and would end the entire investigation into the burning of the Callinicum synagogue, lest the investigation provide an opportunity "to do any injury to Christians" (*Ep.* 1.28 [41.28]).

These two epistles provide a rich narrative about Ambrose's rhetorical efforts to reshape the hegemony of his orthodoxy, as well as his acknowledgment of the power associated with such manipulations. While we know little about the historical events that Ambrose claims to describe in these texts, the explicit and detailed references to recent events that he expects to be familiar to the audience of the letters suggest that like the roughly contemporary oration by Libanius (*Pro templis*) and the stories recorded by Theodoret in the early fifth century, Christian ascetics, sometimes encouraged by local church leaders and with at least the tacit support of the region's bishop, at least occasionally destroyed local places of religious piety, painting the landscape with a new Christian tint. Such physical destruction, most likely very sporadic, went hand in hand with church leaders' much more ubiquitous rhetorical support for and justification of such behavior. Ambrose's earlier involvement in the skirmishes over the location of the altar of Victory in 384 and in the contest over church control in 385–86, and his careful deployment of Gervasius's and Protasius's relics only weeks after the tense conflagration against Valentinian II in 386, complement his epistolary rhetoric of 388. Ambrose emerges from these texts as astutely and deeply engaged in using rhetoric to persuade his audience that control over the city belonged to him, shaping the religious topography in many of the same ways, and for some of the same reasons, as Antioch's leaders in these very years.

SAINTS' RELICS AND SHRINES: JERUSALEM AND NORTH AFRICA

The example of Ambrose and the relics of the martyrs Gervasius and Protasius, like the example of Meletius and the relics of Babylas, demonstrates clearly the force that relics could exercise over regional places, and the role they could play in negotiating contests to control the possession and memory of powerful sites such as church buildings. Events from the episcopacies of Cyril of Jerusalem and Augustine of Hippo are just two of many that further confirm that church leaders deployed relics and martyria around the Mediterranean in the late fourth and early fifth centuries in ways that contributed to the reshaping of local topographies.

Jerusalem's landscape of course had already undergone transformations under the emperor Constantine, with his construction of the Church of the Holy Sepulchre over the newly (re)discovered site where Jesus was said to have been buried.[71] Jan Willem Drijvers has furthermore demonstrated Cyril's active and largely successful redefinition of the city's places during his fourth-century episcopacy, specifying the liturgical changes that took place during his time as bishop, as well as the discovery of relics and the construction of new buildings to house and honor them, and Cyril's self-conscious promotion of the city and its sacred sites.[72] The recognition of these relics and places related to biblical stories in turn brought

71. See the discussion of the architectural development of the city in this period in Annabel Wharton, *Refiguring the Post-Classical City: Dura Europos, Jerash, Jerusalem, and Ravenna* (New York: Cambridge University Press, 1995), 85–104. On the Christianization of Jerusalem, see also Kalleres, *City of Demons,* chap. 4.

72. Jan Willem Drijvers, *Cyril of Jerusalem: Bishop and City* (Boston: Brill, 2004).

pilgrims, such as the fourth-century Spanish woman Egeria, who required places to stay and guides to show them around the city, thus leading to further changes in the makeup of the city, and new building complexes including monasteries, such as those founded by Melania on the Mount of Olives in the late 370s.[73] The emperor Julian's effort to restore the Jewish Temple in Jerusalem in the early 360s during Cyril's episcopacy further demonstrates the potential of a historic religious site to instigate religious praxes.[74] In this case, however, the most relevant comparisons to Antioch come from Cyril's use of narratives and relics to manipulate physical places to shape the outcome of theological and political divides.

When Cyril became bishop of Jerusalem in 350, the city had not yet gained the prestige that it would soon have; a fairly small city, it had not yet grown into its future role as the monumental locus of sacred sites associated with the life and death of Jesus. Constantine had begun the process by having the Church of the Holy Sepulchre built, and there is evidence that relics of the True Cross were in circulation by the time Cyril became bishop.[75] The city's bishopric, however, was inferior in status to the larger and more influential Palestinian see of Caesarea, a see governed by the prominent homoian bishop Acacius, successor to the famous Eusebius of Caesarea, when the Nicene Christian Cyril became bishop in Jerusalem.[76] Cyril spent much of his episcopacy trying to overcome Caesarea's (and Bishop Acacius's) greater authority through his efforts to establish Jerusalem as the

73. For an insightful discussion of the ways in which Christian leaders rhetorically shaped the landscape of the area in and around Jerusalem during the fourth and fifth centuries, see Andrew Jacobs, *Remains of the Jews: The Holy Land and Christian Empire in Late Antiquity* (Stanford, CA: Stanford University Press, 2004); compare also Robert Wilken, *The Land Called Holy: Palestine in Christian History and Thought* (New Haven, CT: Yale University Press, 1992). For a discussion of the development of pilgrimage to the region, see E. D. Hunt, *Holy Land Pilgrimage in the Later Roman Empire, AD 312–460* (New York: Oxford University Press, 1982). While both pilgrims and monasteries contributed to the transformation of the landscape in the late Roman Empire, they do not appear very visibly in our sources for late fourth-century Antioch, outside the examples discussed above, and thus are not part of this project.

74. See David Levenson, "The Ancient and Medieval Sources for the Emperor Julian's Attempt to Rebuild the Jerusalem Temple," *Journal for the Study of Judaism* 35 (2004): 409–60; Yaron Eliav, *God's Mountain: The Temple Mount in Time, Place, and Memory* (Baltimore: Johns Hopkins University Press, 2005).

75. Jan Willem Drijvers, "Promoting Jerusalem: Cyril and the True Cross," in *Portraits of Spiritual Authority: Religious Power in Early Christianity, Byzantium, and the Christian Orient,* Religions in the Graeco-Roman World 137, ed. Jan Willem Drijvers and John Watt (Boston: E. J. Brill, 1999), 79–95; Drijvers, *Helena Augusta: The Mother of Constantine the Great and the Legend of Her Finding the True Cross* (Leiden: E. J. Brill, 1992).

76. Acacius is difficult to classify in a clear theological category, and even the broad term "homoian" is not entirely helpful, since Acacius worked to define a new alternative to the creeds of Nicaea and of the Dedication Council that took place in Antioch in 341. Nevertheless, he was clearly theologically opposed to Cyril and had the support of the emperors Constantius II and Valens.

most powerful see not only in Palestine, but in the empire itself. Given his interest in raising the prominence of Jerusalem, and of many individual places within the city such as the sites associated with narratives of Jesus's suffering, death, and resurrection, it is little surprise that Cyril used relics as one way to raise his own status, as well as that of his see and city.

We have seen the turmoil that was caused around the empire with the vacillation of imperial support from one group of Christians to another over the course of the fourth century, and Jerusalem was no exception. Cyril became bishop during the emperor Constantius II's reign when Acacius of Caesarea had the emperor's strong support, and Cyril found himself sent into exile in 357 and again in 360. He returned to his see in 361 under the emperor Julian, only to face the difficulties that this emperor's reign brought to Christian leaders around the empire. Cyril had a glimmer of hope of imperial support under the brief reign of Jovian, only to find himself back under a homoian emperor with the accession of Valens, under whom Cyril was again exiled in late 366 or early 367. Drijvers argues that he returned to his see in Jerusalem in 377 near the end of Valens's reign.[77] It is easy to see that Cyril was standing on slippery ground in his struggle against Bishop Acacius and Caesarea during these first three decades of his episcopacy, much like Bishop Meletius's own experience in Antioch in 360–78, making it all the more impressive that in these years Cyril succeeded in using relics to increase the importance of Jerusalem dramatically. John Baldovin has demonstrated the constructive ways in which Cyril used the developing stational liturgy to reshape perceptions of Jerusalem in ways that benefited his Christian community, and his personal authority. Baldovin notes that Eusebius of Caesarea and Cyril "helped to create not only an ecclesiastical-topographical arena but also the idea of a 'Holy Land.'"[78] Although Baldovin cannot prove that Cyril organized the stational liturgy in Jerusalem himself, he writes, "The system does seem to have been very well developed by the time he died."[79]

While some relics of the True Cross were already known before Cyril became bishop, Drijvers has persuasively argued that the stories about their discovery by Helena, Emperor Constantine's mother, and the accompanying rise in their and Jerusalem's prominence, originated during Cyril's episcopacy, and quite possibly derive from Cyril himself.[80] Drijvers's careful analysis of the story concludes that "the legend must have originated in Palestine and most probably in Jerusalem in the second half of the fourth century," and he observes, "It is likely that the Helena

77. For Cyril's exiles, see Drijvers, *Cyril*, 39–44.

78. John Baldovin, *The Urban Character of Christian Worship: The Origins, Development, and Meaning of Stational Liturgy* (Rome: Pontificium Institutum Studiorum Orientalium, 1987), 83.

79. Baldovin, *Urban Character*, 85.

80. Drijvers, "Promoting Jerusalem," 79–95; Drijvers, *Helena Augusta;* and Drijvers, *Cyril*, 172.

legend was first put in writing c. 390 by Gelasius, bishop of Caesarea and metro-politan of the church-province of Palestine."[81] Bishop Cyril was Gelasius's maternal uncle and helped his nephew to acquire the influential see of Caesarea after the death of Bishop Acacius in 365, although Gelasius was unable to assume his posi-tion until the death of Emperor Valens in 378. There is no doubt that Cyril was a powerful influence on Gelasius, and that Gelasius would have been intimately familiar with Cyril's efforts to elevate Jerusalem's prominence. Drijvers demon-strates that the legend must have arisen between 351 and 390, during Cyril's epis-copacy, and notes that the legend "served a political purpose in Cyril's endeavors to gain pre-eminence for Jerusalem"; he reasonably concludes that it is "not improbable that Cyril was responsible for the origin and composition of the story of Helena's *inventio crucis.*"[82] If so, this example would point to Cyril's effective use of relics to construct a history and community memory of imperial support. This relics legend contributed to Cyril's efforts to raise the status of Jerusalem and to overturn its inferiority to Caesarea, much as Bishop Meletius deployed Babylas's relics to raise the status of his Nicene Christian community and the new church he had built to compete with the Great Church and the homoian Christians who had controlled it under the emperor Valens.[83]

By the end of Cyril's episcopacy, despite years in exile and other such difficult circumstances that might have impeded him, his efforts "to construct a new image" of his city "to replace either vague or negative images previously held"—to borrow the vocabulary of geographer Briavel Holcomb—had succeeded in raising Jerusa-lem's status not just within Palestine, but around the empire.[84] Although the city's power would again wane in the centuries that followed, Cyril's efforts to redefine his city as the center of the Christian world received dramatic recognition in 381 under the emperor Theodosius. As part of the Council of Constantinople, the council at which Meletius of Antioch died, the bishops from around the empire established not only theological doctrine, but also that Jerusalem was "the mother of all churches."[85] With Jerusalem's symbolic status in our contemporary world as

81. Drijvers, *Cyril*, 169; see also Drijvers, "Promoting Jerusalem," 79–95; Drijvers, *Helena Augusta.*

82. Drijvers, *Cyril*, 172, 173.

83. Although it is difficult to date precisely, compare also the story of the discovery of the relics of the apostle James, situated in 351, which likewise conveniently used newly discovered relics to highlight the primacy of the Jerusalem episcopacy (Jerome Murphy-O'Connor, *Keys to Jerusalem: Collected Essays* [New York: Oxford University Press, 2012], 138).

84. Briavel Holcomb, "Revisioning Place: De- and Re-constructing the Image of the Industrial City," in *The City as Cultural Capital, Past and Present*, ed. Gerry Kearns and Chris Philo (New York: Pergamon Press, 1993), 133. Dayna Kalleres beautifully evokes the multilayered cityscape in its transi-tion from Aelia Capitolina to the Christian city of Jerusalem, and the variety of influences in its devel-opment (*City of Demons*, chap. 4).

85. Drijvers, *Cyril*, 176; Norman Tanner, *Decrees of the Ecumenical Councils*, vol. 1, *Nicaea I to Lateran V* (Washington, DC: Georgetown University Press, 1990), 30; Theodoret, *HE* 5.9.17.

a long-standing center of pilgrimage for Jews, Christians, and Muslims, it is hard to imagine the small backwater city that Constantine inherited at the beginning of the fourth century under the name Aelia Capitolina.[86] As archaeologists and textual scholars alike have shown, it took decades of intentional hard work to present Jerusalem as the most powerful place of Christian pilgrimage and the center of a Christian world, in the way that Meletius, Flavian, and John Chrysostom shaped significant places in Antioch related to the martyr Babylas to their advantage.[87] Cyril was at the heart of that effort, and his self-conscious manipulation of the city's places, including his strategic deployment of relics, was an important part of the processes through which he was so successful.

In addition to hosting celebrations for the discovery and translation of relics, Antioch provided examples of many different forms of Christian practices related to saints' relics and shrines that were common around the Mediterranean. As we saw in chapter 5, John Chrysostom warned that at memorial feasts Antiochene Christians should take care not to imitate too closely behavior at traditional festivals and celebrations of a deceased family member, and such warnings are familiar among Christian preachers in late antiquity. Like Chrysostom, other Christian leaders were quick to note that such celebrations and remembrances were noteworthy for their drunkenness and frivolity, while Christian occasions should be distinct in their somber sobriety.

Augustine famously remembers, for example, Ambrose's criticism of the behavior of the African bishop's mother, Monica, while she was in Milan with her son: "As is the custom in Africa, [my mother] had taken to the memorial shrines of the saints (*memorias sanctorum*) cakes and bread and undiluted [wine], and was forbidden by the attendant" (*Conf.* 6.2); this prohibition came directly from Ambrose, who mentions it in an extant homily (*De Helia et ieiunio* 62).[88] Augustine describes

86. Eliav claims that even the Temple Mount was overgrown and overlooked in this town about halfway between the thriving cultural centers of Alexandria and Antioch (*God's Mountain*, 122, 124, 135–40, 149–50).

87. See, for example, Jacobs, *Remains of the Jews;* and Wharton, *Refiguring the Post-Classical City,* 85–104. Dayna Kalleres also demonstrates the city's evolution beginning with Constantine (*City of Demons,* chap. 4) and through the complex rhetoric and activity of Cyril (*City of Demons,* chap. 5); the latter discussion perceptively highlights the ways in which Cyril taught his congregants to acquire "exegetical vision" or "apocalyptic sight"—another significant way in which he changed their interpretation of and interaction with the cityscape around them.

88. All translations from Augustine's *Confessions* are my own from the Latin edition in James O'Donnell, *Augustine: Confessions,* vol. 1, *Introduction and Text* (Oxford: Clarendon Press, 1992). This incident is frequently referenced in scholarship, yet only rarely contextualized within a larger discussion of similar practices. See, for example, Peter Brown, *The Cult of the Saints: Its Rise and Function in Latin Christianity* (Chicago: University of Chicago Press, 1981); Éric Rebillard, *The Care of the Dead in Late Antiquity,* trans. Elizabeth Trapnell Rawlings and Jeanine Routier-Pucci, Cornell Studies in Classical Philology 59 (Ithaca, NY: Cornell University Press, 2009), 142–53; Maijastina Kahlos, "Comis-

his mother's "African" tradition and her abstemious sobriety, as she would offer only one very small glass of wine, and even that she would taste only out of respect for the saints and not out of any love of wine. Augustine assures his audience that if there were many memorial shrines for her to honor, then she would carry the same single small cup to each site, stretching it out over all of her visits and offering only small sips at each memorial. Particularly in light of ecclesiastical concerns that Christian behavior at rural shrines not imitate the allegedly unruly behavior of traditional celebrations, and thus confusingly blur a boundary that Christian leaders hoped to draw around Christian places and people, Augustine is at pains to emphasize about Monica that "she sought piety, not pleasure," and that when she learned of the bishop's prohibition, she "happily abstained" (*Conf.* 6.2). Peter Brown draws on the discovery of "new" Augustinian texts—those discovered by François Dolbeau in Mainz—to strengthen his observation that while church leaders such as Augustine criticized such alcohol-laden conviviality at the tombs of the martyrs, many Christians understood such behavior to be normative and entirely acceptable.[89]

Later, in his role as the bishop of Hippo, Augustine wrote to Aurelius, the bishop of Carthage, to combat an allegedly pervasive and tenacious tradition of drinking alcohol as part of the feasts at the Christian martyrs' shrines. He insists, "Rioting and drunkenness are so allowed and lawful that they are practiced even in honoring the most blessed martyrs" (*Ep.* 22.3).[90] Augustine further recognizes that while this tradition may be particularly common to Roman North Africa, it had also been found elsewhere before bishops put an end to such practices (*Ep.* 22.4).[91] Keeping in mind that Augustine may have exaggerated North Africa's position for rhetorical effect, he nevertheless bears witness to these widespread practices and other episcopal efforts to change them.

Augustine presents a lurid picture of the strength of such practices in North Africa in his day, suggesting that "the pestilence" would not be cured without

sationes et ebrietates," in *Ad itum liberum: Essays in Honour of Anne Helttula*, ed. O. Merisalo and R. Vainio (Jyväskylä, Finland: University of Jyväskylä Press, 2007), 13–23. The evidence cited by Rebillard (*Care of the Dead*, 142–53) confirms that criticism of such practices was widespread among Western Christian leaders from Tertullian to Ambrose and Augustine (see Rebillard, 151–53).

89. Peter Brown, "Enjoying the Saints in Late Antiquity," *Early Medieval Europe* 9 (2000): 1–24. I am grateful to Geoffrey Dunn and Wendy Mayer for bringing to my attention another relevant sermon by Augustine (on Saint Cyprian), one of the six authentic sermons by Augustine recently discovered by Isabella Schiller, Dorothea Weber, and Clemens Weidmann in Erfurt, Germany.

90. All translations from Augustine's *Ep.* 22 are my own from the Latin edition in CSEL 34.1.

91. Rebillard has collected other references from late antiquity that corroborate Augustine's claim that this practice was common across North Africa but not unique to that region; see, for example, Rebillard's references to Tertullian's third-century treatises from Carthage, Zeno's late fourth-century *Tractatus* from Verona, Gaudentius's condemnations in Brescia, Italy, ca. 390–410, and of course Ambrose's criticisms in Milan (Rebillard, *Care of the Dead*, 142–53).

intervention from a church council, since these "drunken and luxurious banquets (*convivia*) in the cemeteries are believed by the carnal and inexperienced multitude to be not only an honor to the martyrs, but also a solace to the dead" (*Ep.* 22.4, 6). Augustine warns that consequently these Christians would not easily be "dissuaded from such foul and disgraceful" practices (*Ep.* 22.6). Such rhetoric echoes John Chrysostom's strong warnings about what behavior was and was not appropriate for Christians generally, for anyone attending a martyr's shrine, and for the processions to and from such celebrations (e.g., *De s. Pelagia* 3–4). Antiochenes, it seems, were not alone in carrying traditional festivities into the new Christian commemorations, and John Chrysostom was not alone in his efforts to redraw the landscape in order to distinguish the places of martyrs' shrines from temples and gravesites by distinguishing the behavior that took place there.[92]

Antioch's martyria thus stand in a rich web of Christian shrines around the empire that were in the fourth century growing into significant places of Christian practice as the landscape was being remapped through Christian leaders' eyes, and many of these new Christian places were located outside city walls. Some saints drew primarily local pilgrims,[93] but many drew pilgrims from around the empire (and beyond), whether because the number of places associated with them were much more widely spread, such as for Thecla and Stephen, or simply because their authority and renown had the power to draw people to their singular location from great distances.[94] Thus the locations of saints became new Christian sites on the map of the empire that were increasing in both number and fame in this period, participating in the redefinition of the empire's landscape.

CHRISTIANIZING THE CITYSCAPE:
ALEXANDRIA AND MINORCA

By the end of the fourth century and the beginning of the fifth century, Christianity—and specifically Nicene "orthodoxy"—had become more firmly entrenched in

---

92. Éric Rebillard reminds us that what bishops like Ambrose and Augustine often saw as an inappropriate continuation of ancestral traditions among Christians was often seen by their congregants from quite a different perspective: Rebillard, *Christians and Their Many Identities in Late Antiquity, North Africa, 200–450 C.E.* (Ithaca, NY: Cornell University Press, 2012), e.g., 92.

93. See, for example, James Skedros, *Saint Demetrios of Thessaloniki: Civic Patron and Divine Protector, 4th–7th Centuries C.E.* (Harrisburg, PA: Trinity Press International, 1999).

94. Stephen Davis, *The Cult of St. Thecla: A Tradition of Women's Piety in Late Antiquity* (New York: Oxford University Press, 2001); Marios Costambeys and Conrad Leyser, "To Be the Neighbour of St. Stephen: Patronage, Martyr Cult, and Roman Monasteries, c. 600–c. 900," in *Religion, Dynasty, and Patronage in Early Christian Rome, 300–900*, ed. Kate Cooper and Julia Hillner (New York: Cambridge University Press, 2007), 262–87. Compare the wide appeal of Saint Sergius in Elizabeth Key Fowden, *The Barbarian Plain: Saint Sergius between Rome and Iran* (Berkeley: University of California Press, 1999).

Roman culture, legislation, and of course the physical and ideological landscapes of the empire. While the processes of transforming the empire continued, and certainly the efforts to define religious orthodoxy were unending, the particular theological controversies sparked by the decisions at the Council of Nicaea were waning. We end the tour of the empire, then, with two examples of the flagrant destruction of a once wealthy and prominent religious site: the first a temple to the Egyptian god Serapis, and the second a Jewish synagogue. In both cases, in Alexandria and in Minorca, highly rhetorical narratives of Christian destruction shaped the buildings' significance in the memory of the community, highlighting a "Christianization" of the local cityscape.

Texts such as Libanius's *Pro templis* allege a pattern of Christian violence against temples in the late fourth century. One of the most spectacular examples of temple destruction, owing to its size and significance, was the destruction of the famous Alexandrian temple of Serapis, the Serapeum. Ammianus Marcellinus is among those who describe the earlier majesty of the Serapeum, calling the temple "prominent" among Alexandrian temples (*Res gest.* 22.16.12).[95] Although he protests that his words will be insufficient to do justice to the great building, he mentions the "extensive columned halls, with almost breathing statues, and a large number of other works of art," second only to the famous Capitolium in Rome (22.16.12).[96] Even the Christian author Rufinus describes the temple's enormous size and beauty (*HE* 11.23). Located at the top of a hill overlooking the large city, the Serapeum was well known, visually conspicuous, and admired throughout the empire. When a mob destroyed the Serapeum around 392, the skyline of the city was changed forever. Thanks to the ways in which the destruction was narrated by Christian leaders and authors, the ruins of the Serapeum, like those of the temple of Apollo at Daphne but on a greater scale, became not only a highly visible but also a significantly meaningful symbol. The destruction of the Serapeum and the narratives that record it reveal the large scale on which Christians were physically and rhetorically reshaping the religious landscape of Alexandria by the end of the fourth century.[97]

95. All translations of Ammianus Marcellinus are my own from the Latin in *Ammianus Marcellinus: History, XX–XXVI*, ed. John Rolfe (Cambridge, MA: Harvard University Press, 2006).

96. See the discussion of statues as works of art in Kalas, *Transforming Public Space*, chaps. 5 and 6.

97. Although earlier scholars dated the destruction to 391, Johannes Hahn has demonstrated that 392 is a more likely date: Hahn, "The Conversion of the Cult Statues: The Destruction of the Serapeum 392 A.D. and the Transformation of Alexandria into the 'Christ-Loving' City," in *From Temple to Church: Destruction and Renewal of Local Cultic Topography in Late Antiquity*, ed. Johannes Hahn, Stephen Emmel, and Ulrich Gotter (Boston: Brill, 2008), 340–44. Hahn also published some of this scholarship earlier in *Gewalt und religiöser Konflikt: Studien zu den Auseinandersetzungen zwischen Heiden, Christen und Juden im Osten des Römischen Reiches (von Konstantin bis Theodosius II)* (Berlin: Akademie Press, 2004).

Given the power of narratives of community memory to shape identity, as explored in chapter 2, it is not surprising that there are significant differences in the ways that various authors recorded the events surrounding the Serapeum's destruction, although all agree that Christians destroyed the building.[98] Although Johannes Hahn uses the textual descriptions to construct some aspects of the riot and destruction of the temple, he agrees with Jitse Dijkstra that the literary sources cannot be reconciled with one another and are not trustworthy as descriptions of the events.[99] Ulrich Gotter focuses on the literary nature of the descriptions of the destruction of the Alexandrian Serapeum in order to demonstrate that this narrative and others like it were, above all, rhetorical tropes used by early "church historians" to illustrate the "orthodox" (or "heretical") Christianity of the emperor.[100] As a temple to Serapis and the home to numerous statues of gods, the large complex had strong associations with traditional Greek teachings and practices. Edward Watts observes:

> In the later fourth century, the Alexandrian Serapeum had become an intellectual center to which many Iamblichan Neoplatonists were attracted. The site had many features that such men would have found appealing. Not only was the temple fully functional, but the area surrounding it also provided classroom spaces for teachers and, potentially, the largest library in Alexandria.[101]

Eunapius describes the destruction as the unprovoked and unjustifiable violence of a Christian mob under the leadership of the local bishop Theophilus against the unarmed foe of the temple's statues and votive offerings, even accusing the attackers of looting the temple in the process of its destruction (*Vitae sophistarum* 472). Christian narratives, in contrast, describe a heated and violent conflict sparked by Bishop Theophilus's public display and ridicule of some ritual objects discovered in a hitherto secret room of a local temple, a conflict that led to a prolonged series of physical skirmishes, with the supporters of the temple barricaded in the relative safety of the Serapeum until their eventual surrender and the crowd's destruction of the temple complex (e.g., Sozomen, *HE* 7.15; Rufinus, *HE* 2.23).[102]

---

98. Jitse Dijkstra notes that despite this apparent wealth of literary evidence, it is difficult to reconstruct the events: Dijkstra, "The Fate of the Temples in Late Antique Egypt," in Lavan and Mulryan, *Archaeology*, 394.

99. Hahn, "Conversion," 339, 347–60.

100. Ulrich Gotter, "Rechtgläubige—Pagane—Häretiker: Tempelzerstörungen in der Kirchengeschichtsschreibung und das Bild der christlichen Kaiser," in Hahn, Emmel, and Gotter, *From Temple to Church*, 43–89, esp. 43–44, 50, 59, 79–86.

101. Edward Watts, *City and School in Late Antique Athens and Alexandria* (Berkeley: University of California Press, 2006), 189. Watts has collected and analyzed the relevant primary sources on this history, such as Eunapius's *Vitae sophistarum*.

102. Watts, *City and School*, retells these events, as does Christopher Haas, *Alexandria in Late Antiquity: Topography and Social Conflict* (Baltimore: Johns Hopkins University Press, 1997), 160–61, and they each reference the academic literature on the topic.

Christopher Haas has usefully examined the numerous ways in which the Alexandrian bishop Theophilus "Christianized" public space during this time, including building a church "within the precinct of the temple of Serapis," reminiscent of the translation of Christian relics within the *temenos* of the Apollo shrine in Daphne.[103] Haas writes:

> Theophilus stands out as but one member of a long line of Alexandrian bishops who actively sought the thoroughgoing Christianization of Alexandria's landscape. Unlike Rome at this time, the Christianization of Alexandria's urban space was not accompanied by a fundamental shift in the city's design, which might have refocused the urban consciousness on new points such as suburban churches and martyria. The topography of Alexandria was too constrained by natural barriers to permit a reconfiguration of the pronounced design system. . . . Instead, the forceful leaders of the Christian community had a program of converting the existing urban landscape, constructing in stone a reflection of the progressive conversion of the city's populace.[104]

Haas clearly notes the significance of the Serapeum's visibility and importance in the city when he examines the effects its destruction could have had: "This famous complex of buildings crowned the city's most prominent height (sometimes referred to as Alexandria's acropolis). The Serapeum so loomed over the urban landscape that Diocletian chose to set up his victory column here in 297/298. Its conversion into a church presaged the downfall of public paganism in Alexandria and the takeover of several key sites."[105]

In addition to the later church building, Hahn follows the late fourth-century author Eunapius and the late seventh-century author John of Nikiu in describing another building on the temple's site: "As an open demonstration of the permanent victory of the Christian faith, the site [of the destroyed Serapeum] was occupied by a colony of monks. Immediately, or shortly, after the destruction of the Serapeum, the site became a *martyrium* dedicated to St. John the Baptist."[106] Although Eunapius's reference to monks occupying the site (*Vitae sophistarum* 472) and John of Nikiu's reference to the building of a martyrium for John the Baptist (*Chron.* 78) may be literary devices, they reveal at least the rhetorical, if not also the physical, advantages of describing this further transformation of the site of the former Serapeum.

103. Haas, *Alexandria,* 207; more generally, see Haas, 206–14.
104. Haas, *Alexandria,* 207–8.
105. Haas, *Alexandria,* 211. The narrative records of fifth-century physical violence perpetrated and encouraged by Shenoute of Atripe against temples in Upper Egypt are but another of the many examples of this continuing history. For more on transformations in Egypt, see also David Frankfurter, *Religion in Roman Egypt: Assimilation and Resistance* (Princeton, NJ: Princeton University Press, 1998); Stephen Emmel, "Shenoute of Atripe and the Christian Destruction of Temples in Egypt: Rhetoric and Reality," in Hahn, Emmel, and Gotter, *From Temple to Church,* 161–201.
106. Hahn, "Conversion," 352.

The discussion in chapter 2 of the Babylas relics and the Apollo temple in Daphne suggests that the destruction of the Serapeum was significant far beyond the loss of the place of worship of the gods, because the rubble would have presented a constant reminder to passersby of the conquest of the gods' place by Christians, as narrated through Christian histories. While we do not have a local text like John Chrysostom's *De s. Babyla* to describe the role that the Serapeum ruins played in contests to define the memory of the site and its meaning for community identity, there can be little doubt that the monumental temple's destruction, the attribution of the destruction to Christians, and the location of a Christian church in the temple precinct would all reinforce a message of the superior power of Christianity over the gods, a message that it is hard to imagine Bishop Theophilus not pressing to its fullest advantage in coaxing the landscape of Alexandria to reflect the success of his Christian community, and encourage its continued growth.

While the stories about the destruction of the Serapeum in Alexandria demonstrate that occasionally some temples became targets of Christian violence, other texts describe Christian violence against Jewish synagogues, reminiscent of Bishop Ambrose and Emperor Theodosius's exchange regarding the synagogue in Callinicum. Just as relics offered Cyril of Jerusalem, like Meletius of Antioch, a means of claiming physical places and authority over their Christian opponents, the early martyr Stephen's relics ostensibly offered Severus, the bishop of the island of Minorca, a means of claiming Jewish land (and people) for Christianity in the early fifth century. Celebrated as the first "Christian" martyr, Stephen was one of the few "Christian" martyrs whose death was blamed exclusively on Jews (Acts 7), and his death became a powerful legend.[107] Stephen's relics, first identified in 415 in Jerusalem by Lucian, who then wrote a narrative of the events, were involved in numerous controversies in the decades after their initial discovery,[108] and the dispersal of some of these relics from Jerusalem to the island of Minorca, off the coast of present-day Spain, clearly reflects the role that Stephen's relics played in Christian leaders' efforts to gain control over powerful local Jewish places.

Lucian claims that he was allowed to keep some of Stephen's relics after most of them were carried off to be housed in the church of Sion (*Revelatio s. Stephani* 8). Lucian distributed some of the relics that he had kept to Avitus, a Spanish priest in Palestine, who allegedly sent them to Balchonius, the bishop of Braga, by way of Orosius, who was returning to the West from a council at Diospolis/Lydda, west of Jerusalem.[109] There is no evidence that any relics arrived in Braga, but an extant

---

107. Although the term "Christian" is anachronistic for Stephen, he becomes admired within later Christianity as the first "Christian" martyr.

108. See Elizabeth Clark, "Claims on the Bones of Saint Stephen: The Partisans of Melania and Eudocia," *CH* 51.2 (1982): 141–56.

109. See Clark, "Claims," 142.

letter by Severus of Minorca claims that relics from Stephen arrived on his island in early 418 and made the island's Jews and the place of their synagogue building Christian.[110]

The sharp anti-Judaism of Severus's narrative coincides with the particulars of Stephen's first-century martyrdom, during which he insulted a Jewish crowd that then stoned him to death (Acts 7), and of the story of the discovery of his relics, during which the rabbi Gamaliel appeared as a Christian in a vision to Lucian (Lucian, *Revelatio s. Stephani*). It is, however, the story's rich topographical language that is most relevant here. Severus begins his letter by providing his reader with a clear sense of the island's physical location and dimensions: "The isle of Minorca is one of the Balearic Islands. . . . It is located in the open sea almost midway between Mauritania and Spain, and is confined within rather narrow boundaries, being thirty miles long and ten miles wide" (*Epistula Severi* 2).[111] Emphasizing its lowliness, Severus describes the island's "smallness, dryness, and harshness," and explains that the island was the home to "two small towns (*parva oppida*) . . . : Jamona looks to the West, Magona to the East" (2). Severus further explains that Jews, along with "foxes and wolves, and all harmful animals," were "absolutely unable to live" in Jamona, while the town of Magona "swarmed with such a multitude of Jews, as if with snakes and scorpions, that the church of Christ was being stung by them daily" (3).[112] Such is the narrative landscape into which Stephen's relics entered, giving the reader a clear sense that the story that followed would be strongly place-oriented.

Bishop Severus's story of the Jews' adoption of Christianity follows a series of events that are firmly located in their physical surroundings. He narrates that the arrival of Stephen's relics sparked a Christian missionizing spree across the island: "In every avenue (*plateis*), fights were waged against the Jews concerning the Law, in every house battles concerning the faith" (*Epistula Severi* 5). This culminated in a throng of Christians gathering in Jamona and traveling together the difficult thirty-mile journey across the island to Magona in order to confront the Jews (12). Just as the transgressions that followed the Statues Riot in Antioch transformed the city, in John Chrysostom's rhetoric, into a more thoroughly Christian place, the Christians' journey across Minorca and their entry into Magona transformed

110. *Severus of Minorca: Letter on the Conversion of the Jews*, trans. and ed. Scott Bradbury (Oxford: Clarendon Press, 1996).

111. All translations of the *Epistula Severi* are from Bradbury's English translation, with reference to, and with my own occasional modifications from, his Latin edition (Bradbury, *Severus*). For an analysis of Severus's rhetoric, see Jacques Fontaine, "Une polémique stylistique instructive dans la 'lettre encyclique' de Sévère de Minorque," *Eulogia: Mélanges offerts à A. R. Bastiaensen à l'occasion de son soizante-cinquième anniversaire* (Steenbrugis: Abbatia S. Petri, 1991), 119–35.

112. See also E. D. Hunt, "St. Stephen in Minorca: An Episode in Jewish-Christian Relations in the Early Fifth Century AD," *JTS* n.s. 33 (1982): 106–23.

the formerly Jewish town into a Christian place, according to Severus's account. The Christians invited the Jews of Magona to return to their church in Jamona with them, but when the Jews refused, the Christians instead entered the synagogue, physically taking control of the place, although Severus carefully describes the peaceful manner in which the Christian mob entered and occupied the synagogue, despite Jews' efforts to prevent them (12–13). After allegedly little effort, Severus implies, "the Jews had withdrawn and we gained control of the synagogue," after which "fire consumed [the synagogue] itself and all of its decorations, with the exception of the books and silver" (13). While all the Jews "were stupefied by the destruction of the synagogue," the Christians prayed for the Jews to turn away from Judaism and join the Christian community (14). Within days, Severus claims, 540 Jews had become Christian (29).[113] Back in Jamona, Severus notes that the newly enlarged Christian congregation "was in the church, which is located a short distance from the town (*civitate*) in a secluded spot (*loco*) and in which rest the relics of the holy martyr Stephen, recently established [there], waiting for Mass with me" (20).

Severus is explicit about the topographical transformation that the island underwent as a result of the arrival of Stephen's relics and the Christians' transgression into the Jews' town. The place of the synagogue was utterly transformed: "For not only are [the Jews] bearing the expense, first, to level the very foundations of the synagogue, and then for constructing a new basilica, but they even bring in the boulders on their [own] shoulders" (*Epistula Severi* 30). Like John Chrysostom's description of the manual labor he attributes to Bishop Meletius in building the church for Babylas, praising that Meletius "even often brought along stone and dragged a rope" (*De s. hierom. Babyla* 10), Severus's description of the Jews' manual labor in building their new basilica suggests their complete devotion and their Christian humility.

Further, Severus sees in these events a lesson and hope for the broader empire: "Perhaps the Lord wished to kindle this spark from the ends of the earth, so that the whole breadth of the earth might be ablaze with the flame of love in order to burn down the forest of unbelief" (*Epistula Severi* 31). While bishops in Antioch and Jerusalem used Babylas's relics and the relics of the True Cross to transform space to their benefit over their Christian opponents, Stephen's relics effected the redefinition of local space from Jewish to Christian in a story not dissimilar from the transformation described by John Chrysostom in the spatial transgressions that followed the Statues Riot. Whether a synagogue in Minorca or a temple in Alexandria, such destroyed and transformed buildings inevitably became new vis-

---

113. On the role of Jewish women in this narrative, see Ross Kraemer, "Jewish Women's Resistance to Christianity in the Early Fifth Century: The Account of Severus, Bishop of Minorca," *JECS* 17.4 (2009): 635–65.

ible and rhetorical cues to the city's inhabitants, suggesting that the gods had suc-
cumbed to the efforts of forceful Christian leaders and their triumphant God.

These examples are just a few of the many extant narratives of the "Christianization" of places by relics in late antiquity. Stephen's bones were discovered during
the reign of the emperor Honorius, which also saw the translation of Ignatius of
Antioch's relics by Honorius's eastern counterpart, Theodosius II, from the cemetery outside of Antioch into a Tychaeum that had been turned to a church inside
the city. All over the empire in the late fourth and early fifth centuries relics assisted
Christian leaders in gaining control over places that so-called heretics, pagans,
and/or Jews once controlled. Sometimes the manipulation was primarily rhetorical, as Jonathan Yates has shown in the case of Augustine, who manipulated the
community's memory of the martyr-bishop Cyprian in order to win over his Pela-
gian opponents,[114] or as Johan Leemans has shown in the case of Basil of Caesarea,
who manipulated the hagiography of the martyr Gordius to make him particularly
useful in Basil's efforts against traditional religious practices.[115] Other times the
manipulation of relics was physical, such as the transfer of Babylas's relics in Antioch, Bishop Flavian's transference of the saints' bodies in the floor of the Romanesian Gate martyrion, and the translation of Stephen's relics on the island of
Minorca. In numerous ways, relics helped Christian leaders to win control of local
places from their opponents, thus contributing to the definition of Christian
"orthodoxy" and the overall transformation of the empire's religious topography.

CONCLUSION: BEYOND ANTIOCH

Although Antioch remains one of the best recorded and more complex examples,
this chapter demonstrates that Antioch was far from the only place in the empire
where Christian leaders were actively manipulating the local topography in efforts
to secure their authority to define fourth-century religious orthodoxy. The construction of new buildings and the contests over their control in Milan reveal the
sharply politicized struggles between opposing theological parties, most frequently in the second half of the fourth century between those who supported the
outcome of the Council of Nicaea and those whom these Christians termed "Arians." The examples of Cyril of Jerusalem and Ambrose of Milan reveal that these
struggles were sometimes wider than just the bishop's own city, expanding to
regional and even empire-wide contests over prestige and authority, and Cyril

---

114. Jonathan Yates, "Augustine's Appropriation of Cyprian the Martyr-Bishop against the Pelagians," in *More Than a Memory: The Discourse of Martyrdom and the Construction of Christian Identity in
the History of Christianity*, ed. Johan Leemans (Dudley, MA: Peeters, 2005), 119–35.

115. Johan Leemans, "Martyr, Monk, and Victor of Paganism: An Analysis of Basil of Caesarea's
Panegyrical Sermon on Gordius," in Leemans, *More Than a Memory*, 45–79.

adeptly demonstrates the role that relics also played in shaping the outcomes of many of these intra-Christian conflicts. Martyrs' shrines in the rural areas of the empire offer further parallels to Antioch's history, demonstrating that temples were often part of these transition narratives, and that rural martyrs' shrines were particularly effective agents by which Christian places superseded what had come before. The destruction of the Alexandrian Serapeum and Bishop Severus's narrative of the transformations that Stephen's relics effected on the island of Minorca further demonstrate that such contests to control local places sometimes extended—as they did in John Chrysostom's Antioch—to interreligious struggles against temples and synagogues. While the examples from Antioch have their local uniqueness, the imperial legislation preserved in the Theodosian Code and the examples above of other church leaders' efforts reveal that in late antiquity the Antiochene conflicts were being echoed around the empire.

Conclusion

Controlling Contested Places

Perceptions of places are socially constructed and profoundly influential, shaping understandings of the past and thus also expectations for the future. Fourth-century Antioch is a particularly rich site of spatial construction and change, in part because of its complex history during late antiquity, when religious and political upheavals altered the cityscape, in part because of its prominence within empire-wide conversations, and in part because so much textual evidence regarding Antioch survives. Thanks to Libanius, John Chrysostom, and Theodoret, it is possible to investigate these decades of Antioch's history in much more depth and from more perspectives than is usually possible for antiquity. The privilege of hindsight also allows modern readers to examine the long-term repercussions of these leaders' efforts to shape their landscape, and offers useful comparanda for thinking about the religious and political effects of ongoing efforts toward topographical transformation in our world today.

A woman steps across a dry streambed into Arizona and becomes subject to arrest as an illegal alien. Astronauts plant an American flag on the moon, and the implications of that act reverberate from Washington to Moscow. Hijacked planes destroy the Twin Towers, and the site of the World Trade Center becomes Ground Zero, its meaning as indelibly changed as its landscape. The power that places have to shape history, politics, memory, and identity is visible in antiquity and in our world today, as are the contests to control those places and to manipulate the authority associated with them. The news is filled with physical contests to control places of political and religious significance, from Jerusalem's Temple Mount to Cairo's Tahrir Square, with innumerable others etched in our collective memory. Rhetorical contests likewise reflect politicized struggles to control places by shaping the meanings and memories associated with them, from patriotic American claims to be "the land of the free" to George W. Bush's identification of Iraq, Iran, and North Korea as "an axis of evil." Ancient and contemporary, local and global, such physical and rhetorical contests demonstrate the significant and complex politics involved in controlling contested places.

Libanius's fourth-century comments about his struggle to gain access to the most prestigious teaching place in Antioch, as well as his tussles with the praetorian prefect Strategius and the emperor Julian, reveal that early Christian leaders were not alone in recognizing the power dynamics of manipulating places, particularly crowded public places with large audiences, to their advantage. As seen above, Libanius demonstrated his participation in numerous place-related negotiations of power and authority with fellow teachers as well as with local and imperial officials. Similarly, the complexities of the fourth-century episcopal schisms in Antioch meant that at least some of the city's clergy were particularly attentive to the possibilities that the landscape and its prominent religious structures provided for reshaping local perceptions of religious orthodoxy and orthopraxy. Decades of rival bishops, repeated exiles, and shifting control over the city's Great Church laid the foundation for Bishop Meletius's and Bishop Flavian's physical manipulations of saints' relics, and John Chrysostom's vocal rhetorical efforts to reshape and control the topography of Antioch and its surrounding countryside.

Babylas's relics provided one of the most spectacular and long-lasting tools by which leaders in Antioch worked physically and rhetorically to regulate the memories associated with their landscape, and thus its meaning to passersby. As Harriet Flower has shown in another Roman context, the "use of past history for partisan purposes" was not new in fourth-century efforts to define the history of Daphne's Apollo temple; rather, throughout history those "who had the authority to decide about remembering and forgetting" influenced the community identity that ultimately developed.[1]

Geographers Chris Philo and Gerry Kearns note the "tensions and potential conflict" that can arise from spatial manipulations, and their work can be applied productively to the conflicts that arose around Babylas's relics between supporters of Apollo's temple and supporters of the Christian saint, and between homoian and Nicene Christians.[2] Much as other saints' relics did around the empire, Babylas's (and Meletius's) relics redefined the location where they were finally interred, in this case the church that Meletius had built in the field across the river from the city, so

---

1. Harriet Flower, *The Art of Forgetting: Disgrace and Oblivion in Roman Political Culture* (Chapel Hill, NC: University of North Carolina Press, 2006), xxi-xxii.

2. Chris Philo and Gerry Kearns, "Culture, History, Capital: A Critical Introduction to the Selling of Places," in *Selling Places: The City as Cultural Capital, Past and Present*, ed. Gerry Kearns and Chris Philo (New York: Pergamon Press, 1993), 3.

as to connect the place with Meletius's "orthodox" Christian community. Like Bishop Ambrose did years later in Milan, Meletius co-opted for his community the authority of a powerful local saint and then had himself buried with the saint, ensuring that the martyr became inseparable from the Christian faction closely associated with the bishop who had spent his career in the midst of bitter theological and political controversies. By moving Babylas's remains to the church he had built, Meletius created a new local Christian place that thanks to the saints' relics—those of the martyr and of the later bishop—competed with the other most authoritative places in the city, changing how people saw the location where the new church was built, and their behavior, as the new church became a destination for religious devotion. Later in the same decade, Bishop Ambrose did the same in Milan.

In the case of Babylas's relics, however, this translation to their final resting place was the last stage in an already eventful fourth century. Not only a tool in the intra-Christian controversies that split the city, Babylas's relics had previously become the strongest of the local voices against the Greek gods and their temples, thanks to the events of the 350s and 360s under Caesar Gallus and his half brother, the emperor Julian. Gallus's translation of the relics to Apollo's temple precinct in Daphne parallels other Christian efforts to deactivate temples and insert new, Christian interpretations, and in this case perhaps a specific connection with the homoian Christians under the bishop Leontius. Gallus's success was demonstrated by the oracle's silence and the temple's disrepair, such that the emperor Julian forced Christians to remove Babylas's relics from the temple grounds in the hope that the oracle would then be restored. When the oracle remained mute and the temple itself burned soon afterward in a destructive fire, leaders in the region presented competing narratives through which visitors were to understand the ruins. The emperor Julian argued that the charred remains sharply chastised the Antiochenes for their maltreatment of Julian and the gods, whom he claimed had left the city in disgust. Christians such as John Chrysostom, however, argued that all those who entered Daphne would instantly recognize in the ruined temple remains physical evidence of the power and superiority of Christians, and for Chrysostom this meant Nicene Christians, and their God.

Babylas's relics appear in the events of the 350s with Gallus, the 360s with Julian and Libanius, around the time of Theodosius's accession in 379, and through the 380s with Meletius and John Chrysostom. They continued to have multivalent significance throughout their long history in ways that recall what Angèle Smith calls "the politics of perception."[3] Chrysostom was explicit that Babylas's relics were perceived as being as strong in their absence as they were in their presence,

---

3. Angèle Smith, "Landscape Representation: Place and Identity in Nineteenth-Century Ordnance Survey Maps of Ireland," in *Landscape, Memory, and History: Anthropological Perspectives,* ed. Pamela Stewart and Andrew Strathern (Sterling, VA: Pluto, 2003), 71.

arguing that passersby should read the burned ruins and the empty martyrion in ways that recalled the power of the Christian saint (*De s. Babyla* 126–27). The martyr's relics thus affected more than one place; from the time of their removal from Apollo's temple grounds, they spoke loudly in their absence in Daphne and in their presence in Antioch, working to reshape the ways Antiochenes saw their landscape and remembered its history. In Daphne the relics appear to have represented primarily a symbol of Christianity, although which kind of Christianity was under negotiation, in contrast to what John Chrysostom refers to as "Greek superstition," as they competed with Apollo for authority in his temple precinct. After returning to Antioch under Bishop Meletius, the relics were claimed by those following Nicene orthodoxy against Meletius's local homoian opponents. Babylas's relics, at once agents of "Christianization," "orthodoxy," and "orthopraxy," offer an unusual window onto the complexities of Antiochene religious and political controversies in the second half of the fourth century, and the role that physical places—and rhetorical and physical manipulations of them—played in these dynamics.

Like Babylas's relics, the example of Bishop Flavian's rearrangement of saints' remains at the Romanesian Gate participated in the manipulation of memory and religious identity in fourth-century Antioch. As Charles Hedrick notes with respect to the later Roman Empire, "The past could not be accepted without qualification: certain things had to be forgotten."[4] Bishop Flavian's efforts at the martyrion at the Romanesian Gate imitated the so-called Roman *damnatio memoriae* practice, and served to sanction memory in ways helpfully described by Harriet Flower. "Memory sanctions," Flower writes, "are deliberately designed strategies that aim to change the picture of the past, whether through erasure or redefinition, or by means of both."[5] By obscuring the graves of his theological opponents, Bishop Flavian hoped to rewrite the history of Christianity in the city and construct a particular Christian identity for the martyrion at the Romanesian Gate, and for all those who visited it, that was consonant with his own particular version of Nicene Christian orthodoxy. Hedrick's observations about a restored Roman inscription are relevant to this Antiochene martyrion. "Meaning is produced," Hedrick writes, "precisely by the selection of significant detail, the identification and inclusion of what is relevant; or, to put it in a negative way, by the exclusion of what is irrelevant."[6] By excluding the homoian burials and highlighting the "orthodox" burials, Flavian inscribed a meaningful history for his community in the physical structures of the region. Through his efforts, and through the later

4. Charles Hedrick, Jr., *History and Silence: The Purge and Rehabilitation of Memory in Late Antiquity* (Austin: University of Texas Press, 2000), xv.

5. Flower, *Art of Forgetting*, 2–3; cf. Gregor Kalas, "Conservation, Erasure, and Intervention: Rome's Ancient Heritage and the History of SS. Cosma e Damiano," *Arris* 16 (2005): 1–11.

6. Hedrick, *History and Silence*, 34.

rhetorical efforts of John Chrysostom, Christian leaders not only affected the type of Christianity that the martyrion represented, but contributed to the broader project over these decades of making the landscape in and around Antioch more visibly associated with ("orthodox") Christianity.

John Chrysostom's manipulations of Antioch's places, though more oratorical compared with the manual rearrangements of Bishops Meletius and Flavian, likewise reshaped the region's topography. Chrysostom's homilies against "Judaizers" and "Anomeans" from 386–87 demonstrate that the fiery preacher persistently associated Christian identity and orthodoxy with attendance at particular physical places. Most notably, Chrysostom's homilies against the "Judaizers" pressed his listeners to reject any positive connotations that they had with synagogues—and from Chrysostom's comments it seems clear that some in his audience had held synagogues in high regard—and to replace that respect with fear. The positive connotations align with Yi-Fu Tuan's concept of *topophilia,* and I have termed the fear that Chrysostom hoped to instill instead *topophobia* in the hope of highlighting the spatial manipulations at play in Chrysostom's complex rhetoric. Whereas the translations of Babylas's relics and the building of new churches physically changed the city's landscape, Chrysostom rhetorically reshaped how Antioch's inhabitants saw and interacted with the topography of their city, even when the buildings in question remained physically largely unchanged. While some congregants seem to have seen in synagogues holy places that housed sacred scripture, John Chrysostom encouraged them to fear them as places filled with demons and a people prone to murder. Theaters, pubs, athletic competitions, and temples likewise felt the brunt of Chrysostom's polemic as he created a "geography of difference" by identifying certain of the city's places as physically and spiritually dangerous for Christians to attend.[7] Such rhetoric could be every bit as effective as physical manipulations in changing citizens' perceptions of, and patterns of attendance at, the city's places.

A comparison of John Chrysostom's anti-Anomean homilies with those against the Judaizers, however, reveals that his rhetoric contains much more nuance than the binary categories of "Christian" and "Jewish" initially suggest. The complex history of the control of church buildings in fourth-century Antioch appears to have discouraged Christian leaders from associating particular buildings with one Christian group or another, because the sites changed hands among the various Antiochene Christian communities during the course of the century. Reading Chrysostom's homilies against the Anomeans with an eye to their spatial rhetoric, and particularly in light of the homilies against the Judaizers from the same years, reveals Chrysostom's nuance regarding the value of Christian places, a nuance that

7. David Sibley, "Creating Geographies of Difference," in *Human Geography Today,* ed. Doreen Massey, John Allen, and Philip Sarre (Malden, MA: Polity Press, 1999), 126.

is lacking in his blunt evaluation of "Christian" versus "Jewish" places. Against the Anomeans, even John Chrysostom's church, which emerged as the safest place in his other homilies, acquired a potential danger, depending on the behavior of the person in question. Weak Christians could, in these homilies, find their orthodoxy endangered in Christians' homes and even in the church itself, where demons threatened to leap into inattentive Christians from the demon-possessed people who stood at the front of the congregation to receive their prayers. Strong Christians, on the other hand, maintained their orthodoxy wherever they were, and as a result Chrysostom could even safely encourage them to befriend "heretical" Anomeans in the hope that the former would "heal" the latter. Being correctly Christian for Chrysostom thus included vigilant attendance at particular places and absence from others, along with spiritual focus and engagement; being correctly Christian was thus a matter of orthopraxy as well as orthodoxy.

The highly rhetorical nature of place-production becomes clear through comparison of the different conclusions that Chrysostom draws in different situations. When the emperor Julian required that Babylas's relics be removed from the site of the Apollo temple in the hope of reinstating the temple's oracle, he set the stage for Chrysostom's claim that the saint's relics transformed the temple site and prevented worship of the god from continuing there. In his *Adversus Iudaeos* homilies, however, Chrysostom argued that the scriptures shared by Jews and Christians, holy as the texts were, did not transform the synagogue or prevent harmful practices there. In his homilies *De incomprehensibili natura dei,* Chrysostom argued that not even his own church building could guarantee protection from demon possession or Christian heresy for those he called weaker Christians. This comparison highlights the variability in Chrysostom's spatial descriptions, and that his perceptions were socially and rhetorically constructed to fit the needs of each situation. It also, though, suggests that Chrysostom assumed a sharper distinction between Christianity and the worship of the gods than between Christianity and what Chrysostom considered Judaism, on the one hand, and Christian heresy, on the other. According to Chrysostom, "weaker" Christians were safest in his church with their full attention focused on the liturgy, "stronger" Christians could associate with heretics and bring them to Christian orthodoxy, and saints could deactivate sites associated with the Greek gods, but no one under any circumstances should face the moral and physical danger of a Jewish synagogue, or the theater and brothel to which it is compared. It seems that for Chrysostom, Christians should conquer the gods and their places, heal heretics and their places by turning them to Christian orthodoxy, and avoid Jews and their places at all costs.

In addition to his spatial rhetoric regarding Judaism and Christian "heresy," in these same years John Chrysostom also took advantage of the cultural presumption of a significant difference between urban and rural people and places in order to further shape perceptions of religious orthodoxy. The liturgical year contained within it numerous events, such as martyrs' festival days and the Easter baptism of new church members, when Chrysostom's audience consisted of not only urban but also rural congregants. On these occasions, Chrysostom repeatedly inverted the value that he claimed his urban congregants placed on the possession and display of a formal Greek education and of material wealth in order to shame his urban congregants by praising the rural visitors in their midst. Rejecting the wealthy Christians' material luxury, Chrysostom praised rather the hard work and simplicity of the lives of the rural Christians who farmed the land around the city. Rejecting the urban Christians' pride in their *paideia,* Chrysostom praised the simplicity and deeper wisdom embodied by those whose speech and dress his urban congregants mocked in disdain. Criticizing any educated Greek-speakers who would snicker at the visitors, whose speech was apparently less formal and polished and whose appearance reflected their humble and hard-working lives, Chrysostom lauded the ascetic virtues of spiritual over material wealth, humility over pride, natural wisdom over educated sophistication.

Comparing the rural Christians to Jesus' first apostles, and their speech to the simple Greek of the Gospels, Chrysostom praised the abstemious and unadulterated orthopraxy of the rural Christians, and the simple orthodoxy of their belief. Through such rhetoric, Chrysostom challenged the "normative landscape" that he attributed to his urban audience and instead located religious orthodoxy in an idealized form outside the city walls, far from the corruption and licentiousness that he associated with the city and its inhabitants.[8] More than a congratulatory message for the rural visitors, who ostensibly did not understand well the polished Greek of Chrysostom's sermons and who in either case had already returned home on at least one occasion, this rhetoric chastised and shamed Chrysostom's urban congregants as he worked to further delineate clear regulations for Christian orthodoxy and orthopraxy in his contested city.

In light of this definition of urban and rural characteristics, the spatial transgressions that followed the Statues Riot of 387 provided an opportunity for Chrysostom to follow the logic of his rhetoric to its conclusion, the transformation of the city of Antioch into an idealized Christian place. Chrysostom described the chaos of the riot in terms that suggested that the civic order was upended, with the city's inhabitants fleeing into the countryside and those ascetics who lived in the countryside entering into the city, with the first men of the city imprisoned out of view and the first women of the city becoming public spectacles in the city's center. Such migrations not only emptied the city of its inhabitants and brought the rural ascetics into the city, but also reversed the city's traditional social order, much as Chrysostom had portrayed Christian values doing through his praise of ascetic

8. Tim Cresswell, *In Place/Out of Place: Geography, Ideology, and Transgression* (Minneapolis: University of Minnesota Press, 1996), 8.

simplicity and abstinence, and his rejection of material wealth and ostentation. Thus in the days after the riot, the populations of the city and the country traded places, and Chrysostom claimed that the result, logically previewed elsewhere in his sermons, was the momentary transformation of the city. In the absence of the corrupting forces of the urban elite and of the public theater and baths, and with the arrival of pious fear and Christian ascetic saints from the mountains, the city itself became, in Chrysostom's words, a monastery and a church, and those who remained in the city flocked to Chrysostom's church building to pray to God throughout each day, models of Christian piety. The transgression of the urban/rural divide thus allowed in Chrysostom's rhetoric the temporary and utopian Christianization of the city, as Chrysostom again relied on spatial rhetoric to narrate and shape religious orthodoxy and orthopraxy in Antioch.

The city was not, though, the only region redefined through such topographical transformations. The countryside around Antioch was populated with numerous small villages, temples, saints' shrines, and itinerant ascetics, and these likewise became contested sites in the late fourth and early fifth centuries. Theodoret and Libanius map from different perspectives the role that Christian saints, living and dead, could play in reshaping the rural landscape. Although Theodoret's fifth-century Christian texts laud the ability of Christian ascetics to make places and people Christian, Libanius's orations mourn the destruction of rural temples and accuse Christian ascetics of illegally harassing people who were performing traditional rituals (though without blood sacrifice) and celebrating festivals to the gods. The conceptual landscapes that emerge from both authors' texts are neither exclusively "real" representations nor fully "imagined"—a complexity that geographer Edward Soja explores in another context through his concept of real-and-imagined Thirdspace.[9] While Libanius, John Chrysostom, and Theodoret each offer a tinted map of the region, in which temples, martyrs, or ascetics, respectively, are particularly visible, the overall picture from their idiosyncratic representations is that the countryside was becoming more discernibly Christian, and most distinctively Nicene Christian, in the late fourth and early fifth centuries, due in large part to these newly Christian places around the ascetics and the relics of other saints—a conclusion that coincides with the archaeological evidence for the region.

John Chrysostom both confirmed and contributed to these processes in his homilies on the martyrs. On the one hand, he testified to the growing number of saints' shrines, the rituals, processions, and festivals associated with them, and the crowds participating in them, confirming that people perceived the sites of the martyrs' remains as powerful sites of religious ritual and made them more visible through their presence there. On the other hand, Chrysostom's rhetoric strove to

9. Edward Soja, *Thirdspace: Journeys to Los Angeles and Other Real-and-Imagined Places* (Malden, MA: Blackwell Publishing, 1996), esp. 1, 6.

reshape further the behavior of those in his audience, determined as he was to make the people, processions, and their associated places more closely identifiable with his conception of "orthodox" Christianity. Chrysostom's descriptions of idealized Christians whose behavior and very appearance had been transformed by their visit to the martyrs' shrines reveal his concerted effort to reshape religious orthopraxy in the region. While Chrysostom and Libanius wrote most frequently about the city of Antioch itself, the area within the walls was not the only site of the religious and political struggles of this period. From the cemeteries just outside the gates of the city and throughout the region around Antioch, places in the local landscape became important signifiers of religious identity.

The examination of places other than Antioch demonstrates that the city was not alone in late antiquity in having leaders who manipulated local and regional topography in order to promote their own authority, or that of the Christianity that they represented. Because Antioch provides so many rich sources from this period, it offers a broader picture of these processes than most other places do, and Antioch thus provides new insights into the dynamics of religious controversy elsewhere in the empire. Evidence that would perhaps have had less meaning in isolation thus becomes richer through this contextualization, allowing a fuller picture of the spatial dynamics of religious and political controversy in the Roman Empire of late antiquity.

While Peter Brown and others have, for example, noted that church leaders appropriated the charisma inherent in famous ascetics and the relics of famous martyrs in order to strengthen their own authority, often in the midst of sharp political and/or theological conflict, scholars have not always identified the spatial elements of these appropriations, the ways in which they marked the empire's places as Christian (and often a particular type of Christian), or the ways in which the growing Christian devotion at martyrs' shrines was part of the church leaders' wider efforts to manipulate places and behavior in them. Scholarship that focuses primarily on the practices of religious devotion that took place at the shrines, and the people who performed them, contributes significantly to our understanding of early Christianity and the world of late antiquity, but has not fully revealed the role of church leaders' efforts to shape those behaviors as part of a larger interest in topographical transformation. Gathering data from around the Mediterranean, and putting the rhetoric of leaders like Chrysostom, Ambrose, and Augustine together with both the practices of Christian devotion at saints' shrines and other ecclesial efforts to control local places and the behaviors performed there, newly evidences the ways in which church leaders used the shrines, the behavior at them, and the behavior en route to and from them, to differentiate orthodox Christian places, people, and practices. Contextualized within imperial legislation, these individual examples become part of a pattern by which the empire's people and landscape slowly became associated with a particular kind of Christianity. In this respect, this project may contribute to other ongoing conversations about "Christianization" and the late antique transformation of the Roman Empire.[10]

The examples from around the empire demonstrate that the evidence from Antioch is not entirely unique, but that analogous events and efforts were happening elsewhere in the empire in the same decades. This additional evidence also suggests more information about Antioch. The physical confrontations over church ownership that took place in Milan, for example, suggest that it is entirely plausible to consider Bishop Meletius's construction of a new church that contained his own body and the relics of Saint Babylas as an effort to ensure Nicene Christian control over a powerful church building when the political future was unknown. Retrospectively Bishop Meletius's church construction might be understood as the first act that demonstrated his Christian faction's decisive control over the landscape, which the emperor Theodosius's policies enforced and continued to support more strongly in future years. In light of the fact that Meletius could not have known the future, however, his building project shows that he seized an opportunity to control a powerful church building with the expectation that at any moment he and his successors could again be exiled by the changing political tides and lose control once again of Antioch's churches. We do not have narratives of physical standoffs over church buildings in fourth-century Antioch, but the stories about the conflicts in Milan and elsewhere deepen our picture of the possibilities in the decades of complex negotiations that took place in Antioch as church buildings passed from the possession of one group to another. The stories about Milan cast the efforts of Antioch's church leaders—their manipulation of relics and saints' shrines, and their rhetorical efforts to reshape the landscape and behavior in it—in a new light. The events and efforts in Antioch emerge from such an investigation as importantly local but also representing empire-wide phenomena.

Comparison of Antioch with other places in the empire also reveals the significance of the decade of the 380s in these conversations, something that would not have been as clear only from the evidence of a single city. The Theodosian Code reveals that from 380 onward emperors noticeably began to legislate the location of

---

10. The work of Liebeschuetz is foundational in these academic discussions, even if scholars continue to add nuance to his insistence on urban "decline." See, for example, the following works by J. H. W. G. Liebeschuetz: *The Decline and Fall of the Roman City* (New York: Oxford University Press, 2001); *Antioch: City and Imperial Administration in the Later Roman Empire* (Oxford: Clarendon Press, 1972); "The End of the Ancient City," in *The City in Late Antiquity*, ed. John Rich (New York: Routledge, 1992), 1–49; "Transformation and Decline: Are the Two Really Incompatible?," in *Die Stadt in der Spätantike—Niedergang oder Wandel?*, ed. Jens-Uwe Krause and Christian Witschel (Stuttgart: Franz Steiner Press, 2006), 463–83; "The Uses and Abuses of the Concept of 'Decline' in Later Roman History, or, Was Gibbon Politically Incorrect?," in *Recent Research in Late-Antique Urbanism*, ed. Luke Lavan, Journal of Roman Archaeology Supplementary Series 42 (Portsmouth, RI: Journal of Roman Archaeology, 2001), 233–38.

religious orthodoxy and orthopraxy, requiring that church buildings belong to Nicene leaders and forbidding the urban assembly of groups that they considered to be heretical. Naturally this legislation did not appear out of nowhere; church leaders' efforts to control the religious topography of their regions are documented well before this legislation, such as in the conflicts between Damasus and Ursinus in Rome in 366 and 367 and in the multiple translations of Babylas's relics in Antioch. Nevertheless, the legislation created a new legal context that gave imperial support to Nicene efforts and severely compromised those of their opponents. During the 380s, legislation made Nicene Christianity the legally supported version of Christianity in the empire, and then required all church buildings to be relinquished by those considered to be heretical; Bishop Meletius finished the church for Babylas, and was himself buried there by his side; John Chrysostom preached his anti-Judaizing rhetoric depicting the synagogue as a dangerous place; the struggles over church buildings between Bishop Ambrose and Emperor Valentinian II came to a head in Milan; Ambrose successfully prevented the altar of Victory from being restored; John Chrysostom depicted the aftermath of the Statues Riot as the Christianization of his city; and Bishop Flavian and John Chrysostom worked to increase participation at Antioch's martyr shrines while redefining the behavior associated with them.

Of course, other leaders did not easily cede the religious landscape, as can be seen in later legislation forbidding homoian Christians from continuing to meet in the city or on private land inside and outside the city walls. At this time, Libanius likewise made a case in *Pro templis* for the preservation of temples, now devoid of sacrificial practices, and Bishop Ambrose responded to Emperor Theodosius's intention to restore a synagogue in Callinicum. The 380s was a decade of unprecedented success for Nicene Christians' efforts to control the empire's landscape, although it was by no means the end of the story. It is likely not a coincidence that Egeria's pilgrimage in this period focused so explicitly on visiting places associated with her biblically based narrative of Christian history, and that, as Andrew Jacobs has shown, her view of the landscape through which she traveled was so myopically Christian.[11]

Although 415 brought an end to the lengthy Nicene/homoian episcopal schisms within the see of Antioch, when homoian Christians no longer had a separate bishop of Antioch and the two Nicene communities reconciled, it was far from the end of internal ecclesiastical conflict.[12] As the empire settled into some semblance of consistency with regard to the outcome of the first Council of Nicaea, and its implications for Trinitarian theology and doctrine, new conflicts were already under way. The success of the doctrine that the Son was of the same substance as

11. See Egeria, *Itinerarium peregrinatio;* Andrew Jacobs, *Remains of the Jews: The Holy Land and Christian Empire in Late Antiquity* (Stanford, CA: Stanford University Press, 2004).

12. See, for example, Klaus-Peter Todt, *Region und griechisch-orthodoxes Patriarchat von Antiocheia in mittelbyzantinischer Zeit und im Zeitalter der Kreuzzüge (969–1204),* 2 vols. (Wiesbaden, 1998).

God the Father did not yet resolve questions about the vocabulary with which to describe the Son's own status as fully human and fully divine, topics that were debated at the Council of Ephesus in 431 and the Council of Chalcedon in 451, and that would cause new ruptures in the church that remain to this day. The city of Antioch and those who lived there once again found themselves at the center of these new controversies, which were every bit as complicated and politically entangled as those of the fourth century had been. Like the fourth-century controversies, these too were long-lived, with consecutive emperors supporting different church leaders, and leaders of every side of the conflict fighting for the right to define religious orthodoxy. Although Antioch's Christians returned to acknowledging a single local bishop in the early fifth century, by the early sixth century the see was again torn by schism between those Antiochene Christians who supported the Miaphysite bishop Severus, and those who supported his Chalcedonian opponent, Bishop Flavian II, and his successors. Unlike the schism that followed the first Council of Nicaea, this schism has yet to be reconciled; to this day the Greek Orthodox Church identifies their bishop of Antioch as the successor to the see in the line of Chalcedonian bishops who followed the sixth-century Flavian II, while the Syrian Orthodox Church claims that the see rightfully belongs to their bishop of Antioch, successor in the line of the Miaphysite bishop Severus. Later schisms further multiplied these claims to Antioch's influential see.

Between the early fifth-century reconciliation of Antioch's episcopacy and the new schism in the early sixth century, Antiochene leaders continued to use some of the same topographical tactics to claim authority as they had used in the late fourth century. Unfortunately, though, fewer sources survive for this century, making it less possible to reconstruct the changes. The relics of the renowned first-century bishop Ignatius, for example, had a shrine in the cemetery outside the city walls that had become a place for Christian prayer and ritual celebration. Sometime during the reign of Emperor Theodosius II (408–50) Ignatius's relics seem to have been translated from the cemetery into a building that used to be the Tychaeum, and thus an important place of religious ritual with respect to the city's identity and fortune.[13] The building's new role as the resting place of Ignatius's relics reflects the continuing transformation of the city's landscape. Similarly, the relics of the famous ascetic Symeon the Stylite (d. 459) were translated to Antioch during the beginnings of the long-lasting Miaphysite/Chalcedonian schism; and Theodoret's *Historia religiosa* is only one of many sources for the role that Christian ascetics, many of them Miaphysite after the fifth century, continued to play in the Christianization of the Syrian countryside.

---

13. Wendy Mayer and Pauline Allen present and analyze the evidence for sites of Ignatius's remains in *The Churches of Syrian Antioch (300–638 C.E.)* (Walpole, MA: Peeters, 2012), esp. 81, 86, 145–46, 148–49.

The growing visibility of Christianity in Antioch's landscape was short-lived, however, in the long course of history. Despite new Christian churches in the city in the century after John Chrysostom, the sixth and seventh centuries brought with them other radical changes that forever reshaped the city's topography: the city suffered a significant earthquake and fire in 526, and a catastrophic earthquake in 528 that destroyed many of the city's buildings; in 540 Antioch was captured and burned by Persian forces; in 610 the Persians sacked the city; and in 637/8 the city was captured by Arab followers of Muhammad (d. 632), who in the decades that followed began their own projects of reshaping the city's topography. While the city became the center of a Western Christian Crusader state from the late eleventh through the thirteenth century, with Christian narratives claiming that relics again played a notable part in the city's religious transformation, the seventh-century conquest turned out to be the beginning of the end of a Christian city in the ways that John Chrysostom and his contemporaries had imagined.[14]

Work by religious studies scholars such as Jonathan Z. Smith, Kim Knott, and Thomas Tweed reveal that "the spatial turn" is significant to the study of religion far beyond Mircea Eliade's early notions of "sacred space." "Geography matters," geographers have shown, "not for the simplistic and overly used reason that everything happens in space, but because *where* things happen is critical to knowing *how* and *why* they happen."[15] Focusing on the manipulation of places and religious identity in fourth-century Antioch contributes to the sophisticated contemporary discussions in cultural geography in at least two significant ways. First, adding new historical examples to the conversation contributes new evidence of particular ways in which places have played important roles in otherwise well-known historical narratives, and studying examples from the past reveals the long-term effects of such topographical changes and the forces that influenced them. Second, focusing primarily on places associated with religious identity, orthopraxy, and orthodoxy highlights the particular significance of religion to understanding the dynamics of place and politics, and the powerful narratives in which they participate, not only in the ancient world, but also in our world today. Although modern Western concepts of what constitutes "religion" and of religion's

14. For some of this history, see Hugh Kennedy, "Antioch: From Byzantium to Islam and Back Again," in *The City in Late Antiquity,* ed. John Rich (New York: Routledge, 1992), 181–98; Todt, *Region und griechisch-orthodoxes Patriarchat von Antiocheia;* Bernd Andreas Vest, "Les sources médiévales dites 'orientales' (syriaques, arabes, arméniennes et autres) concernant l'histoire de la ville d'Antioche et sa topographie," in *Les sources de l'histoire du paysage urbain d'Antioche sur l'Oronte* (Paris: Université Paris 8, Vincennes-Saint-Denis, 2012), 179–202; Todt, "Antioch in Byzantine Sources of the 8th–13th Centuries," ibid., 203–22.

15. Barney Warf and Santa Arias, "Introduction: The Reinsertion of Space into the Social Sciences and Humanities," in *The Spatial Turn: Interdisciplinary Perspectives,* ed. Barney Warf and Santa Arias (New York: Routledge, 2009), 1.

relation to other components of society, such as politics, are radically different from those in the Roman Empire in late antiquity, studying the latter can still lead to analyses and information that can be productive for the former.

Demonstrating the power dynamics of controlling the places of fourth-century Antioch might, for example, facilitate a deeper understanding of the complex dynamics of Israeli "settlements" in Palestinian territory; explain some of the challenges that a country will face as long as individuals' primary political identity is, for example, Sunni or Shi'i instead of Iraqi; give voice to some of the silent forces at play in, for example, Kurdish bids for, and other nations' opposition to, an independent Kurdistan; and it provides a sharp reminder about the erasure of cultures and people that can too easily happen when places are renamed and redefined without attention to the power dynamics involved and active care for those who are disenfranchised. Studying the spatial politics of religious controversy in fourth-century Antioch thus reshapes traditional narratives about the definition of Christian orthodoxy and the processes of "Christianization" in the Roman Empire in late antiquity, or, more specifically, the means by which the empire's people and places came to be more closely associated with Nicene Christianity. It also, I hope, brings to light some of the powerful physical and rhetorical mechanisms through which the control over and transformation of places contested by any rival communities can shape individual and community identity, and perceptions of religious truth.

BIBLIOGRAPHY

SELECTED PRIMARY SOURCES

Ambrose. *Epistulae.* Text in *Sancti Ambrosi Opera, pars 10, Epistulae et acta,* edited by M. Zelzer. CSEL 82.3. Vienna: F. Tempsky, 1982.

Ammianus Marcellinus. *Res gestae* 22. Text and English translation in *Ammianus Marcellinus: History, XX–XXVI,* edited by John Rolfe. Cambridge, MA: Harvard University Press, 2006.

Augustine. *Confessiones.* Text in *Augustine: Confessions,* vol. 1, *Introduction and Text,* edited by James O'Donnell. Oxford: Clarendon Press, 1992.

———. *Epistula* 22. Text in *Sancti Aureli Augustini Hipponiensis Episcopi Epistulae,* edited by A. Goldbacher. CSEL 34.1. Vienna: Tempsky, 1895.

Basil of Caesarea. *Epistula* 57. Text and French translation in *Saint Basile: Correspondance,* vol. 1, *Letters 1–100,* edited by Yves Courtonne. Paris: Les Belles Lettres, 2003.

Codex Theodosianus. Text in *Codex Theodosianus,* vol. 1, *Theodosiani libri XVI cum constitutionibus Sirmondianis,* edited by Paul Krueger and Theodor Mommsen. Hildesheim: Weidmann, 2000. English translation in *The Theodosian Code and Novels and the Sirmondia Constitutions: A Translation with Commentary, Glossary, and Bibliography,* translated by Clyde Pharr. Union, NJ: The Lawbook Exchange, 2001.

Gregory of Nyssa. *Oratio funebris in Meletium episcopum.* Text in *Gregorii Nysseni Opera,* 9:441–57, edited by Gunter Heil. Leiden: Brill, 1967.

John Chrysostom. *Ad finem ieiunii.* Text in PG 49.197–212.

———. *Adversus Iudaeos.* Text in PG 48.843–942. English translation in *St. John Chrysostom: Discourses against Judaizing Christians,* translated by Paul W. Harkins. FC 68. Washington, DC: Catholic University of America Press, 1979.

———. *Catecheses.* Text and French translation in *Jean Chrysostome: Huit catechèses baptismales inédites,* edited by Antoine Wenger. SC 50. 3rd ed. Paris: Éditions du Cerf, 1985.

English translation of *Cat.* 8 in *John Chrysostom*, edited by Wendy Mayer and Pauline Allen. The Early Church Fathers. New York: Routledge, 2000. English translation of all the homilies in *St. John Chrysostom: Baptismal Instructions*, edited by Paul Harkins. ACW 31. New York: Newman Press, 1963.

———. *De incomprehensibili natura dei, hom.* 1–5. Text and French translation in *Sur l'incompréhensibilité de Dieu*, edited by A.-M. Malingrey et al. SC 28bis. Paris: Éditions du Cerf, 1970. English translation in *St. John Chrysostom: On the Incomprehensible Nature of God*, translated by Paul Harkins. FC 72. Washington, DC: Catholic University of America Press, 1984.

———. *De incomprehensibili natura dei, hom.* 7–12. Text and French translation in *Sur l'égalité du Père et du Fils*, edited by A.-M. Malingrey. SC 396. Paris: Éditions du Cerf, 1994. English translation in *St. John Chrysostom: On the Incomprehensible Nature of God*, translated by Paul Harkins. FC 72. Washington, DC: Catholic University of America Press, 1984.

———. *De Lazaro.* Text in PG 48.963–1044. English translation in *St. John Chrysostom: On Wealth and Poverty*, translated by Catharine Roth. Crestwood, NY: St. Vladimir's Seminary Press, 1984.

———. *De sancta Droside.* Text in PG 50.683–94. English translation in *St. John Chrysostom, The Cult of the Saints: Select Homilies and Letters*, translated by Wendy Mayer with Bronwen Neil. New York: St. Vladimir's Seminary Press, 2006.

———. *De sancta Pelagia.* Text in PG.579–84. English translation in *"Let Us Die That We May Live": Greek Homilies on Christian Martyrs from Asia Minor, Palestine, and Syria (c. AD 350–AD 450)*, translated by Johan Leemans, Wendy Mayer, Pauline Allen, and Boudewijn Dehandschutter. New York: Routledge, 2003.

———. *De sanctis martyribus.* Text in PG 50.645–54. English translation in *"Let Us Die that We May Live": Greek Homilies on Christian Martyrs from Asia Minor, Palestine, and Syria (c. AD 350–AD 450)*, translated by Johan Leemans, Wendy Mayer, Pauline Allen, and Boudewijn Dehandschutter. New York: Routledge, 2003.

———. *De sancto Babyla.* Text and French translation in *Jean Chrysostome: Discours sur Babylas*, edited by M. A. Schatkin et al. SC 362. Paris: Éditions du Cerf, 1990. English translation in *Saint John Chrysostom: Apologist*, translated by Margaret Schatkin and Paul Harkins. FC 73. Washington, DC: Catholic University of America Press, 1983.

———. *De sancto hieromartyre Babyla.* Text and French translation in *Jean Chrysostome: Discours sur Babylas*, edited by M. A. Schatkin et al. SC 362. Paris: Éditions du Cerf, 1990. English translation in *"Let Us Die that We May Live": Greek Homilies on Christian Martyrs from Asia Minor, Palestine, and Syria (c. AD 350–AD 450)*, translated by Johan Leemans, Wendy Mayer, Pauline Allen, and Boudewijn Dehandschutter. New York: Routledge, 2003.

———. *De sancto Meletio.* Text in PG 50.515–20. English translation in *St. John Chrysostom, The Cult of the Saints: Select Homilies and Letters*, translated by Wendy Mayer with Bronwen Neil. New York: St. Vladimir's Seminary Press, 2006.

———. *De statuis* 2–21. Text in PG 49.33–222. English translation of *De statuis* 17 in *John Chrysostom*, edited by Wendy Mayer and Pauline Allen. The Early Church Fathers. New York: Routledge, 2000.

———. *De terrae motu.* Text in PG 50.713–16.

————. *Homilia 3 in Titus*. Text in PG 62.

————. *In ascensionem*. Text in PG 50.441–52.

————. *In martyres*. Text in PG 50.661–66. English translation in *John Chrysostom*, edited by Wendy Mayer and Pauline Allen. The Early Church Fathers. New York: Routledge, 2000.

————. *In s. Ignatium*. Text in PG 50.587–96. English translation in *St. John Chrysostom, The Cult of the Saints: Select Homilies and Letters*, translated by Wendy Mayer with Bronwen Neil. New York: St. Vladimir's Seminary Press, 2006.

————. *In s. Iulianum martyrem*. Text in PG 50.665–76. English translation in *"Let Us Die That We May Live": Greek Homilies on Christian Martyrs from Asia Minor, Palestine, and Syria (c. AD 350–AD 450)*, translated by Johan Leemans, Wendy Mayer, Pauline Allen, and Boudewijn Dehandschutter. New York: Routledge, 2003.

————. *In s. Lucianum*. Text in PG 50.519–26. English translation in *St. John Chrysostom, The Cult of the Saints: Select Homilies and Letters*, translated by Wendy Mayer with Bronwen Neil. New York: St. Vladimir's Seminary Press, 2006.

Julian. *Misopōgōn*. Text and English translation in *The Works of the Emperor Julian*, vol. 2, edited by Wilmer Cave Wright. New York: Putnam, 1923.

Libanius. *Encomium 7*. Text and English translation in *Libanius's Progymnasmata: Model Exercises in Greek Prose Composition and Rhetoric*, edited by Craig Gibson. Writings from the Greco-Roman World 10. Atlanta: Society of Biblical Literature, 2008.

————. *Epistula 6*. Text and English translation in *Libanius: Autobiography and Selected Letters*, vol. 1, edited by A. F. Norman. Cambridge, MA: Harvard University Press, 1992.

————. *Oratio 60*. Text in *Libanii Opera*, vol. 4, edited by Richard Foerster. Leipzig: Teubner, 1908.

————. *Orationes 1, 15*. Text and English translation in *Libanius: Autobiography and Selected Letters*, vol. 1, edited by A. F. Norman. Cambridge, MA: Harvard University Press, 1992.

————. *Orationes 22, 30*. Text and English translation in *Libanius: Selected Orations*, vol. 2, edited by A. F. Norman. Cambridge, MA: Harvard University Press, 1977.

Severus of Minorca. *Epistula Severi*. Text and English translation in *Severus of Minorca: Letter on the Conversion of the Jews*, edited by Scott Bradbury. Oxford: Clarendon Press, 1996.

Sozomen. *Historia ecclesiastica*. Text in *Sozomenos, Historia ecclesiastica: Kirchengeschichte*, vol. 2, edited by Günther C. Hansen. Fontes Christiani 73/2. Turnhout, Belgium: Brepols, 2004.

Theodoret. *Historia ecclesiastica*. Text and French translation in *Théodoret de Cyr, Histoire Ecclésiastique, vol. 1 (I–II)*, edited by Léon Parmentier and Günther C. Hansen. SC 501. Paris: Les Éditions du Cerf, 2006.

————. *Historia religiosa*. Text and French translation in *Théodoret de Cyr, Histoire des moines de Syrie (I–XIII)*, vol. 1, edited by Pierre Canivet and Alice Leroy-Molinghen. SC 234. 1977. Reprint, Paris: Les Éditions du Cerf, 2006. English translation in *A History of the Monks of Syria, by Theodoret of Cyrrhus*, translated by Richard Price. Kalamazoo, MI: Cistercian Publications, 1985.

SECONDARY SOURCES

Adams, Paul, Steven Hoelscher, and Karen Till, eds. *Textures of Place: Exploring Humanist Geographies*. Minneapolis: University of Minnesota Press, 2001.

Alcock, Susan. *Archaeologies of the Greek Past: Landscape, Monuments, and Memories*. New York: Cambridge University Press, 2002.

Alissandratos, Julia. "The Structure of the Funeral Oration in John Chrysostom's *Eulogy of Meletius*." *Byzantine Studies* 7.2 (1980): 182–98.

Allen, John. "Introduction." In *Human Geography Today*, edited by Doreen Massey, John Allen, and Philip Sarre, 43–45. Malden, MA: Polity Press, 1999.

———. "Spatial Assemblages of Power: From Domination to Empowerment." In *Human Geography Today*, edited by Doreen Massey, John Allen, and Philip Sarre, 194–218. Malden, MA: Polity Press, 1999.

Anderson, Benedict. *Imagined Communities: Reflections on the Origin and Spread of Nationalism*. London: Verso, 1983.

Anderson, Kay, and Fay Gale. *Inventing Places: Studies in Cultural Geography*. Melbourne: Longman Chesire/Wiley Halsted Press, 1992.

Ando, Clifford. *Roman Religion*. Edinburgh Readings on the Ancient World. Edinburgh: Edinburgh University Press, 2003.

Andrews, John. *Meaning, Knowledge, and Power in the Map Philosophy of J. B. Harley*. Trinity Papers in Geography 6. Dublin: Department of Geography, Trinity College, 1994.

Antioch-on-the-Orontes. Vol. 1, *The Excavations of 1932*, edited by George W. Elderkin. Publications of the Committee for the Excavation of Antioch and Its Vicinity. Princeton, NJ: Princeton University Press, 1934.

———. Vol. 2, *The Excavations, 1933–1936*, edited by Richard Stillwell. Princeton, NJ: Princeton University Press, 1938.

———. Vol. 3, *The Excavations, 1937–1939*, edited by Richard Stillwell. Princeton, NJ: Princeton University Press, 1941.

———. Vol. 4.1, *Ceramics and Islamic Coins*, edited by Frederick O. Waagé. Princeton, NJ: Princeton University Press, 1948.

———. Vol. 4.2, *Greek, Roman, Byzantine, and Crusaders' Coins*, edited by Dorothy B. Waagé. Princeton, NJ: Princeton University Press, 1952.

Anzaldúa, Gloria. *Borderlands/La Frontera: The New Mestiza*. San Francisco: Spinsters/Aunt Lute Press, 1987.

Assmann, Aleida. *Cultural Memory and Western Civilization: Functions, Media, Archives*. New York: Cambridge University Press, 2011.

L'Association pour l'Antiquité Tardive, ed. *L'Empereur Julien et son temps*. Antiquité Tardive 17. Turnhout, Belgium: Brepols, 2009.

Athanassiadi-Fowden, Polymnia. *Julian and Hellenism: An Intellectual Biography*. New York: Oxford University Press, 1981.

Ayres, Lewis. *Nicaea and Its Legacy: An Approach to Fourth-Century Trinitarian Theology*. New York: Oxford University Press, 2004.

Baker-Brian, Nicholas. "The Politics of Virtue in Julian's *Misopogon*." In *Emperor and Author: The Writings of Julian the Apostate*, edited by Nicholas Baker-Brian and Shaun Tougher, 263–80. Swansea: The Classical Press of Wales, 2012.

Baldovin, John. "Relics, Martyrs, and the Eucharist." *Liturgical Ministry* 12 (2003): 9–19.

———. *The Urban Character of Christian Worship: The Origins, Development, and Meaning of Stational Liturgy*. Rome: Pontificium Institutum Studiorum Orientalium, 1987.

Banchich, T.M. "Eunapius on Libanius' Refusal of a Prefecture." *Phoenix* 39.4 (1985): 384–86.

Barnes, Timothy D. "Ambrose and the Basilicas of Milan in 385 and 386: The Primary Documents and Their Implications." *Zeitschrift für antikes Christentum* 4 (2000): 289–99.

———. *Athanasius and Constantius: Theology and Politics in the Constantinian Empire.* Cambridge, MA: Harvard University Press, 1993.

Bauer, Franz Alto. "Urban Space and Ritual: Constantinople in Late Antiquity." *Acta ad Archaeologiam et Atrium Historiam Pertinentia* 15, n.s. 1 (2001): 27–61.

Baur, Chrysostomus. *John Chrysostom and His Time.* Vol. 1. Westminster, MD: The Newman Press, 1959.

Beard, Mary, John North, and Simon Price. *Religions of Rome.* Vol. 1, *A History.* Cambridge: Cambridge University Press, 1998.

Belayche, N. "Une panégyrie antiochéenne: Le maïouma." In *Antioche de Syrie: Histoire, images et traces de la ville antique, colloque de Lyon [octobre 2001],* edited by B. Cabouret, P.-L. Gatier, and C. Saliou, 401–15. . Topoi Suppl. 5. Lyon: Maison de l'Orient et de la Méditerranée, 2004.

Bidez, J., ed. *La vie de L'Empereur Julien.* Paris: Société d'Édition "Les Belles Lettres," 1965.

———. *L'Empereur Julien, Oeuvres completes.* Vol. 2. Paris: Société d'Édition "Les Belles Lettres," 1932.

Bitton-Ashkelony, Brouria. *Encountering the Sacred: The Debate on Christian Pilgrimage in Late Antiquity.* Berkeley: University of California Press, 2005.

Bonner, Stanley. *Education in Ancient Rome: From the Elder Cato to the Younger Pliny.* Berkeley: University of California Press, 1977.

Boone, Marc. "Urban Space and Political Conflict in Late Medieval Flanders." *Journal of Interdisciplinary History* 32.4 (2002): 621–40.

Bouffartigue, Jean. "Julien entre biographie et analyse historique." *Antiquité Tardive* 17 (2009): 79–89.

———. "L'image politique de Julien chez Libanios." *Pallas* 60 (2002): 175–89.

Bourdieu, Pierre. *Outline of a Theory of Practice.* New York: Cambridge University Press, 1977.

Bowersock, Glen. *Julian the Apostate.* Cambridge, MA: Harvard University Press, 1978.

Bowes, Kim. "'Christianization' and the Rural Home." *JECS* 15.2 (2007): 143–70.

———. *Houses and Society in the Later Roman Empire.* London: Duckworth, 2010.

———. *Private Worship, Public Values, and Religious Change in Late Antiquity.* New York: Cambridge University Press, 2008.

Boyarin, Daniel. *Border Lines: The Partition of Judaeo-Christianity.* Philadelphia: University of Pennsylvania Press, 2004.

Bradbury, Scott. "Constantine and the Problem of Anti-Pagan Legislation in the Fourth Century." *Classical Philology* 89.2 (1994): 120–39.

———. "Julian's Pagan Revival and the Decline of Blood Sacrifice." *Phoenix* 49.4 (1995): 331–56.

Brakke, David. *Athanasius and Asceticism.* Baltimore: Johns Hopkins University Press, 1995.

———. *Demons and the Making of the Monk: Spiritual Combat in Early Christianity.* Cambridge, MA: Harvard University Press, 2006.

Brands, Gunnar. "Antiochia in der Spätantike." Forthcoming.

———. "Antioch on the Orontes." In *Archaeology of Late Antiquity*, edited by Leonard Rutgers, Olof Brandt, and Jodi Magness. Cambridge: Cambridge University Press, forthcoming.

———. "Die spätantike Stadt und ihre Christianisierung." In *Die spätantike Stadt und ihre Christianisierung: Symposion vom 14. bis 16. Februar 2000 in Halle/Saale*, edited by Gunnar Brands and Hans-Georg Severin, 1–26. Wiesbaden: Reichert Press, 2003.

Brands, Gunnar, and Ulrich Weferling. "Ein neuer Stadtplan für Antiochia." *Jahrbuch des Deutschen Archäologischen Instituts.* Forthcoming.

Brennecke, Hanns Christof. *Studien zur Geschichte der Homöer: Der Osten bis zum Ende der homöischen Reichskirche.* Tübingen: J. C. B. Mohr/Paul Siebeck, 1988.

Brock, Sebastian. "Greek and Syriac in Late Antique Syria." In *Literacy and Power in the Ancient World*, edited by Alan Bowman and Greg Woolf, 149–60. New York: Cambridge University Press, 1994.

Brown, Peter. *The Cult of the Saints: Its Rise and Function in Latin Christianity.* Chicago: University of Chicago Press, 1981.

———. "Enjoying the Saints in Late Antiquity." *Early Medieval Europe* 9 (2000): 1–24.

———. *Power and Persuasion in Late Antiquity: Towards a Christian Empire.* Madison: University of Wisconsin Press, 1992.

———. "The Rise and Function of the Holy Man in Late Antiquity." *Journal of Roman Studies* 61 (1971): 80–101.

———. "The Rise and Function of the Holy Man in Late Antiquity, 1971–1997." *JECS* 6.3 (1998): 353–76.

———. *Through the Eye of a Needle: Wealth, the Fall of Rome, and the Making of Christianity in the West, 350–550 AD.* Princeton, NJ: Princeton University Press, 2012.

Browning, Robert. *The Emperor Julian.* Berkeley: University of California Press, 1976.

———. "The Riot of A.D. 387 in Antioch: The Role of the Theatrical Claques in the Later Empire." *The Journal of Roman Studies* 42.1–2 (1952): 13–20.

Burns, Ross. *The Monuments of Syria: A Guide.* New York: I. B. Tauris, 2009.

Butcher, Kevin. *Roman Syria and the Near East.* London: The British Museum Press, 2003.

Cabouret, Bernadette. "Le gouverneur au temps de Libanios: Image et réalité." *Pallas* 60 (2002): 191–204.

Callard, Felicity. "Doreen Massey." In *Key Thinkers on Space and Place*, edited by Phil Hubbard, Rob Kitchin, and Gill Valentine, 219–25. Thousand Oaks, CA: Sage Publications, 2004.

Cameron, Alan. *The Last Pagans of Rome.* New York: Oxford University Press, 2011.

Canfora, Fabrizio. *Simmaco e Ambrogio, o di un' antica controversia sulla tolleranza e sull' intolleranza.* Bari: Adriatica Editrice, 1970.

Carruthers, Mary. *The Craft of Thought: Meditation, Rhetoric, and the Making of Images, 400–1200.* New York: Cambridge University Press, 1998.

Casana, Jesse. "The Archaeological Landscape of Late Roman Antioch." In *Culture and Society in Later Roman Antioch*, edited by Isabella Sandwell and Janet Huskinson, 102–25. Oxford: Oxbow Books, 2004.

Caseau, Béatrice. "Religious Intolerance and Pagan Statuary." In *The Archaeology of Late Antique "Paganism,"* edited by Luke Lavan and Michael Mulryan, 479–502. Boston: Brill, 2011.

Casella, Marinela. "Les spectacles à Antioche d'après Libanios." *Antiquité Tardive* 15 (2007): 99–112.

Castles, Stephen, and Alastair Davidson. *Citizenship and Migration: Globalization and the Politics of Belonging.* New York: Routledge, 2000.

Chadwick, Henry. "The Fall of Eustathius of Antioch." *JThS* 49 (OS) (1948): 27–35.

Chin, Catherine. "The Bishop's Two Bodies: Ambrose and the Basilicas of Milan." *CH* 79.3 (2010): 531–55.

———. *Grammar and Christianity in the Late Roman World.* Philadelphia: University of Pennsylvania Press, 2008.

Chitty, Derwas. *The Desert a City: An Introduction to the Study of Egyptian and Palestinian Monasticism under the Christian Empire.* Oxford: Blackwell Press, 1966.

Ciggaar, Krijnie. "Antioche: Les sources croisées et le plan de la ville." In *Les sources de l'histoire du paysage urbain d'Antioche sur l'Oronte,* 223–34. Paris: Université Paris 8, Vincennes-Saint-Denis, 2012.

Clark, Elizabeth. "Claims on the Bones of Saint Stephen: The Partisans of Melania and Eudocia." *CH* 51.2 (1982): 141–56.

Clegg, Stewart. *Frameworks of Power.* London: Sage, 1989.

Colish, Marcia. *Ambrose's Patriarchs: Ethics for the Common Man.* Notre Dame, IN: University of Notre Dame Press, 2005.

———. "Why the Portiana? Reflections on the Milanese Basilica Crisis of 386." *JECS* 10.3 (2002): 361–72.

Connerton, Paul. *How Societies Remember.* New York: Cambridge University Press, 1989.

Cooper, Kate. *The Fall of the Roman Household.* New York: Cambridge University Press, 2007.

Cosgrove, Denis. "Mapping New Worlds: Culture and Cartography in Sixteenth-Century Venice." *Imago Mundi* 44 (1992): 65–89.

Costambeys, Marios, and Conrad Leyser. "To be the Neighbour of St. Stephen: Patronage, Martyr Cult, and Roman Monasteries, c. 600–c. 900." In *Religion, Dynasty, and Patronage in Early Christian Rome, 300–900,* edited by Kate Cooper and Julia Hillner, 262–87. New York: Cambridge University Press, 2007.

Crawford, Catherine Lyon. "Collecting, Defacing, Reinscribing (and Otherwise Performing) Memory in the Ancient World." In *Negotiating the Past in the Past: Identity, Memory, and Landscape in Archaeological Research,* edited by Norman Yoffee, 10–42. Tucson: University of Arizona Press, 2007.

Cresswell, Tim. *In Place/Out of Place: Geography, Ideology, and Transgression.* Minneapolis: University of Minnesota Press, 1996.

Cribiore, Raffaella. *Gymnastics of the Mind: Greek Education in Hellenistic and Roman Egypt.* Princeton, NJ: Princeton University Press, 2001.

———. *Libanius the Sophist: Rhetoric, Reality, and Religion in the Fourth Century.* Ithaca: Cornell University Press, 2013.

———. *The School of Libanius in Late Antique Antioch.* Princeton, NJ: Princeton University Press, 2007.

———. "The Value of a Good Education: Libanius and Public Authority." In *A Companion to Late Antiquity,* edited by Philip Rousseau, 233–45. Malden, MA: Wiley-Blackwell, 2009.

Cribiore, Raffaella, Paolo Davoli, and David M. Ratzan. "A Teacher's Dipinto from Trimithis (Dakhleh Oasis)." *Journal of Roman Archaeology* 21 (2008): 170–91.

Criscuolo, Ugo. "Libanio e Giuliano." *Vichiana* 11 (1982): 70–87.

Cumont, Franz. *After Life in Roman Paganism.* New Haven, CT: Yale University Press, 1922.

Cunningham, Mary, and Pauline Allen, eds. *Preacher and Audience: Studies in Early Christian and Byzantine Homiletics.* Leiden: Brill, 1998.

Curran, John. *Pagan City and Christian Capital: Rome in the Fourth Century.* Oxford: Clarendon Press, 2000.

Dally, Ortwin. "'Pflege' und Umnutzung heidnischer Tempel in der Spätantike." In *Die spätantike Stadt und ihre Christianisierung: Symposion vom 14. bis 16. Februar 2000 in Halle/Saale,* edited by Gunnar Brands and Hans-Georg Severin, 98–114. Wiesbaden: Reichert Press, 2003.

Dassmann, E. "Ambrosius und die Märtyrer." *JAC* 18 (1975): 49–68.

Davis, Stephen. *The Cult of St. Thecla: A Tradition of Women's Piety in Late Antiquity.* New York: Oxford University Press, 2001.

de Certeau, Michel. *The Practice of Everyday Life.* Translated by Steven Rendall. Berkeley: University of California Press, 1984.

De Giorgi, Andrea. "The Formation of a Roman landscape: The Case of Antioch." *Journal of Roman Archaeology* 20 (2007): 283–98.

DeLyser, Dydia. "When Less Is More: Absence and Landscape in a California Ghost Town." In *Textures of Place: Exploring Humanist Geographies,* edited by Paul Adams, Steven Hoelscher, and Karen Till, 24–40. Minneapolis: University of Minnesota Press, 2001.

Derda, Tomasz, Tomasz Markiewicz, and Ewa Wipszycka, eds. *Alexandria: Auditoria of Kom el-Dikka and Late Antique Education.* Journal of Juristic Papyrology Supplement 8. Warsaw: Journal of Juristic Papyrology, 2007.

Derks, Ton. "The Transformation of Landscape and Religious Representations in Roman Gaul." *Archaeological Dialogues* 4.2 (1997): 126–47.

DeRogatis, Amy. *Moral Geography: Maps, Missionaries, and the American Frontier.* New York: Columbia University Press, 2003.

de Wet, Chris. "The Priestly Body: Power-Discourse and Identity in John Chrysostom's *De Sacerdotio.*" *Religion & Theology* 18 (2011): 351–79.

———. "A Walk through the City with John Chrysostom: Toward a Psychogeography of the Urban Ascetic." *Religion and Theology.* Forthcoming.

Digeser, Elizabeth. "An Oracle of Apollo at Daphne and the Great Persecution." *Classical Philology* 99.1 (2004): 57–77.

Dijkstra, Jitse. "The Fate of the Temples in Late Antique Egypt." In *The Archaeology of Late Antique "Paganism,"* edited by Luke Lavan and Michael Mulryan, 389–436. Boston: Brill, 2011.

Dorival, Gilles. "Cyniques et chrétiens au temps des pères grecs." In *Valeurs dans le stoicism: Du portique à nos jours,* edited by M. Soetard, 57–88. Lille: Presses Universitaires de Lille, 1993.

Douglas, Mary. *Purity and Danger: An Analysis of the Concepts of Pollution and Taboo.* New York: Routledge, 1966.

Downey, Glanville. *Ancient Antioch.* Princeton, NJ: Princeton University Press, 1963.

———. *Antioch in the Age of Theodosius the Great.* Norman, OK: University of Oklahoma Press, 1962.

———. *A History of Antioch in Syria: From Seleucus to the Arab Conquest*. Princeton, NJ: Princeton University Press, 1961.

———. "The Olympic Games of Antioch in the Fourth Century A.D." *Transactions and Proceedings of the American Philological Association* 70 (1939): 428–38.

Drecoll, Carsten. "Sophisten und Archonten: *Paideia* als gesellschaftliches Argument bei Libanios." In *Philosophia Togata: Essays on Philosophy and Roman Society*, edited by M. Griffin and J. Barnes, 403–17. New York: Oxford, 1989.

Drijvers, Jan Willem. *Cyril of Jerusalem: Bishop and City*. Boston: Brill, 2004.

———. *Helena Augusta: The Mother of Constantine the Great and the Legend of Her Finding the True Cross*. Leiden: E. J. Brill, 1992.

———. "Promoting Jerusalem: Cyril and the True Cross." In *Portraits of Spiritual Authority: Religious Power in Early Christianity, Byzantium, and the Christian Orient*, edited by Jan Willem Drijvers and John Watt, 79–95. Religions in the Graeco-Roman World 137. Boston: E. J. Brill, 1999.

Duindam, Jeroen, Jill Harries, Caroline Humfress, and Nimrod Hurvitz, eds. *Law and Empire*. Boston: Brill, 2013.

Dünzl, Franz. "Die Absetzung des Bischofs Meletius von Antiochien 361 N.C." *Jahrbuch für Antike und Christentum* 43 (2000): 71–93.

Durmaz, Reyhan. "Reconstructing the Mount Athos of the East: Christian Hierotopy of Tur ʾAbdin in Late Antiquity." Paper presented at the VI North American Syriac Symposium (Duke University, June 2011).

———. "Tur ʾAbdin at Close: The Church Complex at Zaz, Mardin, Its Architecture, History, and Contemporary Revitalization Process." Masters thesis, Koç University, Turkey, 2010.

Duval, Yvette. *Auprès des saints, corps et âme: L'inhumantion "ad sanctos" dans la chrétienité d'Orient et d'Occident du IIIe au VIIe siècle*. Paris: Études Augustiniennes, 1988.

Duvette, Catherine, Bertrand Riba, and Marion Rivoal. "Évolution démographique et modes d'occupation du sol en Syrie du Nord: Les cas du Ǧebel Waṣṭāni, du Ǧebel Zāwiye et des marges arides (IIe-VIIe s.)." *Antiquité Tardive* 20 (2012): 87–104.

Ebbeler, Jennifer, and Cristiana Sogno. "Religious Identity and the Politics of Patronage: Symmachus and Augustine." *Historia: Zeitschrift für alte Geschichte* 56.2 (2007): 230–42.

Eliade, Mircea. *The Sacred and the Profane: The Nature of Religion*. San Diego: Harcourt Brace Jovanovich, 1959.

Eliav, Yaron. *God's Mountain: The Temple Mount in Time, Place, and Memory*. Baltimore: Johns Hopkins University Press, 2005.

Elliott, Tom. "Was the *Tomus ad Antiochenos* a Pacific Document?" *Journal of Ecclesiastical History* 58 (2007): 1–8.

Elm, Susanna. *Sons of Hellenism, Fathers of the Church: Emperor Julian, Gregory of Nazianzus, and the Vision of Rome*. Berkeley: University of California Press, 2012.

Elsner, Jaś. *Art and the Roman Viewer: The Transformation of Art from the Pagan World to Christianity*. New York: Cambridge University Press, 1995.

Elsner, Jaś, and Ian Rutherford, eds. *Pilgrimage in Graeco-Roman & Early Christian Antiquity: Seeing the Gods*. New York: Oxford University Press, 2005.

Eltester, W. "Die Kirchen Antiochias im IV. Jahrhundert." *ZNTW* 36 (1937): 251–86.

Emmel, Stephen. "Shenoute of Atripe and the Christian Destruction of Temples in Egypt: Rhetoric and Reality." In *From Temple to Church: Destruction and Renewal of Local*

Cultic Topography in Late Antiquity, edited by Johannes Hahn, Stephen Emmel, and Ulrich Gotter, 161–201. Boston: Brill, 2008.

Festugière, A.-J. *Antioche païenne et chrétienne: Libanius, Chrysostome et les moines de Syrie.* Paris: Éditions E. de Boccard, 1959.

Flinterman, Jaap-Jan. "Sophists and Emperors: A Reconnaissance of Sophistic Attitudes." In *Paideia: The World of the Second Sophistic*, edited by Barbara Borg, 359–76. New York: Walter de Gruyter, 2004.

Flower, Harriet. *The Art of Forgetting: Disgrace and Oblivion in Roman Political Culture.* Chapel Hill, NC: University of North Carolina Press, 2006.

Fonrobert, Charlotte. "Jewish Christians, Judaizers, and Christian Anti-Judaism." In *Late Ancient Christianity*, edited by Virginia Burrus, 234–54. Minneapolis: Fortress Press, 2005.

Fontaine, Jacques. "Une polémique stylistique instructive dans la 'lettre encyclique' de Sévère de Minorque." In *Eulogia: Mélanges offerts à A. R. Bastiaensen à l'occasion de son soizante-cinquième anniversaire*, edited by G. J. M. Bartelink, 119–35. Steenbrugis: Abbatia S. Petri, 1991.

Fowden, Elizabeth Key. *The Barbarian Plain: Saint Sergius between Rome and Iran.* Berkeley: University of California Press, 1999.

Fowden, Garth. "Bishops and Temples in the Eastern Roman Empire, A.D. 320–435." *JThSt* 29.1 (1978): 53–78.

Francesio, Maria. *L'idea di città in Libanio.* Stuttgart: Franz Steiner Press, 2004.

Frank, Georgia. *The Memory of the Eyes: Pilgrims to Living Saints in Christian Late Antiquity.* Berkeley: University of California Press, 2000.

———. "Pilgrimage." In *The Oxford Handbook of Early Christian Studies*, edited by Susan Ashbrook Harvey and David Hunter, 826–41. New York: Oxford University Press, 2008.

Frankfurter, David, ed. *Pilgrimage and Holy Space in Late Antique Egypt.* Boston: Brill, 1998.

———. *Religion in Roman Egypt: Assimilation and Resistance.* Princeton, NJ: Princeton University Press, 1998.

———. "Stylites and *Phallobatēs*: Pillar Religions in Late Antique Syria." *VC* 44 (1990): 168–98.

———. "Where the Spirits Dwell: Possession, Christianization, and Saints' Shrines in Late Antiquity." *Harvard Theological Review* 103.1 (2010): 27–46.

Fredriksen, Paula. "Paul and Augustine: Conversion Narratives, Orthodox Traditions, and the Retrospective Self." *JThSt* 37.1 (1986): 3–34.

French, Dorothea. "Rhetoric and the Rebellion of A.D. 387 in Antioch." *Historia: Zeitschrift für alte Geschichte* 47.4 (1998): 468–84.

Fretter, Andrew. "Place Marketing: A Local Authority Perspective." In *Selling Places: The City as Cultural Capital, Past and Present*, edited by Gerry Kearns and Chris Philo, 163–74. New York: Pergamon Press, 1993.

Gainzarain, Pedro. "La lengua de Libanio." *Veleia* 4 (1987): 229–53.

Gesler, Wilbert. *Healing Places.* Lanham, MD: Rowman & Littlefield Publishers, 2003.

Gibbs, Laura, trans. *Aesop's Fables.* New York: Oxford University Press, 2008.

Gibson, Craig. *Libanius's Progymnasmata: Model Exercises in Greek Prose Composition and Rhetoric.* Writings from the Greco-Roman World 10. Atlanta: Society of Biblical Literature, 2008.

Gleason, Maud. *Making Men: Sophists and Self-Presentation in Ancient Rome.* Princeton, NJ: Princeton University Press, 1995.

Goehring, James. *Ascetics, Society, and the Desert: Studies in Early Egyptian Monasticism.* Harrisburg, PA: Trinity Press International, 1999.

——. "The Dark Side of Landscape: Ideology and Power in the Christian Myth of the Desert." In *The Cultural Turn in Late Ancient Studies: Gender, Asceticism, and Historiography,* edited by Dale Martin and Patricia Cox Miller, 136–49. Durham, NC: Duke University Press, 2005.

Goliav, Ana Maria. "Proposal for the Reconstruction of the Golden Octagon." In *Les sources de l'histoire du paysage urbain d'Antioche sur l'Oronte,* 159–77. Paris: Université Paris 8, Vincennes-Saint-Denis, 2012.

Goodwin, Mark. "The City as Commodity: The Contested Spaces of Urban Development." In *Selling Places: The City as Cultural Capital, Past and Present,* edited by Gerry Kearns and Chris Philo, 145–62. New York: Pergamon Press, 1993.

Gotter, Ulrich. "Rechtgläubige—Pagane—Häretiker: Tempelzerstörungen in der Kirchengeschichtsschreibung und das Bild der christlichen Kaiser." In *From Temple to Church: Destruction and Renewal of Local Cultic Topography in Late Antiquity,* edited by Johannes Hahn, Stephen Emmel, and Ulrich Gotter, 43–89. Boston: Brill, 2008.

Grabar, André. *Martyrium: Recherches sur le culte des reliques et l'art chrétien antique.* Vols. 1–2. Paris: Collège de France, 1946.

Grissom, Fred A. "Chrysostom and the Jews: Studies in Jewish-Christian Relations in Fourth-Century Antioch." PhD diss., Southern Baptist Theological Seminary, 1978.

Gross-Albenhausen, Kirsten. *Imperator christianissimus: Der christliche Kaiser bei Ambrosius und Johannes Chrysostomus.* Frankfurt am Main: Marthe Clauss Press, 1999.

Guinot, Jean-Noël. *L'exégèse de Théodoret de Cyr.* Théologie Historique 100. Paris: Beauchesne, 1995.

——. "L'Homélie sur Babylas de Jean Chrysostome: La victoire du martyr sur l'hellenisme." In *La narrative cristiana antica: XXIII Incontro de studiosi dell'antichità Cristiana,* edited by S. Pricoco, 323–41. Studia Ephemeridis Augustinianum 50. Rome: Istituto Patristico Augustinianum, 1995.

Gwynn, David. *The Eusebians: The Polemic of Athanasius of Alexandria and the Construction of the "Arian Controversy."* New York: Oxford University Press, 2007.

Haas, Christopher. *Alexandria in Late Antiquity: Topography and Social Conflict.* Baltimore: Johns Hopkins University Press, 1997.

Hahn, Johannes. "The Conversion of the Cult Statues: The Destruction of the Serapeum 392 A.D. and the Transformation of Alexandria into the 'Christ-Loving' City." In *From Temple to Church: Destruction and Renewal of Local Cultic Topography in Late Antiquity,* edited by Johannes Hahn, Stephen Emmel, and Ulrich Gotter, 335–65. Boston: Brill, 2008.

——. *Gewalt und religiöser Konflikt: Studien zu den Auseinandersetzungen zwischen Heiden, Christen und Juden im Osten des Römischen Reiches (von Konstantin bis Theodosius II).* Berlin: Akademie Press, 2004.

Hahn, Johannes, Stephen Emmel, and Ulrich Gotter, eds. *From Temple to Church: Destruction and Renewal of Local Cultic Topography in Late Antiquity.* Boston: Brill, 2008.

Halbwachs, Maurice. *On Collective Memory.* Edited and translated by Lewis A. Coser. Chicago: University of Chicago Press, 1992.

Hales, Shelley. *The Roman House and Social Identity.* New York: Cambridge University Press, 2003.

Hanson, R. P. C. "The Fate of Eustathius of Antioch." *Zeitschrift für Kirchengeschichte* 95 (1984): 171–79.

———. *The Search for the Christian Doctrine of God: The Arian Controversy, 318–381.* Grand Rapids, MI: Baker Academic Press, 1988.

Harkins, Paul. *St. John Chrysostom: Baptismal Instructions.* ACW 31. New York: Newman Press, 1963.

———. *St. John Chrysostom: Discourses against Judaizing Christians.* FC 68. Washington, DC: Catholic University of America Press, 1979.

———. *St. John Chrysostom: On the Incomprehensible Nature of God.* FC 72. Washington, DC: Catholic University of America Press, 1984.

Harley, J. B. "Deconstructing the Map." *Cartographica* 26.2 (1989): 1–20.

———. "Maps, Knowledge, and Power." In *The Iconography of Landscape: Essays on the Symbolic Representation, Design and Use of Past Environments,* edited by Denis Cosgrove and Stephen Daniels, 277–311. New York: Cambridge University Press, 1988.

———. "Silences and Secrecy: The Hidden Agenda of Cartography in Early Modern Europe." *Imago Mundi* 40 (1988): 57–76.

Harries, Jill. *Law and Empire in Late Antiquity.* New York: Cambridge University Press, 1999.

Hart, Gerald. *Asclepius: The God of Medicine.* Lake Forest, IL: Royal Society of Medicine Press, 2000.

Hartney, Aideen. *John Chrysostom and the Transformation of the City.* London: Duckworth, 2004.

Harvey, Susan Ashbrook. *Scenting Salvation: Ancient Christianity and the Olfactory Imagination.* Berkeley: University of California Press, 2006.

Hedrick, Charles, Jr. *History and Silence: The Purge and Rehabilitation of Memory in Late Antiquity.* Austin: University of Texas Press, 2000.

Henig, Martin, and Anthony King, eds. *Pagan Gods and Shrines of the Roman Empire.* Oxford: Oxford University Committee for Archaeology, 1986.

Hess, Hermann. *The Early Development of Canon Law and the Council of Serdica.* Oxford: Oxford University Press, 2002.

Holcomb, Briavel. "Revisioning Place: De- and Re-constructing the Image of the Industrial City." In *Selling Places: The City as Cultural Capital, Past and Present,* edited by Gerry Kearns and Chris Philo, 133–43. New York: Pergamon Press, 1993.

Honoré, Tony. *Law in the Crisis of Empire, 379–455 AD: The Theodosian Dynasty and Its Quaestors.* New York: Clarendon Press, 1998.

Hope, Valerie. *Roman Death: Dying and the Dead in Ancient Rome.* New York: Continuum, 2009.

Hopkins, Keith. *Death and Renewal.* New York: Cambridge University Press, 1983.

Howard-Johnston, James, and Paul Antony Hayward, eds. *The Cult of Saints in Late Antiquity and the Middle Ages: Essays on the Contribution of Peter Brown.* New York: Oxford University Press, 1999.

Hubbard, Phil, Rob Kitchin, and Gill Valentine. "Editors' Introduction." In *Key Thinkers on Space and Place*, edited by Phil Hubbard, Rob Kitchin, and Gill Valentine, 1–15. Thousand Oaks, CA: Sage Publications, 2004.

Hull, Daniel. "The Archaeology of Monasticism: Landscape, Politics, and Social Organisation in Late Antique Syria." PhD thesis, York University, 2006.

Humfress, Caroline. *Orthodoxy and the Courts in Late Antiquity*. New York: Oxford University Press, 2007.

Hunt, David. "Christianising the Roman Empire: The Evidence of the Code." In *The Theodosian Code*, edited by Jill Harries and Ian Wood, 143–60. Ithaca, NY: Cornell University Press, 1993.

Hunt, E. D. *Holy Land Pilgrimage in the Later Roman Empire, AD 312–460*. New York: Oxford University Press, 1982.

———. "St. Stephen in Minorca: An Episode in Jewish-Christian Relations in the Early Fifth Century AD." *JTS* n.s. 33 (1982): 106–23.

Illert, Martin. *Johannes Chrysostomus und das antiochenisch-syrische Mönchtum: Studien zu Theologie, Rhetorik und Kirchenpolitik im antiochenischen Schrifttum des Johannes Chrysostomus*. Zurich: Pano Press, 2000.

Jackson, Peter. *Maps of Meaning: An Introduction to Cultural Geography*. Boston: Unwin Hyman, 1989.

Jacobs, Andrew. *Remains of the Jews: The Holy Land and Christian Empire in Late Antiquity*. Stanford, CA: Stanford University Press, 2004.

Jensen, Robin. "Dining with the Dead: From the *Mensa* to the Altar in Christian Late Antiquity." In *Commemorating the Dead: Texts and Artifacts in Context—Studies of Roman, Jewish, and Christian Burials*, edited by Laurie Brink and Deborah Green, 107–43. New York: Walter de Gruyter, 2008.

Kahlos, Maijastina. "Comissationes et ebrietates." In *Ad itum liberum: Essays in Honour of Anne Helttula*, edited by O. Merisalo and R. Vainio, 13–23. Jyväskylä, Finland: University of Jyväskylä Press, 2007.

Kalas, Gregor. "Conservation, Erasure, and Intervention: Rome's Ancient Heritage and the History of SS. Cosma e Damiano." *Arris* 16 (2005): 1–11.

———. "Topographical Transitions: The Oratory of the Forty Martyrs and Exhibition Practices in the Early Medieval Roman Forum." In *Santa Maria Antiqua al Foro Romano: Cento anni dopo*, edited by John Osborne, J. Rasmus Brandt, and Giuseppe Morganti, 201–13. Rome: Campisano Editore, 2004.

———. *Transforming Public Space in Rome: The Late Antique Revision of the Roman Forum*. Austin: University of Texas Press, forthcoming.

———. "Writing Restoration in Rome: Inscriptions, Statues, and the Late Antique Preservation of Buildings." In *Cities, Texts, and Social Networks, 400–1500: Experiences and Perceptions of Medieval Urban Space*, edited by Caroline Goodson, et al., 21–43. Farnham, UK: Ashgate, 2010.

Kalleres, Dayna. *City of Demons: Violence, Ritual, and Christian Power in Late Antiquity*. Berkeley: University of California Press, forthcoming.

———. "Imagining Martyrdom during Theodosian Peace: John Chrysostom and the Problem of Judaizers." In *Contextualising Early Christian Martyrdom*, edited by Jakob

Engberg, Uffe Holmsgaard Eriksen, and Anders Klostergaard Petersen, 257–75. New York: Peter Lang, 2011.

Karmann, Thomas. *Meletius von Antiochien: Studien zur Geschichte des trinitätstheologischen Streits in den Jahren 360–364 n. Chr.* Regensburger Studien zur Theologie 68. Frankfurt: Peter Lang, 2009.

Kaster, Robert. *Guardians of Language: The Grammarian and Society in Late Antiquity.* Berkeley: University of California Press, 1988.

Kearns, Gerry. "The City as Spectacle: Paris and the Bicentenary of the French Revolution." In *Selling Places: The City as Cultural Capital, Past and Present,* edited by Gerry Kearns and Chris Philo, 49–102. New York: Pergamon Press, 1993.

Kearns, Gerry, and Chris Philo, eds. *Selling Places: The City as Cultural Capital, Past and Present.* New York: Pergamon Press, 1993.

Kelly, J. N. D. *Golden Mouth: The Story of John Chrysostom—Ascetic, Preacher, Bishop.* London: Duckworth, 1995.

Kennedy, Hugh. "Antioch: From Byzantium to Islam and Back Again." In *The City in Late Antiquity,* edited by John Rich, 181–98. New York: Routledge, 1992.

King, Geoff. *Mapping Reality: An Exploration of Cultural Cartographies.* New York: St. Martin's Press, 1996.

Knapp, Gregory, and Peter Herlihy. "Mapping the Landscape of Identity." *Yearbook: Conference of Latin Americanist Geographers* 27 (2002): 251–68.

Knott, Kim. *The Location of Religion: A Spatial Analysis.* Oakville, CT: Equinox Press, 2005.

Kondoleon, Christine, ed. *Antioch: The Lost Ancient City.* Princeton, NJ: Princeton University Press, 2000. Published in conjunction with the exhibition of the same name, shown at Worcester Art Museum, October 7, 2000–February 4, 2001; The Cleveland Museum of Art, March 18–June 3, 2001; The Baltimore Museum of Art, September 16–December 30, 2001.

Kraemer, Ross. "Jewish Women's Resistance to Christianity in the Early Fifth Century: The Account of Severus, Bishop of Minorca." *JECS* 17.4 (2009): 635–65.

Krause, Jens-Uwe, and Christian Witschel, eds. *Die Stadt in der Spätantike—Niedergang oder Wandel?* Stuttgart: Franz Steiner Press, 2006.

Krautheimer, Richard. *Three Christian Capitals: Topography and Politics.* Berkeley: University of California Press, 1983.

Krueger, Derek. *Writing and Holiness: The Practice of Authorship in the Early Christian East.* Philadelphia: University of Pennsylvania Press, 2004.

Lafferty, Maura. "Translating Faith from Greek to Latin: *Romanitas* and *Christianitas* in Late Fourth-Century Rome and Milan." *JECS* 11.1 (2003): 21–62.

Lagacherie, Odile. "Libanios, rhétorique et politique à propos des discours 50 et 45: Le principe de réalité." In *Approches de la Troisième Sophistique: Hommages à Jacques Schamp,* edited by Eugenio Amato, 460–68. Brussels: Editions Latomus, 2006.

Lassus, Jean. "L'église cruciforme Antioche-Kasoussié 12-F." In *Antioch-on-the-Orontes,* vol. 2, *The Excavations, 1933–1936,* edited by Richard Stillwell, 114–56. Publications of the Committee for the Excavation of Antioch and its Vicinity. Princeton, NJ: Princeton University Press, 1938.

Latham, Jacob. "The Ritual Construction of Rome: Processions, Subjectivities, and the City from the Late Republic to Late Antiquity." PhD diss., University of California, Santa Barbara, 2007.

Laurence, Ray, and David Newsome, eds. *Rome, Ostia, Pompeii: Movement and Space*. New York: Oxford University Press, 2011.

Lavan, Luke. "The *agorai* of Antioch and Constantinople as Seen by John Chrysostom." In *Wolf Liebeschuetz Reflected: Essays Presented by Colleagues, Friends, and Pupils*, edited by John Drinkwater and Benet Salway, 157–67. London: Institute of Classical Studies, University of London, 2007.

———. "Political Talismans? Residual 'Pagan' Statues in Late Antique Public Space." In *The Archaeology of Late Antique "Paganism,"* edited by Luke Lavan and Michael Mulryan, 439–77. Boston: Brill, 2011.

Lavan, Luke, and Michael Mulryan, eds. *The Archaeology of Late Antique "Paganism."* Boston: Brill, 2011.

Leemans, Johan. "Martyr, Monk, and Victor of Paganism: An Analysis of Basil of Caesarea's Panegyrical Sermon on Gordius." In *More than a Memory: The Discourse of Martyrdom and the Construction of Christian Identity in the History of Christianity*, edited by Johan Leemans, 45–79. Dudley, MA: Peeters, 2005.

———. "Preaching and the Arian Controversy: Orthodoxy and Heresy in Gregory of Nyssa's Sermons." *Journal of Eastern Christian Studies* 60 (2008): 127–42.

Leemans, Johan, Wendy Mayer, Pauline Allen, and Boudewijn Dehandschutter. *"Let Us Die That We May Live": Greek Homilies on Christian Martyrs from Asia Minor, Palestine, and Syria (c. AD 350–AD 450)*. New York: Routledge, 2003.

Lenox-Conyngham, Andrew. "The Topography of the Basilica Conflict of A.D. 385/6 in Milan." *Historia* 31 (1982): 353–63.

Leppin, Hartmut. "Steuern, Aufstand und Rhetoren: Der Antiochener Steueraufstand von 387 in christlicher und heidnischer Deutung." In *Gedeutete Realität: Krisen, Wirklichkeiten, Interpretationen (3.–6. Jh. n. Chr.)*, edited by Hartwin Brandt, 103–23. Stuttgart: Franz Steiner Press, 1999.

Leroux, J.-M. "Saint Jean Chrysostome: Les Homélies sur les Statues." *Studia Patristica* 3 (1961): 232–39.

Levenson, David. "The Ancient and Medieval Sources for the Emperor Julian's Attempt to Rebuild the Jerusalem Temple." *Journal for the Study of Judaism* 34.4 (2004): 409–60.

Leyerle, Blake. "Refuse, Filth, and Excrement in the Homilies of John Chrysostom." *Journal of Late Antiquity* 2.2 (2009): 337–56.

———. *Theatrical Shows and Ascetic Lives: John Chrysostom's Attack on Spiritual Marriage*. Berkeley: University of California Press, 2001.

Liebeschuetz, J. H. W. G. *Ambrose and John Chrysostom: Clerics between Desert and Empire*. New York: Oxford University Press, 2011.

———. *Antioch: City and Imperial Administration in the Later Roman Empire*. Oxford: Clarendon Press, 1972.

———. *The Decline and Fall of the Roman City*. New York: Oxford University Press, 2001.

———. "The End of the Ancient City." In *The City in Late Antiquity*, edited by John Rich, 1–49. New York: Routledge, 1992.

———. "Transformation and Decline: Are the Two Really Incompatible?" In *Die Stadt in der Spätantike—Niedergang oder Wandel?*, edited by Jens-Uwe Krause and Christian Witschel, 463–83. Stuttgart: Franz Steiner Press, 2006.

———. "The Uses and Abuses of the Concept of 'Decline' in Later Roman History, or, Was Gibbon Politically Incorrect?" In *Recent Research in Late-Antique Urbanism*, edited by Luke Lavan, 233–38. Journal of Roman Archaeology Supplementary Series 42. Portsmouth, RI: Journal of Roman Archaeology, 2001.

Lieu, Samuel. *The Emperor Julian: Panegyric and Polemic, Claudius Mamertinus, John Chrysostom, Ephrem the Syrian*. Translated Texts for Historians, Greek Series 1. Liverpool: Liverpool University Press, 1986.

———. "Libanius and Higher Education at Antioch." In *Culture and Society in Later Roman Antioch*, edited by Isabella Sandwell and Janet Huskinson, 13–23. Oxford: Oxbow Books, 2004.

Lillios, Katina. "Creating Memory in Prehistory: The Engraved Slate Plaques of Southwest Iberia." In *Archaeologies of Memory*, edited by Ruth Van Dyke and Susan Alcock, 129–50. Malden, MA: Blackwell Publishing, 2003.

Limberis, Vasiliki. *Architects of Piety: The Cappadocian Fathers and the Cult of the Martyrs*. New York: Oxford University Press, 2011.

———. "'Religion' as the Cipher for Identity: The Cases of Emperor Julian, Libanius, and Gregory Nazianzus." *HTR* 93.4 (2000): 373–400.

Locher, Miriam. *Power and Politeness in Action: Disagreements in Oral Communication*. New York: Mouton de Gruyter, 2004.

Lynch, Paul, Jennie Germann Molz, Alison McIntosh, Peter Lugosi, and Conrad Lashley. "Theorizing Hospitality." *Hospitality & Society* 1.1 (2011): 3–24.

MacMullen, Ramsay. *Christianizing the Roman Empire, A.D. 100–400*. New Haven, CT: Yale University Press, 1984.

———. "The Preacher's Audience (AD 350–400)." *JTS* 40.2 (1989): 503–11.

———. *The Second Church: Popular Christianity, A.D. 200–400*. Atlanta: Society of Biblical Literature, 2009.

Maier, Harry. "Heresy, Households, and the Disciplining of Diversity." In *A People's History of Christianity*, vol. 2, *Late Ancient Christianity*, edited by Virginia Burrus, 213–33. Minneapolis: Fortress Press, 2005.

———. "Private Spaces as the Social Context of Arianism in Ambrose's Milan." *JTS* 45 (1994): 72–93.

———. "The Topography of Heresy and Dissent in Late-Fourth-Century Rome." *Historia: Zeitschrift für alte Geschichte* 44.2 (1995): 232–49.

Maraval, Pierre. *Lieux saints et pèlerinages d'Orient: Histoire et géographie des origines à la conquête arabe*. Paris: Les Éditions du Cerf, 2004.

Marrou, Henri. *Histoire de l'éducation dans l'antiquité*. Paris: Éditions du Seuil, 1948.

Martin, Dale. *Inventing Superstition: From the Hippocratics to the Christians*. Cambridge, MA: Harvard University Press, 2004.

Massey, Doreen. *Space, Place, and Gender*. Cambridge: Polity Press, 1994.

Massey, Doreen, and John Allen. *Geography Matters! A Reader*. New York: Cambridge University Press, 1984.

Matthews, John. *The Journey of Theophanes: Travel, Business, and Daily Life in the Roman East*. New Haven, CT: Yale University Press, 2006.

———. *Laying Down the Law: A Study of the Theodosian Code*. New Haven, CT: Yale University Press, 2000.

Maxwell, Jaclyn. *Christianization and Communication in Late Antiquity: John Chrysostom and His Congregation in Antioch*. New York: Cambridge University Press, 2006.

———. "Lay Piety in the Sermons of John Chrysostom." In *A People's History of Christianity*, vol. 3, *Byzantine Christianity*, edited by Derek Krueger, 19–38. Minneapolis: Fortress Press, 2006.

May, Jon. "Globalization and the Politics of Place: Place and Identity in an Inner London Neighbourhood." *Transactions of the Institute of British Geographers* 21 (1996): 194–215.

Mayer, Wendy. "Antioch and the Intersection between Religious Factionalism, Place, and Power in Late Antiquity." In *The Power of Religion in Late Antiquity*, edited by Andrew Cain and Noel Lenski, 357–68. Burlington, VT: Ashgate, 2009.

———. "Female Participation and the Late Fourth-Century Preacher's Audience." *Augustinianum* 39 (1999): 139–47.

———. *The Homilies of St John Chrysostom—Provenance: Reshaping the Foundations*. Rome: Pontificio Istituto Orientale, 2005.

———. "John Chrysostom: Extraordinary Preacher, Ordinary Audience." In *Preacher and Audience: Studies in Early Christian and Byzantine Homiletics*, edited by Pauline Allen and Mary Cunningham, 105–37. Leiden: Brill, 1998.

———. "John Chrysostom and His Audiences: Distinguishing Different Congregations at Antioch and Constantinople." *Studia Patristica* 31 (1997): 70–75.

———. "John Chrysostom on Poverty." In *Preaching Poverty in Late Antiquity: Perceptions and Realities*, edited by Pauline Allen, Bronwen Neil, and Wendy Mayer, 69–118. Leipzig: Evangelische Verlagsanstalt, 2009.

———. "The Late Antique Church at Qausīyeh Reconsidered: Memory and Martyr-Burial in Syrian Antioch." In *Martyrdom and Persecution in Late Antique Christianity: Festschrift Boudewijn Dehandschutter*, edited by J. Leemans, 161–77. Bibliotheca Ephemeridum Theologicarum Lovaniensium 241. Leuven: Peeters, 2010.

———. "Monasticism at Antioch and Constantinople in the Late Fourth Century: A Case of Exclusivity or Diversity?" In *Prayer and Spirituality in the Early Church*, edited by Pauline Allen and Raymond Canning, with Janelle Caiger, 1:275–88. Brisbane: Centre for Early Christian Studies, Australian Catholic University, 1998.

———. "Poverty and Generosity toward the Poor in the Time of John Chrysostom." In *Wealth and Poverty in Early Church and Society*, edited by Susan Holman, 140–58. Grand Rapids, MI: Baker Academic, 2008.

———. "The Sea Made Holy: The Liturgical Function of the Waters surrounding Constantinople." *Ephemerides Liturgicae* 112 (1998): 459–68.

———. "The Topography of Antioch Described in the Writings of John Chrysostom." In *Les sources de l'histoire du paysage urbain d'Antioche sur l'Oronte*, 81–100. Paris: Université Paris 8, Vincennes-Saint-Denis, 2012.

———. "What Does It Mean to Say that John Chrysostom Was a Monk?" *Studia Patristica* 41 (2006): 451–55.

———. "Who Came to Hear John Chrysostom Preach? Recovering a Late Fourth-Century Preacher's Audience." *Ephemerides Theologicae Lovanienses* 76.1 (2000): 73–87.

Mayer, Wendy, and Pauline Allen. *The Churches of Syrian Antioch (300–638 CE)*. Walpole, MA: Peeters, 2012.

———, eds. *John Chrysostom*. New York: Routledge, 2000.

Mayer, Wendy, with Bronwen Neil. *St. John Chrysostom: The Cult of the Saints*. Popular Patristics Series. Crestwood, NY: St. Vladimir's Seminary Press, 2006.

McLynn, Neil. *Ambrose of Milan: Church and Court in a Christian Capital*. Berkeley: University of California Press, 1994.

Meeks, Wayne, and Robert Wilken. *Jews and Christians in Antioch in the First Four Centuries of the Common Era*. Missoula, MT: Scholars Press, 1978.

Meskell, Lynn. "Back to the Future: From the Past in the Present to the Past in the Past." In *Negotiating the Past in the Past: Identity, Memory, and Landscape in Archaeological Research*, edited by Norman Yoffee, 215–26. Tucson: University of Arizona Press, 2007.

——. "The Intersections of Identity and Politics in Archaeology." *Annual Review of Anthropology* 31 (2002): 279–301.

Meyer, Guy. "L'apport des voyageurs occidentaux (1268–1918)." In *Les sources de l'histoire du paysage urbain d'Antioche sur l'Oronte*, 235–58. Paris: Université Paris 8, Vincennes-Saint-Denis, 2012.

Millar, Fergus. *A Greek Roman Empire: Power and Belief under Theodosius II (408–450)*. Berkeley: University of California Press, 2006.

——. "Theodoret of Cyrrhus: A Syrian in Greek Dress?" In *From Rome to Constantinople: Studies in Honour of Averil Cameron*, edited by Hagit Amirav and R. B. ter Haar Romeny, 105–26. Leuven: Peeters, 2007.

Mitchell, W. J. Thomas. *Landscape and Power*. Chicago: University of Chicago Press, 2002.

Monmonier, Mark. *How to Lie with Maps*. 2nd ed. Chicago: University of Chicago Press, 1996.

Moorhead, John. *Ambrose: Church and Society in the Late Roman World*. London: Longman Press, 1999.

Moralee, Jason. "The Stones of St. Theodore: Disfiguring the Pagan Past in Christian Gerasa." *JECS* 14.2 (2006): 183–215.

Muehrcke, Phillip, with Juliana Muehrcke. *Map Use: Reading, Analysis, and Interpretation*. Madison, WI: JP Publications, 1978.

Murphy-O'Connor, Jerome. *Keys to Jerusalem: Collected Essays*. New York: Oxford University Press, 2012.

Nasrallah, Laura. *Christian Responses to Roman Art and Architecture: The Second-Century Church amid the Spaces of Empire*. New York: Cambridge University Press, 2010.

Nauroy, G. "Le fouet et le miel: Le combat d'Ambroise en 386 contre l'arianisme milanais." *Recherches Augustiniennes* 23 (1988): 3–86.

Nevett, Lisa. *Domestic Space in Classical Antiquity*. New York: Cambridge University Press, 2010.

Nock, Arthur Darby. "Sapor I and the Apollo of Bryaxis." *American Journal of Archaeology* 66.3 (1962): 307–10.

Norman, A. F. *Antioch as a Centre of Hellenic Culture as Observed by Libanius*. Liverpool: Liverpool University Press, 2000.

——. *Libanius: Selected Orations*. Vol. 2. Cambridge, MA: Harvard University Press, 1977.

North, John. *Roman Religion*. Greece & Rome: New Surveys in the Classics 30. New York: Oxford University Press, 2000.

O'Donnell, James. *Augustine: Confessions*. Vol. 1, *Introduction and Text*. Oxford: Clarendon Press, 1992.

O'Sullivan, Timothy. *Walking in Roman Culture*. New York: Cambridge University Press, 2011.

Palm, Jonas. *Rom, Römertum und Imperium in der griechischen Literatur der Kaiserzeit*. Lund: Gleerup, 1959.

Palmer, Andrew. "The Mountain of the Seventy Monasteries: The Monastic Geography of Tur 'Abdin." Unpublished manuscript, 2011.

Pamir, Hatice. "Preliminary Results of the Recent Archaeological Researches in Antioch on the Orontes and Its Vicinity." In *Les sources de l'histoire du paysage urbain d'Antioche sur l'Oronte*, 259–70. Paris: Université Paris 8, Vincennes-Saint-Denis, 2012.

Parmentier, Léon, and Günther C. Hansen, eds. *Théodoret de Cyr, Histoire Ecclésiastique, vol. 1 (I-II)*. SC 501. Paris: Éditions du Cerf, 2006.

Pellizzari, Andrea. "'Salvare le città': Lessico e ideologia nell'opera di Libanio." *KOINONIA: Rivista dell'Associazione di Studi Tardoantichi* 35 (2011): 45–61.

Penn, Michael. *Kissing Christians: Ritual and Community in the Late Ancient Church*. Philadelphia: University of Pennsylvania Press, 2005.

Perry, Ellen. "Divine Statues in the Works of Libanius of Antioch: The Actual and Rhetorical Desacralization of Pagan Cult Furniture in the Late Fourth Century C.E." In *The Sculptural Environment of the Roman Near East: Reflections on Culture, Ideology, and Power*, edited by Y. Eliav, E. Friedland, and S. Herbert, 437–48. Leuven: Peeters, 2008.

Petit, Paul. *Les étudiants de Libanius*. Paris: Nouvelles Éditions Latines, 1955.

———. *Libanius et la vie municipale à Antioche au IVe siècle après J.-C.* Paris: Libraire Orientaliste Paul Geuthner, 1955.

———. "Sur la date du 'Pro Templis' de Libanius." *Byzantion* 21 (1951): 285–309.

Pharr, Clyde. *The Theodosian Code and Novels and the Sirmondia Constitutions: A Translation with Commentary, Glossary, and Bibliography*. Union, NJ: The Lawbook Exchange, 2001.

Philo, Chris, and Gerry Kearns. "Culture, History, Capital: A Critical Introduction to the Selling of Places." In *Selling Places: The City as Cultural Capital, Past and Present*, edited by Gerry Kearns and Chris Philo, 1–32. New York: Pergamon Press, 1993.

Poccardi, Grégoire. "Antioche de Syrie: Pour un nouveau plan urbain de l'île de l'Oronte (ville neuve) du IIIe au Ve siècle." *Mélanges de l'École Française de Rome* 106 (1994): 993–1023.

———. "L'île d'Antioche à la fin de l'Antiquité: Histoire et problem de topographie urbaine." In *Recent Research in Late-Antique Urbanism*, edited by Luke Lavan, 155–72. Journal of Roman Archaeology Supplementary Series 42. Portsmouth, RI: Journal of Roman Archaeology, 2001.

Pradels, Wendy, Rudolf Brändle, and Martin Heimgartner. "Das bisher vermisste Textstück in Johannes Chrysostomus, Adversus Judaeos, Oration 2." *Zeitschrift für antikes Christentum* 5 (2001): 23–49.

———. "The Sequence and Dating of the Series of John Chrysostom's Eight Discourses Adversus Iudaeos." *ZAC* 6 (2002): 90–116.

Price, Richard. *A History of the Monks of Syria, by Theodoret of Cyrrhus*. Kalamazoo, MI: Cistercian Publications, 1985.

Puertas, Alberto Quiroga. "Como ángeles venidos del cielo": Los monjes en la homilía XVII (*De Statuis*) de Juan Crisóstomo." *Euphrosyne* 36 (2008): 327–32.

———. "Juan Crisóstomo *De Statuis* XVIII, 2 y Libanio *Or.* XXII, 22: Variaciones sobre un mismo hecho." *Florentia Iliberritana* 16 (2005): 285–95.

———. *La retórica de Libanio y de Juan Crisóstomo en la Revuelta de las Estatuas.* Salerno, Italy: Helios Editrice, 2007.

Rapp, Claudia. "Holy Texts, Holy Men, and Holy Scribes: Aspects of Scriptural Holiness in Late Antiquity." In *The Early Christian Book,* edited by William Klingshirn and Linda Safran, 194–222. Washington, DC: Catholic University of America Press, 2007.

———. "Safe-Conducts to Heaven: Holy Men, Mediation, and the Role of Writing." In *Transformations of Late Antiquity: Essays for Peter Brown,* edited by Philip Rousseau and Manolis Papoutsakis, 187–203. Burlington, VT: Ashgate, 2009.

Rawson, Beryl, and Paul Weaver, eds. *The Roman Family in Italy: Status, Sentiment, Space.* Oxford: Clarendon Press, 1997.

Rawson, Elizabeth. "Roman Rulers and the Philosophic Advisor." In *Philosophia Togata: Essays on Philosophy and Roman Society,* edited by M. Griffin and J. Barnes, 233–57. New York: Oxford University Press, 1989.

Rebillard, Éric. *The Care of the Dead in Late Antiquity.* Translated by Elizabeth Trapnell Rawlings and Jeanine Routier-Pucci. Cornell Studies in Classical Philology 59. Ithaca, NY: Cornell University Press, 2009.

———. *Christians and Their Many Identities in Late Antiquity, North Africa, 200–450 CE.* Ithaca, NY: Cornell University Press, 2012.

———. *Religion et sepulture: L'Église, les vivants et les morts dans l'Antiquité tardive (IIIe-Ve siècles).* Paris: Éditions de l'École des hautes études en sciences socials, 2003.

Rhee, Helen. *Loving the Poor, Saving the Rich: Wealth, Poverty, and Early Christian Formation.* Grand Rapids, MI: Baker Academic, 2013.

Richter, G. "Über die älteste Auseinandersetzung der syrischen Christen mit den Juden." *ZNW* 35 (1936): 101–14.

Ricoeur, Paul. *Memory, History, Forgetting.* Translated by Kathleen Blamey and David Pellauer. Chicago: University of Chicago Press, 2004.

Ritter, A. M. "Erwägungen zum Antisemitismus in der Alten Kirche: Acht Reden über die Juden." In *Bleibendes im Wandel der Kirchengeschichte,* edited by B. Moeller and G. Ruhbach, 71–91. Tübingen: J. C. B. Mohr/Paul Siebeck, 1973.

———. "John Chrysostom and the Jews, a Reconsideration." *Ancient Christianity in the Caucasus* (1998): 141–54, 231–32.

Rives, James. *Religion in the Roman Empire.* Blackwell Ancient Religions. Malden, MA: Blackwell Publishers, 2007.

Robinson, Martha, and Paul Lynch. "The Power of Hospitality: A Sociolinguistic Analysis." In *Hospitality: A Social Lens,* edited by Conrad Lashley, Paul Lynch, and Alison Morrison, 141–54. New York: Elsevier, 2007.

Rose, Gillian. "Contested Concepts of Community." *Journal of Historical Geography* 16.4 (1990): 425–37.

Roth, Catharine, trans. *St. John Chrysostom: On Wealth and Poverty.* Crestwood, NY: St. Vladimir's Seminary Press, 1984.

Rousseau, Philip. *Basil of Caesarea.* Berkeley: University of California Press, 1994.

———. "The Preacher's Audience: A More Optimistic View." In *Ancient History in a Modern University*, edited by T. Hillard, R. A. Kearsley, C. E. V. Nixon, and A. Nobbs, 2:391–400. Grand Rapids, MI: William B. Eerdmans, 1998.

Rouwhorst, Gerard. "The Emergence of the Cult of the Maccabean Martyrs in Late Antique Christianity." In *More Than a Memory: The Discourse of Martyrdom and the Construction of Christian Identity in the History of Christianity*, edited by Johan Leemans, 81–96. Leuven: Peeters, 2006.

Rowell, Geoffrey. *The Liturgy of Christian Burial: An Introductory Survey of the Historical Development of Christian Burial Rites*. London: Alcuin Club/S.P.C.K., 1977.

Rowlands, Michael. "The Role of Memory in the Transmission of Culture." *World Archaeology* 25 (1993): 142–51.

Rutgers, Leonard V. "The Importance of Scripture in the Conflict between Jews and Christians: The Example of Antioch." In *The Use of Sacred Books in the Ancient World*, edited by L. V. Rutgers et al., 287–303. Leuven: Peeters, 1998.

Saliou, Catherine. "Antioche décrite par Libanios: La rhétorique de l'espace urbain et ses enjeux au milieu du quatrième siècle." In *Approches de la Troisième Sophistique: Hommages à Jacques Schamp*, edited by Eugenio Amato, 273–85. Brussels: Editions Latomus, 2006.

———. "À propos de la ταυριανὴ πύλη: Remarques sur la localisation présumée de la grande église d'Antioche de Syrie." *Syria* 77 (2000): 217–26.

———. "Bains d'été et bains d'hiver: Antioche dans l'empire romain." *Topoi* Supplement 5 (2004): 289–309.

———. "L'*Éloge d'Antioche* (Libanios, discours 11 = *Antiochikos*) et son apport à la connaissance du paysage urbain d'Antioche." In *Les sources de l'histoire du paysage urbain d'Antioche sur l'Oronte*, 43–56. Paris: Université Paris 8, Vincennes-Saint-Denis, 2012.

———. "Le palais imperial d'Antioche et son contexts à l'époque de Julien: Réflexions sur l'apport des sources littéraires à l'histoire d'un espace urbain." *Antiquité Tardive* 17 (2009): 235–50.

———. "Les foundations d'Antioche dans l'*Antiochikos* (*Oratio* XI) de Libanios." *ARAM* 11–12 (1999–2000): 357–88.

Saller, Richard. *Personal Patronage under the Early Empire*. New York: Cambridge University Press, 1982.

Salzman, Michele. "*Superstitio* in the *Codex Theodosianus* and the Persecution of Pagans." *VC* 41 (1987): 172–88.

Sandwell, Isabella. "Christian Self-Definition in the Fourth Century AD: John Chrysostom on Christianity, Imperial Rule, and the City." In *Culture and Society in Later Roman Antioch*, edited by Isabella Sandwell and Janet Huskinson, 35–58. Oxford: Oxbow Books, 2004.

———. *Religious Identity in Late Antiquity: Greeks, Jews, and Christians in Antioch*. New York: Cambridge University Press, 2007.

Saradi-Mendelovici, Helen. "Christian Attitudes toward Pagan Monuments in Late Antiquity and Their Legacy in Later Byzantine Churches." *Dumbarton Oaks Papers* 44 (1990): 47–61.

Schatkin, Margaret ,and Paul Harkins. *Saint John Chrysostom: Apologist*. FC 73. Washington, DC: Catholic University of America Press, 1983.

Schemmel, Fritz. "Der Sophist Libanios als Schüler und Lehrer." *Neue Jahrbücher für das klassische Altertum, Geschichte und deutsche Literatur und für Pädagogik* 20 (1907): 52–69.

Scholl, Reinhold. *Historische Beiträge zu den julianischen Reden des Libanios.* Stuttgart: Franz Steiner Press, 1994.

Schoolman, Edward. "Civic Transformation of the Mediterranean City: Antioch and Ravenna, 300–800 CE." PhD diss., University of California, Los Angeles, 2010.

Schor, Adam. *Theodoret's People: Social Networks and Religious Conflict in Late Roman Syria.* Berkeley: University of California Press, 2011.

Schouler, B. "Le rôle politique de l'école au temps de Libanios." In *Antioche de Syrie: Histoire, images et traces de la ville antique; Colloque de Lyon (octobre 2001)*, edited by B. Cabouret, P.-L. Gatier, and C. Saliou, 97–115. Topoi Suppl. 5. Lyon: Maison de l'Orient et de la Méditerranée, 2004.

Seeck, Otto. *Die Briefe des Libanius zeitlich geordnet.* Leipzig: J.C. Hinrichs, 1906.

Sessa, Kristina, ed. "Holy Households: Space, Property, and Power." Special issue, *Journal of Early Christian Studies* 15.2 (2007).

Shepardson, Christine. *Anti-Judaism and Christian Orthodoxy: Ephrem's Hymns in Fourth-Century Syria.* Washington, DC: Catholic University of America, 2008.

———. "Apollo's Charred Remains: Making Meaning in Fourth-Century Syria." *Studia Patristica* 38 (2013): 297–302.

———. "Burying Babylas: Meletius and the Christianization of Antioch." *Studia Patristica* 37 (2010): 347–52.

———. "Controlling Contested Places: John Chrysostom's *Adversus Iudaeos* Homilies and the Spatial Politics of Religious Controversy." *JECS* 15.4 (2007): 483–516.

———. "Meaningful Meetings: Constructing Linguistic Difference in Late Antique Antioch." *Syriac Encounters.* Leuven: Peeters, forthcoming.

———. "Paschal Politics: Deploying the Temple's Destruction against Fourth-Century Judaizers." *VC* 62.3 (2008): 233–60.

———. "Rewriting Julian's Legacy: John Chrysostom's *On Babylas* and Libanius' *Oration* 24." *Journal of Late Antiquity* 2.1 (2009): 99–115.

Sheridan, J.J. "The Altar of Victory: Paganism's Last Battle." *L'Antiquité Classique* 35 (1966): 186–206.

Sibley, David. "Creating Geographies of Difference." In *Human Geography Today*, edited by Doreen Massey, John Allen, and Philip Sarre, 115–29. Malden, MA: Polity Press, 1999.

Simon, Marcel. "La polémique anti-juive de S. Jean Chrysostome et le mouvement judaisant d'Antioche." *Annuaire de l'Institut de Philologie et d'Histoire Orientales et Slaves* 4 (1936): 403–29.

Siniossoglou, Niketas. *Plato and Theodoret: The Christian Appropriation of Platonic Philosophy and the Hellenic Intellectual Resistance.* New York: Cambridge University Press, 2008.

Skedros, James. *Saint Demetrios of Thessaloniki: Civic Patron and Divine Protector, 4th–7th Centuries CE.* Harrisburg, PA: Trinity Press International, 1999.

Slootjes, Danielle. "Between Criticism and Praise: Provincials' Image of the Governor in the Later Roman Empire." In *The Representation and Perception of Roman Imperial Power: Proceedings of the Third Workshop of the International Network "Impact of Empire"*

(Roman Empire, c. 200 B.C.–A.D. 476), Netherlands Institute in Rome, March 20–23, 2002, edited by Lukas De Blois, Paul Erdkamp, Olivier Hekster, Gerda De Kleijn, and Stephan Mols, 138–26. Amsterdam: J. C. Gieben, 2003.

Smelik, Klaas. "John Chrysostom's Homilies against the Jews: Some Comments." *Nederlands theologisch tijdschrift* 39 (1985): 194–200.

Smith, Adam. *The Political Landscape: Constellations of Authority in Early Complex Politics.* Berkeley: University of California Press, 2003.

Smith, Angèle. "Landscape Representation: Place and Identity in Nineteenth-Century Ordnance Survey Maps of Ireland." In *Landscape, Memory, and History: Anthropological Perspectives,* edited by Pamela Stewart and Andrew Strathern, 71–88. Sterling, VA: Pluto, 2003.

Smith, Jonathan Z. *To Take Place: Toward a Theory of Ritual.* Chicago: University of Chicago Press, 1987.

Smith, Warren. *Christian Grace and Pagan Virtue: The Theological Foundation of Ambrose's Ethics.* New York: Oxford University Press, 2011.

Soja, Edward. *Postmetropolis: Critical Studies of Cities and Regions.* Oxford: Blackwell, 2000.

———. "Taking Space Personally." In *The Spatial Turn: Interdisciplinary perspectives,* edited by Barney Warf and Santa Arias, 11–35. New York: Routledge, 2009.

———. *Thirdspace: Journeys to Los Angeles and Other Real-and-Imagined Places.* Malden, MA: Blackwell Publishing, 1996.

Soler, Emmanuel. "Evêque et pasteurs à Antioche sous l'empereur Théodose: L'engagement chrétien dans la défense de la cité après la sédition des statues (387)." In *Vescovi e pastori in epoca teodosiana,* 461–67. Incontro di Studiosi dell'Antichità 25. Studia Ephemeridis Augustinianum 58. Rome: Roma Inst. Patristicum Augustinianum, 1997.

———. *Le sacré et le salut à Antioche au IVe siècle apr. J.-C.: Pratiques festives et comportements religieux dans le processus de christianisation de la cité.* Beirut: Institut français du Proche-Orient, 2006.

———. "Sacralité et partage du temps et de l'espace festifs à Antioche au IVe siècle." In *Les frontières du profane dans l'antiquité tardive,* edited by Éric Rebillard and Claire Sotinel, 273–86. Collection de l'École Française de Rome 428. Rome: École française de Rome, 2010.

Sotinel, Claire. "La sphère profane dans l'espace urbain." In *Les frontières du profane dans l'antiquité tardive,* edited by Éric Rebillard and Claire Sotinel, 319–49. Collection de l'École Française de Rome 428. Rome: École française de Rome, 2010.

———. *Les sources de l'histoire du paysage urbain d'Antioche sur l'Oronte: Actes des journées d'études des 20 et 21 septembre 2010.* Paris: Université Paris 8, Vincennes-Saint-Denis, 2012.

Steer, Carol. "City Slicker versus Country Bumpkin: Farmers in the *Acharnians* of Aristophanes and the *Dyskolos* of Menander." In *Daimonopylai: Essays in Classics and the Classical Tradition Presented to Edmund G. Berry,* edited by Rory Egan, Mark Joyal, and Edmund Grindlay Berry, 383–96. Winnipeg: University of Manitoba, 2004.

Stephens, Justin. "Ecclesiastical and Imperial Authority in the Writings of John Chrysostom: A Reinterpretation of His Political Philosophy." PhD diss., University of California, Santa Barbara, 2001.

———. "Religion and Power in the Early Thought of John Chrysostom." In *The Power of Religion in Late Antiquity,* edited by Andrew Cain and Noel Lenski, 181–88. Burlington, VT: Ashgate, 2009.

Stewart, Pamela, and Andrew Strathern, eds. *Landscape, Memory, and History: Anthropological Perspectives.* Sterling, VA: Pluto, 2003.

Tanner, Norman. *Decrees of the Ecumenical Councils.* Vol. 1, *Nicaea I to Lateran V.* Washington, DC: Georgetown University Press, 1990.

Tate, Georges. *Les campagnes de la Syrie du Nord du IIe au VIIe siècle.* Bibliothèque Archéologique et Historique 133. Paris: P. Geuthner, 1992.

———. "Les relations villes-campagnes dans le nord de la Syrie entre le IVe et le VIe siècle." In *Antioche de Syrie: Histoire, images et traces de la ville antique; Colloque de Lyon (octobre 2001),* edited by B. Cabouret, P.-L. Gatier, and C. Saliou, 311–18. Topoi Suppl. 5. Lyon: Maison de l'Orient et de la Méditerranée, 2004.

Taylor, David. "Bilingualism and Diglossia in Late Antique Syria and Mesopotamia." In *Bilingualism in Ancient Society: Language Contact and the Written Text,* edited by J. N. Adams, Mark Janse, and Simon Swain, 298–331. New York: Oxford University Press, 2002.

Taylor, Joan. *Christians and the Holy Places: The Myth of Jewish-Christian Origins.* New York: Clarendon Press, 1993.

Tchalenko, Georges. *Villages antiques de la Syrie du Nord, le massif du Bélus à l'époque romaine, I-III.* Bibliothèque Archéologique et Historique 50. Paris: P. Geuthner, 1953–58.

Thacker, Alan. "Rome of the Martyrs: Saints, Cults, and Relics, Fourth to Seventh Centuries." In *Roma Felix—Formation and Reflections of Medieval Rome,* edited by Éamonn Ó Carragáin and Carol Neuman de Vegvar, 13–49. Burlington, VT: Ashgate, 2007.

Todt, Klaus-Peter. "Antioch in Byzantine Sources of the 8th–13th Centuries." In *Les sources de l'histoire du paysage urbain d'Antioche sur l'Oronte,* 203–22. Paris: Université Paris 8, Vincennes-Saint-Denis, 2012.

———. *Region und griechisch-orthodoxes Patriarchat von Antiocheia in mittelbyzantinischer Zeit und im Zeitalter der Kreuzzüge (969–1204).* 2 vols. Wiesbaden, 1998.

Torres, Juana. "Emperor Julian and the Veneration of Relics." *Antiquité Tardive* 17 (2009): 205–14.

Toynbee, J. M. C. *Death and Burial in the Roman World.* Ithaca, NY: Cornell University Press, 1971.

Triebel, Lothar. "Das angebliche Synagoge der makkabäischen Märtyrer in Antiochia am Orontes." *Zeitschrift für antikes Christentum* 9 (2005): 464–95.

Trombley, Frank. "Christian Demography in the *territorium* of Antioch (4th–5th c.): Observations on the Epigraphy." In *Culture and Society in Later Roman Antioch,* edited by Isabella Sandwell and Janet Huskinson, 59–85. Oxford: Oxbow Books, 2004.

———. *Hellenic Religion and Christianization, c. 370–529.* Vols. 1–2. Leiden: E. J. Brill, 1993.

Trout, Dennis. "Damasus and the Invention of Early Christian Rome." *Journal of Medieval and Early Modern Studies* 33.3 (2003): 517–36.

———. "Inscribing Identity: The Latin Epigraphic Habit in Late Antiquity." In *A Companion to Late Antiquity,* edited by Philip Rousseau, 170–86. Oxford: Wiley-Blackwell, 2009.

———. "Saints, Identity, and the City." In *A People's History of Christianity,* vol. 2, *Late Ancient Christianity,* edited by Virginia Burrus, 165–87. Minneapolis: Fortress Press, 2005.

Tuan, Yi-Fu. *Topophilia: A Study of Environmental Perception, Attitudes, and Values.* Englewood Cliffs, NJ: Prentice-Hall, 1974.

Tweed, Thomas. *Crossing and Dwelling: A Theory of Religion.* Cambridge, MA: Harvard University Press, 2006.

Urbainczyk, Theresa. "'The Devil Spoke Syriac to me': Theodoret in Syria." In *Ethnicity and Culture in Late Antiquity*, edited by Stephen Mitchell and Geoffrey Greatrex, 253–65. London: Duckworth and The Classical Press of Wales, 2000.

———. *Theodoret of Cyrrhus: The Bishop and the Holy Man.* Ann Arbor: University of Michigan Press, 2002.

Vaggione, Richard. *Eunomius of Cyzicus and the Nicene Revolution.* New York: Oxford University Press, 2000.

Valentine, Gill. "Imagined Geographies: Geographical Knowledges of Self and Other in Everyday Life." In *Human Geography Today*, edited by Doreen Massey, John Allen, and Philip Sarre, 47–61. Malden, MA: Polity Press, 1999.

van de Paverd, Frans. *St. John Chrysostom, The Homilies on the Statues: An Introduction.* Orientalia Christiania Analecta 239. Rome: Pontificium Institutum Studiorum Orientalium, 1991.

van der Horst, Pieter W. "Jews and Christians in Antioch at the End of the Fourth Century." In *Christian-Jewish Relations through the Centuries*, edited by Stanley E. Porter and Brook W. R. Pearson, 228–38. Sheffield, UK: Sheffield Academic Press, 2000.

van Dijk, Teun. "Structures of Discourse and Structures of Power." *Communications Yearbook* 12 (1989): 18–59.

Van Dyke, Ruth, and Susan Alcock, eds. *Archaeologies of Memory.* Malden, MA: Blackwell Publishing, 2003.

Vest, Bernd Andreas. "Les sources médiévales dites 'orientales' (syriaques, arabes, arméniennes et autres) concernant l'histoire de la ville d'Antioche et sa topographie." In *Les sources de l'histoire du paysage urbain d'Antioche sur l'Oronte*, 179–202. Paris: Université Paris 8, Vincennes-Saint-Denis, 2012.

Vinson, Martha. "Gregory Nazianzen's Homily 15 and the Genesis of the Christian Cult of the Maccabean Martyrs." *Byzantion* 64 (1994): 166–92.

Vittinghoff, Friedrich. *Der Staatsfeind in der römischen Kaiserzeit: Untersuchungen zur damnatio memoriae.* Berlin: Junker and Dunnhaupt, 1936.

Volk, J. "Die Predigten des Johannes Chrysostomus über die Statuen." *Zeitschrift für praktische Theologie* 8 (1886): 128–51.

Völker, Harald. "Spätantike Professoren und ihre Schüler: Am Beispiel von Himerios und Libanios." In *Gelehrte in der Antike: Alexander Demandt zum 65. Geburtstag*, edited by Andreas Goltz, Andreas Luther, and Heinrich Schlange-Schöningen, 169–85. Cologne: Böhlau Press, 2002.

Volp, Ulrich. *Tod und Ritual in den christlichen Gemeinden der Antike.* Boston: Brill, 2002.

Vorderstrasse, Tashe. "The Romanization and Christianization of the Antiochene Region: The Material Evidence from Three Sites." In *Culture and Society in Later Roman Antioch*, edited by Isabella Sandwell and Janet Huskinson, 86–101. Oxford: Oxbow Books, 2004.

Walsham, Alexandra. *The Reformation of the Landscape: Religion, Identity, and Memory in Early Modern Britain and Ireland.* New York: Oxford University Press, 2011.

Ward-Perkins, J. B. "Memoria, Martyr's Tomb, and Martyr's Church." In *Studies in Roman and Early Christian Architecture*, edited by J. B. Ward-Perkins, 495–516. London: Pindar Press, 1994.

———. "Reconfiguring Sacred Space: From Pagan Shrines to Christian Churches." In *Die spätantike Stadt und ihre Christianisierung: Symposion vom 14. bis 16. Februar 2000 in Halle/Saale*, edited by Gunnar Brands and Hans-Georg Severin, 285–90. Wiesbaden: Reichert Press, 2003.

———. "Re-using the Architectural Legacy of the Past, *entre idéologie et pragmatism.*" In *The Idea and Ideal of the Town between Late Antiquity and the Early Middle Ages*, edited by G. P. Brogiolo and Bryan Ward-Perkins, 225–44. Boston: Brill, 1999.

Warf, Barney, and Santa Arias. "Introduction: The Reinsertion of Space into the Social Sciences and Humanities." In *The Spatial Turn: Interdisciplinary perspectives*, edited by Barney Warf and Santa Arias, 1–10. New York: Routledge, 2009.

Warrior, Valerie. *Roman Religion*. Cambridge Introduction to Roman Civilization. New York: Cambridge University Press, 2006.

Wartenberg, Thomas. *The Forms of Power: From Domination to Transformation*. Philadelphia: Temple University Press, 1990.

Wataghin, Gisella Cantino, and Hervé Inglebert. "Introduction." *Antiquité Tardive* 20 (2012): 13–23.

Watts, Edward. *City and School in Late Antique Athens and Alexandria*. Berkeley: University of California Press, 2006.

———. *Riot in Alexandria: Tradition and Group Dynamics in Late Antique Pagan and Christian Communities*. Berkeley: University of California Press, 2010.

Watts, Michael. "Mapping Meaning, Denoting Difference, Imagining Identity: Dialectical Images and Postmodern Geographies." *Geografiska Annaler: Series B, Human Geography* 73.1 (1991): 7–16.

Watts, Richard. *Power in Family Discourse*. New York: Mouton de Gruyter, 1991.

Wharton, Annabel. *Refiguring the Post-Classical City: Dura Europos, Jerash, Jerusalem, and Ravenna*. New York: Cambridge University Press, 1995.

Whittaker, C. R. *Frontiers of the Roman Empire: A Social and Economic Study*. Baltimore: Johns Hopkins University Press, 1994.

Wiemer, Hans-Ulrich. "Die Rangstellung des Sophisten Libanios unter den Kaisern Julian, Valens und Theodosius: Mit einem Anhang über Abfassung und Verbreitung von Libanios' Rede Für die Tempel (Or 30)." *Chiron* 25 (1995): 89–130.

———. *Libanios und Julian: Studien zum Verhältnis von Rhetorik und Politik im vierten Jahrhundert n. Chr.* Munich: C. H. Beck'she, 1995.

Wilken, Robert. *John Chrysostom and the Jews: Rhetoric and Reality in the Late 4th Century*. Berkeley: University of California Press, 1983.

———. *The Land Called Holy: Palestine in Christian History and Thought*. New Haven, CT: Yale University Press, 1992.

Williams, Daniel. "Ambrose, Emperors, and Homoians in Milan: The First Conflict over a Basilica." In *Arianism after Arius: Essays on the Development of the Fourth-Century Trinitarian Conflicts*, edited by Michel Barnes and Daniel Williams, 127–46. Edinburgh: T&T Clark, 1993.

———. *Ambrose of Milan and the End of the Nicene-Arian Conflicts*. New York: Oxford University Press, 1995.

———. "When Did the Emperor Gratian Return the Basilica to the Pro-Nicenes in Milan?" *Studia Patristica* 24 (1993): 208–15.

Wintjes, Jorit. *Das Leben des Libanius*. Rahden/Westf.: Marie Leidorf Press, 2005.

Wolf, P. *Vom Schulwesen der Spätantike: Libanius-Interpretationen*. Baden: A. Reiff & Cie. Press, 1951.

Yasin, Ann Marie. *Saints and Church Spaces in the Late Antique Mediterranean: Architecture, Cult, and Community*. New York: Cambridge University Press, 2009.

Yates, Jonathan. "Augustine's Appropriation of Cyprian the Martyr-Bishop against the Pelagians." In *More Than a Memory: The Discourse of Martyrdom and the Construction of Christian Identity in the History of Christianity*, edited by Johan Leemans, 119–35. Dudley, MA: Peeters, 2005.

Yoffee, Norman. *Negotiating the Past in the Past: Identity, Memory, and Landscape in Archaeological Research*. Tucson: University of Arizona Press, 2007.

———. "Peering into the Palimpsest: An Introduction to the Volume." In *Negotiating the Past in the Past: Identity, Memory, and Landscape in Archaeological Research*, edited by Norman Yoffee, 1–9. Tucson: University of Arizona Press, 2007.

Zachhuber, Johannes. "The Antiochene Synod of AD 363 and the Beginnings of Neo-Nicenism." *Zeitschrift für antikes Christentum* 4.1 (2000): 83–101.

Zambon, M. Grazia, Domenico Bertogli, and Oriano Granella. *Antioch on the Orontes: "Where the Disciples Were First Called Christians."* Parma, Italy: Edizioni Eteria, 2005.

Zangara, V. "*L'inventio* dei martiri Gervasio e Protasio." *Augustinianum* 21 (1981): 119–33.

Ziadé, Raphaëlle. *Les martyrs Maccabées: De l'histoire juive au culte chrétien, les homélies de Grégoire de Nazianze et de Jean Chrysostome*. Boston: Brill, 2007.

GENERAL INDEX

Abraham, ascetic, 197–98

Acacius, Bishop of Caesarea, 15, 39, 227–29

Aelia Capitolina. *See* Jerusalem

Aetius, xvii, 14, 59, 116, 211–12

Africa, 29, 167n19, 204, 207, 208, 210, 214, 226, 230–31

agora, 11, 28, 31, 36, 39, 48–49, 53, 54, 113–14, 130, 134, 141, 147–49, 151–56, 158–59, 161–62, 166, 180

Aleppo, Syria. *See* Beroea

Alexander, Bishop of Alexandria, 12

Alexander, Bishop of Antioch, xvi, xix, 19

Alexandria, xvii, xviii, xix, 11n37, 12, 13, 16–17, 19, 29, 32, 33, 53, 173n44, 204, 213, 230n86, 232–36, 238–39, 240

altar, 46–48, 65, 68, 71, 74, 76, 112, 166, 178, 191, 193, 201, 208, 210, 223. *See also* altar of Victory; temple

altar of Victory, 214, 216, 217n36, 224, 226, 251

Ambrose, Bishop of Milan, xvi, xviii, xix, 17, 211, 213–26, 230, 231n88, 232n92, 236, 239, 243, 249, 251

Ammianus Marcellinus, xviii, 21, 50, 51n65, 66n28, 68, 96n8, 135n22, 165n11, 233

ʿAmuq Valley, 167

Anomean Christians, 18, 27–28, 94–95, 97, 99, 116–27, 195, 211, 245–46

Antakya, Turkey, 1, 19–20, 22–23, 152–53n70, 167n18, 174n47

Aphrahat, ascetic, 139, 198

Aphthonius, 132

Apollinaris of Laodicea, xvi, 17

Apollo, xviii, 9–10, 14–15, 22, 27, 50, 55, 58–59, 61–79, 90, 91, 104, 107, 115, 126, 165, 175–76, 191, 201, 204, 221, 225, 233, 235, 236, 242–44, 246. *See also* Daphne, suburb of Antioch; Didyma; temple: of Apollo at Daphne; temple: of Apollo at Didyma

Apollinarians, 212

Apostolic Church. *See* churches of Antioch: Apostolic Church

Aramaic, Syriac, 21, 138–40, 189n85

Arcadius, emperor, xv, xix, 209

Archelaus, 43–44

Arius, Arian, 12–13, 84n80, 209, 211–12, 213, 219n50, 220, 221, 223. *See also* homoian Christianity

Armenia, Armenians, 80, 81, 83n78, 84, 188

asceticism, 17–18n62, 86, 130, 135, 136, 138n30, 142n44, 157, 161, 214n27

ascetics, monks, 22, 25, 28–29, 52, 86, 130–31, 135, 136n24, 138n30, 139–41, 142n44, 146, 147–48, 152–55, 158–61, 163, 164, 167, 170, 172n41, 187, 188–98, 200, 201–3, 204, 208, 225, 226, 235, 247–49, 252

Athanasius, Bishop of Alexandria, xvi, xvii, xviii, 11–12, 13, 14, 16–17, 81, 142n44

Athens, Athenians, xvii, 33–34, 35, 36, 38, 39, 42, 66n28, 165

DISCARDED
CONCORDIA UNIV. LIBRARY

CONCORDIA UNIVERSITY LIBRARIES
MONTREAL